THE
PACIFIC WAR
PAPERS

ALSO BY THE AUTHORS

By Donald M. Goldstein and Katherine V. Dillon:
The Williwaw War (1992)
The Pearl Harbor Papers: Inside the Japanese Plans (1993)
Amelia: The Centennial Biography of an Aviation Pioneer (1997)

By Donald M. Goldstein and Katherine V. Dillon,
with J. Michael Wenger:
The Way It Was: Pearl Harbor: The Original Photographs (1991)
D-Day Normandy: The Story and Photographs (1993)
"Nuts!" The Battle of the Bulge: The Story and Photographs (1994)
Rain of Ruin: The Hiroshima and Nagasaki Atomic Bombs (1995)
The Vietnam War: The Story and Photographs (1997)
The Spanish-American War: The Story and Photographs (1998)

By Donald M. Goldstein and Katherine V. Dillon,
with Gordon W. Prange:
At Dawn We Slept: The Untold Story of Pearl Harbor (1981)
Miracle at Midway (1982)
Target Tokyo: The Story of the Sorge Spy Ring (1984)
Pearl Harbor: The Verdict of History (1987)
December 7, 1941: The Day the Japanese Attacked Pearl Harbor (1988)
God's Samurai: Lead Pilot at Pearl Harbor (1990)

By Donald M. Goldstein and Katherine V. Dillon,
with Masataka Chihaya:
Fading Victory: The Diary of Admiral Matome Ugaki (1991)

By Donald M. Goldstein and Harry J. Maihafer:
The Korean War: The Story and Photographs (2000)
America in World War I: The Story and Photographs (2003)

By Donald M. Goldstein, Phil Williams, and J. M. Shafritz:
Classic Readings of International Relations (1998)

By Donald M. Goldstein, Phil Williams, and Hank Andrews:
Security in Korea: War, Stalemate and Negation (1994)

THE PACIFIC WAR PAPERS

JAPANESE DOCUMENTS OF WORLD WAR II

Donald M. Goldstein
and
Katherine V. Dillon

Potomac Books, Inc.
Washington, D.C.

First Paperback Edition 2006
Copyright © 2004 by Prange Enterprises, Inc.

Library of Congress Cataloging-in-Publication Data

The Pacific War papers : Japanese documents of World War II / [edited by] Donald M. Goldstein and Katherine V. Dillon.—1st ed.
    p. cm.
    Pt. 2 consists of extracts from the diaries of Marquis Kâoichi Kido and Admiral Kichisaburâo Nomura.
    Includes index.
    ISBN 1-57488-632-0 (alk. paper)
    1. World War, 1939–1945—Naval operations, Japanese—Sources. 2. Japan. Kaigun—History—World War, 1939–1945—Sources. 3. Japan. Kaigun—Officers— Diaries. 4. Kido, Kâoichi, 1889–1977—Diaries. 5. Nomura, Kichisaburâo, 1877–1964—Diaries. 6. World War, 1939–1945—Personal narratives, Japanese. I. Goldstein, Donald M. II. Dillon, Katherine V. III. Title.

D777.P33   2004
940.54'5952—dc22   2003028207

Hardcover ISBN-10: 1-57488-632-0
Hardcover ISBN-13: 978-1-57488-632-0
Paperback ISBN-10: 1-57488-633-9
Paperback ISBN-13: 978-1-57488-633-7

(alk. paper)

Printed in Canada on acid-free paper that meets the American National Standards Institute Z39-48 Standard.

Potomac Books, Inc.
22841 Quicksilver Drive
Dulles, Virginia 20166

First Edition

10 9 8 7 6 5 4 3 2 1

Contents

List of Illustrations

Preface

Gordon Prange was the eminent scholar on Pearl Harbor and one of the eminent scholars on the Pacific War. What made his works different was that they presented the Japanese point of view as well as the American side.

At the end of the war, the Japanese armed forces conducted a wholesale destruction of documents. Untold quantities of valuable historical material went up in smoke. During the occupation, the Military History Section of Headquarters United States Army Forces–Far East attempted to reconstruct events on the basis of the memories of survivors and bits and pieces of other documents. For this reason, this particular type of study cannot be adjudged as absolutely officially correct. Some of the studies herein are what Capt. Mitsuo Fuchida, who led the air attack on Pearl Harbor, called "memory documents." There is no reason, however, to question the expertise or good faith of the officers engaged in their preparation, so these memory documents are probably reliable within the powers of human recollection.

Most of the documents herein are available nowhere else. Many have never before been available in English. Indeed, few have been published in Japanese, either. Our purpose in preparing this book has been to make them readily available to scholars and buffs of the Pacific War. This book allows the scholar to use these rare papers without having to go to the library or send for them. Prange was very protective of his sources while preparing his manuscripts, but now that his books have been published, we are sure he would want to share them, so that they can be used to set the record straight from the Japanese point of view.

We believe that *The Pacific War Papers* is the first attempt to put the Japanese story in proper context. The documents herein are primary source material and should be cited as such by any student making use of them. We have made no major changes that would affect the meaning or in any other way compromise the integrity of the material. Our part has been confined to minor grammatical corrections, identification where possible of individuals not fully cited, a few explanatory footnotes, and the introductions to each part and to each individual study.

There are no endnotes in this work because the individual documents are their own sources. They are major extracts from the Prange files, and we are happy to make them available to the layman, so that he or she may

Gordon W. Prange. *Author's Collection*

better understand the war in the Pacific. This is the second of two volumes pertaining to these documents. The first volume, primarily on the Japanese attack, was published in 1997 and titled *The Pearl Harbor Papers: Inside the Japanese Plans*. This volume, *The Pacific War Papers*, covers the Japanese Navy before World War II, pre–World War II diplomacy, and politics and documents pertaining to the post–Pearl Harbor naval war. It is divided into three parts: Part I, "The Japanese Navy before the Pacific War," Part II, "Prewar Diplomacy and Politics," and Part III: "Post–Pearl Harbor."

Specifically, Part I, *The Japanese Navy before the Pacific War*, contains monographs by Atsushi Oi, in 1941 a member of the Navy Ministry's Personnel Bureau; Masataka Chihaya, who may well have been the foremost Japanese naval expert of the 1990s; and Jisaburo Ozawa, who in 1941 was Commander in Chief of the Southern Expeditionary Fleet. These give the reader an early overview of the vastness of the buildup to the war. A second Ozawa essay talks about the development of the Japanese Navy's operational concept against America and makes some startling, telling points. Next, Prange's right hand, Chihaya, discusses the construction of Japanese warships. Ozawa appears once more to discover the tactics and organization of the Japanese carrier force. Finally, Toshikazu Ohmae of the Navy Ministry's Naval Affairs Bureau provides a special study about personnel.

Part II, *Prewar Diplomacy and Politics*, consists of extracts from the diaries of Marquis Koichi Kido, who was Lord Keeper of the Privy Seal in 1941, and Admiral Kichisaburo Nomura, Japan's ambassador to the United States at the time. These are vital to an understanding of the political and diplomatic background of the Pacific War and have never before been published in English.

Part III, *Post–Pearl Harbor*, is important because it relates Japanese accounts of activities after Pearl Harbor, including submarine operations, the movement of Japanese battleships, the Battle of the Java Sea, and the fiasco at Truk early in the war. Again, most of this work was prepared by Chihaya for Prange. Included in this section are some enlightening opinions about the war by Nobutake Kondo, Commander in Chief of the Second Fleet.

We would at this time like to acknowledge and thank Lisa Gillette for her support and input; Masataka Chihaya, who was one of the real stars of the Prange team; John Michael Wenger, our colleague on seven other Brassey's books, who encouraged us to do this book; Bob Cressman, who read the entire manuscript; Doug and Carol MacPhail for their support on all projects; Jack Grater, who has been there for our last two projects; and Emily Walker, who typed and edited the whole manuscript. A special thanks to our man at Brassey's, Don McKeon.

The book is dedicated to all those who died in the Pacific War on both sides of the ocean; to our old mentor, Gordon Prange, one of the best and without whom our works would never have been successful; and to all historians who seek the truth.

Donald M. Goldstein, Ph.D.
Professor, Public and International Affairs
Pittsburgh, Pa.

Katherine V. Dillon
CWO USAF (Ret.)
Arlington, Va.

Part I

The Japanese Navy before the Pacific War

Introduction

As the title implies, this group of documents concerns the Imperial Japanese Navy before the outbreak of the war. Together, they give the reader an excellent background in its organization, strategy, ships, and psychology. All were written by former officers of the Imperial Japanese Navy who served long and honorably in key positions, so their expertise is unquestionable.

The essays reveal that while in its early days the Japanese Navy was happy to learn what the West had to teach, it did not rely mindlessly upon Occidental examples and teachings. Top Japanese naval officers did not need Homer Lea, Hector Bywater, Billy Mitchell, or anyone else to prime their mental pumps; they were quite capable of working out their own strategy. Put through the test of time and combat, some of those strategies might have proved exceedingly ill conceived, but they were the Japanese Navy's own ideas.

These studies are arranged in more or less chronological order so that the material concerning the history and background of the organization appears first, followed by those items most closely related to plans, preparations, and activities immediately preceding the Pacific War.

The Japanese Navy in 1941

Atsushi Oi

1951

Introduction

Capt. Atsushi Oi was a member of the Personnel Bureau, Navy Ministry, from 1941 to 1943. From 15 November 1943 to the end of the war, he was an operations staff officer in Combined Escort Force General Headquarters. He has been published in the *United States Naval Institute Proceedings*. It is obvious from the text of this study that he was respected and his opinions sought.

This essay serves as a succinct introduction to the Imperial Japanese Navy—its history, traditions, strategy, training and education, types of ships, and the beginnings of its air power. Of particular interest is the concept of luring the U.S. Pacific Fleet westward to engage in a once-and-for-all encounter with the Japanese fleet—a concept discussed by several of the experts quoted herein. Long before World War II broke out, the Japanese postulated taking the Philippines at the outset to (1) deny the United States use of Manila Bay, and (2) to lure out the U.S. Pacific Fleet. Devotion to this all-out battle concept helps explain why Yamamoto's Pearl Harbor plan was so revolutionary and occasioned bitter opposition in the Navy.

Oi points out several Japanese strategic errors, such as neglecting to protect their own commercial shipping and destroy the enemy's. He also notes that between world wars, Japanese national pride degenerated into self-righteousness, forcing out of the Navy many fine officers who had trained abroad.

This essay repays detailed study for it is crammed with facts and theories that help explain what made the Japanese Navy tick in 1941.

History and Tradition

The origin of the Japanese sea forces dates far back into the mythological ages of more than 2,000 years ago. But in spite of their being an island nation, the Japanese ancestors failed to bequeath any worth-mentioning naval tradition to their 20th Century posterity. Since Oriental philosophy teaches man to conform to nature instead of overcoming it, it seems natural that the science of conquering the sea, i.e., navigation, did not develop in Asia as it did in the Occidental nations. Japan's Asiatic neighbors seldom offered any serious threat of invasion against her. Moreover, in the days of scattered population, agricultural Japan had little life-and-death necessity to expand overseas. No matter what the reason, Japanese military history was largely of the ground forces.

Worse still, what is found in the scattered naval records is not flawless. In the middle of the 7th Century the Japanese expeditionary forces sent to Korea ended in failure chiefly due to a naval defeat at the mouth of the River Kum. In the 4th quarter of the 13th Century the navyless [sic] Japan was invaded by the Mongolian forces. Though the Mongolians' final failure came in 1281 due to wholesale destruction of the invading armada, what was mainly instrumental for the destruction was not the quickly-assembled piratical Japanese sea forces, but a severe typhoon which every Japanese knows by the name of Kami-Kaze (divine wind)—the name given to the famous suicide-attack air unit in the Pacific War. Another Japanese expedition to Korea made in the last years of the 16th Century presents us with an ignominious naval record. During the expedition the Japanese fleet was decisively defeated by the Korean sea forces near Masan, South Korea.

Fortunately, or unfortunately, these ancient naval traditions came to an end due to self-imposed international seclusion started in the 1630s to last for more than 200 years. The Tokugawa Shogunate imposed a strict ban on the building of all oceangoing vessels as well as on overseas travel of her nationals. True, the hermitage could not preclude a threat from outside. European warships and merchant ships frequently appeared off the Japan coast. But these Europeans seem to have been casual strays, or, for some reason or another, did not carry out any threat. The Tokugawa Shogunate was satisfied with its navyless defense.

The introduction of steam power into seafare by the Western nations helped revolutionize the position of Japan. Well situated as stations for supply of coal and water to steam-driven ocean traders, Japan could no longer remain isolated from the maritime activities in the world. Commodore Perry's visit in 1853 awoke Japan from her long slumber in the hermitage. Japanese began to study Western civilization intensely. The Tokugawa Shogunate established a naval training school in 1857 under the tutorship of the Dutch, the only Christian nation which had been allowed to keep a trading post near Nagasaki under the pledge that no Christian propagation would be attempted. Progressive-minded and thriving local feudal lords acquired warships of their own. Soon after this, however, the feudal ages of

Japan were brought to an end, and in 1868 an entirely new era of Meiji was opened with vigorous national innovations.

The new government under Emperor Meiji unified all of the separate navies of the feudal lords, founding His Imperial Japanese Majesty's Navy. The new Navy, amounting to about 14,000 tons in all by the end of 1871, began to learn preponderantly from the British Navy. By both inviting instructors and sending students, Japan inherited not only the system but also the tradition from the Mistress of the Seven Seas. To a lesser extent, tutelage was furnished also by the U.S. Navy. The Sino-Japanese War of 1894–95 and the Russo-Japanese War of 1904–05 were fought by the Japanese Navy under the strong influence of Anglo-American sea traditions.

With the victory in the Russo-Japanese War, the Japanese Navy became recognized at home and abroad as having attained her maturity. By this time the traditions of British origin had been thoroughly digested and absorbed into the body of the national character. The Japanese Navy was naturally so proud of what had been displayed during the Sino-Japanese War and the Russo-Japanese War, that the spiritual achievements in the two wars became generally regarded as examples to posterity. The most prominent among these were symbolized in the persons mentioned below:

1. Torajiro Miura, a seaman aboard the Japanese CinC's flagship *Matsushima* in the Battle of Yalu on 17 September 1895, who, dying of his serious wounds and in his last breath, asked the executive officer of the ship, who happened to pass by his side, whether or not the enemy battleship *Chen Yien* had been sunk, instead of saying anything about his wounds or any other personal matters.
2. Commander Takeo Hirose, who, in his third attempt to sink a ship in the entrance of Port Arthur to block up the Russian Fleet inside in the spring of 1904, did not leave the sinking ship in defiance of the hail of enemy fire before he had done his best in searching every corner of the ship for his missing subordinate, Warrant Officer Sugino.
3. Vice Admiral Hikonojo Kamimura, who, in his victorious chase of the Russian fleet on 14 August 1904 off the southeastern coast of Korea, suspended the chase, at the cost of tactical advantage, to rescue the lives of the drowning crew of the Russian cruiser *Rulik* [Rurik?], which was sinking due to damage by Japanese fire.

The abovementioned episodes were fondly told in stories and sung in songs. But the most outstanding personification of the Japanese naval traditions which developed through the Sino-Japanese and Russo-Japanese Wars is seen in the person of Admiral Heihachiro Togo. Togo was the son of samurai of Satsuma Province (Kagoshima Prefecture), where the teaching of Bushido was most flourishing. While a lieutenant commander, he was educated for many years in the British Navy. It can be said therefore that Togo's character as a naval man is a blend of Bushido teaching and British naval tradition.

Probably the strongest point of Togo's character was out-and-out faithfulness to his naval profession. The hero of the Battle of Tsushima could have occupied any political position on which he cast a covetous eye. Except that he was appointed to a non-political post as chief tutor of the Crown Prince (the present Emperor) for a time at the special request of the Imperial household, Togo's career, which lasted as long as thirty years from the victory in the Russo-Japanese War, was wholly confined to the Navy.

In the World War of 1914–18, the Japanese Navy displayed the superiority of her tradition all over the world. Many warships joined the British Navy in escorting convoys of the Allied powers in the Indian Ocean and in the Mediterranean. Many precious qualities of a seagoing fighter were fully recognized world-wide—self-sacrificing spirit, bravery, assiduity, efficiency and rigid discipline.

By the standard of the Japanese nation as a whole, the Navy was respected as one of the best communities where the people were to send their sons. Let alone the officer personnel, common sailors were recruited from the cream of the lads. Partly due to the tradition of the feudalistic ages when the men in the fighting profession were classified as the top caste of the people—*Samurai* by name—to be enlisted in the military services was an honor and a matter of pride. The Emperor Meiji made it a rule that every son of the Imperial families was to be sent to the Army or the Navy. Moreover, military service men were given many social privileges, probably far more exorbitant than those given to military men in foreign countries.

Of the two fighting services, the Army and Navy, the popularity of the Navy fairly exceeded that of the Army in the eyes of the general public, in spite of the weakness of its political influence. The reasons were many, and may vary according to the persons who interpret. Some persons may point out the romantic temptation of sea life. The opportunity of visiting foreign ports no doubt fascinated the dreams of young lads. The mechanized navy was looked upon as something more highly civilized than the foot soldiers of the Army. But far more important than various other reasons this should not be overlooked: The naval education policy was more humanistic or closer to the national standard than the Army's educational policy. As the famous statesman-soldier General Issei Ugaki recollects in his book *Shorei Seidan*, the educational policy of the Army which closely followed the Prussian example disregarded human rights. In 1900 the Army went so far as to establish the Army Education Superintendent General's Office independent of the authority of the War Minister, thus alienating the Army education entirely from the general policy of the nation's education. The Army, moreover, started the education of future Army leaders at the preparatory military academy (*Yonen Gakko*) where teenagers in their sensitive and formative years were rigidly cast in the purely military pattern. The Navy refused to follow the example of the Army in these regards, and conformed character building with the general national pattern as much as possible, professional training apart.

Japanese writers in general were also more sympathetic with the Navy than with the Army. The most outstanding example is seen in a fiction entitled *Fujoki* ("Better Return"), also known as *Hototogisu* ("Nightingale"). The author was Roka Tokutomi, one of the most popular novelists and greatest literary critics of the Meiji-Taisho era. After its first appearance in 1898, it was so widely read that the 100th reprinted publication was issued in 1909 with the following reprinting still continuing unabatedly. Not only by print, the story was made popular through films and theatrical shows as well as songs, until every Japanese could tell the story by heart. The hero of the story is a young Navy officer, Ensign Takeo Kawashima. He married a daughter of an Army general, a sweet girl named Namiko, who chooses the naval ensign in spite of an ardent courtship by an Army officer of the Army General Staff, a cousin of Takeo. Namiko soon falls ill, suffering from consumption. The Army officer persuaded Hamiko's [sic] mother-in-law to force the divorce of the young Kawashima couple by inspiring in the old woman's mind a fear of consumption and taking advantage of Takeo's absence from home. Disappointed with the forced separation, Namiko dies amidst a burning affection toward Takeo. After a long absence from home due to the Sino-Japanese War and subsequent Navy duty, Takeo visits Namiko's tomb, and, as if she were still alive, says to the tomb, "Why have you died, O Nami-san?"

The main motive of the author seems to have been to point out a conventional Japanese family conception which was cruel and unhumanistic to its individual members, especially a bride. But at the same time, by presenting a naval officer as an exemplary man against some fascinating backgrounds of Navy life, the author did a great service in favor of the Navy. And in Japan, "Takeo" became a symbolical name for young Navy officers.

But having attained full maturity of development at World War I, the Japanese naval tradition began to show an internal decay. The words, "Invincible Navy," began to be used by its own spokesmen, themselves, as well as by the people. Indeed, the nation as a whole became so self-conceited with the strength and system of Japan that the national pride degenerated into self-righteousness. Everything genuinely Japanese was respected while everything bred in the West was despised. The Japanese seem to have forgotten the lesson of their own history in which Japanese civilization throve only when they ceaselessly tried to harmonize their own traditions with the civilizations learned from abroad. The trend seriously affected the Navy. Many of the best brains who drew deeply from the rich wells of Western civilizations were ousted from the service early in the 1930s and men of limited vision were often given highly responsible positions of naval leadership.

True, it was the Navy which spearheaded and represented Japanese superiority more than any other branch of the Japanese nation, thus was chiefly responsible for the national self-conceit. But it is not correct to conclude that the Navy was the most committed to self-righteousness. Though it may sound strange, it was the Navy which the ultra-nationalists accused of having been too influenced by foreign civilization, or being too much pro-British and pro-American.

It goes without saying that the naval traditions were reared predominantly in the service at sea. But despite the rapid increase of shore-based naval units in the form of shore-based flying units, landing parties, base forces, etc., since the outbreak of the Sino-Japanese Incident in 1937, the sea-reared naval traditions were generally maintained throughout the Navy. When the Pacific War threatened and then broke out, raw recruits including those of inferior qualifications flowed into the service on a gigantic scale and in a short period of time. Even the officer personnel were hastily replenished from among civil college graduates. Due to the urgency of the war situation there was neither sufficient time nor an adequate number of instructors to train these recruits fully for the naval customs and traditions. The result was some appreciable degradation in the efficiency and skill in various fields. But thanks to the high reputation and soundness of the long-established traditions as well as thanks to war psychology, the recruits were easily as well as willingly assimilated among their old comrades in the service, thus precluding any serious problem of order and discipline. If the tradition was inevitably thinned out, it was not to any degree of serious danger.

Strategy and Tactics

The basic study of strategy and tactics in the Japanese Navy was made in the Naval War College. Of all the instructors of the college, which was first opened in 1888 and finally closed in 1944, two great figures shone out. They were Shinshi Akiyama and Tetsutaro Sato (both later promoted to Vice Admiral). It can well be said that Japanese naval strategy and tactics were based on the teachings of these two, and that the later development of Japanese naval strategical [sic] and tactical conceptions were only a slight modification of their teachings. Having graduated from the naval academy (Japan's Annapolis) in 1887 and 1890 respectively, Sato and Akiyama were almost contemporary with each other. Akiyama studied tactics and strategy in the United States from 1897 to 1900. He was fortunate in joining the Spanish-American War on board the U.S.S. *New York* and in enjoying the private tutorship of Admiral Alfred T. Mahan. During almost the same period, Sato was sent to Britain (for a short time also to the United States) to study how important the influence of sea power was in relation to the rise and fall of nations. After returning to Japan, both of them were appointed as instructors at the Naval War College. Akiyama taught tactics while Sato strategy, or rather naval history. But they were not mere instructors. Akiyama drafted a guidebook on fleet tactics which he later improved. To his disciples and colleagues it became a tactical bible of the Japanese Navy. This Navy bible was called the *Kai-Sen Yomu-Hei (Essential Instructions on Naval Battles)* and continued to be used until the last days of the Pacific War with slight modifications in principle.

Sato wrote a voluminous book entitled *Historical Study for the Defense Problems of the Japanese Empire (Teikoku Kokubo Shiron)*. No Japanese either before or after him ever made such a profound study on naval history as he did. By his book he ably explained that Japanese national defense should depend on sea power rather than on ground troops. Sato's book was very much appreciated by Navy Minister Gombei Yamamoto (Count, Admiral, and twice premier later), who was seeking to place the naval position on an equal footing with the Army. The book was circulated among national leaders first and then among the nation in general in an abridged form. It is generally recognized that it helped Navy Minister Yamamoto achieve his aim of obtaining the Imperial sanction on 28 December 1903 to have the chief of the Naval General Staff independent of the chief of the Army General Staff, who at that time exercised a war-time control over the naval command. Generally speaking, the Japanese like a deductive approach. Akiyama's method was of this tendency, while Sato followed a Western way of inductive approach. But unlike Admiral Mahan, both of them had tremendous experience in practical service at sea and in administrative jobs. Sato's brilliant command of a small gunboat, I.J.M.S. *Akagi*, during the Battle of Yalu on 17 September 1894 was so famous that the brave and tenacious conduct of *Akagi* was sung in a song of which Japanese naval men were very fond. In the Russo-Japanese war, Akiyama was a key staff officer (operations) of Togo's Combined Fleet and Sato was the senior staff officer of the Second Fleet Headquarters. After the victorious return from the Russo-Japanese War both Akiyama and Sato were again appointed as instructors at the Naval War College. It was during this stage of their second-time instructorships that they founded tactical and strategical doctrines for the Japanese Navy in a complete blend of Eastern tradition, Western teaching, and actual war experience. Indeed both Akiyama and Sato were excellent scholars of Chinese classics. Both were very well versed in the teachings of Sun-tzu, the ancient (B.C. 500) Chinese Clausewitz. For instance, Sato was so great a scholar of Sun-tzu that he was selected to lecture to the Emperor on the classic Chinese Sun-tzu.

Even in its embryo stage, the Japanese Navy showed ability in creative tactics. Before the Sino-Japanese War, Western naval teachers taught the Japanese Navy the lessons of the Battle of Lissa. In this battle of July 20, 1866, the Italian fleet maneuvering in line ahead was miserably defeated by the Austrian fleet which advanced in a wedge-shaped formation in order to use rams. But Hayao Shimamura (graduated from the naval academy in 1883, later Fleet Admiral), as an Instructor in the Naval War College concluded, after his own experiments, that the lessons of Lissa had to be recovered by the Japanese fleet in the coming war with China. In the Battle of the Yalu on 17 September 1894, the Chinese fleet, which had in its line such formidable battleships as the *Ting-Yuen*, with the German and British advisers on board, and the *Chen-yueni*, commanded by a United States naval officer, followed Tegethoff's tactics off Lissa with a wedge-shaped formation. But the Japanese fleet adopted Shimamura's advice and maneuvered in line ahead, using broadside fire power to the best advantage and discarding the use of ramming. These Japanese tactics in conjunction with superiority of gunnery won the day.

After the Russo-Japanese War, the Japanese Navy considered the United States Navy as her probable enemy. The great disparity of strength which developed between the United States Navy and the Japanese overtaxed the tactics and strategy of the Japanese fleet. According to Tetsutaro Sato's study, there was no hope for the Japanese Navy to cope with the United States fleet under the naval ratio set at the Washington Conference (Admiral Sato was fired from active service because of his opposition to the ratio of the Washington Conference). Still, the Japanese Navy continued to consider the United States as a probable enemy. (Such grand national defense policy was formulated only in 1909, 1921, and 1930. In all of the three, the U.S. Navy was selected as a most probable invader of the Western Pacific, while Russia and China were considered military menaces in the Far East.) Indeed, rare in Japanese politico-military history, the Japanese leaders formulated a national defense plan immediately after the Washington conference [sic], thereby prescribing that the naval mission of Japan was to secure command of the Western Pacific with the tacit understanding that the United States Navy would be the probable invader of the sea area.

Since then, until the outbreak of the undeclared war between the Chinese Republic and Japan, the Japanese naval strategy and tactics were aimed at fighting the U.S. Navy in the Western Pacific. With a marked inferiority in strength, it became very difficult to pursue orthodox or common-sense principles of strategy and tactics. Therefore, the Japanese Navy had to place undue emphasis on "surprise." To achieve surprise, she had to take the "initiative." Being an inferior party, she could not bring her forces to the Eastern Pacific. In other words, she was forced to take a defensive position geographically. But otherwise, she adopted the concept of the offensive in order to secure initiative.

It seems that the policy of surprise and offensive matched the Japanese national temperament very well, too. Compared with the Americans, the Japanese people are romantic and illogical. To sit in a defensive position without fighting is very detrimental to the maintenance of Japanese morale.

Fortunately for the Japanese Navy, already in the 1920s the intelligence service knew that the United States fleet would advance her fleet into the Western Pacific to seek a decisive battle as soon as possible. (Somehow the Japanese naval intelligence service obtained documents through which the strategic ideas of such American naval strategists as Captain Pye and Commander Frost could be fully detected.) If the Japanese Navy had been uncertain about whether the U. S. Navy would dare bring her fleet to the Western Pacific to seek an early naval decision or would only send submarines to Japanese waters to destroy Japanese sea communications while retaining her main fleet to the east of Hawaii, the Japanese naval planners would have been put in an extremely difficult position.

It goes without saying that the Japanese naval planners made some efforts to devise a method positively to induce the American fleet into the Western Pacific. To send an expeditionary army to reduce the Philippines at the earliest opportunity was thought necessary for various reasons. The bases of the American submarines or other commerce raiders had to be eliminated in order to secure the safety of Japanese sea communications. The use of Manila Bay as an advanced base had to be denied to the American fleet. But the Japanese naval strategists reasoned that the attack on the Philippine Islands would help induce the American fleet to come to an early decisive battle in the Western Pacific.

This does not mean, however, that the Japanese Navy was confident in the decisive naval battle in the Western Pacific. Far from it! The disparity between the American fleet and the Japanese fleet was too great. It was thought essential that this disparity be reduced to a reasonable degree. For this purpose the Japanese Navy decided to use submarines against the American main fleet in every possible manner. The submarine forces were to be used not only for scouting purposes but also for sinking or damaging battleships and aircraft carriers with torpedoes. The larger-type submarines were to be sent out to the American west coast or Hawaii, depending upon where the American main fleet assembled at the outbreak of war. These submarines were to lie in ambush not only at the exit of the American anchorage, but also ahead of the cruising course in the ocean. Ordinary submarines whose radius of action was limited were to be used in the theater of the decisive battle.

It was expected that the disparity could not be sufficiently reduced by the use of submarines. To further reduce the enemy strength before the decisive daylight battle was fought, the Japanese Navy planned to launch a large-scale night action on the eve of the decisive battle. In this respect the Japanese Navy had both good traditions and weapons. Almost from the first stage of Japanese naval development, the torpedo branch occupied a very important position, almost equal to that of the gunnery branch in the Japanese Navy's composition. Such prominent persons as Kantaro Suzuki (Admiral, Baron, and Premier in 1945) and Keisuke Okada (Admiral, and Premier in 1935–36) were torpedo officers in their younger days and contributed to establishing the traditions and technical developments. Early in 1930 (Vice Admiral Kaneji Kishimoto was a promoter of the invention of this weapon), oxygen-propelled torpedoes made a successful debut. This encouraged the Japanese Navy a great deal. To remedy the inferiority in gunpower of big warships, the Japanese Navy armed all cruisers and destroyers very heavily with torpedo armaments, even at the cost of the protective elements in ships' construction. The Japanese Navy finally went to the extreme of converting some of her old light cruisers into torpedo ships at [the] sacrifice of gun armaments. Since torpedo attack required a close approach to the target, the call for night action became more and more great.

Overtaxed and engrossed with the preparations for a decisive battle with the main fleet of the United States, the Japanese Navy unwittingly disregarded another essential naval mission—the protection of sea communications. In the days of the Sino-Japanese War (1894–95) [and] the Russo-Japanese War (1904–05), Japan was primarily an agricultural and self-sufficient nation. Therefore, in these tradition-making wars the problem of trade protection did not come to the fore. But [with] the rapid growth of population and industrialization as well as the acquisition of overseas territories in the later generations, the island nation of Japan, like Great Britain, became increasingly dependent upon seaborne [sic] trade. But, as a matter of fact, the Japanese neglected to make any appreciable effort toward preparing for the mission in this field. Moreover, the colorless, monotonous, and entirely defensive warfare of trade protection, no matter how important, did not suit the temperament of the Japanese nation. Not only were no escort ships built on the pretext of a small naval appropriation, but planning and education, which could be done with little monetary expense, were similarly slighted.

During World War I, the Japanese Navy did an excellent job in escorting Allied shipping, thus obtaining precious lessons and experience in this field. But the post-war study was concentrated on colorful fighting such as the battles of Jutland, Coronel, and the Falkland Islands. In the 1930s the Japanese Navy went so far as to defy the international disarmament agreements and built such very costly battleships as the *Yamato* and the *Musashi* despite her light purse of national wealth. Still, the Japanese did not care for the building of any escort ships in which she would be deplorably lacking in case of war. The fact that in successive disarmament negotiations the United States concurred with the British insistence on the abolition of submarines might give a deceptive impression to Japan that U. S. submarines would present no serious menace. Indeed, an opinion was current among the Japanese that the Americans had neither adaptability nor liking for submarine life.

Moreover, the Japanese Navy placed little importance on commerce-destruction warfare. The primary reason was that the submarine tonnage permitted to Japan by the disarmament treaties was too small to let her allocate enough submarines for the mission, since submarines had to be used against the main fleet of the enemy. Of course, in the minds of the Japanese naval men was this idea—that submarines sufficiently trained for fleet action could be more effectively used against enemy merchant ships. It was also expected that the American shipping volume on the Pacific side would reach no great amount in wartime. As for the Atlantic side, the Japanese Navy could only send very limited numbers of submarines for a more diversionary purpose.

After 1936, Japan broke away from the international disarmament agreements. This drastic measure, far from helping improve her relative strength with the U. S. Navy, plunged her into a hopeless race of naval building. The only relief coming from this drastic measure was the building, in great secrecy, of *Yamato* and *Musashi*. The battleship admirals of the Japanese Navy certainly eased their minds to a great extent with the progress of this building. But ironically enough, it was the same Japanese Navy which developed, during this same period, very effective airborne torpedoes capable of sinking any battleship if used in numbers.

After 1937, when Japan launched an undeclared war against China, Japan became increasingly involved in the clash of interests in China with Britain and began consciously challenging the British hegemony in the Far East. Anti-British feeling in Japan rose high, guided by some of the militarists and industrialists, more and more dark with pro-Axis sentiment. It was thus that the Japanese Navy, traditionally pro-British, came to regard the British Navy as a probable enemy in addition to the American Navy. But the Japanese Navy anticipated that most of the British fleet would be retained in the European theater. The Japanese view that the main enemy in the Pacific theater would be the American fleet did not change, thus no substantial change was made in her naval strategy and tactics except that Singapore and Hong Kong had to be reduced, that the sea lanes of the British Commonwealth had to be destroyed in the Indian Ocean, and that the oil resources of the Dutch East Indies had to be secured at all costs. This change of strategy called for a gigantic joint operation with the Army, and the protection of sea communications added logically to its importance to a large extent. But the Japanese continued to slight the menace to her own sea communications, underestimating the enemy's power of submarine warfare.

As for joint operations with the German and Italian navies, there were practically no preparations or enthusiasm, despite the military alliance. Only a loose understanding was made with the German Navy that certain submarine forces were to be diverted for commerce raiding operations in the Indian Ocean.

Maneuvers and War Games

The Japanese Navy started its training year on 1 December, to last until 30 November of the next year. During the period from about 1 November to around 1 December, large personnel shifts and promotions took place. From mid-December to mid-January, each fleet crew enjoyed about two weeks' vacation in two shifts. With 1 December as the middle, a period of about three months saw no major fleet activities. Individual ships composing the Combined Fleet were permitted to return to their respective mother ports—Yokosuka, Kure, Maizuru and Sasebo—to be repaired and supplied. Each Japanese warship had her permanent mother port where her enlisted crew underwent their initial naval education at the naval barracks.

After this pleasant sojourn of three months at the mother ports, each ship was ordered by the fleet commanders to assemble at a prescribed anchorage. The date of assemblage usually fell sometime around 20 January and the anchorage was selected somewhere in the western part of the Inland Sea. Thus the Combined Fleet was regrouped to start its annual training.

Initial training in the assemblage area took about two months, for the personnel shifts of the preceding autumn were generally very extensive. This period was devoted to individual training. With the completion of individual training late in March, the Combined Fleet went out for a cruise rife with incessant battle practices day and night.

After a brief rest in the mother ports as shown above, the Combined Fleet held the so-called "A" class competition battle practice. The base of the practice was usually selected in a good harbor within several hours cruising distance from Yokosuka, Kure, or Sasebo (Tateyama, Saeki, or Terajima-suido). Lasting during May and June in general, the "A" practice was for departmental technical training (gunnery, damage control, engineering, communication, etc.). To be given a finishing touch in the "B" class competitive battle practice in August and September, the "A" practice was aimed at training for simple conditions of actual battle. Live shells were shot in gunnery practice, but with a reduced charge.

Expert instructors of the gunnery school, torpedo school, communications school, etc. were sent by the Navy Ministry to inspect and criticize the skill and efficiency of the fleet crews. Exhaustive studies and discussions were made between the school instructors and fleet personnel to acquire lessons from each practice. The results were carefully recorded and later published all over the Navy from the Navy Ministry (the Education Bureau). This publication helped Navy officers keep their technical knowledge up to date. Indeed, the battle practice was the main event for both the fleet crew and the rest of the Navy personnel.

During the period between the "A" and "B" practices, the Combined Fleet again went out for a cruise during which, as in the cruise in early April, the emphasis of the training was placed on day and night tactical maneuvers. Usually the cruising was interwoven with calling at pleasure ports such as Beppu, Osaka, Keirun (Formosa), and Tsingtao (China).

The "B" class competitive battle practice was held in the same system as the "A" practice. The only difference was that the "B" practice was more advanced and was held in conditions resembling as closely as possible those expected in a heated battle. Live shells were shot at full charge and engines steamed at maximum horsepower.

But the culmination of the fleet training was reached in a maneuver which was held in October. The maneuver was not for mere technical training, but rather for an advanced tactical training such as was needed for fleet leaders at high level. The Combined Fleet was divided into two, friend and foe, in the maneuver. The foe, i.e., the theoretical enemy fleet, was composed of a very few ships, each assumed to be representing a large strength. The umpires of the maneuvers were supplied from the faculties of the Naval War College and the Naval General Staff.

Once every four years the Emperor, aided by the Chief of the Naval General Staff, presided over such autumn maneuvers of the fleet. In the Emperor-presided maneuvers, a different fleet from the Combined Fleet was temporarily organized to act as a hostile fleet. In time of peace, many warships under complete conditions were retained in ordinary with a reduced complement. Of these reserve warships, the temporary fleet was composed. (Unlike the U.S. warships, the ships of the Combined Fleet were manned with full wartime complement even in peacetime.) The leadership personnel of the "enemy" fleet were supplied from the Naval War College, other naval schools, and the Naval General Staff.

By the "enemy," the Japanese Navy usually meant the U.S. Pacific Fleet. The problem of the maneuver varied in accordance with the requirements in the planning of the Naval General Staff. Generally speaking, however, the maneuvers progressed along the following line: The Combined Fleet searches out the enemy fleet which is reported entering the western Pacific (submarine forces, tender-based flying boats or seaplanes, and temporarily requisitioned fishing boats are used for this purpose); the main combatant body of the Combined Fleet then sorties to seek out and destroy the enemy fleet; in doing so the Japanese combatant forces are divided into two groups, with the 2nd Fleet (heavy cruisers as a backbone strength) acting as the advanced body and the 1st Fleet (battleships as backbone strength) following in the rear, keeping a distance [of] some 50 to 80 seamiles [sic] from the 2nd Fleet. The 2nd Fleet tries to make contact with the enemy main fleet toward sunset, so as to launch a night torpedo attack. Both the 1st and 2nd Fleets try to regroup into one body as a preparation for fighting a decisive daylight action with the enemy fleet crippled through the night action. In the process of regrouping, the 2nd Fleet tries to induce the enemy to the area where friendly submarines are lying in ambush, or to fire torpedoes taking advantage of her retreating course.

It was thought as a more or less foregone conclusion that there would be no chance whereby the enemy fleet could be surprised while in its base. The idea of the Pearl Harbor attack was exclusively that of Admiral Isoroku Yamamoto in 1941.

Another important pattern of naval maneuvers was a joint maneuver with Army forces. From the early stages of the Japanese Imperial Navy, the escorting of Army expeditionary forces was taken as one of the Navy's most important missions. As early as 1874, only two years after the inauguration of the Navy Ministry with the total naval strength of a mere 13,812 tons, the Imperial Japanese Navy took as her first warlike activity the escorting of an Army convoy to Formosa by two warships. Both in the Sino-Japanese War and the Russo-Japanese War, the Navy's cooperation with the Army in escorting the Army convoys and helping establish beachheads was exemplary. In the Japanese war plan against the United States, the invasion of the Philippines by the Japanese Army was an important factor. Almost every year a joint Army-Navy maneuver was held in some form or another with a view to training for the Philippine invasion. Moreover, between the Naval War College and the Army General Staff College a close contact of strategical and tactical study was maintained, with the expected Philippine invasion as a main problem of their joint study. And this was certainly instrumental in cultivating friendly intercourse between the two sister services, since the graduates of these colleges occupied key positions in the services. (Note: Though, in the administrative field, a bitter rivalry between the two services came to the fore frequently, friendly relations were generally maintained between them in the field of operational planning.)

As for the naval stations and minor naval stations which were responsible for defensive missions, they held annual maneuvers, anti-invasion tactics and shipping protection. But the Navy in general gave these maneuvers slight importance. Unlike in the British Navy, no large-scale shipping protection maneuvers in which merchant ships joined were held in the Japanese Navy.

The first anti-British war games were held in 1938 on the map between the Combined Fleet headquarters and the Naval War College, under the auspices of the Naval General Staff. The assumption was that Japan went to war against the British Commonwealth with Germany and Italy maintaining a benevolent neutrality in favor of Japan, while the United States and Holland were in favor of the British Commonwealth. The greatest difficulty involved in the Japanese Navy's training and maneuvers was the shortage of fuel oil. The area of maneuvers and the speed of ships were strictly limited. Many problems of maneuvers had to be solved only by theoretical studies. Therefore, thoroughgoing appraisals of the value of such-and-such tactics were difficult to obtain. This, together with the scanty budgetary appropriations for other training expenses (e.g., limited amounts of live shells, etc., permitted for training), handicapped the Japanese Navy in developing realistic tactical doctrines.

Combined with the Japanese dislike of things defensive, the fact that no thoroughgoing experiments could be made to ascertain the effect of shells and bombs led the Japanese Navy to slight the importance of protective measures and damage control. While the United States Navy learned very much from World War I various lessons on damage control, the Japanese Navy long neglected this phase of war lessons. It was only through the result of intelligence information that the Japanese Navy began realizing the importance of damage control drill in the 1930s.

The acute necessity to economize fuel necessitated the Japanese Navy to make fleet cruises packed full of training programs. The instant the anchor was aweigh, the bugle sounded "clear for action" to start a series of battle trainings. As long as the fleet was steaming, the fleet crew could enjoy little time for rest. Night was more important for training than daytime, so that it was not at all rare for a ship's crew to spend all night at the battle stations. The severity of training was one of the prominent traditions of the Japanese Navy. Immediately after the Russo-Japanese War was over, the Combined Fleet with Admiral Goro Ijuin as the CinC held such a severe training that a saying became current among the crewmen that a week of the Japanese Navy consisted of "Monday, Monday, Tuesday, Wednesday, Thursday, Friday, and Friday." (And this saying became later spread among the Japanese people in general.) But in the Japanese fleet of oil-burning days, there was even no bedtime for the crew.

What Composed Naval Strength

The types of combat ships which the Japanese Navy had in 1941 were almost the same as those of the United States Navy, because of the naval armament treaties to which the two countries were among the parties. But there were some minor differences in the detail characteristics in each type of ship. Generally speaking, the Japanese combat ships placed more emphasis on offensive armaments and top speed, the U. S. ships on protective elements and radius of action. The volcanic temper of the Japanese might be more responsible for the slight of protective measures in favor of the offensive, though we may also count among the reasons Japanese eagerness to compensate [for] the inferior naval ratio by having an individual ship armed more heavily than that of the rival country's. The reason why the Japanese Navy sacrificed radius of action is obvious. In the Washington naval treaty both the United States and Britain were strictly limited in building up adequate naval bases in the Western Pacific where the Japanese homeland with many naval bases lay. And the Japanese naval strategists were contented with fighting a defensive war in the western Pacific.

a. *Battleships*. Despite the fact that it was the Japanese Navy which first proved that aircraft could sink battleships as in the case of her Pearl Harbor attack and of the sinking of *Prince of Wales* and *Repulse*, it was also the Japanese Navy which clung to the idea that the battleship was the backbone of naval strength to the last minutes of the Pacific War. From the fall of 1943 to 31 March 1944, Admiral Koga, Commander in Chief of the Combined Fleet, was apparently ready to fight a decisive war in the central Pacific although his carrier strength was not at his disposal. On 31 March 1944 he seemed to learn that this policy was wrong because, in spite of his order to his surface fleet to be ready for a decision off Palau, he shifted his flag ashore from his flagship *Musashi*. And, although an American fast carrier task force raided the island for three consecutive days, inflicting heavy damage to Japanese shipping and installations, no order was given to his surface fleet to counterattack the enemy carrier strength. But Admiral Koga and his Chief of Staff Fukudome were among the most outstanding battleship admirals. In the sea battle off the Marianas on 19–20 June 1944, Admiral Ozawa divided his fleet into two major groups—a carrier group and a battleship group—placing daytime emphasis on the former but attempting a night attack with the battleship group in vain. After this ill-fated battle, many young admirals and captains in the Navy Ministry cried for recapturing Saipan with battleship strength in defiance of enemy air supremacy.

The sea battle that took place on 25 October 1944 off Samar and *Yamato*'s sortie toward Okinawa on 17 April 1945 were more marked illustrations of the Japanese naval tactical doctrine in which the Japanese believed that the battleship could to something in the face of the enemy's mighty air supremacy. Of course there were only suicidal attempts. But still, the Combined Fleet resorted to such tactics in spite of a great sacrifice in fuel oil and manpower which could be favorably diverted to escort-of-convoy warfare and shore-based air warfare.

The fact that the Japanese Navy had *Yamato* and *Musashi* is believed to be partly, if not primarily, responsible for making the Japanese admirals so obsessed with a "battleship first" idea. Then why did the Japanese Navy build these mammoth battleships? Because the superiority of the U.S. fleet over the Japanese naval forces was so great that the Japanese Naval General

Staff, as already explained in the section on tactics, tried to discover various sorts of tactical measures to reduce this U.S. superiority before a final fleet encounter was fought. But it was considered that, after all sorts of attempts to reduce the American superiority were made, a pitched battle between the battleships of the two fleets must be fought after all. To win this battle, the Japanese thought, ships which could outrange the enemy ships would be useful. It was also considered that the American Navy would be loath to build battleships that could not pass through the Panama Canal.

Maybe it was in the fall of 1934 (this writer remembers that argument pro and con on the building of such battleships exchanged in the Naval General Staff sometime in the summer of 1934) that a blueprint of such a battleship started. In the naval armament conference held in London in 1935 Japan made clear her intention that she would not adhere to the existing treaties on naval armament after they expired. The dockyard facilities in which to build the *Yamato* class had to be augmented and extended to a great degree. Machinery by which to produce 18-inch guns had to be procured from Germany. A special crane ship to transport the big guns had to be built. Many of these new preparations were needed, quite different from building another battleship of the *Nagato* class.

In view of the light purse of the Japanese nation, the sacrifices made to other defense measures for building *Yamato* and *Musashi* were indeed tremendous. Also we must not forget another sacrifice which the building of *Yamato* and *Mushashi* brought about. Quite different from producing atomic weapons or radar, which were of real scientific innovation, the building of these mammoth battleships which called for little scientific innovation would be easily cancelled by such a big industrial power as the United States as soon as a mere hint that such ships were being built in Japan was made to the American authorities. Therefore, an extraordinary secrecy had to be kept, and an extremely strict anti-spy measure had to be enforced. Within the service, discussions on tactical problems which involved the use of these mammoth ships could not be fully made except by a very limited group of personnel. In the field of foreign relations, the exchange of information and inspection of naval facilities were strictly limited, to the detriment of otherwise friendly relationships with the United States and the British Empire.

b. *Air force and aircraft carriers.* Speaking before students of the Naval War College in 1935, Admiral Nobumasa Suetsugu, currently the most prominent naval tactician and formerly CinC of the Combined Fleet, reminded his audience as follows:

> The Japanese Navy at present lags manifestly behind the American Navy in aviation and communications. While Commander in Chief of the Combined Fleet and that of the 2nd Fleet, I repeatedly referred to this matter. Though efforts are being made at present by the central authorities of the Navy, our

backwardness on these points cannot be remedied easily no matter what efforts are made. We lag behind not only in equipment but also in many points of the arts concerning aviation and communication.*

Japanese naval carrier aviation made its debut as early as 1913, with a converted seaplane tender *Wakamiya* carrying two seaplanes. But it was not until a British air force mission comprising 30 aviators were [sic] invited to teach the Japanese Navy at the aviation groups at Kasumigaura and Yokosuka for two and a half years beginning from 1921 that naval air strength worth mentioning became capable of claiming existence in the Japanese Navy. It must be said that the Japanese Navy was greatly indebted to this British mission.

By the Japanese standard, the Japanese Navy men were the most air-minded. In the 1920s and 1930s the Japanese Army placed so much emphasis on the spiritual (or morale) factor of military strength that that [sic] service neglected to improve its air forces as well as its mechanized units. Civil aviation saw little improvement. But the Navy did its best for its air force, building aircraft carriers up to the limit of the treaty allowance. The training of young naval officers as aviators began intensively due to the impetus given by the British mission. The proportion of naval academy graduates to become aviators had been very little before the British teaching was given. But beginning with the classes of 1922 and 1923, the proportion jumped up. It was a sort of surprise that Ensign Kurio Toibana (who was killed in action on 18 April 1943 over Bougainville while accompanying Admiral Isoroku Yamamoto as aviation staff officer of the Combined Fleet) was selected as an aviation cadet "in spite of his being a head graduate from Etajima in his class, the position which promised him a great naval future without costing him dangerous and hazardous service as an aviator."

Indeed, the life of aviators was full of danger, not only because the material weakness and technical backwardness were still great, but also because the training was especially severe. In order to try to catch up with the world standard of aviation progress, the Japanese Navy produced many experimental types of airplanes one after another. Moreover, Japanese fleet training was very hazardous both on the surface and in the air, in defiance of bad weather and poor preparations. From top brass down to ensign, the Japanese Navy believed that the only way to make up for the inferior tonnage ratio imposed by the naval armament treaties was to intensify training far above that of the American and British navies.

But, as aptly stated by Admiral Suetsugu, the Japanese Navy failed to keep pace with the U.S. Navy in aviation and radio communications. The

*From lecture given by Admiral Nobumasa Suetsugu, CinC of the Yokosuka Naval Station on 12 March 1935.

national technical standard in these highly scientific fields was so low that the Navy alone could compete fairly well with such highly industrialized nations as the United States and Britain.

(Note: In the fall of 1943, a problem arose whether naval aviation could be advantageously merged with that of the Army. This problem was taken up in the Naval General Staff by Commander Minoru Genda, who seemed to have been influenced by his Army colleagues as well as his own studied conviction. This writer, then also in the Naval General Staff, was secretly ordered to study the problem by Admiral Nagano, Chief of the Naval General Staff. It seemed to this writer that Admiral Nagano was from the first opposed to the idea of the merger. He secretly confided to this writer that when he was Minister of the Navy he took General [Hisaichi] Terauchi, then War Minister (Commander in Chief of the Southern Army in the Pacific War), to the Naval Aeronautical Research Laboratory at Yokosuka. He remembered a great lack of knowledge as well as surprise revealed by the War Minister. He said that Army aviation was so poorly developed that to merge with Army aviation would only mean the retrogression of naval aviation.)

Ironically enough, this lack of air-mindedness on the part of the nation as a whole, especially on the part of the Army, resulted in one advantage to naval aviation. The Navy could develop her land-based aviation as she wanted. In Japan the Army's influence in the political field was very, very strong. There was nothing that the Army could not attain by persistent political pressure. Therefore, had the Army been interested very deeply in aviation in the 1920s and early 1930s, land-based aviation would have been monopolized by the Army just as the American Navy became limited to sea-based aviation alone due to the U.S. Army Appropriation Act of 1920.

Mainly due to the fact that Japanese naval strength became more severely limited after the London Naval Treaty, Japanese naval men considered it necessary to compensate the surface inferiority by land-based aviation. The effort to develop a long-range land-based bomber was thus strenuously made in the naval building programs. The effort bore such rich fruit that by 1936 heated enthusiasts began to insist that carrier aviation ought to give way to land-based air. For instance, this writer was sent, in March 1936, a letter to this effect by Lt. Cmdr. Yasuna Kozono, his classmate (class of 1923).

Lt. Cmdr. Kozono was then the No. 1 flyer, especially majoring in bombing and torpedoing, of the Japanese Navy. (In 1942, then Commander Kozono was awarded by the Navy Minister for his invention of tactics and devices to shoot down B-17s, then the severest menace to Japanese aviation. In August 1945 he, as a captain, was commanding officer of Atsugi Air Field, where General MacArthur was to arrive as SCAP [Supreme Commander Allied Pacific]. Due to his strong nationalistic belief, he would not admit Japan's surrender. His subordinates also followed his preaching. He was told, however, that the Emperor was much concerned about his disobedience. The dilemma drove him to insanity. Later, he was court-martialed for his insubordination and sent to prison.) Kozono's letter to this writer advocated not only the abolition of battleships but also of aircraft carriers. He advocated the concentration of the entire naval budget to the increase and development of land-based air forces.

Along with the development of the medium land-based bomber, the airborne torpedo made great strides in its improvement. Thanks to the traditional superiority of the Japanese Navy in the torpedo field, it was just one stride from cruiser's torpedo to airborne torpedo. But it must not be forgotten that the Naval Aeronautical Department made especial studies and experiments of its own. Lt. Cmdr. Fumio Aiko, the classmate of Yasuna Kozono and Kurio Toibana, was the central figure in the development of the airborne torpedo. The sinking of *Prince of Wales* and *Repulse* off the Malay Peninsula and the attack on Pearl Harbor were thus planned on the basis of these developments.

But a more fundamental weakness of Japanese naval aviation was of quantity rather than of quality. The scarcity of aircraft was inevitable, not only due to the shortage of material resources but also to the insufficient development of the aircraft industry. The latter deficiency included the small scale of the so-called *shadow* industries such as the automobile industry which can be easily converted to produce aircraft engines. (Note: Probably in the first half of the war period, the scarcity of aircraft factories was more responsible for the slow supply of airplanes. But it was without question that in the latter half of the war the shortage of raw material was the bottleneck of the production of aircraft. In other words, the exorbitant loss to the American submarines of ships importing bauxite from Bintang Island became the real cause of the Japanese failure to produce a sufficient number of airplanes).

In terms of manpower, Japanese aviation was not happy, in spite of the large population. The Japanese in general lacked training in sciences and in the handling of machines. To train them as aviators took much time after an uneasy selection. Mass recruiting and training on such a big scale as can be seen in the United States were impossible. (Note: This writer was a member of the Personnel Bureau of the Navy Ministry from 1941 to 1943, and shared responsibility in the training of aviation personnel. Before 1940, to train elementary aviation one instructor was in charge of four pupils. In 1941, teaching methods were improved, and one instructor became able to teach eight, and then twelve in one class. As far as this writer remembers, the last figure, twelve, was said to be the maximum which one instructor could efficiently teach flying techniques in class. Thus, it was thought that the rapid increase of air power of the Japanese Navy depended on the number of aviation instructors. At that time the Combined Fleet and the Naval General Staff were demanding as many aviators as possible to man carriers and operational flying groups. These men could not be used to train raw recruits. Therefore, it was impossible to obtain the required number of aviation instructors in training air groups. This writer believes that one of the important reasons why Japanese naval air strength became suddenly degraded, to be unretrievable forever after the defeat at Midway, is attributable to the negligence of training a backlog of aviators at the outset of the war).

Types of Naval Vessels

With the battlecruiser *Kongo* as the last warship built by British shipbuilders, all the warships of the Japanese Navy were built in Japanese yards. (Note: *Kongo* was completed in 1913. Several years later, the electrically propelled naval transport *Kamoi* was built in the United States. The Japanese Navy wanted to know something about the electric propulsion engine with which many American naval vessels were equipped. Though *Kamoi* was converted to a seaplane tender some years later, this ship should be excluded from the present discussion due to the nature of the subject.) The genius of Shipbuilding Vice Admiral Baron Motoki Kondo gave the Japanese Navy independence in warship building. It was not merely independence, it was independence accompanied by qualitative superiority second to none. The battleships *Yamashiro*, *Fuso*, *Hyuga*, and *Ise* were successively launched in Japanese shipbuilding yards soon after the battlecruisers *Haruna*, *Kirishima*, and *Hiei*, the sister ships to the British-born *Kongo*, had been completed by imitation-clever Japanese hands. If these four battleships could not claim the world's applause, *Nagato* and *Mutsu* could.

Without the able support of Shipbuilding Vice Admiral Yuzuru Hiraga (Kondo's eleven years' junior), Baron Kondo would never have been so successful in giving the Japanese Navy such a brilliant shipbuilding record. Baron Hiraga, who was later appointed President of Tokyo Imperial University, was a genius both in practical administration and shipbuilding science. When the Washington Naval Treaty brought about a holiday to battleship building, the center of gravity of naval shipbuilding fell on cruiser building. Hiraga's genius gave birth to the light cruiser *Yubari*, which displaced only 2,890 tons in terms of the naval treaty, but could easily compete in combat strength with a light cruiser of 5,100 tons *(Kinu, Yura, Kitakami, Tama, Oi, etc.)* with which the Japanese Navy was abundant. It was on the model of *Yubari* that the Japanese cruisers to be completed later, 7,100 tonners and 10,000 tonners, were built. Even destroyers and torpedo boats largely followed the model of *Yubari*.

In this connection it must be noted that one of the main factors which enabled the Japanese shipbuilding designers to succeed in giving a small ship big fighting power was the sacrifice of radius of action. Since the Japanese strategists were contented with the defensive strategy in the western Pacific where the Japanese Navy was in an advantageous position to the American and British navies in the abundance and propinquity of bases, small demand was made on the radius of action. By saving the fuel-carrying capacity and allocating the tonnage thus saved to the superstructure, the stability of the entire ship was affected. Moreover, tacticians naturally demanded strongly that fire-control stations, range-finders, searchlights and the like be installed as high as possible and be substantiated as much as possible. Always subject to these tactical demands, shipbuilding experts could not or dared not rightfully insist on their position. Japanese ships became increasingly top-heavy until on 15 March 1934 the torpedo boat *Tomozuru* capsized off Sasebo in a storm not necessarily in that region, to the tragedy of the crew and the shame of the Navy.

Like the United States Navy and unlike the Royal British Navy, the Japanese Imperial Navy did neglect to build ships to escort convoys along shipping lanes vital to her economic subsistence. In explaining the reason for the neglect, the authorities concerned said, after exorbitant havoc had been done by submarines to shipping in the Pacific War, that they had been too busy building up the first-line strength to pay attention to the preparation for shipping protection.

In contrast to the neglect in building antisubmarine vessels, the building of submarines themselves was most earnestly pushed forward. The building program became so gigantic by 1941 that it was problematical whether or not the training of commanding officers could keep pace with the building program. According to the estimate of the personnel bureau of the Navy Ministry, by 1943 a young officer who would have finished only three years or so of naval life after graduation from the Naval Academy, would have been assigned as commanding officer of a fleet submarine of 1,000 tons or even over, if the building program had fair going. It was believed such little experience of naval life could not produce a competent submarine commander. In the personnel bureau planning, all Naval College graduates whose physical and mental capacity met the standard for aviators were reserved for aviation service. The rest of the Naval College graduates would be divided into surface duty and submarine duty. Moreover, due to the stringent economy of the naval budget, as well as the Navy's abhorrence of seeing premature retirement of naval officers, the number of naval cadets was strictly limited from 1923 to 1938. This caused a great shortage of officer personnel (especially in the rank of lieutenant commander) in the Pacific War. This writer believes this is one of the fundamental weaknesses of the Japanese Navy in the Pacific War.

As a whole, however, the types of Japanese naval combat vessels were almost the same as those of the American equivalents. It is true that the

Japanese Navy built such mammoth battleships as *Yamato* and *Musashi*, while the size of the aircraft carriers was a little smaller compared with that of the American. The Japanese Navy converted old cruisers to torpedo ships, and there were no ardent advocates to building antiaircraft cruisers which the American Navy built. The Japanese built a few very big submarines which might have been better called cruiser-submarines and, at the same time, many midget submarines. Still it can be generally said that the types of Japanese naval vessels were analogous to those of the Americans.

Navy Ministry and Naval General Staff

The Navy Ministry came into existence in February 1872, when the Defense Ministry was divided into the War and Navy Ministries, with the total naval expenditure of Y 1,190,000 as against the Army's Y 8,000,000 per month (17 ships with a total displacement of 13,812 tons as against 20 battalions of 12,000 troops of the Army). The first Navy Minister was Admiral Awa Katsu, the former samurai of the Tokugawa shogunate and a graduate of the naval training center at Nagasaki, the instructors of which were furnished by the Dutch. (Note: 1872 was also the year when the Japanese Navy shifted its system from the Dutch pattern to the British pattern.)

At this time the forerunner of the Naval General Staff was only a division within the Navy Ministry. In November 1878, the Army General Staff became independent of the War Ministry at the urgent recommendation of Taro Katsura (later general, premier in the days of the Russo-Japanese War, president of the Seiyukai Party, the forerunner of the present Liberal Party), who returned from Germany under the strong influence of the Prussian Army. This was the origin of the so-called "independence of the military command" which became instrumental to the predominance of the Army over the civil government. The Navy did not follow suit because the British pattern prevailed in the Navy. But the naval leaders had no rival in national politics. In 1886 the Army leaders forced the Navy leaders to transfer the power of the naval command to the Army General Staff. The Army's argument was that national defense strategy should be one and integral [sic]. Thus under the Chief of the General Staff (an Army general was appointed), an admiral served as the deputy chief for the Navy.

A strong resentment developed among Navy circles over the fact that naval strategy was subjected to the Army strategy. In March 1889, just the next month after promulgation of the Meiji Constitution, the Navy recovered from the Army General Staff the power of the naval command. The Minister of the Navy at that time was Judo Saigo, who was originally an Army general but later shifted to become a naval leader, and was one of the political leaders representing the Satsuma clan as against General Aritomo

Yamagata and Taro Katsura of the Choshu clan. Thus the Navy Ministry again absorbed the office of Naval Staff within the framework of the ministry.

Due to the gradual growth in size of the duties of the office of naval staff, and also due to the necessity to display a semblance of equality with the Army General Staff, the Navy finally established the Naval General Staff independent of the Navy Ministry on 19 May 1893. Unfortunately for the Navy, however, the Army's political dominance was so strong that the Army succeeded in subjugating the Naval General Staff to the Army General Staff in time of war. In other words, the same month as the inauguration of the Naval General Staff, the Regulation of Imperial General Headquarters was promulgated, with its Article 2 providing that "he who plans a grand army-navy strategy at the Imperial GHQ shall be the Chief of the Army General Staff."

In 1889, Admiral Gombei Yamamoto, a young and spirited naval administrator, was appointed Navy Minister as a representative of the Satsuma clan in the Yamagata Cabinet. The War Minister was General Taro Katsura, a representative of the Choshu clan. The Navy's fight to free the Naval General Staff from the war-time control of the Army General Staff—indeed the Navy's independence of the Army—began. Both Yamamoto and Katsura appealed and counter-appealed to Emperor Meiji on this great problem. Yamamoto was not a soft man as was usually the case with the Navy men. He was also a great logician. As seen in the section on "strategy and tactics," he also set a long-range plan for winning this fight through sending Commander Tetsutaro Sato to England to study the history of the influence of sea power on the nation's rise and fall. On the eve of the Russo-Japanese War, the Army leaders finally yielded to the tenacity of Navy Minister Yamamoto. On 28 December 1903, the Regulation of the Imperial GHQ was revised so as to give equal footing to the Chief of the Naval General Staff with the Chief of the Army General Staff.

In the Army, the Army General Staff enjoyed complete independence of, if not predominance over, the War Ministry. But in the Navy, the Navy Minister was always an ultimate master of the entire Navy. Nobody in the Navy could rival the great Navy Minister, Admiral Gombei Yamamoto, who carefully laid a firm cornerstone for the Navy tradition that military matters should be subject to the overall policy of the general government. Though Admiral Togo was made a national hero and No. 1 admiral of the Navy he was nothing but an obedient follower of Admiral Yamamoto. Naturally Admiral Yamamoto invited the deep hatred of the Army leaders and a political intrigue was staged against him. In January 1914, the enemies of Admiral Yamamoto struck a chance. Yamamoto had been Navy Minister from 1898 to 1906, and made his able follower Admiral Makoto Saito his successor as Navy Minister from 1906 to 1914. (Note: Viscount

Makoto Saito was assassinated in the 26 February 1936 Incident by Army rebels while he was Lord Keeper of the Privy Seal. He was one of many naval men who studied in the United States. Because of his profound pro-American attitude, it is believed no further explanation on him is needed here.) In 1913, Yamamoto was appointed Premier with Admiral Saito as Navy Minister. In January 1914, some politician overheard that the Chief of the Kure Naval Arsenal (Vice Admiral Matsumoto) was involved in a mean transaction with the Seamens [sic] Company of Britain. An intrigue was at once organized to discredit both Yamamoto and Saito. As was usually the case, the Diet members were utilized to attack the Yamamoto Cabinet. In Japan, to criticize a man on monetary matters was a most effective weapon. The Yamamoto Cabinet fell in April 1914 in a single political stroke, though no evidence was traced either to Yamamoto or to Saito. It was generally believed that General Yamagata was behind the anti-Yamamoto intrigue. Though Yamamoto retired from the political scene for some time, and though the post of the Navy Minister was temporarily (about one year and four months) occupied by an anti-Yamamoto admiral (Rokuro Yatsushiro), he soon recovered his control over the Navy by the appointment of Admiral Tomosaburo Kato (representative at the Washington Conference) in August 1915. After that time until the abolition of the Navy Ministry in 1945, the position of Navy Minister was occupied mostly by Yamamoto's followers. There were some Navy Ministers who were not direct followers of Yamamoto, for instance Admiral Murokami (six months in 1924) and Admiral Nagano (about eleven months in 1936–37). But even these men were not anti-Yamamoto; they were just neutral.

Due to the tradition founded by G. Yamamoto, the Chief of the Naval General Staff was always faithful and obedient to the policy laid down by the Navy Minister. It was the Navy Minister who recommended to the Emperor who should be Chief of the Naval General Staff. The Chief of the Naval General Staff had no voice in selecting the Navy Minister.

In 1930, indignant over the government's attitude toward the London Naval Conference, the Navy rose in revolt against the Government and its Navy Minister, Admiral Takeshi Takarabe. Admiral Takarabe was a son-in-law of Admiral Gombei Yamamoto and was then one of the delegates to the London Conference. The problem of the self-preservation of the Navy and also of the Army was involved in the subject of the dispute. Disarmament meant not only the retirement and slow promotion of naval personnel, but there was another point which the Army and Navy did not like. The Government had the power to make treaties. But to make a treaty at a disarmament conference meant to decide the size of armaments. The Japanese Constitution was so interpreted by the military that the size of armaments could not be decided without the consent of the Chief of the Navy (and Army for Army armament) General Staff. In other words, this was a collision between the Government's power and the military power.

The Government was headed by Yuko Hamaguchi, president of the Minseito Party. Those were the days of dirty political struggles. The opposition party, the Seiyukai Party, took advantage of the Government-Military quarrel. Admiral Kanji Kato, Chief of the Naval General Staff, and Vice Admiral Nobumasa Suetsugu, the Vice Chief, raised an open opposition against the Government. The Seiyukai Party and newspapers tried to egg these admirals on. Admiral Togo and Prince Fushimi were influenced by Kato. Young naval officers were also sympathetic to Kato and Suetsugu.

Though Navy Minister Takarabe ousted Kato and Suetsugu after he returned home, the opposition within the Navy was so strong that he could not help resigning from his post at last. The incident dealt a tremendous blow to the prestige of the Navy Minister.

But if the Manchurian Incident had not taken place in 1931, things must [sic] have been quite different from what actually developed. In the Manchurian Incident, the Army in the field defied the authority of the Government. Already young officers who occupied key positions in the Army organized the Cherry Party (*Sakura-kai*) to do away with government by political parties and pro-Anglo-American diplomacy. The Manchurian Incident was nothing but a business by a group of these officers. By this time, for reasons which are not explained here, ultra-nationalistic sentiment began increasingly gaining strength among the nation. And the sentiment of the nation was found to be sympathetic with the Manchurian Incident. Many politicians and journalists were quick to support the Army officers. Thus, the days of the Army began. There were many "smart" Navy men who were quick to ride the "bandwagon" of the Army. The tendency was aggravated in the early months of 1932 when the Manchurian Incident expanded to Shanghai. The Chief of the Naval General Staff, Admiral Naomi Taniguchi, who had been picked by a compromise between Admiral Togo and Admiral Takarabe, was ousted from the post. Prince Admiral Fushimi was then appointed Chief of the Naval General Staff after the pattern of Prince General Kanin, who had been Chief of the Army General Staff since after the outbreak of the Manchurian Incident. In Japan no one could vie with the power and prestige of a prince of royal blood in such an office. The appointment of Prince Fushimi was a suspension of the practice established by Gombei Yamamoto—the practice that in the Navy, the Naval General Staff should be obedient to the Navy Minister.

As soon as Prince Fushimi was seated at the Naval General Staff, a regulation governing the relations between the Navy Ministry and the Naval General Staff was changed according to the Army pattern. In order to oust the influence sympathetic with Britain and America as well as with Admiral Takarabe, many admirals of outstanding ability and vision were sent into retirement. Indeed, the seed was sown for the war coming in 1941. Prince Fushimi quitted the office only after Prince Kanin had been impeached by the Emperor and resigned in September 1940 because of the Army's unauthorized armed invasion into North French Indochina. But after him, Admiral Nagano, who was a master of "bandwagon riding" and was at the top of the seniority list of the active-service admirals, was made Chief of the Naval General Staff. In October 1941, Admiral Shimada, who was No. 1 "yes man" of Prince Fushimi, and who was a son-in-law of General Kumashichi Tsukushi, top "adviser" to the Emperor of Manchukuo, was appointed Navy Minister. Thus, until Admiral Yonai came back to the Navy Ministry in the summer of 1944 with his protégé, Admiral Oikawa, as Chief of the Naval General Staff, the golden rule set by Gombei Yamamoto ceased to work. (Note: In 1924 when he was appointed Premier for the second time, Gombei Yamamoto succeeded in opening a way to the appointment as War Minister and Navy Minister of a retired general and admiral. But this rule was cancelled in 1936 at the time of the Hirota Cabinet by the Army's demand. No man in Japanese history was appointed War Minister and Navy Minister who was not on active service—one of the important factors which caused the military control of the Government.)

Naval Education

The system of the education of naval personnel was almost the same as that in the U.S. Navy. Maybe the major difference was that in the U.S. Navy the fleet has its own school system for various technical educations such as for gunnery, engineering, etc., while in the Japanese Navy the entire school education was held at schools established ashore. To explain, in Yokosuka, for instance, there were the Gunnery School, Communications School, Torpedo School, Mining School, Navigation and Seamanship School, Manufacturing School (for repair work and damage control), etc. In these schools, not only young officers but also petty officers and men were educated after they had acquired some experience at sea. There were two or three grades for these school educations: the ordinary course, higher course, and special course.

It goes without saying that there were the Submarine School (in Kure) and the Aviation Training Group (in Kasumigaura and Yokosuka) for submarines and aviators respectively.

What the fleet gave to its crews was training and drills and such basic education as was given at the schools ashore. All the fleet program was so thickly packed that few could enjoy time for basic study or initiation of technical skill. The atmosphere in the Japanese fleet was not suitable for basic education.

Until just immediately before the Pacific War, the naval cadets who underwent education at the Naval College at Etajima were not qualified for engineering duty or paymaster duty. The officers of the engineering branch were the graduates of the Engineering School at Maizuru (formerly at Yokosuka) and those of the paymaster corps were graduates of the Paymaster School at Tenkiji, Tokyo. These officers were educated in such specialized fields alone from their cadet stage. The engineering officers demanded that they be permitted to serve as line officers with the same qualifications as the Etajima graduates. For the future of engineering officers were [sic] limited compared with that of the line officers. The struggle continued more than ten years. Finally the Engineering School was abolished, and the discrimination between the engineering officers and the line officers was removed. As for the paymaster officers, no such change took place.

There was no marine corps in the Japanese Navy. The key personnel of the landing parties were educated at the Gunnery School at Tateyama. But before the Sino-Japanese Conflict started in 1937, the scale of the Japanese landing party was very small. There was no Gunnery School at Tateyama. The Gunnery School at Yokosuka gave a limited education in landing party tactics. A few key officers who were to constitute the real core of the landing party were educated at the Infantry School of the Army. These officers were very few, less than one every [sic] Naval College graduate.

Probably the greatest weakness of the educational practice in the Japanese Navy as compared with that in the U.S. Navy was the weak coordination between the Naval War College and the Army General Staff College. In the Naval War College, matters about the Army were little taught by only two visiting instructors who appeared in the college for the duration of their assigned hours. The Navy did not send full-time instructors, either, to the Army General Staff College.

Ozawa Essays

Introduction

VADM Jisaburo Ozawa was a far-sighted officer of great determination. On 15 November 1939, as a Rear Admiral, he became commander of the First Carrier Division, which at that time comprised only *Akagi,* and was under the First Fleet commanded by Yamamoto. Four months in office convinced Ozawa that the current carrier organization was inefficient. He proposed organizing all major carriers under one command, with a guard force of destroyers. Not until December 1940, however, did Yamamoto approve the plan.

At the time of Pearl Harbor, Ozawa had been promoted to Vice Admiral and was CinC of the Southern Expeditionary Fleet. He served throughout the war in responsible positions, culminating in May 1945 as CinC of the Navy and, concurrently, as CinC of the Combined Fleet and of the Marine Escort.

This section consists of an extract from a larger Ozawa study and covers the setup of the Naval General Staff.

The translator was Capt. Toshikaze Ohmae.

Vice Adm. Jisaburo Ozawa. *Author's Collection*

The Naval General Staff

Jisaburo Ozawa

Adm. Ozawa's work

(Note:This is condensed as deemed necessary)

2. Naval General Staff

It was in 1886 that the Naval General Staff was for the first time established in the General Staff as the branch to take charge of naval operations. The Chief of the Naval General Staff, however, was under the Chief of the General Staff—an Army general.

In 1889 this command setup was switched so as to have the Naval General Staff under the Navy Minister, and in 1893 it was again changed so that the Naval General Staff for the first time became an independent office. However, according to the Wartime Imperial General Headquarters Regulation (*Daihonei* in Japanese) which was formulated in May 1893, the Chief of the Naval General Staff was to receive orders from the Chief of the Army General Staff in case of war. This system naturally caused much discussion, particularly after the Sino-Japanese War. Thereupon Marshalls Yamagata and Ovama, who worried over the situation, submitted a recommendation to the Emperor in favor of changing this system, and in 1903 this system was revised so that the Naval General Staff became an independent office directly under the Emperor.

In October 1933 the Naval General Staff setup was expanded as follows:

Chief of Naval General Staff
    Vice Chief
    Adjutant's Office
    First Bureau
    Special Branch under the direct control of the Bureau Chief:
    Matters pertaining to war direction, national matters concerning military affairs, matters concerning military agreements.

First Section: national defense policy, operational policies and plans, wartime organization, matters concerning necessary strength for national defense, defense matters, joint operations, materials for operations and matters concerning naval history.

Second Section: missions and movements of fleets, guard duty, commission of ships, organization, complements, system, regulations, training, discipline, traffic escort, security, inspection, manuals and directions.

Second Bureau

Third Section: war preparations, studies and experiments of warships, planes and weapons, installations.

Fourth Section: mobilization, transportation and supply plans; inspection (excluding fleets), hydrographical and meteorological matters.

Third Bureau

Special Branch under direct control of the Bureau Chief: intelligence plans, intelligence administrations, summary of intelligence, matters pertaining to operational materials and maps and counter-intelligence.

Fifth Section: intelligence towards North and South Americas, propaganda against those concerned countries.

Sixth Section: towards China and Manchuria.

Seventh Section: towards Soviet Russia

Eighth Section: towards Britain, European countries and Thai [sic].

Fourth Bureau

Ninth Section: communication plans, communications control, training and inspection pertaining to communications, communications intelligence and counter-intelligence.

Tenth Section: matters concerning codes.

Special Branch: radio intelligence.

Simultaneously with this revision of the Naval General Staff, a regulation ruling overlapping business between the Navy Ministry and the Naval General Staff was formulated.

In view of the tense international situation in 1941, defects in preparations for anti-sub operations were keenly felt. Accordingly, the Second Section was expanded so as to concentrate on anti-sub operations and business other than anti-sub operations was gradually turned over to the First Section.

7. Naval Stations*

The first naval station in the Japanese Navy was established in Yokosuka in September 1876. In May 1886 naval stations were also established in

*This jump from paragraph 2 to paragraph 7, without break, occurs in the translation.

Kure and Sasebo, and three years later, in May 1889, a naval station was established in Maizuru.

The commanding officer of a naval station was made responsible for guard and defense of his jurisdiction area and preparations for mobilization. As for administrative matters, he was responsible to the Navy Minister and, as for operational plans, to the Chief of the Naval General Staff.

Toward the end of the war, the Yokosuka Naval Station commander had under his command the following units and offices:

Garrison Squadron
Defense Squadron
Personnel Bureau
Accounts Bureau
Construction Bureau
Supplies Bureau
Ship Maintenance Bureau
Naval Yard
Naval Powder Arsenal
Aeronautical Arsenal
Aeronautical Research Arsenal
Naval Fuel Depot
Naval Clothing and Provision Depot
Naval Medical-Material Depot
Naval Hospital
Court-martial
Naval Prison
Harbormaster Office
Naval Barracks
Submarine Base Unit
Air Group
Communications Unit
Vessels and Units
Gunnery School
Torpedo School
Anti-Sub School
Navigation School
Communications School
Engineering School

Chihaya Essays

Introduction

Masataka Chihaya was a former commander in the Japanese Navy who served through the Pacific War. His brother was at Pearl Harbor and killed in the Battle of Midway. After the war, he worked for Gordon Prange as a freelance researcher while Prange was on the staff of Douglas MacArthur. Not only was he a researcher for Prange, but he had much to do with the writings of *At Dawn We Slept*, *Miracle at Midway*, *God's Samurai*, and *The Way It Was*. He was Prange's man Friday in Japan, acting as his administrator and translator. It was because of Chihaya that Fuchida, Genda, and other Japanese pilots granted Prange sole interviews and gave Prange their diaries and papers.

He translated the Ugaki diary and has written several works in Japan about the Pacific War. An excellent researcher, with twenty years of service in the Japanese Navy, Chihaya worked for the *Reader's Digest* in Japan as a researcher and administrator. He was like a brother to Gordon Prange and spent much time at Prange's home in Maryland. When Prange died, he became chief advisor for Goldstein and Dillon until his death in 1997. At the time of his death, he was considered the most knowledgeable Japanese historian on naval warfare. He knew everyone who was anyone who had served for the Japanese in World War II. It was fortunate for Prange and Dillon and myself, because without him, we could not have written our most famous works on the Pacific War. His analyses, none of which were published in English, are the best in the field and demonstrate both depth and breadth and for the first time are published here in this major section. We hope that they give the reader much insight into the running of the Japanese Navy before and during the war. The following are articles by Chihaya depicting the organization of the Naval General Staff Headquarters in Tokyo, the organization of the Japanese Naval Department, and the importance of Japanese naval bases overseas, to name a few.

Organization of the Naval General Staff Headquarters in Tokyo

Masataka Chihaya

19 December 1947

The Japanese Naval Staff Headquarters had peculiar characteristics. According to Japanese naval regulations, the Chief of the Japanese Naval Staff had the responsibility of aiding the Emperor in operating the Japanese Navy. The Emperor was the Generalissimo of the Imperial Navy as well as of the Imperial Army. Each CinC of the fleets directly belonged to the Generalissimo.

In this sense, the Chief of the Naval General Staff was no more than a staff officer and had no right to issue orders from his initiative. In fact, the Chief of the Naval General Staff took the form of either issuing orders "in the name of the order of the Emperor" or issuing instructions, when he intended to give instructions to the Imperial Navy. He never took the form of issuing an order on his initiative, whatever it might be.

* * *

Extract from the regulation of the Naval General Staff:

1. The Naval General Staff will deal with matters concerning state defense and operations.
2. The Chief of the Naval Staff directly belongs to the Emperor and aids the Emperor in important operational matters. He will control the Naval General Staff.

3. The Chief of the Naval General Staff will take the responsibility of planning the state defense and operations.

Yet the Chief of the Naval Staff ought to have been said to have all the responsibilities of naval operations, because he was the only man in the Imperial Navy who could offer his opinions to the Emperor as far as operations were concerned. Even any CinC of the Japanese fleets could offer his opinions only to the Chief of the Naval General Staff, but not the Generalissimo directly, of whom he was under the direct command.

It was the customary understanding in the old Japanese Constitution that neither the Prime Minister nor the War and Navy Ministers had any right to offer any opinion concerning operations to the Emperor. What's more, the Generalissimo never used his veto to the opinions made by the Chief of the General Staff.

This peculiar system of the General Staff was not inaugurated from its beginning. It was in 1886 that the General Staff for the first time was inaugurated into the Japanese Army and Navy. The General Staff of that time had Army and Navy branches and the chief of that headquarters had rights of controlling both branches.

In 1889 the Navy branch was separated from the Army branch, but the Naval Staff was put under the command of the Navy Minister. It is noteworthy that at this time the operation of the Navy was not outside of the Navy Minister but within his jurisdiction.

But four years later, in 1893, one year before the Sino-Japanese War, the Naval General Staff was established independent from the Navy Department. Since then, the peculiar system of the General Staff remained unchanged.

The position of Chief of the Naval General Staff had long been assumed by Prince Fushimi, until he was relieved by Admiral Osami Nagano in April 1941.

Admiral Nagano was a man worth mentioning a little. He was born in Kochi Prefecture, Shikoku, in 1880. He entered the Naval College in 1898 to begin his naval life. At the time of graduation from that college he was awarded the Imperial prize. Later he received courses at the Gunnery School and the Naval Staff College.

He was in America twice. The first time was from 1913 to 1915, the second time was from 1920 to 1923 as a naval attaché in Washington. During his second tenure he attended the Washington Naval Treaty.

From 1926 to 1930 he served as President of the Naval College. From 1930 he was transferred to the post of Vice Chief of the General Staff. In 1931 he was relieved of his post and was given the mission of attending the Geneva Naval Conference. In 1935 again he was assigned to attend the London Naval Conference.

In 1936, he got the post of Navy Minister and one year later, in 1937, he became CinC of the Combined Fleet. In April 1941 he was appointed Chief of the General Staff and remained in this post until he was relieved in February 1944.

After the surrender of Japan he was charged as a war crimes suspect, but he died in the early part of 1945.

Admiral Nagano was assisted by Admiral Seiichi Ito.

* * *

VADM Seiichi Ito was born in Fukuoko Prefecture in 1890. His naval career began when he entered the Naval College in 1908. He started his naval life as a torpedo man but later he received the course of the Naval Staff College in Tokyo. He was in America from 1927 to 1929. He spent most of his naval life in the Personnel Bureau of the Navy Department and educational circles.

In 1937 he became Chief of Staff of the 2nd Fleet and in April 1941 he became Chief of Staff of the Combined Fleet, the most important post of the Combined Fleet at the forthcoming world crisis, as the successor to the then RADM Shigeru Fukudome. But five months later, in September 1941, he jumped to Vice Chief of the General Staff to assist Admiral Nagano.

He had previously been a good assistant to Admiral Nagano as well as this time. In 1929 when I was a cadet of the Naval College in Etajima, he was the general manager of the school, assisting the then Vice Admiral Nagano, the president of the school. I can easily recall his doing well in assisting the president. He remained at his post as Vice Chief of the General Staff until, in late December 1944, he was appointed CinC of the 2nd Fleet, the remnant of the once armada of the west Pacific. He commanded the one-way sortie of the *Yamato* and other ships to Okinawa in April 1945 and died on board the *Yamato*.

* * *

Generally speaking, the General Staff was divided into five groups. They were: operations, war preparations, intelligence, communications and radio observation. Those bureaus were headed by RADMs Shigeru Fukudome, Yoshio Suzuki, Minoru Maeda, Shigeharu Kaneko and Gonichiro Kakimoto, respectively.

* * *

Shigeru Fukudome was born in Tottori Prefecture in 1891 and entered the Naval College in 1909. He was a navigation officer and also received the course at the Naval Staff College. He spent most of his naval life in the General Staff.

In 1939 he became Chief of Staff of the Combined Fleet and in April 1941 he was relieved of his post by Vice Admiral Ito, and he became Chief of the First Bureau of the General Staff. He retained his post until in May 1943 he was transferred to be Chief of Staff of the Combined Fleet again. In June 1944 he was appointed CinC of the newly organized 2nd Air Fleet and after the Leyte campaign he was transferred to be CinC of the newly organized 10th Area Fleet. He is still in Singapore.

The First Bureau headed by Rear Admiral Fukudome was divided into two sections. One was called the First Section, headed by then Captain Tomioka, which had all the responsibilities for naval operations. The First Section was really the brain of the Imperial Navy. Members of that section at the outbreak of the war were: Capt. Shigenori Kami, Cmdr. Prince Takamatsu, Cmdr. Yuki Yamamoto, Cmdr. Sadamu Sanagai, Cmdr. Seishi Uchida, Lt. Cmdr. Tatsukichi Miyo, Lt. Cmdr. Ryonosuke Ariizumi.

As to their personalities, characters and abilities, I commend you to refer to Mr. Tomioka who was then Chief of that section.

There was another group which directly belonged to the chief of the First Bureau. They dealt with war policy.

The Second Section was headed by Capt. Taro Taguchi, having the responsibility of complement, state guard and education.

The Second, Third and Fourth Bureaus were as follows:

The Second Bureau headed by Rear Admiral Suzuki

Third Section	Capt. Kuro Sugiura War preparation	
Fourth Section	Capt. Etsuzo Kurihara Mobilization	

The Third Bureau headed by Rear Admiral Maeda

Fifth Section	Capt. Bunjiro Yamaguchi Intelligence concerning America	
Sixth Section	Capt. Shigeto Kuwabara China	
Seventh Section	Capt. Tadashi Maeda Soviet Union	
Eighth Section	Capt. Kanei Chudo Great Britain	

The Fourth Bureau headed by Rear Admiral Kaneko

Ninth Section	Capt. Ichiro Aitoku
	Communications
Tenth Section	Capt. Shinju Ogura
	Codes and ciphers

The Special Bureau headed by RADM Gonichiro Kakimoto dealt with matters concerning radio observation. Radio observation aimed at gathering information through observing enemy radio activities. This method proved for the Japanese Navy the most useful information source during the war.

Supplement: Members of the General Staff at the Time of the Outbreak of the War
1 February 1948

1. First Bureau (*Dai Ichi Bu*)
   a. Second Section
   Capt. Taro Taguchi, Chief
   Capt. Yoshihiko Takasaki
   Cmdr. Yoriichi Uozumi
   Lt. Cmdr. Nobutoshi Minakawa
   Lt. Cmdr. Takumi Takao
   Lt. Cmdr. Takeo Nakamura

2. Second Bureau (*Dai Ni Bu*)   RADM Yoshio Suzuki
   Chief of Staff
   a. Third Section
   Capt. Juro Sugiura, Chief
   Cmdr. Kikuta Seto
   Cmdr. Umejiro Inoue
   Cmdr. Minato Nakajima
   Lt. Cmdr. Shigeru Iwaki

   b. Fourth Section
   Capt. Etsuzo Kurihara, Chief
   Cmdr. Yoshiji Doi
   Cmdr. Tooru Nishikawa
   Cmdr. Ikutora Masaki

3. Third Bureau (*Dai San Bu*)   RADM Minoru Maeda, Chief
   Chief

a. Special Group

Capt. Kanji Ogawa
Capt. Seishi Kojima
Lt. Cmdr. Itaru Tachibana
Lt. Cmdr. Hirohide Fushimi

b. Fifth Section

Capt. Bunjiro Yamaguchi, Chief
Cmdr. Senmi Muchaku
Cmdr. Yoshiro Kanamoto
Cmdr. Ichiji Higo
Lt. Cmdr. Tadashi Yamada

c. Sixth Section

Capt. Shigeto Kuwabara, Chief
Cmdr. Shinsaku Hidaka
Cmdr. Kaoru Kawase
Lt. Cmdr. Osamu Tsukada
Lt. Cmdr. Isamu Teshima
Lt. Cmdr. Taiichi Yasamura

d. Seventh Section

Capt. Tadashi Maeda, Chief
Cmdr. Toshio Usui

e. Eighth Section

Capt. Kanei Cyudo, Chief
Cmdr. Kikuo Yamakazi
Cmdr. Syutei Tonaki
Cmdr. Michinori Yoshii
Cmdr. Keisuke Matsunaga
Lt. Cmdr. Takao Inami

4. Fourth Bureau (*Dai Yon Bu*)
   Chief

RADM Shigeharu Kaneko

a. Ninth Section

Capt. Ichiro Aitoku, Chief
Cmdr. Saburo Tamura
Cmdr. Kosuke Nagai
Lt. Cmdr. Kaoru Imanaka

b. Tenth Section

Capt. Shinji Ogura, Chief
Cmdr. Okina Yasuda
Cmdr. Hiroo Yoshine

5. Special Bureau (*Tokumu Han*)
   Chief

RADM Gonichiro Kakimoto
Capt. Sei Mizoguchi
Lt. Cmdr. Hideo Ozawa
Lt. Cmdr. Toshiaki Shigekawa

The Organization of the Japanese Naval Department

Masataka Chihaya

18 January 1948

In the International Tribunal for the Far East, it was revealed that all military affairs concerning operations were, in this country, under the jurisdiction of the Chief of the General Staff, but not in that of the Navy Minister. This may seem very strange to foreigners, but it was quite true in the former Japanese Army and Navy.

It was stated, however, in my previous report that the fact that operational matters were entirely under the control of the Chief of the General Staff was not definitely based upon the old Japanese Constitution, but upon the customary understanding of it. Yet it is a very difficult matter to divide all military affairs very clearly into either operations or administration. As I will mention later, the Navy Minister also had responsibilities of war preparations and mobilization. So there were some overlaps between the jurisdictions of the Chief of the General Staff and the Navy Minister, which naturally needed a certain adjustment. In fact, there was an agreement between them which read:

> Article 3. The amount of strength will be planned by the Chief of the General Staff, and, with the agreement of the Navy Minister, will be offered to the Emperor as decided.

> Article 4. The following matters will be planned by the Chief of the General Staff and, with the agreement of the Navy Minister, will be offered to the Emperor to be authorized. After their authorization by the Emperor, they will be related by the Chief of the General Staff to the necessary sections and also to the Navy Minister. In case the Navy Minister finds a necessity of dispatching naval warships and troops, he will consult concerning it with the Chief of the General Staff.

Dispatch, mission and movement of warships and troops in reference to operations

Mission and movement of fleets in reference to operations

Dispatch of ships and troops to overseas areas and their missions and movements with regard to operational matters.

Article 5. The following matters will be planned by the Chief of the General Staff and, with the agreement of the Navy Minister, will be offered to the Emperor to be authorized. After their authorization by the Emperor, they will be related to the Chief of the General Staff, to the necessary sections and also to the Navy Minister.

Naval organization at wartime

Maneuvering and training

Instruction of sea battle

Article 6. The following matters will be planned by the Chief of the General Staff and, with agreement of the Navy Minister, will be offered to the Emperor to be authorized. After their authorization by the Emperor, they will be related to the Navy Minister, who will take the responsibility of executing them.

Organization of fleets and air forces at peacetime

Organization of destroyer divisions, submarine divisions, torpedo divisions, minesweeper divisions, air corps and marines

Instruction of fleet movement and regulation of maneuvering

Regulation concerning the chain of command.

Article 7. The following matters will be planned by the Navy Minister and will be consulted by the Chief of the General Staff. In case the authorization of the Emperor is needed, the Chief of the General Staff will offer them to the Emperor, and after the Emperor's authorization of them, they will be related to the Navy Minister, who will take the responsibility of executing them. The Chief of the General Staff will consult with the Navy Minister about matters as necessary.

Dispatch, mission and movement of warships and troops except those mentioned in Article 4.

Article 8. The following matters will be planned by the Navy Minister and will be consulted by the Chief of the General Staff. In case the authorization of the Emperor is needed, the Navy Minister will offer them to the Emperor and, after the Emperor's authorization of them, they will be conducted by the Navy Minister. The Chief of the General Staff will consult the Navy Minister about matters as necessary.

Complement of warships, troops and schools

Appointment of staff officers

Manuals.

Article 10. As regards important installations concerning stationing of forces, mobilization, national defense and operations, the Chief of the General Staff and the Navy Minister will consult with each other.

Article 13. The Chief of the General Staff and the Navy Minister will consult with each other concerning the following matters:
Such matters in reference to the strength of powers such as equipment and types of warships and weapons, and important installations.
Important experiment and study.

Article 14. The Chief of the General Staff and the Navy Minister will investigate in studying reports concerning training, experiments, and important missions.

* * *

Article 17. Other than mentioned above, the Navy Minister will maintain close contact with the Chief of the General Staff with regard to discipline, education, training, important affairs referring to national defense or operations and regulations.

* * *

Admiral Shigetaro Shimada headed the Navy Department since the Tojo Cabinet assumed its regime on 18 October 1941. Admiral Shimada was assisted by VADM Yorio Sawamoto, later Admiral, the then Vice Minister of the Navy. Under the control of Vice Admiral Sawamoto, the Navy Department was divided into nine groups. They were:

Office of the Secretary
Bureau of Military Affairs
Bureau of Military Preparation
Bureau of Personnel
Bureau of Education
Bureau of Supply
Bureau of Medical Affairs
Bureau of Accounting
Bureau of Legal Affairs

These bureaus were again divided into several sections, which were:

Office of the Secretary
   Aide-de-Camp   Capt. Katsuhei Nakamura
   Library
   Investigative Section
   Communications Section

Bureau of Military Affairs* RADM Takajumi Oka
  Preparations for War Capt. Toshitane Takada
  Policy Capt. Shingo Ishikawa
  Engineering Capt. Kakazu Urano
  Propaganda Capt. Hideo Hiraide

Bureau of Military Preparations RADM Zenshiro Hoshina
  Mobilization Capt. Syozo Hashimoto
  Policy of Supply Capt. Fumichika Okazaki
  Transportation Capt. Chikaya Hayashi

Bureau of Personnel RADM Giichiro Nakahara
  Appointments Capt. Wataru Nakase
  Rewards Capt. Syozo Tominaga

Bureau of Education RADM Sakae Tokunaga
  General Policy Capt. Shinzaburo Hase
  Technical Affairs Capt. Zyoichiro Hitomi

Bureau of Supply RADM Ko Misyuku
  Quartermaster Capt. Ichiro Kuzyu
  Fuel Capt. Mizuhiko Watanabe

Bureau of Medical Affairs
  Administration
  Planning

Bureau of Accounting
  Budget Estimate
  Inspection
  Accounting
  Contract
  Raising

Bureau of Legal Affairs

*Translator's penciled note: "Most powerful bureau in N. Min."

The Principal Propelling Power in the Former Japanese Naval Department

Masataka Chihaya

31 January 1948

My previous statement that the principal propelling power in the former Japanese Navy Department was focused in the Military Affairs Bureau interested you very much, so I want to add something about it.

It was a traditional feature that the principal propelling power of the Navy Department, if not of all the Navy, was focused into the Military Affairs Bureau. At some times in Japanese naval history, the bureau seemed to have even more power than any other bureau including the Naval General Staff. In fact, as was stated in my previous report, from 1889 to 1893 the Naval Staff Headquarters was even placed under the command of the Navy Minister.

Since 1893 the Naval General Staff was separated from the Navy Department, though the Navy Department had some influence on the former. It climaxed in the controversies fought between both departments just following the London Naval Treaty in 1930. In that Naval Treaty, Japan conceded the ratio of auxiliary vessels, including cruisers and destroyers, as 70% of the United States and the Great Britain [sic] navies, with the decision of the Japanese delegate to the Treaty, the then Navy Minister Admiral Tsuyoshi Takarabe.

This decision of Admiral Takarabe, made without any consultation with the General Staff, naturally caused heated controversies between him and the Chief of the General Staff, the then Admiral Kanji Kato. Because in Article 3 of the Japanese naval regulations concerning the liaison service

48

between the Navy Department and the Naval General Staff, which was also mentioned in my previous information, it was stated as follows:

"Article 3. The amount of strength will be planned by the Chief of the General Staff and, with an agreement of the Navy Minister, will be offered to the Emperor to be decided."

This heated friction was at last settled by relieving both chiefs of both Departments and leaving the following understanding about the matter concerning the amount of naval strength:

> The Instruction of the Navy Minister No. 157 dated 2 July 1930.
>
> Matters concerning naval strength will be dealt with in accordance with the following line as well as regulations in reference with it:
>
> Matters concerning naval strength will be dealt with in accordance with the existing custom. In this case, the agreement between the Navy Minister and the General Staff will be requested.

This instruction of the Navy Minister was followed by the following explanation by the Vice Minister of the Navy Department:

> As to naval strength, it was agreed when the Naval General Staff was established that it would be consulted with each other between the Navy Minister and the Chief of the General Staff, in accordance with the regulation concerning the liaison service between both Departments, to which line matters have hitherto been executed customarily. It was studied recently at the conference of the Naval Military Advisers Council in order to make the situation clear and also to wipe out any doubt and suspicion about it, with the result that it was unanimously agreed that this matter would be dealt with the same line as ever. So that it was instructed by Instruction No. 157 with the authorization of the Emperor.

The jurisdiction of the Military Affairs Bureau was, however, rather moderate according to the Japanese naval regulation which said:

a. War preparation and matters concerning general military administration
b. Complements and service of warships, troops, and officers and schools
c. Organization and missions of warships and troops
d. Discipline
e. Maneuvering
f. Inspection
g. Military ceremony, salute and flag
h. Principal matters concerning warships, weapons and equipment
i. Martial law and guard

The Second Section

a. Policy of national defense
b. International law and regulations

Notwithstanding, the Military Affairs Bureau of the Navy Department had such powers as to effect some influence to any matters concerning the administration of the Navy. For instance, even such minor matters as replacing a 13 mm machine gun were not to be carried out without the permission of the Military Affairs Bureau.

In wartime, the bureau sometimes exercised some influence even over operational matters. Because, as the war progressed, the war, not battles, came more to depend upon the abilities to produce and replenish weapons, men, equipment and supplies, which, in the Japanese viewpoint, were under the responsibility of the Navy Minister. To what extent the Military Affairs Bureau had powers in the Navy Department could be briefly shown in the following table: Extracted from the charge table of the Navy Department First Section of the Military Affairs Bureau:

Chief	General matters concerning naval administration
Member A	Military preparation
Member B	Complements of ships, troops, offices and schools
	Discipline and service
	Association and union
	Budget in the Bureau
	Conference of the Chief of Staff
Member C	Preparation, organization and complements of naval air forces
Member D	Organization, mission and movement of warships and troops
	Register of warships
	Maneuvering
	Martial law, guard and air defense
	Inspection
	Capture of ships in wartime
	Fuel
Member E	Ceremony, salute, flag, uniform and medals
	Protection of military secrets
	Counterintelligence
	Protection of mobilization secrets and war material secrets

	Prisoners of war, examination of ship and prohibited materials
Member F	General matters concerning ships and weapons except submarines
Member H	General matters concerning submarines and their weapons Preparation, organization and complement of submarine forces
Member I	Defense, defense sea area, and protection of merchant ships Part of guard and air defense Part of preparation and organization concerning defense Part of complements of warships and troops General books and war records Materials for statistics and year book
Member P	Preparation, organization, system and complement concerning convoy escort
Member S	General matters concerning war supply Engineering except electric power engines and gasoline, diesel engines Repairing Systems and complements of engineering and repairing Equiping ships Conference of Chiefs of Ship Maintenance Emergency repairing of ships
Member T	Electric power engines and gasoline and diesel engines Registering of miscellaneous ships Equiping of submarines Matters concerning personal matters

The Second Section of the Military Affairs Bureau

Chief	General matters concerning policies of the national defense
Member J	War policy Matters concerning the Supreme War Steering Council
Member K	Policy of foreign except regarding Manchuria and China
Member L	Policy of domestic affairs

Member M	Policy concerning Manchuria, China, and Inner South Sea Archipelago
	Matters concerning the Liaison Committee of the Great Asia Ministry
	Matters concerning the Investigation Committee of establishing Great Asia
Member N	Increasing war strength
	Policy concerning transportation and communications
Member O	Policy concerning Southern Area Occupation
Member P	Diet
	Policy concerning thought of people
	Part of domestic policy
	Part of increasing war strength

You can easily imagine how extensively the Military Affairs Bureau covered under its jurisdiction. It was not too much exaggeration to say that the Military Affairs Bureau had such powers in the former Japanese Navy as to exercise some influence upon nearly every aspect of naval affairs.

It was not, however, the Military Affairs Bureau itself, nor the Chief of that Bureau, but the Navy Minister himself, who represented the Japanese Navy to those outside the Navy. The Navy Minister was literally the boss of the Japanese Navy, if not in all senses. Although the boss of the operations field was the Chief of the General Staff, the Navy Minister could be called, in some senses, the boss of the Navy.

The other day I told you that the then Navy Minister at the time of the Russo-Japanese War 1904–05, Admiral Gombei Yamamoto, demanded of the then C-in-C of the Combined Fleet, Admiral Soonojo Hidaka, to turn over his post to Admiral Heihachiro Togo. I want to add here one more instance of the power of the Navy Minister.

Towards the beginning of August 1945 when Japan was driven on the verge of the final decision, facing successive disasters of atomic bombs and Russian participation in the war, the Cabinet headed by Baron Suzuki considered the problem of Japan's surrender in the utmost seriousness.

Of all four military persons of the Supreme War Steering Council, Admirals Yonai and Toyoda, Generals Umezu and Anami, Admiral Yonai was the only person who gave approval to accepting the surrender terms. Naturally, there was [sic] aroused heated discussions, even some sparks. One day Admiral Yonai got angry with the behavior of the then Vice Chief of the General Staff, Vice Admiral Onishi. The latter, who was quite discontented with the surrender, seemed to have revealed his opposition to the surrender to someone in the Army.

Admiral Yonai immediately requested both the Chief and the Vice Chief of the General Staff to report to his office. Furiously he blamed the behavior of Admiral Onishi as acting ultra vires [sic]. Admiral Onishi, however, admitted it quietly. And Admiral Toyoda advanced to tender his apology for Admiral Onishi's misconduct. It was quite against the expectation of Vice Admiral Hoshina who was there as Chief of the Military Affairs Bureau. This story was also revealed by Admiral Hoshina himself.

Short History of the Japanese Naval Bases in the Homeland

Masataka Chihaya

5 January 1947

Japan did not awake from her long dream, which had lasted more than 218 years under the regime of the Tokugawa Shogunate, until in July 1853 Commodore Mathew C. Perry appeared off the coast with a squadron of ships of the United States Navy. His sudden appearance was literally an alarm bell which awakened the Japanese people not only politically but strategically.

The next year they decided to throw away their long-cherished "closed door" policy and also issued permission to build large ships which had been strictly prohibited. In 1855 they established a naval training board at Nagasaki, in which about 120 students received Western-style naval training guided by the Dutch Navy. Among those directors and students of that training board were such persons as Count Awa Katsu, VADM Buyo Enomoto and Admiral Sumiyoshi Kawamura, who later played important roles as Navy Minister in the early history of the Japanese Navy.

They also established an ironworks at Nagasaki in 1861 and another one at Yokosuka in 1866. In later years the former became the Mitsubishi Shipbuilding Yard, the biggest civil shipbuilding yard in this country, and the latter became the Yokosuka Naval Yard.

After the restoration of the Meiji regime in 1868, the armed forces, sea powers inclusive, which had been under the power of the Tokugawa Shogun and its subordinate feudal lords, became reorganized under the control of the Meiji Government. With the establishment of the Navy Ministry on 27 February 1872, the Japanese Navy was born, consisting of two steel ships, one composite ship, and 17 others, totaling only 13,832 tons.

At this time when the Japanese Navy set up its first step, it seemed that there were two different opinions about naval bases. In 1878 the naval authority sent an opinion to the Cabinet to the effect that a naval base would be established at Otsu, south of Yokosuka. The next year, another opinion was sent to the Cabinet. The opinion said:

> If Japan happened to suffer from an invasion by other countries in the future, it would be from the west through Hongkong [sic] to the Kanmon Area or to the Osaka-Kobe Area, to the Tokyo-Yokohama Area. If we hold strong naval bases at such places as Kagoshima and Tsushima, invasion forces doubtless would have to attack both bases as their first step of the invasion. This is most desirable for the defense of our country. We the naval authority, therefore, asked the Cabinet to establish naval bases at Kagoshima, Tsushima and Otsu.

To this requirement of the Navy Ministry, the Cabinet decided to establish a naval base only at Kagoshima, but in practice it did not go ahead.

In 1876 it was decided to establish two naval bases, Tokai Naval Base (meaning Eastern Sea Base) and Seikai Naval Base (meaning Western Sea Base). The site of Tokai Naval Base was set at Yokohama, but that of Seikai Naval Base was not yet fixed.

On 15 December 1882, the site of the Tokai Naval base was changed to Yokosuka. This was the beginning of Yokosuka Naval Base.

After investigations were made as to the site of Seikai Naval Base, Kure and Sasebo were selected in 1886. On 1 July 1889, both Kure and Sasebo were opened.

The capacities of these naval bases were so remarkably developed and expanded that these bases, especially Sasebo Naval Base, played important roles in both the Sino-Japanese War (1894–95) and the Russo-Japanese War (1904–05).

In 1901, three years before the outbreak of the Russo-Japanese War, the Maizuru Naval Base was established.

In 1905, the Ominato Naval Base was established.

Although both Maizuru and Ominato Naval Bases had good anchorages, they lacked elements of naval yards, because of their poor hinterland as manufacturing center, also because of their snowy climate [sic]. In consequence, they made comparatively little contribution to the great expectations of the Japanese Navy after the Russo-Japanese War, while shares played by the other three bases, Yokosuka, Kure and Sasebo, were surprisingly remarkable.

In addition to these bases, in 1939 a new naval base was established in Osaka. The Osaka Naval Base was, however, not worthy of the name. It was no more than the representative of the Navy in that area, having no facility of base, yard and supply.

Sources of this information

History of Japanese Naval Organization, published by the Navy Ministry in 1939.

History of the Japanese Navy, published by the Naval Reserve Association in 1938.

Biography of Admiral Gombei Yamamoto

Importance of Japanese Naval Bases in the Homeland

6 January 1947

Yokosuka Naval Base was the oldest one and the role it played in Japanese naval history was great.

Let us first consider particular features of the organization of the base at the first step. Each Japanese naval base except Ominato and Osaka used to be organized by the following elements:

Headquarters   Hospital
Guard Vessels   Prison
Reserved Vessels   Harbormaster
Personnel Section   Naval Barrack
Supply Section   Defense Corps
Ship Superintendent Section   Flying Corps
Naval Yard   Communications Corps

In addition to these usual elements, Yokosuka Naval Base had two outstanding features. One was [the] concentration of naval technical schools in Yokosuka, and the other was the Naval Aero Technical Institution.

There were such schools in Yokosuka as Gunnery, Torpedo, Navigation, Communications, Engineering, Antisubmarine and Radar Schools. In these schools, not only technical knowledge of each technique was taught to officers and enlisted men, but research and experiment about [sic] each technique were also carried out. Furthermore, in the Yokosuka Flying Corps, a higher course of flying education was taught. Thus Yokosuka was the center of naval technique.

Research in the Naval Aero Technical Institution covered from researching of materials to be used for aircraft to testing new model craft. How great a role this institution played in the development of Japanese naval air strength can hardly be exaggerated.

However, Yokosuka Naval Base had some defects. Its anchorage was not only insufficient to accept a task force, but it was so exposed in such a populated area as Tokyo and Yokohama that it was very difficult to keep the whereabouts of a fleet secret. Moreover, it faced the menace of enemy carrier-borne air forces. In consequence, the Japanese Navy did not pay much attention to Yokosuka as a fleet operating base.

As the war progressed, Yokosuka Naval Base began to reveal an important fault which had been little recognized before the war. That was the ability to load and unload materials to transport ships. There was no wharf capable of bringing large-type freighters alongside and poor capacity of railway and vehicle transportation. The more the speed and the amount of transportation were needed as the war progressed, the more acutely this grave fault came to be realized.

Although it is not a main point, I want to put in here my private opinion about the future importance of Yokosuka. Some time ago, an American correspondent was said to have reported to the effect that Captain Decker, the present commanding officer of Yokosuka Base, would urge an important opinion about Yokosuka. His claim would be:

1. That in the next war, if it happens, the Yokosuka area would be more important than the Marshalls and the Marianas.
2. That constructing a base at Yokosuka would cost less than that of the Marianas, because cheap Japanese labor would be available in Yokosuka.
3. That in order to obtain this, the United States ought to hold Yokosuka on lease for about a quarter of a century.

This is a very important opinion indeed. But I have a different one. Nobody doubts nowadays that the next war, if it happens, would be chiefly fought in the air. One can easily realize also that the principal task of the United States Navy in the Pacific theater when the next war comes would be the maintenance of a large supply of ammunition, food and fuel chiefly to the areas of Hokkaido, Kanto, northern Kyushu, southern Kyushu, and the advanced Dairen area. In such operations, it is obvious that the most important thing is the capacity to unload materials at terminal ports. There is therefore little doubt that, judging from this point of view, Yokohama is far more valuable than Yokosuka.

Moreover, I believe that the most powerful defense wall to the United States in the next war is not the fortification of Japan proper but the sincere cooperation of the Japanese people with the United States. If the United States merely helps the Japanese people to restore Yokohama harbor instead of holding Yokosuka on lease, one can easily imagine how favorable a sentiment would be impressed upon the Japanese people. It might grow to become a beautiful cooperation of the Japanese people, and also might become a very strong wall in the time of the next war.

Peculiar features of the Kure Naval Base were the Naval College, the Submarine School and its large-scaled Naval Yard. As to details of the Naval College, I want to describe it in another report. Here I am going to refer only to the outline of it. The Naval College was situated on Etajima, the island opposite Kure, and there was no establishment except the college. Its environment was calm and excellent. The effects of its environment upon the cadets were so remarkable that we could not neglect them in analyzing the tradition of the Japanese Navy.

In its width and depth, the Bay of Hiroshima was so suitable for small-craft maneuvering that submarines of the Japanese Navy were trained there from its beginning. Midget-type submarines which had been used in the Pearl Harbor attack for the first time and which would have been used in large numbers in the defense of the homeland, were all taught and trained in the Submarine School.

The Kure Naval Yard was not only the greatest dockyard but the largest arsenal, especially in such heavy industries as manufacturing steel armor plates and large-caliber guns. The thickest armor ever made in this country and 18-inch guns, the greatest naval guns ever made, both of which were made for the *Yamato* and the *Musashi,* were made in Kure arsenal.

Moreover, the Kure Naval Base had a large portion of war stocks of ammunition and fuel. Thus, the Kure Base was both in name and reality the biggest and most important base in this country.

In addition, it had other peculiar advantages that Yokosuka and Sasebo did not have.

1. Its anchorage was not only sufficient for a large fleet but suitable anchorages were elsewhere in the Bay of Hiroshima that were not so exposed to the common view.
2. Compared to Yokosuka and other bases, it was not comparatively exposed to the direct menace of enemy carrier-borne attacks.
3. Near the Bay of Hiroshima there is the Suoo-Nada, the western part of the Inland Sea, the only area where fleet maneuvering could be carried out without any fear of enemy submarines.

Consequently the Kure Naval Base had been used as a fleet operating base from the beginning of this war, until in the spring of 1945 the remaining Japanese fleet was annihilated in the Bay of Hiroshima by Halsey's powerful task forces.

From the early time of Japanese naval history, Sasebo Naval Base was strategically important. In all wars and incidents except the last war, it played important roles as a fleet operating base. It was one of the strategies of our naval authority in those days to utilize the Sasebo Naval Base most effectively in the event of wars or incidents, until in this war the situation changed. However, it seems to me that the future importance of Sasebo would be prosperous. Because, as I have discussed in the phase of Yokosuka, in the event of a future war, maintenance of communications in the Yellow Sea would be important, and Sasebo Base would be more important than now in order to fulfill this aim.

Compared with other bases, the Maizuru and Ominato Naval Bases were less important and there was almost nothing to say about them.

Importance of the Japanese Naval Bases Overseas

Masataka Chihaya

14 January 1947

It was in the Bay of Chinkai that in 1905 Admiral Togo trained his fleet completely and sortied for his victorious battle of Tsushima. At the time of the Russo-Japanese War, the Bay of Chinkai was the next important place to Sasebo in that area, because it was not only situated in a position to cut down communications between Port Arthur and Vladivostok but it had sufficient anchorage for a powerful fleet of that time. The anchorage of that bay was so wide that the Japanese fleet could even practice its training in that bay.

The glorious victory of the Battle of Tsushima, however, brought so drastic a change in the field of naval strategy that the Bay of Chinkai was no longer as important as it had been during the war, because the Battle of Tsushima resulted in complete control of the sea power of the Far East in the hands of the Japanese Navy.

It was the same with Port Arthur. As a harbor it was not so important, because its harbor was narrow and shallow. At the time of the Russo-Japanese War it was an important base only because it was the only Russian all-weather base in the Yellow Sea able to operate the Russian fleet. But the war changed its situation.

Thus both Port Arthur and Chinkai lost their importance after the Russo-Japanese War. The Japanese Navy kept naval bases there chiefly from the political point of view. Soon after the surrender of Port Arthur in 1905, Japan established a naval base there, although in April of 1914 its rank was reduced to a minor naval base. At Chinkai, a minor naval base was established in April of 1916. Both bases retained their functions until the surrender of Japan in the summer of 1945.

Japan gained Formosa as a result of the Sino-Japanese war of 1894 to 1895. Japan made some efforts to exploit it, with considerable success. Japan also established a minor naval base at Bako, the Booko Archipelago, in 1902, two years before the outbreak of the Russo-Japanese War. The Bako Naval Base, however, made little contribution to encountering the Russian Baltic Fleet, first, because Admiral Togo concentrated his fleet at the Strait of Tsushima with a firm confidence that the Russian Fleet would never fail to pass that strait; second, because the Russian Fleet passed around Formosa, passing the Bassi Strait and east off that island.

The Bako Naval Base was the only anchorage capable of harboring a fleet in Formosa, for Formosa had such a monotonous coast line that there were few harbors worthy of the name except Kiirun and Takao. Even these harbors were narrow and needed much construction and equipment for harbors.

The Bako Naval Base, however, had a vital defect. The Booko archipelago consisted of low sand islands engulfing the Bako harbor in their midst. In winter, a raging northwest monsoon prevailed there. One could hardly find trees taller than such shelters as houses and walls, for in winter the raging, sandy wind prevented trees from growing. Wilderness itself was everywhere almost without even bushes and grass. There was scarcely anything more.

As the Sino-Japanese Incident progressed since 1937, there arose, therefore, the necessity of constructing a more useful base than Bako in Formosa. The Japanese Navy thereupon decided to construct an artificial harbor just north of the town of Takao. The general plan of the Takao Naval Base was:

1. Its construction began in 193 [sic] and would be expected to be completed in 194.*
2. Its harbor was to be divided into outer and inner harbors, and the former, engulfed by large-scale breakwaters, would contain more than 6,000,000 square meters and the latter one made by dredging the inland area would contain a 2,000,000-square-meter pond of which the northern half would be 6 meters deep, and the southern half, 9 or 10 meters deep.
3. Two large and three small docks would be built in the inner harbor and of these, in fact, only construction of a small dock was begun, but it was not completed.
4. In addition, necessary loading facilities and oil storage equipment, etc., would be built.

The Japanese Navy also planned to construct two large airfields near Takao Naval Base, at Takao and Tainan. Until the outbreak of this war,

---

*The author omitted the fourth digit.

however, little of what is mentioned above had been completed except the Takao and T'ainan airfields.

Both the Takao and T'ainan airfields had such good capacities that these bases might become strong springboards at the outbreak of this war. Just before the outbreak of the war in 1941, the Japanese Navy concentrated there the main forces of the 11th Air Fleet, powerful land-based naval air forces consisting chiefly of "O" Type fighters and "I" Type land-based twin-engined naval bombers. From both Takao and Tainan bases, those forces sortied for the air of the Philippines. Breaking through the mist in the morning of 8 December 1941, they achieved remarkable success, completing the neutralization of the Philippines in a few days.

In April 1943 the Takao Naval Base was opened and simultaneously the Bako Naval Base was closed, although the construction of the Takao Naval Base was not completed yet. The Takao Naval Base retained its function until the end of this war.

Truk Island is one of the greatest lagoons, shaping nearly a triangle of which each side is more than 30 miles. In the midst of the lagoon are many islands, not sand islands or coral reefs, of which more than 8 of the bigger islands are more than one square mile. It not only provides a sufficient anchorage for a whole Japanese fleet of that time but it also provides enough area in the lagoon for maneuvering several vessels for training. In those islands there is enough area for several airstrips. In fact, the Japanese Navy established more than four strips in those islands by the end of the war. Its climate is mild though it belongs to a typical tropical one. In addition to these advantageous features, it is situated in a most important key position in the middle Pacific area, able to control Midway Island to the north, the Marshalls to the east and Rabaul and New Britain to the south. From every point of view Truk Island is indeed one of the most important bases in the Pacific.

During the occupation of those islands in World War I and the mandated administration of them that followed, the Japanese Navy had well realized the importance of Truk. Having held a comparatively strict attitude toward the treaties, however, the Japanese Navy did almost nothing to establish a naval base there. It seems hard to believe, but believe me, it is quite true. At the outbreak of this war there was only one-half a completed airstrip in Takeshima, a small island less than 1,000 meters long. There was no underground oil storage, no repair facilities on land. There was no naval establishment worthy of the name of land except a half-completed small airstrip.

Even after the outbreak of the war, the Japanese Navy was rather lazy in strengthening the Truk Naval Base. As soon as the United States Navy landed their first step of the offensive on Guadalcanal Island in the summer of 1942 and the area around the Solomon Islands became the main theater of fighting of both countries, Truk Island immediately began to be the center of the Japanese naval operation. Almost all Japanese naval vessels gathered there. Japanese naval vessels sortied there for fighting around the Solomon Islands and returned there for refueling or repairing when damaged. Never before had the need of repair facilities and oil tanks been more urgently realized in Truk. There the Japanese Navy concentrated their repair ships and oil tankers and also endeavored to build repair facilities and oil tanks quickly. But it was too late. How much the schedule of oil transportation from the southern area to the homeland was disturbed by the fact that the Japanese Navy always at that time suspended several tankers at Truk with the aim of using them as only oil tanks, was hardly overestimated. At that time, the *Yamato* and the *Musashi,* which should have been the main bodies of the Japanese fleet, were often nicknamed "the tankers *Yamato* and *Musashi*" because at that time they used to serve as tankers supplying fuel to small vessels instead of engaging in any operation.

As there were no available repair facilities at Truk, it was not seldom also that Japanese naval vessels were forced to go back to the homeland for repair, with the result that it affected the reduction of Japanese naval forces which would engage in fighting around the Solomon Islands.

It was as late as the summer of 1943 that the Japanese Navy at last started to construct three more strips at Truk, two on Harushima, which meant a spring island, and one on Kaede-shima, which meant a maple-tree island. When the United States Navy made a sudden attack on Truk on 17 February 1944, those three bases had been almost completed, but they lacked such adequate equipment as radars and commanding equipment necessary for utilizing those bases perfectly.

As a result, it was an entirely surprising attack for the Japanese forces in Truk when on the morning of 17 February 1945 United States carrier-borne airplanes began to attack Japanese vessels, diving from the blue like bolts. The Japanese Navy lost one light cruiser, 4 destroyers, 26 transport ships, 3 oil tanks, 2,000 tons of food and more than 180 planes. Of those planes lost, more than 100 were lost on the ground.

As a result of the fiasco of the Truk Islands in February 1944 in addition to the fall of the Gilberts and Marshalls, the once most important naval base suddenly began to lose its importance as a naval base. The Japanese fleet which had long used to gather in Truk went westward to the Carolines, Singapore and also the homeland just before the fiasco of Truk. The Japanese naval land-based air forces withdrew to the Marianas and Carolines save for a short period just following that fiasco. The Truk Islands was no longer a worthy naval base, nothing but a stepping-stone between the Marianas and Rabaul.

The bad situation became the worst [sic] when the United States forces began to invade the Marianas in June 1944. During the battle around the Marianas, Truk Island could contribute little to the battle. After the fall of the Marianas, the Truk Islands were forced to be isolated perfectly from the outside except for a very few urgent transportations by means of submarines and flying boats. Since then, the Japanese forces on Truk had to fight not only restless, powerful Allied air forces but daily increasing starvation and disease until the end of the war in August 1945.

Then let us turn our eyes on Rabaul. Even after the occupation by the Japanese forces at the outbreak of the war, Rabaul had still kept quiet, though in May 1942 at the Coral Sea a large-scale fierce battle was fought for the first time between both American and Japanese carrier-borne forces. But it was not long before in August 1942 the United States Navy suddenly landed their crack Marine 1st Division on Guadalcanal. All of Japan's attention began to be focused on the Solomon Islands and New Britain, with the result that the magnificence of Rabaul suddenly began to be realized by the Japanese, especially by the Japanese Navy.

In Rabaul there were several areas suitable for a large-scale strip and a good anchorage, too. The land thereof was suited for cultivation. Also it was situated in the center of that theater. At that time, when both powers were fighting a desperate battle around the Solomon Islands, Rabaul was often compared by the Japanese to the rivet of a fan, which meant that it was so important that if it happened to be lost, the whole situation would be changed at once, like a fan when the rivet was broken off.

Such being the case, Japan, especially the Japanese Navy, did everything possible to reinforce Rabaul since the autumn of 1942. The Japanese Navy endeavored to pour into Rabaul as many weapons, ammunitions, and planes as possible until in February 1944 Japan at last was forced to give up maintaining the Rabaul area. The Japanese Navy reinforced surprisingly great amounts of weapons, ammunition and planes to Rabaul and exhausted almost all of them, so that in February 1944, when Japan at last decided to withdraw air forces from there, Japan hardly had a firm plan to encounter the powerful Allied Powers.

Just after the fiasco of Truk in February 1944, Japanese air forces in the Rabaul area withdrew to Truk and the Marianas. It was the end of February 1944 when the Allied Powers penetrated through Dampier Strait and invaded Admiralty Island even without meeting any effective counterattack by Japanese forces. Admiralty Island is situated in such a position as to cut Rabaul's communication line. In consequence, the once-famed base was left isolated in the southern Pacific, and came to be nothing but a training target of the Allied air forces.

Admiralty Island possesses not only an important position in that area but it has a good harbor in Manus, one of the most magnificent bays in the southern Pacific. Why did the Japanese forces let the Allied Powers invade that important island even without any effective counterattack? Why did the Japanese forces not make some effort to fortify there, to be able to encounter the enemy? Didn't the Japanese forces, especially the Japanese Navy that had ever been claiming the importance of that theater, realize the importance of that island?

One cannot but doubt it. I once asked the reason for it of Capt. T. Ohmae, who was then a staff officer of that theater. He replied, "It was not that the Japanese Navy did not realize the importance of that island. It was because, however, that according to some survey that island was found not entirely suitable for human habitation. Therefore we had to give up constructing a base there." This was one of the great blunders indeed. For the Allied Powers succeeded in constructing a magnificent naval base at Manus after its occupation.

The fate of the once-famed Rabaul after the fall of Admiralty Island in February 1944 suddenly went from worse to the worst. Since then the Japanese garrison of Rabaul had to make up their minds to go literally underground. They completed the underground fortification of Rabaul, constructing even factories and storages underground. Thus, when the war ended in August 1945, Rabaul was found to be one of the strongest bases in the Pacific.

Importance of the Inland Sea

Masataka Chihaya

20 January 1947

Last autumn I went to Kagoshima, and on my return trip to Tokyo I preferred to take a ship from Beppu to Kobe instead of a jammed train. It was in the summer of 1942 that I sailed the Inland Sea last on board a battleship, the *Musashi*. Since then just three-and-a-half years have passed, but to me, perhaps also to most of the Japanese people, it seems to be far more than three years. Nay, it seems even more than thirty years.

I left Beppu in the afternoon on board a small merchant ship of less than 1,00[sic] tons. Toward the evening she passed north off a lighthouse at the tip of Sata Cape. There seemed to be little change in passing islands, and lighthouses flashed as it had ever been. The sea was a little rough with the northwest wind prevailing already, just as it had been in this season. Apparently little change was observed in its natural circumstances.

But what a great difference it was! For I, who once used to sail everywhere at will on board Japanese warships, was now sailing the same sea on board a small merchant ship only as a passing traveler. The steamer made her way alone, guided by leading buoys in the sea once crowded by coming and going vessels, for there was only one available passage in that sea owing to remaining American mines dropped by B-29s during the war. We did not meet any passing vessel nor [sic] even fishing boats. The sea once crowded with vessels had become very quiet.

When the steamer was crossing the Suoo-Nada, the western part of the Inland Sea, I could not help recalling the status of that sea several years ago. Before the war, the western part of the Inland Sea, together with Bungo Strait, was the center of training of the Japanese Navy. The Japanese Navy used to gather at Sukumo Bay, Saeki Bay and Ariake Bay for training almost the whole year. From those training bases they sailed south off Shikoku or east off Kyushu for practice of fleet maneuvers. Sometimes they went to Beppu for recreation and to Tokuyama and Kure for refueling or repairs.

From just before the outbreak of the war, the Japanese Navy began to use the Inland Sea as its base. It was from Hiroshima Bay that Admiral Yamamoto sortied for his first operation just before the outbreak of the war. As soon as the war broke out, the Inland Sea became only a training sea for the Japanese Navy, as the Inland Sea was the only area wide enough to enable fleet training without fear of enemy submarines. It was in the Inland Sea that just three-and-a-half years ago the *Musashi*, on whose board [sic] I was, made her first trial voyage.

In the Inland Sea there were once such important bases as Kure and To-kuyama. As I have mentioned in my No. 2 report, the Kure Naval Base was the greatest naval base in this country. In Tokuyama there was a great naval oil refinery and also oil storage. In Hikari, east of Tokuyama, there was a naval arsenal though it was not completed.

There had also been a weaving traffic of merchant vessels in the Inland Sea, until in the early summer of 1945 it was completely blockaded by American mines, especially magnetic and hydraulic pressure type mines dropped by B-29s. The Inland Sea was often called by the Japanese the artery of Japan. It meant that the Inland Sea was such an important trans-portation route of Japan. Most of that transportation was from Kyushu to Kansai and vice versa. Transportation from Kyushu to Kansai was mostly of coal which was needed in Kansai badly. One could not overestimate how much the industries in Kansai depended upon coal from Kyushu. As the American minelaying [sic] operation in the Inland Sea progressed from the early summer of 1945, it immediately began to sever Japanese industries in Kansai and finally nearly to stop them. It was almost vital to Japanese abil-ity to continue the war.*

It is the same at present. Although a passage through the Inland Sea has been opened by efforts of both Allied Powers and Japanese, few ships are passing the sea. Not only is the so-called artery of Japan not in the pink, but on the contrary there are a lot of ominous indications that it would [sic] stop in the very near future. Almost all Japanese industries are not at work at present because of the severe shortage of all materials and also because of fears of reparation. Japan today is indeed on the verge of its crisis.

For seamen the Inland Sea was once famous for being not easy for sailing, not only because there are many islands and complicated passages, but be-cause there were too many fishing boats. But when the steamer made her way, we scarcely met any of them. The steamer continued her way alone in the dark sea in the middle part of the Inland Sea.

At dawn of the next morning, the steamer was sailing west of Awajis-

---

*I have made efforts to make clear in figures how badly the Japanese ability to continue the war was destroyed by the mine-laying operation of the United States Navy, but so far in vain, to my great disappointment.

hima, the eastern part of the Inland Sea, when we met for the first time a Japanese war-built merchant ship in the same small area. This very ship was one of the "Guinea Pig" ships that were doing dangerous tasks of clearing mine-suspected areas, to the sacrifice of their own ships. This was a peculiar scene of defeated Japan that could not be neglected in looking over the reconstruction of Japan today.

At about noon of that day, the steamer passed through Akashi Strait and approached the outer harbor of Kobe. There we found several wrecked ships exposing their ugly damaged hulls on the surface. In the inner harbor there were only a few Japanese ships and American ships instead of the crowded shipping of the days before the war. On the wharf were American jeeps and trucks.

From the chimneys of remaining factories on war-devastated areas of Kobe where once many factories concentrated, almost no smoke was observed. This was indeed a scene of the defeated Japan of today.

In Japan there is a popular saying to the effect that in a defeated country there remain only mountains and rivers as ever. Never before did I more seriously realize the meaning of this saying than when I disembarked on Kobe after finishing a trip on board a merchant ship crossing the Inland Sea.

Ozawa Essays

Introduction

Here we have three more studies by Admiral Ozawa. The first is primarily devoted to what Dr. Prange called "The Great All-Out Battle" concept, with which other essays included in this book also deal. Ozawa also stressed the Japanese attachment to the tactic of night engagements.

The second Ozawa essay is especially interesting, pertaining as it does to the development of the Japanese Navy's carrier force, with which Ozawa was so closely associated.

The third essay covers the major reorganization of the Japanese Navy that took place in April 1941, listing the composition of all [of] Japan's fleets.

Development of the Japanese Navy's Operational Concept against America

Jisaburo Ozawa

(Writer's note: This was made mostly based on the writer's own memories supplemented by those of former naval officers who were concerned with studies of the naval strategy against America.)

Until World War I, the relationship between the United States and Japan was kept relatively good, without much friction and misunderstanding. But since then troubles such as the 21-articles ultimatum to China, Japan's sending troops to Siberia, and the Shantung Province problem began to deteriorate the relationship between the two countries. After World War I, both countries began the naval armament race which became hot as time went on. As a result, the Japanese naval authorities started earnest studies of operations against America.

1. Development of the operational concept.
When it was first formulated in 1920, the original basic strategical concept against America was as follows:

a. To control the command of the sea in the Orient in order to secure the traffic between the Asia continent and the southern district.
b. To invade Guam Island at the beginning of the war, thus laying patrol lines from the Bonin Islands extending south to the Marianas.
c. To invade the Philippines.
d. To have the fleet wait at Amamioshima, expecting to have the decisive

sea battle somewhere from the Nansei Islands down to east of the Philippines.

Planes and submarines of that day were so primitive that operations solely depended upon the surface force; patrol ships to be used for patrol missions were to be composed of merchant ships converted into patrol ships. As to the American Navy's strategy, the Japanese Navy thought that the main force of their fleets would make preparations at the West Coast and come to attack after joining with its element which had been in Pearl Harbor at the sea near Hawaii. The Japanese Navy thought at that time that Pearl Harbor had not enough accommodations for the whole fleet.

An early decisive battle was what the Japanese Navy most wanted to have. The most painstaking problems we faced in this connection were how to lure the enemy into the western Pacific and how to know when the enemy fleet left the Hawaii area. As to the former, the Japanese Navy thought that an invasion of the Philippines would be enough to lure the enemy, while as to the latter, intelligence was the sole means to be depended upon.

As to the operational lines to be taken by the American Navy in their offensives, the Japanese Navy estimated as follows:

a. Directly to Okinawa or the homeland via a northern route from Hawaii.
b. To the Philippines through the Marianas from Hawaii.
c. To Celebes passing south of the Carolines.
(Note: Possibilities of the Americans launching a major operation via the Aleutian area were not taken into much consideration, in view of the adverse weather conditions in that district.)

In the event of the American fleet taking either of the aforementioned (a) and (b) lines, it was believed they would positively seek the decisive battle with the Japanese Navy. On the other hand, in case of the (c) line being taken, they would first take a stand on the Philippines, and after preparations being made there, they would seek the offensive. In either case, base forces directly supported by old-type ships and others would separately launch successive invasions of the Marshalls and Carolines.

The above was the outline of the Japanese Navy's strategical idea against America. Though it was, to some extent, not much more than a table plan, its basic idea did not change at all. Its details, however, developed along with the improvement and the expansion of naval power.

a. With the Washington Naval Conference in 1922 as the turning point, the naval air and submarine powers were gradually increased. In or around 1927, it was planned to have submarines stay outside of Pearl Harbor to watch and, when opportunities arose, attack the American fleet. This was about the same time the fleet base of Amamioshima was shifted to Chujo-wan in Okinawa, as the Amamioshima base became too narrow for the fleet. It was also in about 1930 that a plan was initiated of preparing air bases in the Southern Mandated Islands area so as to deploy airplanes there for patrol and attack missions. The construction of air bases, however, was hardly started until the beginning of the war because of the defense limitation provision of the Washington Naval Conference.

b. Around 1934, as the capacity and number of submarines increased, an idea of so-called *Zengen-sakusen* by means of submarines watching, chasing and attacking the enemy fleet after its departure from Pearl Harbor was initiated for the first time. Around this time, chiefly from the viewpoint of the anti-air and submarine alert, a suggestion was made to the effect that the fleet for the decisive battle should better stay in the Inland Sea instead of Chujo-wan. Other contributing factors were the increase of the radius of action of the fleet and also concernings [sic] over training and supplies while staying in the base.

(Note: The refueling at sea that had been started in 1927 became generally in practice about this time.)

c. In about 1937, in view of the increased ability of air power, it was feared that American occupations of Rabaul, the Gilberts, Ocean and Wake Islands would bring a grave consequence upon Japan's strategy of encountering the American fleet in those areas. A plan was consequently initiated of rapidly occupying those points in case of war. By this time, most of the patrol vessels, hitherto assumed the most important role in the encounter strategy, had been replaced by land-based air forces and submarines. Air patrols were to be extended from islands on the fronts. At the same time, the Japanese Navy thought a possibility was great that the American Navy would come first to take the Marshalls under the support of its decisive force. The period that they were concentrating on the invasion was considered a good opportunity for the Japanese Navy to launch the decisive battle upon them; accordingly, a plan was initiated of having its decisive battle force advance to Truk at an appropriate time from the Inland Sea and there await further orders, expecting the decisive battle to be made on the sea north of the Marshalls. The above was the traditional basic idea of the Japanese naval strategy against America. But the actual plan that was applied to the actual war differed a good deal from this, because Japan not only launched war against the United States, Great Britain, the Netherlands and China, but the Pearl Harbor operation.

2. Development of the tactical concept.

The Japanese Navy had long thought that naval fighting strength was composed of the following elements:

$F \propto M \times A \times S$
 F: Fighting strength
 M: Mechanical strength
 A: Efficiency (the extent of training)
 S: Mental strength

In other words, they believed that mechanical inferiority could be covered by the troops' efficiency and the men's mental strength. Seeing their inferiority in mechanical strength to the United States Navy, they naturally placed much importance on the naval forces' efficiency and mental strength. Besides, they endeavored to improve the quality of their fighting strength by building powerful and characteristic ships such as the *Yamato*-class super-battleships and others, organizing well-balanced and characterized fleets and preparing new weapons. Night engagements, air and submarine operations were also stressed.

The origin of the Japanese Navy's tactic of stressing the night engagement was pretty old; in both the Sino-Japanese and Russo-Japanese Wars this tactic was used. With the subsequent progress of ships and torpedoes, this tactic accordingly was improved and expedited. In the early 1900s, a torpedo-boat squadron was organized to command torpedo boats. Around 1922, in view of the battle lessons learned at the Jutland Sea Battle, cruisers were added to the night engagement force, hitherto exclusively composed of destroyers and torpedo boats. In about 1939, battleship-cruisers were also to participate in night engagements as supporting forces. The tactic went so far in about 1941 as to dare to have even the whole fleet participate in night engagements if the situation required.

The original idea of the night engagement was to reduce the enemy by it and facilitate the subsequent decisive battle between both fleets. But subsequent studies and training showed that much could not be expected in a night engagement unless powerful strength was used; in consequence, powerful strength began to be used.

With their increased ability, submarines were organized into squadrons in 1920, and since approximately 1934 training for observing enemy bases for a long time and tracking enemy fleets was made. Chiefly from the viewpoint of *zengen-sakusen* the submarine fleet was organized in 1940. But they could not feel assured about tracking and attacking a powerful American fleet protected by sufficient air forces.

When the Japanese Navy organized a carrier division in 1928 to participate in naval operations, the Japanese Navy was the first of all navies to do so. But the mission assigned them at that time was mostly reconnaissance and patrol. It was only after about 1936 that they became confident enough for almost every tactical battle scene. As I said the other day, the carrier force of those days was still considered the auxiliary force and it was only in 1941 that an air fleet was organized for the first time in the Japanese Navy.

In 1935 land-based medium bombers were adopted and before long they became the main body of the Japanese naval land-based air forces. In 1937 when the China Incident broke out, they were for the first time used in real combat. Their expansion was remarkable; in 1938 an air flotilla made of them was organized and in 1941 they were made into an air fleet.

Outline Development of Tactics and Organization of the Japanese Carrier Air Force

Jisaburo Ozawa

(Writer's note: This was made mostly based upon the writer's own experience supplemented by some records and hearsays [sic] by others.)

Development of tactics of the carrier air force.

1. It was in 1928 that carriers were organized for the first time into carrier divisions which in turn were put into the fleet organization of that day. The period since then to 1934 was the cradle time of the Japanese carrier air force, and most able admirals of the Japanese Navy used to be appointed as its commanders. The first commander of that carrier division was later Admiral Sankichi Takahashi who was successively succeeded by Takayoshi Kato, Koshiro Oikawa and Isoroku Yamamoto, all of them later becoming admirals.

The striking range of carrier-borne planes of those days did not exceed 60 to 70 miles. Even though the first air strike was launched from as far as possible in a sea battle between both fleets, therefore, the second air strike could hardly reach the scene of battle much earlier than just as the engagement commenced. The first air strike usually aimed at carriers or battleships, while the second air strike directed its attacks mainly to enemy battleships in cooperation with the decisive battle to be launched by friendly fleets.

In usual cases the carrier division used to stay, generally as a group, within the visibility limit from the battleship group on the latter's noncombat side. Its aim was to give air cover over the latter as well as over itself, in addition to its own mission of attacking the enemy. Another reason for keeping the carrier division quite near the battleship group was not to let it separate from the main force, while making flexible movements as a carrier group in accordance with the prevailing wind, lest it should offer a chance of being attacked separately.

But this school of tactics had a disadvantageous aspect which before long was uncovered through further subsequent studies. This disposition of a carrier division in fact contained the battleship's movement too; the latter came to lose its flexibility of movements for the decisive engagement. Moreover, on many occasions both the battleship group and the carrier division were simultaneously discovered by the enemy, thus increasing the chance of the vulnerable carriers being attacked almost 100%. The method of giving one fighter cover over both the battleship group and the carrier division also proved not so effective. As a result, carrier tactics began to change in 1934 as follows:

2. In 1934 studies began to be made so as to dispose carrier groups separately. Notable points of this tactic were:

a. Carrier divisions, usually divided into one carrier division each, operated independently from the battleship group so as to encircle enemy carrier groups.
b. Each carrier division was appropriately supported by light strength (cruisers and others).
c. Each carrier division was disposed so as to be generally an equal distance from the enemy. But, depending upon the situation, they were purposely disposed at different distances from the enemy.
d. Each element simultaneously launched a forestalling attack upon the enemy.
e. For the purpose of giving fighter cover to the battleship group, a carrier was dispatched separately.

The aim of this tactic was to strike all carriers present with the first attack, aiming at least to put them all out of commission. At the same time, it aimed to prevent all friendly carriers from simultaneously being attacked. Another school of tactics of disposing carriers different distances from the enemy aimed to lure enemy attention to a nearer carrier from the enemy, while others intended to attack the enemy by surprise.

(Note: This idea was initiated in 1934 by later Capt. Kurio Toibana, who had been known among naval officers as one of the big figures in Japanese naval aviation. He later became a staff officer of Admiral Yamamoto and died with him. The fundamental idea envisaged in this tactic did not change virtually up to this war.)

Reconnaissance of the enemy situation and concealment of our side's intention were prerequisite for the successful employment of this tactic. Co-operation of land-based air forces and submarine forces, interception of enemy submarines and planes, and utilization of radio intelligence—all these possible means had to be used to catch the enemy by surprise. But they could not always be expected to bring a successful result, so that the fleet had to launch its own reconnaissance.

The progress of a sea-air battle was so swift that, when fleets in a great formation intended to deploy its [sic] forces after approaching the enemy, there were ample reasons for fearing that it might be too late.

Therefore, steps were to be taken so as to have fleet formations pretty well spread out while approaching, thus reducing the chances of all forces being discovered simultaneously and also making it possible to encircle the enemy or its element after the approach was made.

As there was a limit to carrier-borne reconnaissance, carriers as a matter of course couldn't launch reconnaissance in all directions. All these things added up to this: Unless they were within effective patrol zones from land bases, they could expect pretty great possibilities of attacking the enemy by surprise by means of using the so-called disposed disposition of carriers.

Development of the Organization of the Carrier Group

1. Since 1928 usually two carriers supported by one destroyer division were organized into a carrier division. The strongly prevailing naval tactical view in those days throughout the Japanese Navy was to launch the decisive bat-tle with the battleships as the main fighting strength, the carrier forces only playing the secondary role of assisting them. This view was [sic] right up until the carrier force became strong enough in 1936 or about that time as to change the picture.

But, in fact, the obsolete idea of the battleship power centering did not yield so easily. The 1st and 2nd Carrier Divisions were attached to the 1st and 2nd Fleets respectively as they had been. Training and studies were made independently; there was no systematic study whatsoever.

2. It was in 1940 when Admiral Yamamoto became CinC of the Com-bined Fleet that studies and training were actually made on the combined use of carrier and land naval air forces. In fleet maneuvers, the 1st Carrier Division commander, then the senior officer of all fleet air forces, was or-dered to take command of the 1st and 2nd Carrier Divisions which were all of the fleet carrier forces at that time. But this temporarily established com-mand system did not necessarily work so well; air communications were not smoothly made and cooperation between concerned forces was unsatis-factory.

In view of this, I who was then the 1st Carrier Division commander keenly felt the necessity of establishing a permanent air fleet command, taking charge of all carrier divisions under one control, and submitted the recommendation to this effect. My recommendation, however, met [with] strong opposition, first from staffs of the Combined Fleet, and in particular Admiral [Mineichi] Koga, then CinC of the 2nd Fleet, was dead against it.

They argued that, in view of the great possibilities that the 1st and 2nd Fleets would operate separately in the strategical stage, each fleet needed its own carrier division to provide it a fighter cover. In order to concentrate all carrier forces for attacks, they argued, a temporary authorization of command to the senior carrier division commander of all divisions when deemed necessary would be enough.

To their argument, I countered that an air engagement in the early stage of a sea battle would bring about the decisive consequence on the subsequent course of the battle, and fighter covers could be provided by sending carriers to the fleet when necessary.

Since there were no indications observed on the part of the fleets to adopt my recommendation, I sent it directly to the Chief of the General Staff and the Navy Ministry. The General Staff took it up and finally agreed to it as a result of studies with the Naval Aeronautical Department and the Navy Ministry. In April 1941 the 1st Air Fleet was organized for the first time in the Japanese Navy.

(Note: Since such a step as a division commander sending his recommendation directly to the central authorities in Tokyo without going through his senior Commander in Chief was a violation of the formal procedure, I was scolded by Yamamoto, Commander in Chief. By the way, it seemed to me that Admiral Yamamoto himself was not against my idea in his own mind, though he did not show any such indication as favoring it, out of respect to the opposition entertained by his staffs and the CinC of the 2nd Fleet. This was quite apparent from his remark to me that "he was glad to hear" that the decision had been made with regard to the organization of an air fleet when it was made.)

One problem we had to face at the time of the inauguration of the Air Fleet was which ship under his command the Commander in Chief of the said fleet should be on board. Some old-type naval strategists argued that he should be on board a ship strongly defended enough to keep on fighting until the last stage of a battle, instead of on board a vulnerable carrier apt to be destroyed in the early engagement. This was finally dominated, however, by a school of advocates for a carrier flagship who asserted that air operations were so complicated and, moreover, the first air strike had so great implications that an air fleet commander should be at all times well informed of the actual conditions of carriers and air groups as well as of air communications.

The inauguration of the Air Fleet thus constructed did not mean, however, that the main striking force of naval power was shifted to the carrier force. The 1st Air Fleet thus organized only consisted of carrier divisions supported by a destroyer division each.

3. With this organization of the carrier force Japan entered the war. According to the Japanese Navy's organization, the 1st Air Fleet had not sufficient and necessary supporting forces. In other words, it lacked prerequisite units as a strategical naval force. When it was planned to use this fleet in the Pearl Harbor attack, necessary supporting forces were therefore given to it by a Combined Fleet operational order. The thus reinforced Pearl Harbor attack force was actually as follows:

Commander:	1st Air Fleet commander in chief
Air Striking Force:	1st Air Fleet (1st, 2nd and 5th Carrier Divs.)
Guard Force:	1st Destroyer Squadron
Supporting Force:	3rd Battleship Division (2 battleships) with Cruiser Division (2 heavy cruisers)
Patrol Force:	2nd Submarine Division (3 I-type subs)
Midway Bombardment Force:	7th Destroyer Division (2 destroyers)
8 tankers	

It was only after the defeat at the Midway sea battle that some progressive step was made in the Japanese carrier air force organization. The 3rd Fleet was newly activated to replace the 1st Air Fleet. This time such supporting units as a battleship and a cruiser division, as well as a destroyer squadron, were organized into the fleet organization as integral parts. Even this reorganization did not mean, however, that the carrier task force assumed the main role of the whole naval forces. The 1st and 2nd Fleet still remained separate, at least in the organization system.

It was only as late as April 1944 that, after finally realizing the full implications of the new naval strategy with carrier force as its nucleus, the 1st Mobile Fleet was organized to command almost all naval decisive battle forces.

Annex: Admiral Yamamoto's remarks concerning air operations and my comments upon them.

a. At the result-studying conference following the joint war games studying operations against America between the General Staff, Navy Ministry and Combined Fleet held in May 1933, later Admiral Yamamoto, then 1st Carrier Division commander, remarked to the following effect: "The key to victory in an air battle is a matter of course whether we could launch a forestalling attack upon the enemy. In view of the fact that the radius of attack by our bombers is less than that of the enemy, I as a commander of the carrier force am firmly resolved to have our boys launch the so-called one-way attack and am training them for that end."

When Admiral Yamamoto made that statement, his opinion was so radical from the general viewpoint that it seemed to have been taken as what appeared to be some kind of bluff. But I believe that, judging from the admiral's sincere character, it was his real intention without any exaggeration.

b. One day in February 1941 the admiral told me that the most impressive lesson he learned when he had studied the Russo-Japanese War was the fact that the Japanese Navy launched the night assault against enemy ships in Port Arthur at the very beginning of the war. He believed this idea was the most excellent strategical initiative ever envisaged during the war, but it was a regrettable thing that the Japanese were not thorough-going in carrying out the attack, with the result that they failed to achieve a satisfactory result.

In view of the gradually increasing tension between America and Japan, this statement of Admiral Yamamoto was enough to make me understand his idea. I thought his idea was to attack Pearl Harbor at the beginning of the war when it came.

c. In April of the same year, the admiral asked my opinion about the Pearl Harbor attack. I replied to him that, in the event of war with several countries, the hitherto-conceived strategy of encountering the American fleets would be hard to be carried out, and that the Pearl Harbor attack should be carried out by all means from the overall point of view.

d. I want to add here that during the war the admiral told me more than once—about twice—in an unusually apprehensive tone, that he was wondering whether or not the ultimatum was actually delivered to the United States before the Pearl Harbor attack commenced.

Fleet Organization

Jisaburo Ozawa

Since the China Incident broke out in 1937, the relations between the U.S. and Japan became increasingly tense. Efforts were therefore made to expand the naval strength, and at the same time vigorous studies were made for an operational plan against the U.S. Accordingly, the fleet organization was successively but drastically revised.

a. In 1938 an air flotilla composed of land-based planes was first set up.

b. According to the long-studied *yogeki-sakusen*, submarine forces were to keep watch upon the U.S. fleets in the Hawaii district and make contact it when it came out [sic]. In 1940 the Japanese Navy reached a conclusion that a fleet headquarters should be established to effectively control those submarine operations. The Sixth Fleet was then organized and placed under the Combined Fleet.

c. Previously the Japanese Navy's carriers were divided into the First and Second Fleets, each comprising a carrier division. Those carrier divisions were to cooperate or operate under the unified command when necessary. In view of the disadvantage inherent in that command setup from the nature of air operations, [sic] however the 1st Air Fleet was set up in April 1941 to command carrier divisions and screening [sic] destroyer divisions, but it did not include battleships and cruisers. For the same reason mentioned above, the land-based air forces were incorporated under the unified command of the 11th Air Fleet in August 1941.

d. Previously the CinC of the Combined Fleet had a concurrent duty as the CinC of the First Fleet. In April 1941, however, the CinC of the First fleet was newly appointed and the former was to directly command only two battleships of the 1st Division, one of which was his flagship.

e. In December 1939 the Fourth Fleet was established to take charge of the South Seas Islands. It comprised old-type light cruisers, auxiliary vessels and land-based air forces.

f. In April 1941 the Third Fleet was established for the southern area operations and the Fifth Fleet for the northern area operations.

g. With the occupation of southern French Indo-China in July 1941, the Southern Expeditionary Fleet was established to take charge of that district and also to make preparations for future operations in that district. Its headquarters stationed in Saigon [sic].

The Japanese Navy's fleet organization as of the outbreak of war was as follows:

CinC of the Combined Fleet
2 BBs of 1st Battleship Div.
CinC of the 1st Fleet
    2nd Battleship Div. (4 BBs) under direct command of CinC
    3rd Battleship Div. (4 BBs)
    6th Cruiser Div. (4 CAs)
    1st Destroyer Squadron (1 CL and 4 DD Divs.)
    3rd Destroyer Squadron (1 CL and 4 DD Divs.)
    3rd Carrier Div. (2 CVLs and 1 DD Div.)
CinC of the 2nd Fleet
    4th Cruiser Div. (4 CAs)
    5th Cruiser Div. (4 CAs)
    7th Cruiser Div. (4 CAs)
    8th Cruiser Div. (2 CAs)
    2nd Destroyer Sqdn. (1 CL and 4 DD Divs.)
    4th Destroyer Sqdn. (1 CL and 4 DD Divs.)
CinC of the 3rd Fleet
    16th Cruiser Div. (1 CA and 2 CLs) under direct command of CinC
    17th Minelayer Div. (3 Minelayers)
    5th Destroyer Sqdn. (1 CL and 2 DD Divs.)
    6th Submarine Sqdn. (1 sub-tender and 2 SS Divs.)
    12th Seaplane Tender Div (3 seaplane tenders)
    1st Base Force (2 anti-sub net-layers, 1 Minesweeper Div., [sic] 4 Sub-chaser Divs., 1 Gunboat Div., defense unit, communications unit, harbormaster office and 3 auxiliary vessels)
    2nd Base Force (1 Torpedo Boat Div., 3 Minesweeper Divs., 4 Sub-chaser Divs., 2 Gunboat Divs., defense unit, communications unit, harbormaster office and 9 other vessels)
CinC of the 4th Fleet
    18th Cruiser Div. (3 CLs) under direct command of CinC
    19th Minelayer Division (3 minelayers)
    6th Destroyer Squadron (1 CL and 2 DD Divs.)
    7th Submarine Squadron (1 sub-tender and 3 SS Divs.)
    24th Air Flotilla (2 land-based air groups and 1 seaplane-tender
    3rd, 4th, 5th and 6th Base Forces
CinC of the 5th Fleet
    21st Cruiser Div. (2 CLs) under direct command of CinC

22nd Cruiser Div. (2 converted cruisers)
7th Base Force
CinC of the 6th Fleet
    1 cruiser (flagship)
    1st, 2nd and 3rd Submarine Sqdns.
CinC of the 1st Air Fleet
    1st Carrier Div. (2 CVs and 1 DD Div.)
    2nd Carrier Div. (2 CVs and 1 DD Div.)
    4th Carrier Div. (1 CVL and 1 DD Div.)
    5th Carrier Div. (2 CVs and 1 DD Div.)
CinC of the 11th Air Fleet
    21st, 22nd and 23rd Air Flotillas
    1 DD Div. and five transports also attached.
CinC of the Southern Expeditionary Fleet
    2 corvets [sic]
    9th Base Force

In addition, there were the following forces under the direct command of the Combined Fleet:

    11th Seaplane-tender Div. (2 seaplane-tenders)
    4th Submarine Squadron (1 CL and 2 Submarine Divs.)
    5th Submarine Squadron (1 CL and 2 Submarine Divs.)
    1st Combined Communication Unit (Tokyo, Takao and Chichijima Communications Units)
CinC of China Area Fleet
    1st China Expeditionary Fleet
        10 gunboats
        Hankow Base Force
        Kiukiang Garrison Unit
    2nd China Expeditionary Fleet
        15th Squadron (1 CL, 2 gunboats, 2 torpedo boats and 1 Minesweeper Div.)
        Canton and Amoy Base Forces
    3rd China Expeditionary Fleet
        1 cruiser, 1 Torpedo Boat Div.
        Tsingtao Base Force
    Hainan Guard District
        1 Torpedo Boat Div.

In addition the following units were attached to the China Area Fleet:

Shanghai Base Force
Shanghai Naval Landing Force.

Chihaya Studies

Introduction

These three studies by Masataka Chihaya pertain to the construction of Japanese warships. The first covers briefly the battleships constructed before and after World War I, as well as the later superbattleships, and appends a useful list of battleships, carriers, and cruisers.

The last two studies concern the superbattleships *Yamato* and *Musashi*, their characteristics and armaments, and some enlightening details about the problems involved in the construction of such mammoth ships.

Concerning the Construction of Japanese Warships

Masataka Chihaya

10 January 1947

From its early beginning in history, the Japanese Navy naturally used foreign-made ships. Four battleships and six armored cruisers, which comprised the main strength of the Japanese naval forces at the time of the Russo-Japanese War, were all constructed in England, Germany, and France.

After the Russo-Japanese War, however, Japan began to construct her ships by her own hand and succeeded in constructing the *Tsukuba*, a first-class cruiser, at the Kure Naval Yard in 1907 and also the *Satsuma*, a battle-ship, at the Yokosuka Naval Yard in 1910.

Since then, all Japanese ships except the *Kongo* were constructed in this country. The *Kongo*, a battle-cruiser, which in 1913 was built in England, was the last foreign-made warship and at the same time the first in the world that mounted 14-inch guns. This was the same ship that was sunk south off the coast of Formosa in the autumn of 1944, although she had been much improved compared to when she had been first made.

From 1914, Japan constructed one after another four 30,000-ton battle-ships, the *Fuso, Yamashiro, Ise* and *Hyuga,* and also three battle-cruisers, the *Hiei, Haruno* and *Kirishima,* all of which were sister ships of the *Kongo.*

Japan also succeeded in building a 16-inch-gun battleship, the *Nagato,* at the Kure Naval Yard in 1920, and a sister ship, the *Mutsu,* at the Yokosuka Naval Yard in 1921.

At that time, when the *Mutsu* was being constructed, in the world there was [sic] only the *Maryland,* a United States battleship, that might be equivalent to the *Nagato* and the *Mutsu.* At the Washington Conference held in the same year, both America and Great Britain urged the abandonment of the *Mutsu* on the grounds that she was not completed yet. However, it was changed after-

86

ward so that the *Mutsu* remained in the Japanese Navy on the condition that both countries got the right of constructing two more 16-inch-gun ships.

In 1921 the *Kaga* and the *Tosa,* both 39,900-ton battleships, were launched at the Kawasaki Dockyard and the Nagasaki Mitsubishi Dockyard respectively. The keels of the *Amagi* and the *Akagi* were laid down in 1920. Of those ships, the *Kaga* and the *Akagi* were converted into carriers afterward, and the remainder were abandoned in accordance with the Washington Naval Treaty.

When the Japanese decided to walk out of the Naval Treaty in 1936, they had a plan of constructing four monster battleships, the *Yamato* class, with 18-inch guns mounted on the biggest ships ever made in the world. Japan did everything to build these ships. The first ship, the *Yamato,* was constructed in Kure just after the outbreak of this war, and the *Musashi* was constructed at Nagasaki in the summer of 1942. The keel of the third ship, the *Shinano,* was laid at the Yokosuka Naval Yard's constructing dock, but in 1942 she was converted into a carrier as the result of the fiasco of Midway Island. She met her doom in the autumn of 1944 by the hand of the United States Navy when she was sailing off the Kii Peninsula in her first voyage from Yokosuka for Kure after construction. The fourth one, which was being constructed at Kure, was abandoned before launch.

The Washington Naval Treaty meant the stoppage of constructing battleships as far as Japan was concerned. So the Japanese concentrated their efforts on constructing cruisers. The *Furutaka* class cruisers, which were first built under the terms of the treaty, had such remarkable features that they might astonish naval experts of other countries. Japan seemed to take the lead in the race to construct auxiliary vessels, constructing the *Ashigara** class cruisers, the *Mogami* class cruisers and the *Fubuki* class destroyers one after another.

At the same time, the Japanese Navy made efforts to modernize their battleships. Chief improvements were:

1. Enlarging their radius of action by adoption of oil-burning boilers.
2. Strengthening antiaircraft defense.
3. Enlarging the elevation of the main guns.

In the appendix table 1 will show you the list of the construction of Japanese ships bigger than cruisers which engaged in this war.

Sources of this information

History of the Japanese Navy published by the Naval Reserve Association in 1938.

Official records of construction of the Japanese naval ships.

*Chihaya did not include *Ashigara* in his list of cruisers (see appendix). She was completed on 20 August 1929 at Kawasaki. The ships of her class were *Haguro, Myoko,* and *Nachi.*

Appendix

List of Construction of Japanese Warships

Table 1   Battleships

Name	Place of Construction	Date of Completion
Kongo	Vickers, England	16 Aug. 1913
Hiei	Yokosuka	4 Aug. 1914
Haruna	Kawasaki	10 April 1915
Kirishima	Nagasaki	15 April 1915
Fuso	Kure	8 Nov. 1915
Yamashiro	Yokosuka	31 March 1917
Ise	Kawasaki	15 Dec. 1917
Hyuga	Nagasaki	30 April 1918
Nagato	Kure	25 Nov. 1920
Mutsu	Yokosuka	24 Oct. 1921
Yamato	Kure	16 Dec. 1941
Musashi	Nagasaki	5 Aug. 1942
Shinano	Yokosuka	1944
(On 7 April 1940 her keel was laid and in July 1942 she was changed to a carrier)		
No. 111	Kure	Abandoned

Table 2   Carriers

Name	Place of Construction	Date of Completion
Hosho	Launched at Asano Dock Completed at Yokosuka	27 Dec. 1922
Akagi	Kure	25 March 1927
Kaga	Launched at Kawasaki Completed at Yokosuka	31 March 1928
Ryujo	Launched at Yokohama Dock Completed at Yokosuka	9 May 1933
Soryu	Kure	29 Dec. 1937
Hiryu	Yokosuka	5 July 1939
Shoho (former *Tsurugizaki*)	Yokosuka	15 Jan. 1939 as a submarine tender, was converted to a carrier in Jan. 1942
Zuiho (former *Takasaki*)	Yokosuka	27 Dec. 1940 as a submarine tender; was converted to a carrier in Nov. 1942

Ryuho (former *Taigei*)	Yokosuka	31 March 1934 as a submarine tender; was converted to a carrier in Nov. 1942
Chitose	Kure	25 July 1938 as a seaplane tender; was converted to a carrier in Jan. 1944
Chiyoda	Kure	15 Dec. 1938 as a seaplane tender; was converted to a carrier in Oct. 1943
Shokaku	Yokosuka	8 Aug. 1941
Zuikaku	Kawasaki	25 Sep. 1941
Taiho	Kawasaki	7 March 1943
Unyo (former *Yahata-Maru*)	Nagasaki	31 Aug. 1942
Chuyo (former *Nitta-Maru*)	Nagasaki	20 Aug. 1942
Taiyo (former *Scharnhorst*)*	Kure	15 Dec. 1942
Kaiyo (former *Argentina-Maru*)	Nagasaki	15 Nov. 1943
Hiyo (former *Izumo-Maru*)	Kawasaki	31 July 1942
Junyo (former *Kashihara-Maru*)	Nagasaki	31 July 1942
Ibuki	Kure	After being launched, was converted to a carrier and construction stopped in the spring of 1945.
Unryu	Yokosuka	6 Aug. 1944
Amagi	Nagasaki	10 Aug. 1944
Katsuragi	Kure	15 Oct. 1944
Kasagi	Nagasaki	After being launched, construction stopped in spring of 1945.
Aso	Kure	After being launched, construction stopped in spring of 1945.
Ikoma	Kawasaki	After being launched, construction stopped in spring of 1945.

*Former German luxury liner, not the famous battle cruiser of the same name.

Table 3   Cruisers

Name	Place of Construction	Date of Completion
Furutaka	Nagasaki	31 March 1926
Kako	Kawasaki	20 July 1926
Aoba	Nagasaki	20 Sep. 1927
Kingugasa	Kawasaki	30 Sep. 1927
Nachi	Kure	26 Nov. 1928
Haguro	Nagasaki	25 April 1929
Myoko	Yokosuka	21 July 1929
Atago	Kure	30 March 1932
Takao	Yokosuka	31 May 1932
Chokai	Nagasaki	30 June 1932
Maya	Kawasaki	30 June 1932
Mogami	Kure	28 July 1935
Mikuma	Nagasaki	29 Aug. 1935
Suzuya	Yokosuka	21 Oct. 1937
Kumano	Kawasaki	21 Oct. 1937
Tone	Nagasaki	20 Nov. 1938
Chikuma	Nagasaki	20 May 1939
Katori	Yokohama	20 April 1938
Kashima	Yokohama	31 May 1938
Kashii	Yokohama	15 July 1939
Tenryu	Yokosuka	20 Nov. 1919
Tatsuta	Sasebo	31 March 1919
Kuma	Sasebo	31 Aug. 1920
Tama	Nagasaki	29 Jan. 1921
Kitakami	Sasebo	15 April 1921
Oi	Kawasaki	3 Oct. 1921
Kiso	Nagasaki	4 May 1921
Nagara	Sasebo	21 April 1922
Isuzu	Uraga	15 Aug. 1923
Natori	Nagasaki	15 Sep. 1922
Yura	Sasebo	20 March 1923
Kinu	Kawasaki	10 Nov. 1922
Abukuma	Uraga	26 May 1925
Naka	Yokohama	30 Nov. 1925
Sendai	Nagasaki	29 April 1924
Jintsu	Kawasaki	31 July 1925
Yubari	Sasebo	31 July 1925
Agano	Sasebo	31 Oct. 1942
Noshiro	Yokosuka	20 June 1943
Yahagi	Sasebo	29 Dec. 1943
Sakawa	Sasebo	10 Nov. 1944
Oyodo	Kure	28 Feb. 1943

General Characteristics of Yamato Class Battleships

Masataka Chihaya
15 January 1947

1. Principal Dimensions

Lpp	244.0m
Lou WL (trial condition)	256.0m
Max breadth on trial water line	35.9m
Depth (from bottom of keel to flying deck at side)	18.915m
Displacement (trial condition)	69,100 tons
Draft	10.4m
Displacement (full)	72,809 tons
Mean draft (full)	10.86m
Oil fuel	6,300 tons
Radius of action	16 kts—7,200 miles
Speed	27 kts
S.H.P.	150,000

2. Ordnance

46 c/m ⌄○⌄ guns	3
15.5 c/m ⌄○⌄ guns	4
12.7 c/m ○ H.A. guns	6
25 m/m ○ machine guns	8
18 m/m ○ machine guns	2

After launching, their auxiliary batteries were improved as follows:

Yamato (14 July 1944)
15.5 m/m × 2,   12.7 c/m HAG × 12,   25 m/m MG × 29,
25 m/m MG × 26   12 m/m MG × 2

Musashi (14 July 1944)
15.5 m/m × 2   12.7 m/m HAG × 6,   25 m/m MG × 35,
25 m/m MG × 25,   13 m/m MG × 2

3. Aeroplanes and Their Gear
   Seaplanes   7
   Catapults   2

4. Optical
   15m range finder   1 (top of fore mast)
   10m range finder   3 (main turrets)
   4.5m range finder   2 (HAG predicators)
   1.5m range finder   3 (bridge)
   18c/m binoculars   2
   15c/m binoculars   2
   12c/m binoculars about   30

5. Electrical Instruments
   Diesel dynamoes[sic]   600 KW, 225V × 4
   Turbine "   600 KW, 225V × 4
   150 c/m searchlights   8

6. Machinery
   Main turbines   4 sets
   S.H.P.   ahead   150,000
            astern [sic]   45,000
   H.P.M.   225
   Dia. of propellers   6.0m
   Boilers   12
   Steam pressure   25 Kg/cm^2
   Steam temperatures   325°C

7. Protection
   a. Magazine space
      D*k*   [sic]   200 m/m MNC
      Side   410 m/m MNC (20° inclined)
                                      270 m/m NVNC
                                       90 m/m NVNC (20° inclined)

b. Machinery space
   Dk   200 m/m NNC
   Side   410 m/m MNC (20° inclined)
                                  200 m/m NYNC (15° inclined)
                                  75 m/m NVNC

c. Steering engine room
   Dk   200 MNC
   Side   350 VC

8. Men (including members of headquarters) about 2,200

9. Weight at trial condition

Hull	20,213 tons
Armor	21,266 tons
Protection	1,620
Fittings	1,756
Equipment	417
Ordnance	9,224
Ammunition	2,434
Torpedoes and c. [sic]	75
Water in hydraulic tanks and pipes	297
Navigating equipment	19
Optical	76
Electrical	1,036
Wireless	72
Aeroplanes and equipment	111
Machinery	4,827
Water and oil contained in machinery	4,730
General equipment	641
Fuel oil	4,210
Gasoline oil	48
Lubricating oil	61
Reserve feed water	212
Total	69,100 tons

Some Stories Concerning the Construction of the Yamato Class Battleships*

Masataka Chihaya

1. An account of the decision of the preliminary plan.

It was in the year 1934 that, according to the Naval General Headquarters' demand concerning construction of a new battleship which would mount 18-inch guns, the study of its preliminary plan was first set up. It had been 14 years since the plan of the *Kii*, which was last designed as a battleship in 1920.

The period from the setting up of the preliminary plan to its decision might arbitrarily be divided into two stages. The first stage covered the period from the setting up of the preliminary plan in 1934 to its decision in 1936. In this period more than 20 types of models were studied.

In the end of the first stage in July 1936 the following plan was concluded finally. That final plan was:

Displacement (trial condition)	65,200 tons
Low WL	253m
Max breadth	38.9m
Depth	18.667m
Draft	10.4m

*Note: I have made this report based upon the information which was obtained from the most reliable source of the former Japanese naval shipbuilding authorities. I am afraid, however, that I may fail to relate the information completely owing to my meager knowledge of shipbuilding.

Ordnance

46c/m ⓨ Guns	3
15.5c/m ⓨ guns	4
12.7c/m ⓞ guns	6
25m/c ⓑ guns	12
13m/m ⓑ guns	4
Aeroplanes	6
Speed	27 knots
Radius of action	16 kts—7200 miles
G.H.P.	135,000

Engine   Turbine   2 sets 75,000 HP
            Diesel   2 sets 60,000 HP

Protection would be such as that able to protect 18-inch-gun shells fired at the distance of 20,000–30,000 meters.

In studying this preliminary plan, the Japanese Navy also studied possible measures which the American Navy would take to counter this type of ship. And they reached the following conclusions:

a. That the American Navy could not build this type of ship because the breadth of this ship would be wider than the breadth of the Panama Canal that was 33.3 meters.
b. That a ship which the American Navy would be able to build on the limit of being able to pass the Panama Canal could be 63,000 tons in displacement and less than 23 knots in speed, counting about ten 18-inch guns.

At first the Japanese Naval General Headquarters wanted 30 knots against 23 knots of the supposed American new battleship, but on account of its displacement and necessary horsepower it was finally fixed at 27 knots.

Compared with the *Nagato* class 34,000-ton battleship that was the largest ship in action built in this country, the *Yamato* class 65,000-ton battleships were nearly twice in displacement, so that the Japanese naval authorities had to take every minute care for its construction. However, they had a firm confidence about it because, first, they had the experience of having constructed the *Kaga*, *Akagi* class 40,000-ton ships designed in

1920, second, . . . they had continued the study of constructing a 35,000-ton battleship even during the period when constructing battleships was prohibited by the naval treaties, and finally, . . . by that time two large merchant ships, the *Queen Mary* and the *Normandy*, were successfully launched in other theaters of the world.

In making the design of this ship, the point that needed the hardest application was to make its length as short as possible. To make its length short was urgently needed for strengthening its protection, for if its length were too long, there was no means of designing its protection. In the following table, comparative figures of displacement, length and breadth of several famous ships will be shown:

Name	Displacement (tons)	Length (m)	Breadth (m)	Draft (m)
Yamato	65,200	253	38.9	10.4
Nagato	34,000	212	29	9.15
Akagi	41,000	250	32.1	9.45
Kii	47,500	259	32.4	9.68
Normandy	67,500	294	35.9	11.2
Queen Mary	70,000	312	36.0	11.0

As shown in the above table, the *Yamato* had a comparatively short length and a small draft but a wide breadth for its heavy displacement. In order to strengthen its protection, the Japanese naval authorities after all adopted this peculiar type although this type of ship was not favorable for high speed.*

Thus, the preliminary plan was decided in 1936, but in its subsequent study there arose a problem of the main engines. The period, even though only four months, that followed the decision of the preliminary plan in July 1936 until the problem of its main engines was settled in November the same year could be called the second stage of the study of its construction.

In the original plan decided in July 1936 it was planned that several sets of diesel engines in addition to two sets of turbine engines were to be equipped. Diesel engines to be used were large-scale double-acting ones capable of putting out nearly 10,000 HP a set. As to such powerful diesel engines, the Japanese naval authorities at first did not have any doubt, for

*I think this was indeed a revolutionary change in the thoughts of the Japanese Navy concerning shipbuilding. For, as I should like to describe in a future report concerning the tradition of the Japanese Navy, the Japanese Navy traditionally insisted on high speed which in turn caused comparative vulnerability in defense. Even the *Shinano*, the last-built *Yamato* class ship, which should have been the strongest in defense because of being converted into a carrier after the tragedy of Midway Island in which battle the vulnerability of Japanese ships in defense was completely revealed, was sunk by less than several hits of torpedoes fired from an American submarine.

they had experience already of equipping such diesel engines on the *Taigei* and the *Tsurugizake* with satisfactory results, both of which were originally submarine tenders and were converted into light carriers after the war broke out.

However, it was not long before vital faults of this type of engine were suddenly revealed. The Japanese naval authorities faced a most important problem of solving in a limited period whether such diesel engines could be adopted as the main engines of the *Yamato* or not, for the setting up of its construction was expected in less than a year. After careful and sincere examination, it was finally decided in November 1936 that the *Yamato* was to be equipped with four turbine engines only. The final plan thus decided was:

Displacement (trial condition)	68,200 tons
Low WL	256m
Max. breadth	38.9m
Draft	10.4m
S.H.P.	150,000
Speed	27 kts
Engine turbine	4 sets

2. An account of the decision concerning main guns.
As to its main guns, there were [four] problems. They were:

a. Would its size be 16 inches or 18 inches?
b. Would its length be 45 or 50 calibers?
c. Would its turret be triple mounted or double mounted?
d. What disposition would they be?

In order that Japan would take superiority in the battleship powers against America, there were no other means but to outrange American battleships by means of bigger guns, because there was little hope that Japan would take the lead in the race to construct battleships. It was obvious, too, that 18-inch guns were most favorable for this purpose. Then, the problem lay in whether it would be possible to manufacture such big guns in reality. For this aim the Japanese Navy made careful examinations. The fact that the Japanese Navy had made a 19-inch gun for trial and also had tested it around 1920 contributed much to giving confidence of manufacturing 18-inch guns to the Japanese naval authorities. Eighteen-inch guns were then adopted as the main guns of the *Yamato* class battleship.

The Japanese Navy also paid all attention to keeping the manufacture of 18-inch guns top secret, because bigger guns than 16 inches were prohibited by the naval treaties [sic], and also if it happened to disclose even its slightest indication, the Japanese Navy would fail to achieve superiority in a supposed gun-fire duel between the American and Japanese Navies.

After close examination, the length of an 18-inch gun was after all decided to be 45 caliber and the turret to be a triple-mounted type.

3. An account of the protection plan.

As the *Yamato* class battleship was to be equipped with not only the thickest armor plate ever made in this country, but new armor plates such as VH and KNC, there were many problems to be solved. The Japanese Navy made large-scale experiments and studies to solve these problems. They made real-sized armor tests and also tests against structures that supported armor, using the 19-inch gun. They also made an experiment concerning protection of many holes such as smoke vents, air ventilators and other pipes that would be drilled through armored decks. They achieved success in these experiments.

The *Yamato* was planned to protect her vital parts, a conning tower and a rudder room inclusive, perfectly from 18-inch gun shells fired at the distance of 20,000–30,000 meters.

The vital part designed to protect from 18-inch-gun shells perfectly was also strong enough to protect against any big bombs conceivable. The other part besides the vital part had 85 m/m CNC deck armor capable of protecting it from less than 250 kg bombs.

Underwater protection of the *Yamato*, however, was not so perfect as protection from shells. She had no underwater armor protection save for bottom areas of magazine rooms. But the *Yamato* was designed to have more water-proof [sic] separated rooms than any other ship. In the following table, water-proof separated rooms of several ships will be shown:

Name	Rooms below Armored Deck	Rooms above Armored Deck	Total
Yamato	1,065	82	1,147
Nagato	865	224	1,089
Yamashiro	574	163	737

This table shows that compared to other ships considerable efforts were paid to strengthen underwater protection of the *Yamato*. However, the war proved later than even these improvements were not sufficient to prevent the traditional vulnerability in protection of the Japanese warships.

4. Other characteristics from the shipbuilding point of view [sic].

The *Yamato* might also be regarded as one of the most excellent ships ever built in this country, even from the shipbuilding point of view. Her metacentric height was more than 3.8 meters. This figure would not necessarily be a surprising one to experts of foreign countries. To experts of this country, however, this was a very surprising one. For it was not seldom in this country that Japanese warships suffered from an ominous trend to be top-heavy, owing to the fact that additional equipment was required to be added one after another even beyond their capabilities. The Japanese Navy had two records of most deplorable fact that ships were overturned on account of their top-heavy stabilities.

In order to increase her stability capacity, some efforts were also directed to reducing the dimensions of her foremast as much as possible.

Let us look now at this in figures:

Name	Foremast Fore Dimensions (m²)	Side (m²)	Aftermast Fore (m²)	Side (m²)
Yamato	159	310	59	98
Nagato	162	372	61	97
Fuso	150	351	68.5	135.3

As to her revolution capacity, the *Yamato* had a satisfactory figure, too.

Thorough investigations were made to find out the most suitable type of ship hull too, and the number of models being used for tests were as many as 48. The bulbous bow type was also adopted for her.

5. An account of the launching.

Of three *Yamato* class battleships, the *Musashi* was launched at the Nagasaki Dockyard while the other two, the *Yamato* and the *Shinano*, were built in the constructing docks of the Kure and the Yokosuka Naval Yards respectively. In the case of the *Yamato* and the *Shinano*, there was little question, for the ships were to float in the docks after completion. On the contrary, there were many problems in the case of the *Musashi*.

The launch of the *Musashi* would be one record of shipbuilding not only in this country but in the whole world. How difficult the launching of the *Musashi* was will be sufficiently shown in the following table.

Name	Weight of Hull (tons)	Breadth of Launching Bay (feet)	Pressure upon Pivot (tons)
Kaga	21,575	9.0	2,000
Musashi	33,384	12.5	7,488
Lexington	28,897	7.8	5,070
Queen Mary	36,700	10.5	8,300

Therefore, every minute care was paid in launching the *Musashi* in Nagasaki and the launching of the *Musashi* was done with great success in 1940. However, there were still many problems to be solved in equipping the *Musashi* even after her launch. First, there was a need for a large dry dock capable of docking such a large ship, and a large dry dock was built in the Sasebo Naval Yard for this purpose. Second, there was a need for a large floating crane capable of lifting more than 300 tons in order to equip such large guns and armor to the *Musashi*, for each gun and piece of armor plate weighed often more than 100 tons. Finally, there was also a need to build a special transport ship capable of transporting 18-inch gun turrets from Kure to Nagasaki, for those guns were manufactured in the Kure Naval Arsenal and at that time there was no available transport ship capable of transporting such big guns. For this purpose the Japanese Navy built a special transport ship named *Kashino* that was specially designed to transport an 18-inch turret on board at the time. The *Kashino* made several voyages between Kure and Nagasaki during the period of its construction. Notwithstanding, the construction of the *Musashi* progressed nearly as scheduled. She was completed in August of 1942.

Personnel Study

Toshikazu Ohmae

Introduction

In 1941, Capt. Toshikazu Ohmae was a member of the Naval Affairs Bureau, Navy Ministry. During the war, he served as a staff officer in several combat organizations, and ended his war career as a member of the First Department, Naval General Staff. He was highly respected as a most knowledgeable and intelligent naval officer. Ohmae, who spoke and wrote excellent English, prepared this study in that language. On 29 November 1961, Dr. Prange wrote to Ohmae asking for clarification of certain points, and Ohmae submitted this report as of 16 December 1961. It is based upon Ohmae's interviews with eight of his former colleagues, as well as "all available documents of Military Hist. Department in the Defense Agency, Army Hist. Association and Mobilization Bureau," as Ohmae expressed it in his covering letter to Prange.

This study explains when certain key personnel of the Army and Navy first learned of the Pearl Harbor (PH) operation. Attachments list the staffs of various organizations with brief biographies.

Personnel Study

(1) Lt. Gen. Tsukada (Osamu), Vice Chief of the Army Naval Staff since Nov. 1940, was appointed as the Chief of Staff Southern Army, on 4 November 1941, and Lt. Gen. Tanabe (Moritake) succeeded him as the new Vice Chief. Lt. Gen. Tanabe, a well-known gentleman of fine character, was an authority on mobilization and war preparations, having served in various important posts of that nature. At the rank of Lieutenant General, he participated in the China Incident as the Division Commander (Shan-si Province in North China) and then as CofS of the North China Area Army until he came back to Tokyo as the Vice Chief. His wife was a sister of

General Imamura's wife. Maj. Gen. Seizo Arisue, your friend, was the Assistant Chief of Staff, North Area Army in 1941–2.

(Statement by Col. Nishimura and Col. Imoto)

(2) The list of Army officers who were informed about Pearl Harbor, which you sent me as (Col. Takushiro) Hattori's statement, contains some clear mistakes. Names and posts mentioned in the first paragraph of the statement by Colonel Hattori should be revised as follows:

Lt. Gen. Akira Muto, Chief of the Military Affairs Bureau (Sep. '39–April 42) (Instead of Maj. Gen. Kenryo Sato)

Maj. Gen. Kenryo SATO, Chief of the Military Affairs Section (Feb.'41–April '42) (Instead of Col. Susumu Nishimura)

Col. Joichiro Sanada, Chief of the Army Affairs Section (Feb. '41–April '42) (As he was informed about PH)

Col. Susumu Nishimura, Aide-de-Camp to General Tojo. (Nishimura succeeded Sanada in April '42. Nishiura was informed about PH but only several days before the attack in the capacity of aide.) (By Official Record and Statement by Col. Nishimura)

(3) According to Captain (N) Onoda, he informed the outline of the entire Fleet Operation Plan to Col. Yadoru Arisue around late November '41 in order to discuss the timing for the moment of delivery of the so-called ultimatum to the U.S. Government. Colonel Tanemura had no recollection whether he participated in the discussion or not. Captain Onoda denied having leaked the PH plan to any others including Colonel Kumabe who had no direct connection with the initial naval operations.

(4) Army Officers who knew the PH plan before the actual operation (other than Hattori's statement and staffs of the Operations Section and War Direction Section):

(a) Southern Army (refer to attached paper No. 2, "List of Staff Members, Southern Army"):

Commanding General, Hisaichi Terauchi
Chief of Staff, Tsukada
Assistant Chiefs of Staff, Aoki and Sakaguchi
Col. Masami Ishii (Chief, lst Section [Operations])
Lt. Col. Okikazu Arao (Senior Operations Staff)
Col. Kazuo Tanigawa (Chief, 4th Section [Air])
Maj. Takashi Kagoshima (Operations Staff)

According to Colonel Arao, he was informed of the PH plan by Colonel Hattori before he was appointed as the operational staff of the Southern

Army in early November '41. At the time, he was an attached officer to the Army Section, Imp. GHQ and scheduled to be the Southern Army's key staff. Having been appointed to the post, he informed the top secret plan only to the above-mentioned officers. At the time of the Army-Navy Agreement at the Army Staff College in early November '41, Colonel Ishii was informed by the Combined Fleet staff members, but they knew the outline beforehand. The Southern Army did not disclose the secret plan to any officers of subordinate forces, such as the Malay or Philippine Invasion Force.

The reason why the above-mentioned officers were informed beforehand was for the overall operational timing which should restrict the starting time of combat in all other operations to be only after the PH attack. The Southern Army actually controlled all timing of the combat in Malay and the Philippines. Colonel Arao recalled that the Southern Army denied the proposal of the Malay Invasion Force in early December when the Malay Force advanced the opinion that the landing should be started on the 7th (Japan time) to avoid the anticipated typhoon.

(b) Malay Invasion Army:

(i) According to Colonel Tanemura, Lt. Col. Masanobu Tsuji might probably have been informed by Colonel Hattori or some staff officers as he was a very able staff officer within the Operations Section, Imperial GHQ until 25 September '41. (Statement by Col. Tanemura)

At present he has been missing since April this year when he was traveling in Southeast Asia and there is no means for interrogation at present.

(ii) Colonel Sugita, your good friend and the present Chief of Staff of the Ground Self-Defense Force, answered that no one of his colleagues within the Malay Invasion Force knew about PH beforehand.

(c) Philippine Invasion Force, China Army:

None was informed, as the planned operations of the above forces had no need to adjust the combat timing with PH by the command themselves, as the higher command and the China Area Fleet could control them.

(d) Chief Aide-de-Camp to the Emperor, General (Shigeru) Hasunuma:

Even though the report to the Emperor concerning the Imperial GHQ Navy Order No. I and Navy Directive No. 1 did not touch on the PH plan and the table maneuver in the presence of the Emperor on 15 November did not include the PH theater, the PH plan could not be kept secret from the Emperor too late. On 21 November, when the Navy Order No. 5 (Deployment Order) was submitted for Imperial assent, Chief of the Naval General Staff Admiral Nagano explained the PH plan to the Emperor. At the time, General Hasunuma attended upon the Emperor and so could hear the report of the PH plan to the throne. (Statement by Vice Admiral Fukudome)

(5) Date when Admiral Nagano first heard of the PH operation.

Just after the wargame was completed in the middle of October at the

Naval Staff College, Chief of the Operational Department of the Naval General Staff, Rear Admiral Fukudome, went to the Chief Staffs [sic] room in the Naval General Staff and reported to Admiral Nagano about the Combined Fleet Headquarters' PH plan. As Admiral Fukudome could not agree to the PH operation (too risky), his report was of a somewhat negative-natured tone. After having heard the report, Admiral Nagano said only one word, "Risky," in Japanese "*Abunai na.*"

Although Admiral Fukudome was informed about the conception of the PH attack while he was CofS, Combined Fleet, he said nothing about it to the Naval General Staff members as it was thought too risky, together with the difficulties of supply and secrecy. (Statement by Fukudome)

Statement by Captain Sanagi is almost the same as that by Fukudome. Statement by Admiral Tomioka was that the first hearing was sometime between April and July 1941, but later he agreed to the statement by Fukudome, as Tomioka had never explained directly to the Chief of the Naval General Staff. Fukudome and Tomioka had a joint study for the above answer and so the above-mentioned statement by Fukudome is thought to be the most authoritative one.

(6) Army Officers who attended the so-called "Ten Section Chiefs Meeting:"

Colonel Hattori
Col. Joichiro Sanada, Chief of Army Affairs Section, Army Department
Col. Yadoru Arisue, Chief of War Direction Section, Army Gen. Staff
Col. Isao Takeda, Chief of 8th Section (Stratagem), Army Gen. Staff
Col. Kenryo Sato, Chief of Military Section, Army Department

They discussed only about the war direction matters and did not touch about operations.

Attached Paper No. 1

Members of the Operations Section and War Direction Section, Army Section Imperial GHQ (concurrently Army General Staff) as of 8 Dec. '41)

Operations Section (officially called 2nd Section)
Chief: Col. Takushiro Hattori (deceased)
Staff: Lt. Col. Masao Kushida (in charge of Logistics)
      Lt. Col. Kumao Imoto (in charge of Operations)
      Lt. Col. Seishi Okamura (in charge of Operations)
      Maj. Tsunenori Takeda (in charge of Operations)
      Maj. Zenshiro Hara (in charge of Logistics)
      Maj. Tadao Shudo (in charge of Operations Air)

Capt. Makoto Haruke (in charge of Operations) (deceased)
Lt. Col. Aribumi Kumon (in charge of Air) (deceased)
Lt. Col. Keiji Takase (in charge of Operations)
Maj. Nobutake Takayama (in charge of Logistics & Operations)
Maj. Denpachi Kondo (in charge of Operations) (deceased)
Maj. Ryuzo Sejima (in charge of Operations)
Maj. Fumitada Shirai (in charge of Logistics)

War Direction Section (officially called 20th Group, directly under Vice Chief of the Army Section, Imperial GHQ).
   Chief: Col. Yadoru Arisue (deceased)
   Staff: Col. Isao Takeda (concurrently Chief, 8th Sec.—Stratagem)
          Lt. Col. Sako Tanemura
          Lt. Col . Takuji Suziki
          Capt. Shiro Hara
          Capt. Binju Yamaguchi

Note 1. Lt. Col. Masanobu Tsuji left the Operations Section in late September 1941, but surely he had been informed about PH by Colonel Hattori. (Statement by Colonel Imoto)
Note 2. Colonel Kumabe was not in the Operations Section and there could not be such a fact that he was informed about PH. (Statements by Colonel Nishimura and Captain Onoda). At the time, he was Section Chief of the Army Aeronautical Department and concurrently Instructor in the Army Staff College in 1941. (Statement by Colonel Nishiura)

Attached Paper No. 2

Staff Members, the Southern Army, as of 1941

Chief of Staff	Lt. Gen. Osamu Tsukada (deceased)
Asst. CofS (General Affairs)	Lt. Gen Shigemasa Aoki (promoted to Lt. Gen. on 1 November 1941) (deceased)
Asst. CofS (Air)	Lt. Gen. Yoshitaro Sakaguchi (promoted to Lt. Gen on 1 November 1941)
Chief, lst Section (Operations)	Col. Masami Ishii (deceased)
Operations Staff	Lt. Col. Okikazu Arao
	Maj. Masanori Shibuya
	Maj. Takashi Kagoshima
	Capt. Taro Watanabe
Chief, 2nd Section (Intelligence)	Col Shinryo Kobata
Intelligence Staff	Lt. Col. Akira Ohtsuki
	Lt. Col. Sei Hashida (deceased)

| | Maj. Akira Kobayashi |
| | Capt. Iwaichi Fujiwara |

Chief, 3rd Section   Col. Akiho Ishii
(Logistics and Military Administration over the Occupied Area)
     Logistics & MA Staff   Lt. Col. Kazuo Iwahashi
                                           Lt. Col. Hiroo Sato
                                           Lt. Col. Masao Orita
                                           Maj. Nobuo Shigeno
Chief, 4th Section (Air)   Col. Kazuo Tanigawa (deceased)
     Air Staff   Lt. Col. Tomoo Saito
                                           Lt. Col. Kyo Suzuki
                                           Maj. Mizoo Matsumae

Brief Service Records of Concerned Army Officers

(A) General Shigeru Hasunuma.
    1904   Graduated from Military Academy and Sub-Lt (Cavalry)
    1911   Graduated from Army Staff College
    1925   Colonel, Aide-de-Camp to Emperor
    1935   Lt. Gen., Inspector of Cavalry
    1938   Commanding General, Mongolian Army
    1940   Full General
    (I checked detailed year-by-year records on him kept by Demo. Bureau, but could not find his service as aide to the Emperor while he was Lt. Col. and Major General.)

(B) Staff Members of the Operations Section.
    (a)   Lt. Col. Kushida
        Born in 1902. Sub-Lt (Inf.) in 1923. Graduated from Army Staff College. Served as an aide to the Army Minister Sept. '41–Feb. '42. Staff of the Operations Section (as the successor to Col. Tsuji) Feb. '42–Jan. '43. Chief of War Direction Sec. Operation Staff of Southern Army at the end of the war.
        (Very cheerful, intelligent gentleman. Not tall but fat. Good drinker.)
    (b)   Lt. Col. Kumon
        Born in 1903. Sub-Lt (Inf.) in 1924.
        Graduated from Army Staff College.
        Residential Officer in Great Britain.
        Transferred from infantry to air.
        Then Staff Operations Section in 1941.
        Died in an aeroplane accident near Kuril Is. in 1942.
    (c)   Lt. Col. Imoto
        Born in 1904. Sub-Lt (Inf.) in 1928.

Graduated from Army Staff College.

1935–39 Operations Staff.

1939–Oct. '40 China Army Staff.

Oct. '40–Dec. '42 Operations Staff.

Dec. '42 –June '43 8th Area Army Staff (Solomons, New Guinea).

June '43–Nov. '43 Operations Staff.

Nov. '43–Apr. '45 Personal Secretary to Army Minister.

Apr. '45–2nd General Army Staff.

(Very clever, fine officer. Reliable and cooperative but strict on the important matters. All white hair and looked soft. Baptised by atomic bomb at Hiroshima. Good drinker.)

(d) Lt. Col. Takase

Born in 1905. Sub-Lt (Inf.) in 1926.

Graduated from Army Staff College 1937.

Member, Military Affairs Section.

1941–45. Operations Staff.

1945. Instructor, Army Staff College.

(e) Lt. Col. Okamura

1926. Sub-Lt (Inf.)

1936. Graduated from Army General Staff College.

Apr. '40–May '42. Operations Staff.

May–June '42. Southern Army Staff.

June '42–Nov. '42. Instructor, Army Staff College.

1943–44. Mongolian Army Staff.

1945. Regimental Commander.

(Not so attractive).

(f) Major Takayama

Born in 1906. Sub-Lt (Artillery) in 1929.

Graduated from Army Staff College.

1938. 21st Army Staff (Southern China).

1939. Operations Staff.

1940. Residental [sic] Officer in Germany.

1941. Operations Staff.

1945. Member, Military Affairs Section.

(Careful, gentle, clever.)

(g) Major Takeda (Prince)

Born in 1909. Sub-Lt (Cavalry) in 1930.

Graduated from Army Staff College.

As Cavalry Captain fought in the China Incident with distinguished merit. Operations Staff of the Imperial GHQ in 1941 and on, as staff in charge of Pacific Front.

(h) Major Kondo

Born in 1909. Sub-Lt (Inf) in 1928.

Graduated from Army Staff College.
1937. Served in the Education Inspectorate [sic] General.
1938–39. China Expeditionary Army Staff.
1939–42. Operations Staff of the Imperial GHQ, when he died as a result of an aeroplane crash in Hainan Is.

(i)   Major Hara (Zenshiro)
Born in 1907. Sub-Lt in 1928.
Graduated from Army Staff College.
1939–40. Served as Kwantung Army Staff.
1941–43. Operations Staff of the Imperial GHQ.

(j)   Major Sejima
Born in 1911. Sub-Lt. (Inf.) in 1932.
Graduated from Army Staff College.
1940–43. Served as 4th Division Staff, Operations Staff of IGHQ.
1944. Staff of Combined Fleet.
1945. Kwantung Army Staff and captured by USSR. Now in Japan.

(k)   Major Shudo
Born in 1911. Sub-Lt (Inf.) in 1932.
Graduated from Army Staff College.
Transferred from Inf. to Air.
1941–43. Air Operations Officer in IGHQ. Then Air Army Staff.
1959–60. Worked in U.S. Foreign History Div.

(l)   Major Shirai
Born 1912. Sub-Lt. (Transport) in 1933.
Graduated from Army Staff College.
Expert on logistics.
Logistics Staff in Operations Section, 1941–42.

(m)   Captain Haruke
Born 1913. Sub-Lt. (Inf.) in 1936.
Graduated from Army Staff College.
1938–39. China Expeditionary Army.
1940–   Operations Staff in IGHQ.

(C) Staff Members of the War Direction.

(a)   Col. Yadoru Arisue
Sub-Lt in 1920. Graduated from Army Staff College. Served as residential officer in Great Britain, Operations Section Chief of Kwantung Army. Oct. 1940–Feb. '42. Chief of newly organized War Direction Section. Mar. '42–June '43. Chief of Staff, Hong-kong [sic] Governor General. June–Aug. '43. Asst. Chief of Staff, 8th Area Army (Solon, New Guinea).
He died by an air accident in New [sic] Britain in August '43 and was promoted to Lieutenant General.

(Gentle, attractive, nice-looking but firm will and active. Much more popular and beloved than his brother, Seizo.)

(b) Col. Isao Takeda

Sub.Lt. in 1923. Served as a residential officer in Soviet Russia for several years. Chief of 8th Sec., Army General Staff (and concurrently war direction staff) in Oct. '40–Aug. '42.

2nd Sec. Chief of Kwantung Army and Chief of Staff, Hangkow Area Army while in the war. Died after war.

(c) Lt. Col. Sako Tanemura

Sub-Lt (Cavalry) in 1925 Graduated from Army Staff College in 1934.

Participated in Manchurian and China Incidents.

Dec. '39–Oct '40. Operations Staff.

Oct. '40–Apr. '45. War Direction Staff, IGHQ. (Section Chief from June '44–April '45).

Apr.– Aug. '45) [sic] Member, Military Affairs Section.

Aug '45. 17th Area Army Staff. Captured by USSR in North Korea.

(Clever, quick decisions, gentle and cheerful. Working together with Ohmae & Nishiura as part-time consultant of Self-Defense Agency.

(d) Lt. Col. Takuji Suzuki

Sub-Lt in 1923.

Graduated from Army Staff College.

Residential Officer in China.

1940–Feb. '42. War Direction Staff.

Feb. '42–Oct. '43. Chief of 7th Sec. (China Intelligence, IGHQ).

1943–'44. 43rd Division Chief of Staff.

Died in the Saipan defense combat.

(e) Capt. Shiro Hara

1932. Sub-Lt.

1939. Graduated from Army Staff College.

1939–'40. Kwantung Army Staff.

Nov. '40–Nov. '42. War Direction Staff, IGHQ.

Nov. '42–'44. 8th Area Army Staff.

1945. Operations Staff, IGHQ.

(As he was in the Historical Section, GHQ, you may know him quite well.)

(D) Staff Members of the Southern Army (besides CofS and Asst. CofS).

(a) Col. Masami Ishii

Sub-Lt (Engineer) in 1918.

Graduated from Army Staff College.

1929–'31 Army General Staff.

1931–'37. Residential Officer in Germany (Last half as Asst. Attaché).

1939–'41. Instructor at Army Staff College.

Nov '41–'43. Staff, Southern Army.

Early 1944. Instructor, Army Staff College. Maj. Gen. Instructor, Army Staff College.

Last half, 1944. Chief of Staff, 36th Army.

1945. Chief of Staff, 11th Area Army.

Died after the war.

(b) Col. Kazuo Tanigawa

1921. Sub-Lt (Cavalry).

1926. Transferred to Air from Cavalry.

Graduated from Army Staff College.

1939–40. Assistant Attaché in USSR.

1940–Nov.'41. Instructor of Army Staff College.

Nov . '41–'42. Staff, Southern Army.

Last half 1942. 2nd Air Army Staff.

1943–'44. 8th Area Army Staff.

1945. Assistant Chief of Staff, Combined Fleet. He died after the war.

(Not so good-looking but attractive, kind and gentle. I worked together [with him] in Rabaul and Tokyo. He divorced his wife after the war and lived with his sweetheart [hostess of a restaurant].)

(c) Col. Okikazu Arao

Sub-Lt (Inf.) in 1923. Graduated from Army Staff College.

1934–'36. Residential Officer in USSR.

1936–'37. Residential Officer in Germany.

July–Nov. '41. Operations Staff in IGHQ.

Nov. '41–May '42. Staff of Southern Army.

May '42–Apr. '45. Chief, Shipping Section, IGHQ.

Apr. '45– Chief, Army Affairs Section.

(Able, active, fine gentleman. My good friend.)

(d) Maj. Akira Kagoshima

Sub-Lt (Inf.) in 1930. Graduated from Army Staff College.

1937–'41. Operations Staff, IGHQ.

Nov. '41–Aug. '43. Staff, Southern Army.

Aug. '43–Feb. '44. Member, Aerial Department.

Feb. '44–Aug. '45. Op. (Air) Staff, IGHQ.

Aug. '45. Staff, Air General Army.

(e) Col. Masanobu Tsuji

Sub-Lt (Inf.) in 1924. Graduated from Army Staff College. Staff, Kwantung Army; Op. Staff of Imperial GHQ; Staff, Malay Invasion Force; Op. Staff, IGHQ; Staff, China Expeditionary Army and 15th Army Staff (Burma) in the China Incident and Pacific War.

Part II
Prewar Diplomacy and Politics

Introduction

Anyone who has followed this volume through Part I is likely to have formed the opinion—correctly, we believe—that for most if not all of 1941 Japanese-U.S. diplomacy was irrelevant. Japan's extremist, saber-rattling elements were in the saddle. It was a cliché of the time that the Emperor of Japan was a puppet; there was less realization that the Prime Minister and Foreign Minister were almost equally so. The military had a stranglehold on the Japanese government so that any agreement reached between the Foreign Ministry and the State Department would be meaningless unless the Japanese military supported it. And the Japanese military—particularly the Army—was not interested in peace; it was interested in conquest and power.

Inevitably the diplomatic negotiations between Tokyo and Washington were long and frustrating. The United States could not possibly acquiesce in Japan's takeover of Asia. In particular, the brutality of the Japanese occupation of China revolted Americans, and Japan's membership in the Tripartite Pact placed her in the camp of the enemies of freedom. For their part, the Japanese believed they had the right to anything they had the strength to take and, indeed, a divine mandate to rule Asia.

Into this virtually hopeless situation, Tokyo sent an honorable, intelligent, and well-disposed ambassador, Admiral Kichisaburo Nomura. Nothing would have pleased him better than to arrange a rapprochement between Japan and the United States, for he was convinced that the friendship and support of the latter would far outweigh any advantages that might accrue to Japan through armed conquest. But the Foreign Ministry kept him on such a short leash that he was probably the most frustrated man in Washington.

The United States had a man of equal good will in Tokyo as ambassador. Joseph C. Grew had spent many years there, had seen Japanese governments come and go, and had known just about every Japanese of real importance. While he deplored Japan's current policies, he loved the Japanese people and, like Nomura, would have been delighted to see Tokyo and Washington clasp hands in sincere friendship. Unfortunately, Grew was just as badly

situated in Tokyo as Nomura was in Washington, and for the same reason—
the Japanese Army was calling the tune.

The first part of this section is devoted to a portion of the diary of
Marquis Koichi Kido. It gives what might be called a "meanwhile, back at
the ranch" view of official activities at court. The second part of this section
covers the months of Nomura's diary from June to December 1941. The
reader interested in Grew's view is referred to his book *Ten Years in Japan*.

Extracts from the Diary of Marquis Koichi Kido

Introduction

As Lord Keeper of the Privy Seal, Kido held an important and responsible position at the court of Emperor Hirohito. He arranged all audiences with the Emperor, except for those two laws unto themselves, the War and Navy Ministers, who had free access to the Throne. He acted as the channel between the Emperor and his ministers and kept Hirohito posted on what was going on outside the palace enclave.

The Kido diary has long been an invaluable source for historians and is one of the most important source documents of the Showa era. Kido had been close to the Emperor since childhood. As befitting a man holding a highly confidential position near the Throne, Kido was exceedingly discreet in what he put on paper. Nevertheless, the diary gives an enlightening account of official life behind the Imperial moat before and during World War II.

These extracts cover the period of July through December 1941. The translator of the version presented herein is unknown to us.

Extracts from Diary of Marquis Kido

July 2, 1941 (Full)

Mr. Ando, Governor of Kyoto Prefectural [sic], visited me at nine in the morning. A *Gozen Kaigi* (council in the Imperial presence) was held in the palace at ten in the morning to discuss and decide the national policy to cope with the new phase of the international situation created by the war between Germany and Soviet Russia. Finance Minister Isao Kawada called on me at 12:20 P.M. to explain the matter relating to allowing a credit in favor of the Wang Ching-wei Government, the amount of which would triple the former one. Prince Fumimaro Konoye came at one P.M. and said that he found it very difficult to grasp the true intention of Foreign Minister Matsuoka. I visited the Emperor from 2 P.M. to 3:10 P.M. to hear about the progress of the council in the Imperial presence. At 3:20 P.M. I made arrangements with the Chief Aide-de-Camp about the establishment of the *Dai Honye* (Imperial G.H.Q.) in the palace and the coming Imperial visit to Hayama. Mr. Sekichi Shimozon called at my office at 3 P.M. Mr. Hisatada Hirose visited me at 7:30 P.M.

July 5, 1941 (Full)

Foreign Minister Matsuoka proceeded to the palace at 2 P.M. and we talked after his leaving the Imperial presence. He said information of the diplomatic parley between France and Japan relative to the Japanese Army's entry into French Indochina seemed to have leaked out, for Ambassador Craigie* lodged a protest with us through Mr. Chuichi Ohashi, Vice Foreign Minister, saying that if the understanding reached between France and Japan were true, England would consider it as a serious problem. Therefore the negotiations which had been originally scheduled to start today or thereabout was [sic] decided to be postponed for another five days in order to watch the necessary development.

July 15, 1941 (Extract)

Mr. Matsudaira† visited from Tokyo at eight A.M. He came to report on the outcome of his meeting with Premier Konoye. Still there was something not quite understandable about Foreign Minister Matsuoka's attitude towards the proposed formula, for Japanese-American understanding. Under the circumstances, up to yesterday the Premier was of the opinion that should the Foreign Minister agree to that formula prepared by the Director of Military Affairs and the Director of Naval Affairs, with a few alterations he would push the policy it were. Although [the] Foreign Minister had no objection to the formula, he insisted on giving instructions to Ambassador Nomura in Washington to the effect that the Government would reject the oral statement of Mr. Cordell Hull, as it was of the disgraceful nature to Japan. After that he said that he would wire a compromise formula to Admiral Kichisaburo Nomura. But Prince Konoye was of the opinion that our formula should be wired at the same time, because if we followed Matsuoka's idea, there is a possibility that America might take it as our intention to discontinue the negotiations. Mr. Yoshie Saito, an adviser to the Foreign Office, was in favor of the Foreign Minister's proposal, but the Premier contra-

*Sir Robert Craigie, British Ambassador to Japan
†Marquis Yasumasa Matsudaira, Kido's Chief Secretary

dicted him and sent him to Mr. Matsuoka in order to persuade the Foreign Minister to agree to the Premier's opinions. Such was the condition up to 10:50 yesterday evening. At 1:30 this morning, Prince Konoye telephoned me to say that he had waited long for Matsuoka's answer in vain, so he sent Director of the American Bureau Taro Terasaki to Mr. Matsuoka to hold an enquiry into the circumstances, with the result that he had sent his instructions by himself and not through the medium of the competent director, and that he intended to call me at Hayama to work out remedial measures. I had a conference with the Chief Secretary as to the matter of the resignation en bloc of the Cabinet which was expected under the circumstances. At this time when the tension prevailing over the people regarding the present political situation was so strong that even the higher schools were closed throughout the country lest an unexpected disturbance should arise, the resignation en bloc for some hidden reason, unknown to the people, should be avoided by all means. For this purpose, we would have to try whatever is possible to obtain, first of all the resignation of the Foreign Minister, but we resolved to prevail upon the Emperor and issue the Imperial command to form a new cabinet to Prince Konoye again to tide over the difficult political situation for fear of our failure in our effort to make the Foreign Minister resign, and the resignation en bloc of the cabinet as a result of it.

I went to my office at 11 A.M. I was received in audience by the Emperor from 1:35 P.M. to 2 P.M. to report the above circumstances. Prince Konoye visited me from Tokyo at 3 P.M. We had a talk until 4:20 P.M. What I had heard from the Premier was almost the same as the information I had received from the Chief Secretary.

I thought it was advisable to urge Mr. Matsuoka's resignation to avoid the change of the cabinet, but the Premier disagreed with me, saying that if it should be done Mr. Matsuoka and his party would make propaganda that the cause which had compelled his resignation was nothing but pressure upon our government on the part of the U.S.A., thus leading to the utter failure of the parley at Washington.

July 16, 1941 (Full)

At 4 P.M. Marquis Matsudaira telephoned me to say that the resignation en bloc of the Cabinet had been decided at a special cabinet meeting. I had my audience with the Emperor from 4:10 P.M. to 4:20 P.M. Prince Konoye tendered the general resignation of his ministry at 9 P.M. I proceeded to the palace in response to a summons from His Majesty to receive the Imperial order as to the incoming cabinet as follows: As the premier tendered the general resignation of his ministry, we ordered the Lord Chamberlain to invite the President of the Privy Council and the ex-premiers to gather at the palace and to ask their opinions in order to reply to our question as to who was the suitable person for the post of Premier in the coming cabinet. I talked with the Chief Secretary to arrange tomorrow's procedure and went back home at 10:30 P.M.

July 17, 1941 (Extract)

I left for Tokyo by train, leaving at 8:44 P.M. and proceeded to the palace. I met Mr. [Yoshimichi] Hara, President of the Privy Council, Mr. [Reijiro] Wakatsuki, Admiral [Keisuke] Okada, General [Nobuyuki] Abe, Admiral [Mitsumasa] Yonai, General [Senjiro] Hayashi and Mr. [Koki] Hirota at 1:00 P.M. Mr. Kanroji, Vice Lord Chamberlain, delivered the Imperial message, and then I expressed my opinion as follows:

> The Emperor ordered me to gather your opinions before I should make a reply to the throne regarding the Premier of the succeeding cabinet. I, therefore, would like to have your frank opinions on this matter as I had in the previous case. Of course as you all know, this is not a formal conference and no resolution would be passed, but I should like to have a heart-to-heart talk in a friendly atmosphere. And our utterances in the place were expected to be kept in confidence.

The copy of the Premier's resignation was circulated for reference.

Mr. Wakatsuki questioned me as to the purpose of the resignation and the diplomatic problems, and the breach of opinions between the Premier and the Foreign Minister; General Abe stressed the necessity of having Prince Konoye as Premier; Admiral Okada recommended Prince Konoye, saying that no other person but Prince Konoye could exercise general control over both the Army and political circles; General Hayashi had the same opinion as General Abe and Admiral Okada; Mr. Hara had no different opinion from the above mentioned; Mr. Hirota laid particular stress upon the reinforcement of G.H.Q. Admiral Yonai said that Prince Konoye was the most suitable man to cope with the present difficulty. Mr. Wakatsuki supported Prince Konoye unanimously and closed our meeting at 2 P.M.

The Emperor and Empress returned to Tokyo from Hayama Villa. I visited the Emperor from 3:20 to 4:10 P.M. to report on the progress of our meeting, while the Lord Chamberlain telephoned to Prince Konoye to request his presence at the palace. At 5:05 P.M. Prince Konoye proceeded to the palace to receive the Imperial command to form a cabinet. Mr. Ohashi, Vice Foreign Minister, visited me at 5:50 P.M. to explain the compromise bill between the U.S.A. and this country.

July 31, 1941 (Full)

From 10:15 A.M. to 11 A.M. I was received in audience by the Emperor, and His Majesty was pleased to explain the report of Admiral Osami Nagano in reply to the Imperial question as to our policy toward the U.S.A., as follows:

1. His opinion regarding the war was the same as that of former Chief of the Naval General Staff, Prince Hiroyasu Fushimi, in that we should try to avert the war as much as possible.
2. He seemed very strongly opposed to the Tripartite Alliance. He also seemed to be of the opinion that as long as such an alliance existed, the adjustment of Japan[ese]-American diplomatic relations would be impossible.
3. Suppose the adjustment of diplomatic relations between the U.S.A. and Japan were impossible and we would be cut off from supplies of oil, our oil stored up would run out in two years. In case a war with the U.S.A. breaks out, the supply of oil would be only sufficient for one and a half years. Under these circumstances, there would be no alternative but to take the initiative in operations against them.
4. According to the written report submitted, I believe that we could win, as it is so explained therein. Asked if it would be possible to win a sweeping victory as was the Russo-Japanese War, Admiral Nagano replied to the Throne that it was very doubtful whether or not we could win at all, to say nothing of a great victory such as in the Russo-Japanese War.

I was filled with trepidation by the Imperial anxiety in that it was indeed dangerous to have to wage a desperate war.

My answer to the Imperial speech was as follows:

1. Admiral Nagano's opinion was too simple.
2. The U.S.A recognized the existence of the Triple Alliance pact in our previous parley with America, and I was very doubtful whether we could deepen the confidence of the U.S.A. in us by the act of annulment of the treaty, as the U.S.A. was a nation which showed respect for an international treaty. We would only be held in contempt by the U.S.A. We were not quite out of means of restoring friendship between America and Japan. We must deliberate on the matter in a constructive manner. I would demand the Premier's careful consideration on this point. I met with Navy Minister Admiral Koshiro Oikawa at noon to talk over Admiral Nagano's report to the Throne. The Chief Aide-de-Camp to the Emperor visited me at 1 A.M. to talk with me on the same subject.

August 2, 1941 (Extract)

I went to my office at 10 A.M. Prince Konoye visited me at 11 A.M. He said he was annoyed to find that there was an observable tendency for the tough elements in the Navy to gather strength, a tendency which would be a great hindrance in the war in maintaining harmony between the Supreme Command and the Government. If the U.S.A. adopted decisive measures such as to cut us off from supplies of oil, we would run out of oil. Under these circumstances, we would be threatened by an acute national crisis, if we made a mistake in our diplomatic movements. Hence, the understanding with the War and Navy Ministers concerning our fundamental national policy should be secured as soon as possible, and if a complete agreement were not reached, there would be no way for the government but to resign en bloc.

And it would be the Army and the Navy that assumed charge of the administration of the country. I talked with the Chief Secretary on the same matter.

August 5, 1941 (Full)

At 11:30 A.M. I received a message from Prince Konoye, saying that he had decided to go to the U.S.A. to see President Roosevelt and to take over the pending problems on Pacific affairs, and a memorandum of his intention was handed to the Army and Navy.

August 7, 1941 (Full)

Prince Konoye proceeded to the palace at 3:30 P.M. We talked after his talk with the Emperor from 4 P.M. to 4:30 P.M. I expressed my opinion as follows:

1. The situation we are facing now is very serious.
2. We must decide our national policy immediately, by holding a meeting between the Government and the Army, without idling away the time.
3. According to the reports that have come up to now, we are not strong enough to fight the U.S.A. and the Soviet [sic] at the same time.
4. We are facing a very serious situation which we could easily have reduced to a simple problem such as oil, by making a little difference in our viewpoint.
5. The quantity of oil in store is so moderate that it would barely supply us throughout two years during peace, but in case of war we could have enough only for 1½ years.
6. If the above mentioned were true, we had to reach the conclusion that our war with the U.S.A. would be a hopeless one.
7. The Dutch East Indies and the northern part of the Saghalien would

be the chief source of oil supply after we were cut off from our supplies from the U.S.A.

8. To secure a sufficient quantity of oil in one and a half years would
   be a very difficult task, owing to the destruction of oil fields in parts
   of the Dutch East Indies.
10. If we attacked the Dutch East Indies, the U.S.A. would declare war
    against Japan. Long-distance transportation of oil under a constant
    menace of submarines and airplanes would be very dangerous and
    the result would fall short of our expectations.
11. If there were miscalculations about oil supplies, we would face a
    very serious situation which might lead to our defeat.
12. We couldn't do what we wanted, on account of the shortage of our
    national power. Although the situation was different in external ap-
    pearances, we might be compelled to exercise the same self-restraint
    that we had after our victory in the Sino-Japanese war in 1895.
13. We should resolve to bear through ten years of hard struggles.
14. Meanwhile we should do everything to restore the friendly relation-
    ship between the U.S.A. and Japan. And we must try to secure war
    materials which are in demand.
15. Our ultimate objective in the country will be Japan's advance to
    Southern Regions, and in order to attain this object, a ten-year plan
    has been mapped out as follows:
    a. Establishment of heavy industries and machine tool industries.
    b. Establishment of synthetic oil industry.
    c. Expansion of ocean liners.

August 28, 1941 (Extract)

Mr. Michinao Kubo visited me at 9:30 A.M. Admiral Nagano visited me at
11:30 A.M. and detailed the Government's policy towards the U.S.A. and
England. General Teiichi Suzuki, President of the Planning Board, visited
the Emperor at 2:30 P.M. After his leaving the presence of the Emperor, I
heard a material mobilization plan from him. At 3 P.M. War Minister Lt.
Gen. Hideki Tojo visited the Emperor. I had a talk with him after he retired
from the presence of the Emperor. Mr. Genki Abe visited me to talk about
the recent situation at home and abroad.

September 5, 1941 (Extract)

At 4:30 P.M. the Premier proceeded to the palace and submitted to the
Throne a plan relative to the holding of a council in the Imperial presence.
The Premier said that as the Emperor had many questions as to our policy
towards the U.S.A. from the point of view of war strategy, he had advised

the Emperor to summon the Chief of the Army General Staff and the Chief of the Naval General Staff. I, therefore, proceeded to the palace to advise the Emperor to follow the Premier's advice. I requested Aide-de-Camp Yokoyama to call to the Palace the Chief of the Army General Staff and the Chief of the Naval General Staff and the Premier. At 6:00 P.M. they were granted audience by the Emperor to answer Imperial questions.

September 6, 1941 (Full)

From 9:40 to 9:55 A.M. I visited the Emperor in response to the Imperial summons. The Emperor said that he would like to ask questions. Then I advised His Majesty that since Mr. Hara, the President of the Privy Council, would ask important questions on His Majesty's behalf, the Emperor should only give a warning in conclusion that the Supreme War Command should exert its full-fledged efforts in order to bring about a diplomatic success, inasmuch as the present decision was such an important one that it might lead to a war staking our national fortunes. I visited the Emperor again from 1:10 P.M. to 1:30 P.M. and then I was made acquainted with the progress of the council in the Imperial presence.

It is understood that the Supreme War Command had just kept quiet to the questions put by the President of the Privy Council. At the closing of the meeting, the Emperor declared it was regrettable that the Supreme War Command did not give any reply. After quoting Emperor Meiji's poem entitled "The Sea at the Four Sides," His Majesty emphasized that wholehearted efforts should be made in the conduct of diplomatic negotiations with the United States. It was added that the Navy Minister made an answer to Mr. Hara's questions.

September 11, 1941 (Full)

War Minister Tojo visited me after his retirement from the presence of the Emperor and explained the result of an investigation concerning the preparation for war against the U.S.A.

September 25, 1941 (Extract)

Ambassador Mamoru Shigemitsu visited me to talk about the negotiations between the U.S.A. and this country at 9 A.M. The Chief Aide-de-Camp visited me at 1 P.M. and explained the matter relative to the report of the Chief of the Army General Staff to be submitted to the throne.

September 26, 1941 (Extract)

I met Prince Konoye at 4 P.M. and talked with him until 5:15 P.M. He stated that he had no confidence, and there was no choice for him but to think of resigning if the military insists on starting a war on 15 October. I urged his prudence.

September 27, 1941 (Extract)

I visited the Emperor from 10:55 A.M. to 11:35 A.M. The Emperor requested me to make an investigation regarding the amount of rubber reserves in the U.S.A. and the output and tin resources in the South and Central Americas and the places where the United States would be able to obtain these resources. Hence I contacted the President of the Planning Board through the Chief Secretary of the Cabinet. President of the Privy Council Hara said that as our diplomatic parley with Washington would end in entire failure, and we would have to make our final resolution as to the war against the U.S.A., the coming council in the Imperial presence should not be such a formal one as we usually had, but we must have a full discussion of the matter instead, including the ex-Premiers. I promised him my consideration.

October 1, 1941 (Extract)

General Suzuki, President of the Planning Board, visited me to talk about our national policy towards the U.S.A.

October 2, 1941 (Extract)

I talked with the War Minister about the matter regarding the Premier's resolution from 1:10 P.M. to 1:40 P.M.

October 7, 1941 (Extract)

Mr. Tomita, the Chief Secretary to the Cabinet, visited me at 12:40 P.M. to talk about our negotiations with the U.S.A. He said as follows: The Army was of the opinion that there was no room left for the continuance of the parley, while the Navy held the reverse view. But the officers in medium standing of the Army and Navy were agreed in their anti-American attitude. The Navy's desire for the Premier was that he should immediately declare his resolution and assume the leadership in order to meet the serious situation. First of all, the Premier should talk with the War Minister, who had a strong anti-American attitude, in order to promote a better understanding between them. After that, a meeting among the Premier, War Minister and Navy Minister would be desirable to settle our national policy as to the war against the U.S.A.

October 9, 1941 (Extract)

I met Prince Konoye at 10:30 A.M. following his audience with the Emperor. He was quite uneasy about the future of the parley with Washington, and his prospects as to a satisfactory compromise were very discouraging. I expressed my opinion for his information as follows:

1. The resolution of the Council in the Imperial presence on the 6th of September seemed to me too extravagant. It was not the conclusion of exhaustive discussion, in my opinion.
2. Judging from the situation both at home and abroad, war with the U.S.A. would offer little chance of our victory, so we had better reconsider it.
3. It would be inadvisable to declare war against the U.S.A. immediately.
4. The Premier should clarify his intention to concentrate our national efforts upon the completion of the Chinese Incident.
5. We should acquire freedom without paying any attention to the economic oppression of the U.S.A.
6. The Premier should demand ten or fifteen years of hard struggles on the part of our nation to establish a highly defensive nation.
7. If it is necessary, we were [sic] ready to put belligerency in action to promote the completion of the Chinese Incident and to put the whole military force into the Chinese front, realizing our plans to obtain Kunming and Chungking.

Mr. Hachiro Arita visited me to talk about the American problems and the general resignation of the Cabinet.

October 12, 1941 (Extract)

At 10 A.M. Mr. Kango Koyama called on me to express deep resentment at the recent political situation, urging all possible efforts of the Premier. Major General Kato visited at my house to explain the Military Police's interpretation of the present condition. Mr. Kenji Tomita, Chief Secretary of the Cabinet, visited me to say as follows: The War and Navy and Foreign Ministers were going to hold a meeting in the Prince's house at Ogikubo at 2 P.M. to discuss the adjustment of the diplomatic relations between the U.S.A. and Japan.

The War Minister opined that as there was little room for a compromise between these countries, we should determine our attack upon the U.S.A. as soon as possible; yet as it was not for the Army's own pleasure that they had been expressing their demand for a war, they were quite ready to follow the Premier's opinion, if what he would say was convincing enough. The Navy Minister said that we should try to avoid war as much as possible. Now this country was standing at a crossroads, having two ways to choose: one is [sic] the restoration of a friendly relationship by diplomatic negotiations; the other was the declaration of war on the U.S.A. If the former was our choice, we must bring about a full understanding between the two countries by convincing the U.S.A. of the bona fide nature of our friendship toward the U.S.A., for a war after a patched-up compromise would be most undesirable. Anyway, the Premier's strong determination was the most urgent matter. The Premier expressed his firm conviction as to the successful conclusion of the parley, asking [for] their cooperation with his policy. The Foreign Minister was of the opinion that he was not quite sure of the outcome of the parley, although he could not flatly deny the completion of the meeting in success. They made the following agreement among themselves on the advice of the War Minister: Our demand regarding the stationing of troops should not be altered; the acquired result of the Chinese Incident should be secured by all means; we should further our parley on these agreements, leaving off our preparation for war.

October 13, 1941 (Extract)

I talked with the Emperor from 11:35 A.M. to 11:45 A.M., the center of our conversation being our talks with Washington. The Emperor said as follows: Under the present conditions, there would be practically no hope of the successful conclusion of the negotiations between the U.S.A. and this country. And we would have to issue an Imperial proclamation of war on the morrow of our declaration of war upon the U.S.A. As for the attitude of the people towards an Imperial message, there was much to be desired, for they had always ignored his intention to emphasize world peace and hearty cooperation of the pen and the sword for that purpose, the intentions which were specially stressed in the message issued on the retirement from the League of Nations and that issued when the Triple Alliance pact had been signed. It was very regrettable that they were interpreting these messages as a challenge to both the U.S.A. and England, refusing to take notice of the real meaning of them. He said that it was his earnest desire that his real intentions be materialized in the message of the proclamation of war by the aid of Prince Konoye and me.

When we were going to make our decisions regarding war against the U.S.A., we would have to pay much more attention to the European situation.

We should use diplomacy to prevent Germany from making peace with England and Soviet Russia, leading her to cooperate with us in the war against the U.S.A.

It was quite necessary to establish adequate measures to meet the armistice beforehand. For this purpose we should cultivate friendly relations with the Vatican, dispatching our envoy to the Pope.

At 2 P.M. Prince Konoye proceeded to the palace and was received in audience by the Emperor from 3 P.M. to 4 P.M.; following his audience exchanged notes chiefly about the American problems. The Foreign Minister visited the Emperor at 5 P.M. I talked with him from 5:30 to 6:30 P.M. General Suzuki, President of the Planning Board, visited me at 8 P.M. to talk about his political views which might contribute in some way to the making of a new turn in our political condition. I expressed my opinion to him. Our conclusion of the talk was this: The Premier should make an effort to promote mutual understanding with the War and Navy Ministers.

October 15, 1941 (Not indicated but probably full)

Mr. Yakata visited me at 9 A.M. At 9:30 A.M. General Suzuki, President of the Planning Board, visited me to deliver War Minister Tojo's message, the purpose of which is [sic] as follows: If the Premier would not change his mind, the general resignation of the Cabinet could not be avoided. And as for the succeeding premier, although the War Minister did not mention the name, he made it essential to the next premier that he should harmonize the Army and the Navy with the Imperial will. When one considered this point, it would be very difficult to find a suitable person among the Japanese subjects. He mentioned Prince Naruhiko Higashikuni as an example of the next premier. To this, I answered that we should be very careful for it was a matter concerned with the Imperial family. And if we had to ask the Prince's acceptance of premiership, a common policy between the Army and the Navy should be worked out beforehand; the establishment of an independent policy would take precedence of all others. I asked if the War Minister had any reasonable prospects on this point.

I went to the office at 11 A.M. Prince Konoye visited me to ask my opinion regarding the Higashikuni Cabinet. I answered that it was still under consideration. I requested Mr. Matsudaira, Chief Secretary, to study the procedure for materializing the Higashikuni plan. I visited the Emperor from 1:15 P.M. to 2 P.M. to report upon the pressing political situation. Premier Konoye visited me at 4 P.M. to say that he could no longer hold his premiership, for the breach with the War Minister was becoming deeper every day, until at last the War Minister gave vent to his discontent, saying that he did not like to hold any further conversation with the Premier, as he was not sure if he could stifle his feelings. Finally he asked my opinion regarding the proposed Higashikuni Cabinet, so I opined that I did not know whether the War Minster had changed his opinion in order to effect a compromise with the Navy or whether he intended to put the Prince's shoulder to the wheel, and I had yet to know the real intention of the War Minister.

I telephoned to the President of the Planning Board to request his visit.

I visited the Minister of the Imperial Household Department to talk about the Higashikuni Cabinet plan. The astonished Minister strongly objected to this plan. At 4:30 P.M. General Suzuki, President of the Planning

Board, visited me. I asked him the real meaning of the War Minister's intention, but in vain. I urged him to supply me with a definite report on this matter. The Premier, who joined our conversation on his leaving the presence of the Emperor, said that the Emperor had not shown any particular objection to the Higashikuni Cabinet, a cabinet which might be said to be an outcome of necessity, not of choice.

I talked with the Premier until 8:30 P.M. regarding the political situation. At night Gen. Suzuki telephoned to report on the result of his conversation with War Minister Tojo. According to his report, Tojo's purpose was to establish harmony between the Army and the Navy by the Prince's influence, and not to realize the desired harmony to pave the way for the Cabinet. So I objected to the plan. The Premier also telephoned me to say that he wanted to secure an informal consent from Prince Higashikuni. I answered that it would be too early to do so, though I had no objection to him as long as his action was in his capacity as Premier. At midnight the Premier telephoned to say the that Prince Higashikuni asked for a few days consideration on his part and a meeting with the War Minister and me. From 5:35 A.M. to 5:50 A.M. I made a report to the throne concerning Prince Konoye's talk and asked the Imperial opinion as to the matter.

October 16, 1941

(Not indicated but probably an extract as it does not cover an important conversation between Kido and Konoya that evening)

At 8:30 A.M. President Gen. Suzuki visited me to express his negative opinion regarding a proposed "peer cabinet," saying as follows:

1. The Higashikuni Cabinet should not be brought into existence until* although there was no difference in view between the Army and the Navy, but they were badly in need of the help of a prince of the blood to forget all that had happened between them.
2. To shuffle every responsibility on the shoulders of the prince, leaving all difficulties unsettled, should be avoided by all means.
3. On the one hand, the Higashikuni Cabinet would be a sad sign of a dearth of talent among the subjects, and on the other hand it would make a pretty bad mess of it, if war with the U.S.A. broke out. In that case, the Imperial house would become an object of common hatred. He raised strong objections to the idea of asking the help of a prince of the blood to solve the problem which had some unknown reason to prevent the decision of Prince Konoye in the Council of the Imperial presence.

*Evidently something has been omitted here.

At 2 P.M. I talked with Foreign Minister Admiral Teijiro Toyoda.

At 3 P.M. War Minister Tojo visited me to report on the pressing political situation. I expressed my objection to his idea of the Higashikuni Cabinet from the same standpoint which I had made clear to Gen. Suzuki. I emphasized the revision of the resolution of the Council of the Imperial presence and the unity of the Army and Navy in their policies, two fundamental factors without which no national progress would be expected.

At 4 P.M. Prince Konoye telephoned to say that the Cabinet was going to resign en bloc. I was astonished by its suddenness. I visited the Emperor at 4 P.M. to report upon the general resignation of the Konoye Cabinet. At 5 P.M., Prince Konoye tendered the Cabinet Ministers' resignations to the Throne. I was received in audience by the Emperor from 5:30 P.M. to 5:45 P.M. to answer the Imperial questions regarding the succeeding cabinet.

October 17, 1941 (Not specified but probably an extract)

At 11 A.M. Mr. Matsudaira, Chief Secretary, visited me to make arrangements for a senior statesmen's conference. It was held from 1:10 P.M. to 3:45 P.M. in the west antechamber of the palace. Those present were Viscount Keigo Kiyoura (92 years old), Mr. Wakatsuki, Admiral Okada, Gen. Hayashi, Mr. Hirota, Gen. Abe, Admiral Yonai, ex-premiers, and Mr. Hara, President of the Privy Council. I explained the situation of the general resignation. Mr. Wakatsuki recommended Gen. Issei Ugaki as the succeeding premier. Gen. Hayashi recommended the Higashikuni Cabinet.

I asserted that the most important things were the revision of the decision of the last council in the Imperial presence and the unity of opinion between the Army and Navy. I offered the Tojo Cabinet as a solution to these problems. I met with no objection to my proposal, Mr. Hirota, Gen. Abe, Mr. Hara, giving me positive approval. The meeting broke up at 4 P.M. I reported to the Emperor the details of the progress of the ex-premiers' conference and talked until 4:15 P.M. The War Minister proceeded to the palace at the request of the Emperor to receive the Imperial Order to form a new cabinet. It was followed by the visit of Navy Minister Oikawa to whom the Emperor gave a speech to the effect that the unity of opinions between the Army and Navy was very desirable. I delivered to them in an anteroom the Imperial wish as follows: Deep consideration, a careful attitude and freedom from the decision of the council on the 6th of September were things wished for in the establishment of the fundamental policy of this country.

October 19, 1941 (Extract)

General Suzuki, President of the Planning Board, visited me at 8 P.M. to talk about his political views which might contribute in some way to taking a new turn in our political condition. I expressed my opinion to him. Our conclusion of the talk was this: The Premier should make an effort to promote mutual understanding with the War and Navy Ministers.

October 20, 1941 (Not specified but probably an extract)

I said that I recommended the Tojo cabinet as a preventive to a rush war, after thoughtful consideration of the situation. The Emperor approved my answer, saying "Nothing ventured, nothing gained."

October 25, 1941 (Extract)

The Chief Aide-de-Camp visited at 11:30 A.M. to inform me of the matter regarding the age-limit law for the Board of Marshals and Fleet Admirals.

Admiral Yoshizawa called on me at 3 P.M.

Finance Minister Okinori Kaya visited me to talk about the liaison conference (*Renraku Kaigi*) at 6 P.M.

October 29, 1941 (Extract)

At 9 A.M. General Suzuki, President of the Planning Board, called on me to report on the progress of the liaison conference. Mr. Hara, President of the Privy Council, visited me at 10:30 A.M. to consult about the recommendation to the throne of Mr. Seihim Ijuda as a member of the Privy Council. At 11:30 A.M. I heard from Premier Tojo about the progress of the liaison conference and the extension of the Anti-Comintern Pact and our political move toward Yen Hai-shan. The Chief Aide-de-Camp visited me at 12:45 to talk about the latest political situation. The *Juichi-Kai* (the eleventh party) was held to exchange views regarding the political situation. Those present were Prince Konoye, Mr. Tadataks [sic] Hirohata, Mr. Uramatsu, Viscount Nagakage Okabe, Mr. Kuroki, Count Sakai, Count Oda and Count Yamagisawa.

November 5, 1941

(The translations available to us for November and the part of December we have selected do not specify whether the entries are full or extracts, so we have ceased to so specify in this format. [sic])

The council in the presence of the Emperor (*Gozen Kaigi*) was held at 10:30 A.M. and continued until 3:10 P.M. and a policy towards the U.S.A., England and the Netherlands was then decided. At 3:40 Premier Tojo visited me to inform me of such matters as the formation of the Southern Army (*Nampo Gun*) and the dispatch of Mr. Kurusu to the U.S.A. Mr. Hirose visited me at 7 P.M.

November 19, 1941

Wednesday, rainy.

From 10:50 A.M. I was received in audience by H.M. the Emperor and submitted to the Throne a summary of my opinions as follows: The prospects of the negotiations with America that war were [sic] to break out with America by the end of this month, the existence of any of the following diverse phases might be foreseen:

1. The phase in which the negotiations remain stagnant in the preliminary stage as they have been up to the present.
2. The state of affairs in which our demands had [sic] been partially accepted, that is to say:
   (a) Only a very small portion of same admitted.
   (b) Nearly a half portion accepted.
   (c) Almost the whole accepted.
3. The case where America, although herself coming to an agreement, still seeks to obtain the consent of Britain and the Netherlands.

Thus several phases of the situation must be foreseen and it would appear that there is left enough ground for controversy with regard to our rushing into the war headlong on the mere automatic grounds that the last day of the month of November has passed. If we did so, it is feared that it might exercise an undesirable influence. Accordingly, in the case when the Premier solicits His Majesty's final decision, if possible, I advised His Majesty, the Premier should be ordered to hold the council in the Imperial presence with the participation thereat of all the Primary Vassals of State.

At noon attended the luncheon party given by Baron Inakura at the restaurant Chikuyo, which Prince Konoye, Marquis Hosokawa and Marquis Matsudaira also attended. At 2:00 P.M. came back to the official residence and saw and had a talk with Mr. Nishihara Kamezo. Takazumi received informal order to be transferred to Osaka.

November 26, 1941

Wednesday, fine.

At 9:30 A.M. visited Baron Ito and conferred on the proposal of marriage requested by Mr. Kaneko. At 10:30 A.M. went on duty and conferred with Mr. Hara, President of the Privy Council, about the convocation of the Council of the Primary Vassals of State.

From 11:15 to 11:45 was received in audience. His Majesty told me as follows:

Concerning the prospects of the negotiations with America I fear that, to my great regret, we are now confronted by the worst stage. I think it would be better to hold once more a Council of the Primary Vassals of State and refer the matter to it for deliberation before making the final decision. So I should like to tell this to Tojo. What do you think about it?

So I answered as follows:

Once the final decision is made, this time it would truly be the last and irretrievably final one. Thus if there should be any doubt, or any better idea to surmount the difficulties in your Majesty's mind, I pray that your Majesty be pleased to elucidate the same without the least reserve and appropriate steps which your Majesty might not report of afterwards [sic].

I therefore pray that your Majesty convey to Tojo without reserve anything and everything connected with this question of great moment.

As H.I.H. the Princess Dowager Kayanomia died at 6:30 A.M. this morning I went to H.H.'s palace to register my name and then met Mr. Matsuura, the Chief Attendant to the Prince, to express my condolences.

At 2:30 P.M. met Premier Tojo after his audience and he asked my opinion as to the convocation of the Council of the Primary Vassals of State, concerning which he had been questioned by H.M. the Emperor. Thereupon I told him what I had addressed to the Throne previously and hoped that he would do his best for the attainment of His Majesty's august wishes.

At 3:30 P.M. went to the official residence of the Vice Minister for Foreign Affairs to attend the thirtieth anniversary of Marquis Komura. At 5:00 saw and had a talk with Mr. Junichi Korematsu.

November 29, 1941

Saturday, fine.

At 9:00 A.M. saw and had a talk with Mr. Hideo Ikeda, who called on me at home. At 10:00 A.M. went on duty and conferred with the Grand Chamberlain on the present situation.

It had been arranged that the Government would hold a round table conference together with the Primary Vassals of State at Court today from 9:30 A.M. to discuss the question of the negotiations with America and other relevant important matters of the moment and after its close all present at the conference would receive the honor of being present at the Court dinner.

However, the round table conference consecutively continued its sitting up to 1:00 P.M. and went into recess. We then finally attended the Court dinner. Such being the case, it appeared that they discussed all the questions with glowing enthusiasm.

After the Court dinner there, in the Imperial study, H.I.H. the Emperor was pleased to listen to the Primary Vassals of State expressing their views and opinions for about one hour from 2:00. The outline was as follows:

The conversations were started by His Majesty's remark: "The situation has become grave, has it not?" Thereupon, Baron Wakatsuki and others immediately replied as mentioned below:

Wakatsuki: I have nothing to say about our nation's spiritual power. But how is it in the sphere of our material strength? It well deserves scrupulous study as to whether it will stand a protracted war or not. I am still much concerned about this point, although an explanation was given by the Government during the forenoon.

Okada: Today we are confronted with a truly grave situation. I am very anxious about whether we have the necessary self-support in materials or not. Notwithstanding, I have been unable to understand this point.

Hiranuma: His Excellency Wakatsuki has referred to the spiritual strength of our nation. I agree with him. Nevertheless, the fact is that we have already been prosecuting a war for these four years. If today we have to wage another protracted war, we will have to suffer more hardships and distress. I think it a matter of great importance to adopt more powerful measures and efforts commensurate with the requirements of the times, especially to tighten the war-mindedness of the general public.

Konoye: It is to my deep regret that I could not do anything towards the adjustment of American-Japanese relations, despite my sincere efforts since last April. But I feel very grateful to the present Cabinet for their fervent efforts to attain this aim. According to the explanations given by the Government this morning, I cannot help judging, to my great regret, that the continuance of diplomatic negotiations would be hopeless.

But still, it is (not) inevitable that we resort to war at once, now that the diplomatic negotiations have failed. Is it not possible for us to find some way or other out under the present state of things, by persevering to the utmost under difficulties? I should like to enquire of the Government regarding this point later on.

Yonai: I cannot advance any concrete opinion, as I have not sufficient data, but I pray that sufficient caution be exercised so that we do not fall into the uttermost poverty in trying to avoid becoming gradually poor.

Hirota: (After having talked on conditions of each of the world powers since the World War) Japan adopted every possible means to avoid the intervention of Britain and America in the China Incident. In spite of this, the diplomatic situation has become as serious as it is today. According to the explanations of the Government, we seem to stand now face to face with a diplomatic crisis. Though the diplomatic crisis has a close relationship with the possibility of the outbreak of hostilities, I think the true intentions of both sides in the diplomatic negotiations are only revealed after the repetition of several crises. Why should we hastily rush into war immediately, after facing a crisis only once? Even granting that war is inevitable for argument's sake, and even if actual fighting were to break out, we should always be on the watch to seize the opportunity to solve the problems by means of diplomatic negotiations.

Hayashi: Though I have no data, I think generally speaking we have no alternative other than to rely upon the conclusions reached by the Government after full cooperative study with the Imperial Supreme Command.

Abe: According to the explanations of the government, it seems to be difficult to continue the diplomatic negotiations any further and now we are standing at the grave crossroads of fate. It seems to me that the government has made a scrupulous study of the matter from every angle and any further study can in no way be expected. But it would be vital for U.S.* to pay much more attention to the mental attitude of the Chinese people. What we have gained could be lost at once. Any false step on our part towards them might cause the total loss of our gains in China all at once.

Wakatsuki: Now a great moment indeed has arrived. There is one thing to which I should like to draw your serious attention. It is this: It is not necessary to tell anyone that we must fight even until the country be reduced to ashes and with ultimate defeat staring us in the face, if it were a question of the necessity of maintaining our very existence or one of defending our empire, or in sight [sic]—if when the war were absolutely necessary for the self-existence and the self-defense of our empire, but it is very dangerous indeed to execute state policy or to make use of the national strength to achieve such conjured-up ideas and ideals as the "Establishment of the Great East Asia Coprosperity Sphere" or of the "Stabilizing Power of East Asia." On this point I must pray that Your Majesty be so pleased as to ponder scrupulously.

At 4:00 P.M. it was reported that the Government's explanations to the Primary Vassals of State had been finished and Prince Konoye came to see me at my office and we had a close conversation, primarily on our relations with America and on other matters of importance.

At 7:00 P.M. proceeded to the Palace of H.I.H. the Prince Kayanomiya and attended the funeral service for the late Princess Dowager.

November 30, 1941

Sunday, fine.

At 1:30 P.M. proceeded to the palace of H.I.H. the Prince Takamatsu. I was received in audience by H.I.H. the Prince Mikasa, and reported on the recent situations evolving from our diplomatic policies towards America.

At 2:30 P.M. went on duty. At 3:30 P.M. at the Imperial Command I repaired to the Throne and was asked as follows: "H.I.H. the Prince Taka-

---

*It is not clear from the translation whether this should be U.S., the United States or, "us," i.e. the Japanese, which makes better sense.

matsu came up to see me this morning, and told me that the Navy had been fully occupied after all and it appeared to have been disposed to avoid war with America if possible. What on earth was the real intention of the Navy in this regard?"

So I replied as follows: "His Majesty's decision at this time would be of so grave a nature that, once decided, it would be irrevocable. So if Your Majesty felt any anxiety over the matter, Your Majesty would do well to take every possible precaution so as to do away with any bit of doubt or anxiety. Accordingly, I pray that Your Majesty be so pleased to send for the Navy Minister and the Chief of the Naval General Staff at once, to make sure of their true intentions. I pray that this matter be frankly conveyed to the Premier also."

At 3:30 P.M. met with the Chief Aide-de-Camp and at 6:00 P.M. the Grand Chamberlain. At 6:35 P.M. was summoned and received in audience. I was ordered to the following effect: "The Navy Minister and the Chief of the Naval General Staff have answered my question about the previous matter with considerable confidence, so instruct Tojo to proceed as pre-arranged."

I contacted the Premier on the phone at once and delivered the message to that effect.

Kaneo and his wife went back to Zushi.

December 1, 1941

At 2 P.M. the council in the presence of the Emperor (*Gozen Kaigi*) was held and at last war of Japan on the U.S.A. was decided. At 4:30 P.M., the Premier visited me to consult about the Imperial proclamation of war.

December 7, 1941

At 9:30 P.M. Mr. Naoki Hoshino, Chief Secretary of the Cabinet, visited me to consult about the war with the U.S.A. and England.

December 8, 1941

Monday, fine day.

At 0040 A.M., Foreign Minister Shigenori Togo told me by telephone that Mr. Grew had a cablegram addressed to the Emperor and that he wanted to consult with me over it. I replied to him saying that he had better consult with the Premier about its diplomatic effect and that the Emperor would be in readiness to receive him in audience at any time, even at midnight.

At 1:30 A.M., Tsuneo Matsudaira, the Minister of the Imperial Household, called me by telephone and inquired about the aforesaid matter. I gave him my view. Was notified that Foreign Minister Togo proceeded to the

Court. I therefore proceeded to the Court, too, at 2:40 A.M.; I had a talk with the Foreign Minister in the Court and returned home at 3:30 A.M.

At 7:15 A.M., was on duty at the office. It was an unusually fine day. When I was going up the Akasaka Mitsuke slope toward the Miyako-Zaka, I saw the rising sun above a building. From today, our country is going to enter upon war against America and Britain, the two greatest powers in the world.

Already at daybreak, this morning, an air unit of our Navy had made a raid on Hawaii. I who know it am anxious about its result. Now seeing the rising sun, I close my eyes and pray.

At 7:30 A.M. met the Premier, the Chief of the Naval General Staff, and the Chief of Naval Operations and heard the good news of the success of the raid, and I deeply felt the blessings of divine grace.

From 11:40 to 12 P.M., was received in audience. Even at the moment of our entering upon so gigantic a war as this one, risking the fate of the country, I found the Emperor perfectly calm, unmoved and self-possessed. Felt it a matter for which we all should really be thankful. The announcement of the declaration of war was issued. Was called on by Count Nobuaki Makino at 12:30 P.M. Talked with him.

3:05–3:25 P.M., was received in audience.

At 6 P.M., accompanied by Tsuroku, attended Count Ogtu's announcement banquet.

Diary of Admiral Kichisaburo Nomura, June–December 1941

Introduction

The Nomura diary has been published in Japan in Japanese, but not in the United States in English. This translation, headed "RPS Document Division" under [the] date of 18 July 1946, and identified as Document No. 1686, originated in the records of the International Military Tribunal for the Far East, International Prosecution Section. The translator is given as Kotaro Kurosawa. We understand that Admiral Nomura himself gave this copy to Prange, who held Nomura in affectionate esteem.

There is little of the personal in this diary, which is rather in the nature of a series of aide-mémoire of Ambassador Nomura's conversations with members of the State Department and copies of telegrams. For students of the Pacific War and of U.S.-Japanese relations, this diary provides a valuable cross-check upon the memoranda of conversations for this period available in the Cordell Hull papers in the Library of Congress, and the exchanges of telegrams between the Tokyo Foreign Office and its Embassy in Washington found in the Department of Defense multivolume work entitled *The "Magic" Background of Pearl Harbor*, and those contained in Volume 12 of the record of the *Congressional Investigation of the Pearl Harbor Attack*. Many messages in the diary, however, do not appear elsewhere. Considering the mutual misunderstandings that marked the U.S.-Japanese diplomatic relations of the day, the ambassador's diary dovetails surprisingly well with the American documentation.

Diary of Admiral Kichisaburo Nomura, June–December 1941

Tuesday, June 3, 1941

At 9 P.M. met the Secretary of State at his private residence and made preliminary arrangements as to the instructions to be given to our subordinates

Adm. Kichisaburo Nomura, the Japanese ambassador
to the United States at the time of Pearl Harbor.
Author's Collection

for amending the wording of the American counterproposal which was
handed to us by Valentine [sic]* at 6 P.M., last Saturday (our amendment
was submitted to them on Monday).

According to the Secretary of State, there are many on the American side
who doubt whether Japan has the sincerity to maintain peace in the Pacific
in view of Foreign Minister Yosuke Matsuoka's statement.

The Secretary disclosed that he found himself in a very hard plight and
he emphasized that the maintenance of peace in the Pacific was the basis of

---

*Joseph W. Ballantine, a State Department expert on Japanese affairs. Henceforth for sim-
plicity's sake we have changed "Valentine" to "Ballantine" whenever the former appears in
this diary.

the present understanding and that the same applied to the relations between Japan and Australia and others, and not to speak of Japanese-American relations.

As he repeated his past opinion regarding the "anti-Comintern" stationing of troops, I explained that it was the inflexible policy of the Japanese Government and then I said that, as for Japan, it would be well if the U.S.A. would advise China to make peace with Japan and, if China should refuse it, suspend American support of China. Thereupon the Secretary expatiated on that he was racking his brains in regard to the treatment of this problem. The point to be aimed at, he said, is to so adjust Japanese-American relations as to make China not discontented and to bring about Sino-Japanese amity. He added that this was the most arduous task.

Finally, he wished me to report to Tokyo that the maintenance of peace in the Pacific was the basis.

Wednesday, June 4, 1941

Held a meeting of both countries, attended by Hamilton, Ballantine, Wakasugi, Matsudaira and Iwakuro (accompanied by Ikawa).*

Attended and delivered a speech at the dinner party given under the auspices of the Japanese Chamber of Commerce at Waldorf-Astoria, New York. Admiral Pratt,† General O'Ryan and Mr. Zelders also made speeches. The party was a great success, attended by 800 people, including the hosts and guests.

Friday, June 6, 1941

Returned to Washington at noon.

Saturday, June 7, 1941

At 8:30 P.M. called accompanied by Iwakuro and Ikawa on the Secretary of State.

The stand taken heretofore by the other side has been as follows:

(1) The maintenance of peace in the Pacific being the basis of the present understanding, they wish to make this point so clear that everybody will be convinced of this; they do not wish to create the impression that there was

*Maxwell M. Hamilton, Chief of the State Department's Far Eastern Affairs Division; Kaname Wakasugi, Minister-Counselor of the Japanese Embassy; Col. Takeo Iwakuro, a Japanese Army officer temporarily with the Embassy; Tadeo Ikawa, a Japanese businessman married to an American. Iwakuro and Ikawa were active in the Drought-Walsh proposals. For a brief account, see Prange's *Pearl Harbor: The Verdict of History*, pp. 154–57. For an in-depth treatment, see R. J. C. Butow, *The John Doe Associates: Backdoor Diplomacy for Peace, 1941.*
†Adm. William V. Pratt, former Chief of Naval Operations.

bamboozlement. If this is done, they can fully persuade business circles to participate in financial and economic cooperation between Japan and the U.S.A. The Secretary repeated this two or three times.

(2) The Pacific question includes the relations of Japan and of the U.S.A. to the European war and the China Affair.

Saying that the China problem was the subject of his greatest worries, the Secretary of State said that the improvement of the relations of the three pairs, that is, the relations between Japan and the U.S.A., China and the U.S.A., Japan and China, was what was aimed at, but that caution must be taken not to cause Chinese bad feelings toward the U.S.A.

To my query as to whether the President could advise China to make peace for the sake of peace in the Pacific and for the happiness of whole mankind, he replied that it all depended on whether the two countries could come to a spiritual agreement on the present proposal for understanding.

(3) As to the European war, he repeated several times the self-defense argument *characteristic of the U.S.A.*, saying that Hitler was thinking of conquering the world. If Britain should give in, the Atlantic Ocean would be at his mercy and South America would turn out to be his supply base of materials. This would endanger the U.S.A. Fifteen countries have been destroyed because they had sat with folded arms till their borders were invaded. The United States cannot follow their steps, he declared. (I have tried hard to check this conception along the line of your instructions, but for the present there is no hope of success. The U.S.A., however, is not likely to enter the war so soon. Holding the United States in restraint is the main point of our future diplomatic policy toward the U.S.A.) Moreover, the view is held that the time for peace has not come yet. Winat's* return to America is giving currency to various rumors, but the President denied them positively.

(4) Attaching importance to the principle of nondiscrimination in trade and commerce in the Pacific area, he said that the United States was applying this principle to the other countries of America. By adopting it Japan would become prosperous and lose nothing, he said, adding that the United States had no reason to check Japan's development.

On the night of June 7 (Sat.), the Secretary of State stated with much courtesy to me and Capt.† Iwakuro, who accompanied me, that our private friendship would suffer no change in future. This gave me the impression that he was hinting that the Japanese-American parley would be discontinued.

He stated that unless there is an understanding on these fundamental points the United States has no interest in the proposal for understanding.

*John G. Winat, U.S. Ambassador to Great Britain.
†Probably translator's error. Iwakuro was an Army colonel, not a Navy captain.

Monday, June 9, 1941

At Tokyo's request wired the other party's proposal of May 31 (accompanied by a telegram giving some explanation). At the other party's wish this proposal was originally not intended to be wired to Tokyo.

That day we had a talk for about two hours, but he was confined to bed by illness since the following [sic] day, the 8th. From the 22nd or 23rd he went to Greenbrier for a change of air.

He declared positively that he had no interest whatever in the trifles of wording so long as we could not come to a mutual understanding for the maintenance of peace in the Pacific, the question of the right of self-defense, and the principle of nondiscrimination in trade and commerce (extending over the whole Pacific).

Tuesday, June 10, 1941

Colonel [sic] Iwakuro and I discussed tonight the telegram from Tokyo with much indignation.*

Wednesday, June 11, 1941

Made out the following draft of telegram, but decided to put it off in accordance with Naval Attaché Capt. Iwakuro's† advice.

For Your Excellency's information only:

> I had a dream last night. You must be well aware that I, who have been your friend for thirty years, am not a man who acts ultra vires or who would do anything that hurts others. Nevertheless, picking up a roadside rumor, you demanded my explanation of it last time. The words you used then were such as one would not dare to use in talking to even a common soldier. I obey your instructions to the end, but in carrying them out I am only using my discretion as to the order in which they should be put. Now when I have already received your dignified instructions and am carrying them into effect why should there arise an affair of ultra vires over a matter akin to obtaining tickets? This is absolutely not that heroic Matsuoka. In view of the circumstances which led me to come out of my retirement, the real Matsuoka should put more trust in me.
>
> Another world developed before me and there appeared God. "I sympathize with you in your predicament," said He. "You have lost your prestige toward your subordinates, and, moreover, you look very tired. But remember, now that you have been dispatched to a foreign land as an envoy with a great

---

*The telegram that excited their ire was a harshly worded rebuke from Matsuoka accusing Nomura of exceeding his authority and remarking, among other things, that adherence to the Tripartite Pact was more important than good relations with the United States.

†Col. Iwakuro had diplomatic status as Assistant Military Attaché.

mission on this important occasion by the Imperial command, you should with patience and prudence try not to fail in the fulfillment of the Imperial order, even at the risk of injuring your fair name as a man of spotless integrity, which you have enjoyed for the past fifty years."

To this, I answered: "I will always keep your advice in my mind and I promise you that I will not do anything that will not be justified before heaven and earth."

Friday, June 13, 1941

Towards evening I obtained the following confidential information from the Postmaster General:

(1) From noon he had a talk with key officials of the State Department. The gist of the problems discussed was:

(A) Chinese question.

If the stationing of troops in North China and Inner Mongolia is an exercise of Japan's right of self-defense, this would be justified no matter how long it may be carried out. But it is another question if Japan intends to carry it out for an indefinite period on political grounds. Therefore, the United States wishes to understand that the withdrawal of troops in connection with the China Affair will be completed by the withdrawal from North China and Inner Mongolia as the last.

(B) Question of coping with the European war.

Although the deletion of the words "the right of self-defense, etc." may be all right so far as it goes, their deletion deserves careful consideration because it is likely to be construed as a kind of "threat" to the U.S.A. Therefore, in case these words are to be deleted, /the United States/ desires to make some modifications to the other clauses, or else modify the wording in question in such a way as to satisfy both sides.

(C) The Pacific question.

/The United States/ wishes to extend the application of the principle of nondiscrimination, Secretary of State Hull's cherished opinion, to China and the South Sea Islands. Therefore it is desired that Japan make clear that Japan has no intention of seeing a monopoly in China, nor of restricting the rights of third countries there, as was stated in the Konoye statement.

Though /the United States/ will consider letting Japan share legitimately some of the rights and interests the U.S.A. has in the South Sea Islands she wishes to avoid the insertion in the written understanding of anything that will infringe [on] the sovereignty of Britain or the Netherlands. This does not mean that the United States is unwilling to mediate between Japan and these countries.

The Postmaster General will talk over with the Secretary of State tonight the following items in the American proposal of May 31st:

(a) *The right of self-defense, etc.* (as aforesaid).

(b) *The item regarding the China Affair will be as it is in the Japanese proposal of June 8*, but the name "Chiang Kai-shek Regime" will be changed to "Chungking Regime."

(c) *The other items will be the same as the original American proposal.*

(2) Both the President and the Secretary of State wish the adoption of the draft of understanding.

Saturday, June 14, 1941

At 1 P.M. called on Under Secretary of State Sumner Welles (re Tachibana Incident).*

At 5 P.M. called on Chief of Naval Operations Stark (ditto).

Sunday, June 15, 1941

At 10:30 A.M. met the Postmaster General and Father Mr. James M. Drought.

At 11:00 A.M. met the Secretary of State at his request (accompanied by Iwakuro and Nakagawa;† Ballantine sat in company). (The Secretary was in bed on account of illness).

As he asked me about the state of affairs in Tokyo, I showed him the Japanese proposal of May 10 in accordance with the Government's instructions. I told him that since the receipt of the American proposal of May 31st I had been negotiating without going beyond the bounds of the Government's instructions, not being influenced at all by what others said.

Thereupon he mentioned Mr. Matsuoka's message to Italy and said that he had obtained information that in Tokyo Mr. Matsuoka and his followers were trying to break down the present understanding.

Then as to the Pacific question, he talked of peace between Japan and Britain as well as peace between Japan and America and of "no discrimination." As to the China Affair, the opinions of citing Chinese statesmen, he urged amicable relations between Japan and China and said that the United States demanded nondiscrimination in trade. In regard to the right of self-defense, he said nothing, but this is a pending question.

The Secretary said that if peace could be maintained in the Pacific, it would hasten the peace of the world and that he had been coping with this problem with sincerity without resorting to any tactics. But being confined in bed now, he asked me to send a wire to Tokyo based on my own judgment.

---

*The FBI arrested Lt. Cmdr. Itaru Tachibana for spying on the U.S. Navy. Hull granted Nomura's request that he be deported without trial.

†Hull's record of this conversation indicates it was Ikawa who accompanied Iwakuro and Nomura.

To this I replied that his answer was vague and promised to make some routine arrangements later.

Tuesday, June 17, 1941

At 10 A.M. Admiral Husband E. Kimmel (the Commander in Chief of the U.S. Fleet) called on me, accompanied by his Chief of Staff.

At 5:30 P.M. had a talk with the Postmaster General. He complained that, whereas the U.S.A. entertained a special goodwill toward Japan, as may be seen in the President's fireside talk, in the freezing of the Axis funds, and in the closing out of consulates, Japan on the other hand had not returned any goodwill at all as seen in Matsuoka's statements. He said that the problems now pending were:

(a) The right of self-defense in connection with the Tripartite Alliance.

(b) The stationing of troops in North China and Inner Mongolia against the communists.

(c) The adoption of the principle of nondiscrimination in trade.

If agreements on the aforesaid three points could be reached, we would be able to arrive at an understanding, said he. Upon this, I fully explained the Japanese attitude and set forth in detail that, while I was prepared to make a strong recommendation in respect to item (c) some means must be devised in respect to items (a) and (b), since these were very difficult matters.

Wednesday, June 18, 1941

Wakasugi and Hamilton had a talk. The Tachibana question was settled.

Hamilton is said to have stated that, in view of the Ambassador's request and out of consideration for the Ambassador's "earnest endeavor" to adjust Japanese-American diplomatic relations, they will close the case, in spite of definite proof, on condition that he /Tachibana/ [sic] immediately return to Japan.

Thursday, June 19, 1941

At 1 P.M. called on Under Secretary of State Welles and thanked him for his efforts. He told me the same thing that Hamilton had told Wakasugi (yesterday).

I told him that, in respect to the understanding now pending, too, I was confident of success and believed in providential protection. I added that if the understanding is reached, millions of "silent masses" would surely rejoice. To this he showed an attitude of concurrence.

I called on and tended [sic] my thanks to the Chief of Naval Operations.

Saturday June 21, 1941

At 12:30 called on the Secretary of State and received an "oral statement" and the revised American proposal.

According to him, Hitler, not being satisfied with the conquest of fifteen countries, is trying to conquer others. He is, as it were, a "wild tiger." It is fair and proper as a matter of self-defense to "resist" him.

Europe now stands on a "precipice" and will be confronted with "anarchy" and "bankruptcy." It goes without saying that peace in the Pacific is necessary, but frequent reports indicate that in Tokyo, on the contrary, many responsible persons are opposing Japanese-American understanding along the present "line."

The Secretary of State said that he wanted the Japanese Government to show more sincerity one way or the other.

Hereupon, I told him positively that these were groundless, and explained that I was negotiating within the bounds of the government's instructions.

Sunday, June 22, 1941

At 11 A.M. called (with Iwakuro and Ikawa) on the Postmaster General. The important matters in our talk were as follows. Took our leave at 1 P.M.

(1) There are some in Tokyo who obstruct Japanese-American understanding. It is necessary to remove this misunderstanding, since the U.S. Government is worried about this.

(2) In connection with the Tripartite Alliance, the U.S. Government, insisting on the right of self-defense, has attached an annex. It is difficult for Japan to agree to it.

(3) The anti-Comintern stationing of troops is a troublesome matter to the United States as it is contrary to the American principle of nonstationing of troops in foreign lands.

(4) Principle of nondiscrimination in trade and commerce.

At 8:30 P.M. called on the Secretary of State, gave him our "oral statement" in response to the documents handed to us yesterday (Ballantine sat with us), and explained the four items over which I had talked with Walker this morning.

As to (2), he said that the United States did not like to annoy Japan, nor did she like to be annoyed by Japan. As to (3), he stated that even if Japan and the U.S.A. should come to an understanding, it would place the U.S.A. in an awkward situation if Japan and China should disagree with each other.

He talked very courteously, showing full enthusiasm for reaching an understanding.

Monday, June 23, 1941

At 6:30 p.m. had a talk with the Postmaster General.

He remarked that he revered the Secretary of State as he did his own father, that Hull was a man of sincerity and not a double-tongued man. He also regretted that Hull was ill. According to him, Hull hopes for the consummation of an understanding, but, with the obstinacy of old age, Hull desires to make sure of the true intentions of the Tokyo Government. Then saying that the anti-Comintern stationing of troops was the most difficult issue, he asked whether there was some way of making it consistent and taking it up as a problem between Japan and China.

To this I gave the same reply as I had given to Secretary Hull last night, namely, that I could not "commit" myself, inasmuch as this policy was a fixed policy of Japan, having been decided at a cabinet meeting.

And again, he talked of the enthusiasm of both the President and the Secretary of State for the consummation of an understanding.

Today wired to Tokyo the "oral statement" which I had received the day before yesterday, and others. (Secret No. 424)

Tuesday, June 24, 1941

Was invited to dinner by Admiral and Mrs. Ingersoll.*

Wednesday, June 25, 1941

Regarding the "oral statement" telegraphed the day before yesterday (Mon.), wired my opinion for the confidential information of the Minister only, because rumours had come to my ears that Ambassador Grew had given the following incredible information to the Secretary of State:

As Ambassador Grew submitted to the Secretary of State secret information to the effect that Foreign Minister Matsuoka had stated that Ambassador Nomura's efforts for adjusting Japanese-American relations are ultra vires and hence he would "torpedo" whatever agreement might be reached, the State Department authorities were much puzzled, and the people close to the President wanted to ascertain the Japanese Government's true intentions before submitting the American Government's final proposal because they thought that, if such were the case, there would be great danger of the understanding being broken; however, the United States might endeavor to make the American proposal come closer to the Japanese proposal, and that in that case would raise a grave question of responsibility. Thus reference was made to this matter in the "oral statement" of the Secretary of State.

*Adm. Royal E. Ingersoll was Deputy Chief of Naval Operations.

Thursday, June 26, 1941

Called on Mrs. Benson (2420 Trancy Pl., N.W.). . . . Admiral Benson, who died seven or eight years ago, was Chief of Naval Operations during my service as naval attaché here.

Saturday, June 28, 1941

Drew up the (following) draft today and dispatched it to the Minister on the 29th:

> I am waiting for your instructions with reference to my telegram of the 23rd. The Soviet-German war having broken out since then, I suppose you must be worried about various questions. I hereby forward my opinion once again.
>
> The U.S.A. does not wish to make double-front operations. Consequently it goes without saying that she desires peace in the Pacific, but, as you know, she is hastily making provisions for the time when this may become impossible.
>
> As for her attitude toward the European war, she is trying to reserve freedom of action in her proposal for Japanese-American understanding, but as a practical question, she will probably not participate in it for the time being. If a Japanese-American understanding is reached, there will be room for us to hold her in restraint against participation in war by diplomacy.
>
> Since the outbreak of the Soviet-German War she has been paying special attention to the activities of Japan, and she seems to have concluded that Japan would take a policy of wait-and-see for some time, judging that, free as Japan is now on account of the removal of the Soviet Union's pressure on Japan, it will be difficult for her to advance into Siberia on a large scale as long as the China Affair is going on, and that she will be very cautious in making her advance to the south, as this is likely to cause a large-scale war against Britain and the U.S.A., now that Britain, the U.S.A., and the Netherlands have fortified those districts by airplanes and submarines, with the result that the defenses of these areas have been strengthened more than they were a few months ago. And I add that the underestimation of the strength of the Japanese air force is also one of the reasons for their above-mentioned judgment.
>
> As I have already reported to you, the U.S.A. is very scrupulous in supporting the Soviet Union; this, however, would not be so easy, even if she tried to carry it out.
>
> Now, if the U.S. Government should lose hope in the realization of a Japanese-American understanding, efforts for the improvement of the relations between Japan and the U.S.A. would be stopped. There is considerable danger that this would *naturally bring about the severance of economic relations, then our advance to the south, and finally our clash with Britain and the U.S.A.* Under these circumstances, trade and communications between Japan and all the countries of America and the British possessions would be difficult to maintain, and eventually all diplomatic relations would be severed.

As I understand it, our fundamental policy is to make the Tripartite Alliance our keynote and to avoid Japanese-American War. So long as there is no change in this policy, I believe that the Tripartite Alliance and peace in the Pacific will be compatible as the result of the realization of the proposed understanding.

As stated above, the realization of a Japanese-American understanding will be not only advantageous from a long-range viewpoint, but also provide a way of settling the three pending questions mentioned in my last telegram. So I wish that you would at once think out some means /for realizing this understanding/.

And again, it is my desire to make it clear to the other side that the Japanese Government also desires the realization of a Japanese-American understanding as I think it unwise to postpone this and keenly feel the greatness of my responsibility. I hereby ask for your instructions.

Thursday, July 3, 1941

Made a representation of my opinion to the following effect:

Representation of Opinion*

If Japan should, at this time when she is in a delicate situation, resolve to use armed force against the Soviet Union and prematurely participate in the war, and that in concert with Germany, who can say that this will not aggravate Japanese-American relations and to a critical point short of war?

Therefore, even when such a resolve is made, I wonder if it might not ease in some measure the aggravation of the relations between Japan and the U.S.A. if Japan should send the troops in the name of the maintenance of peace in East Asia and from Japan's own independent standpoint at a period of political confusion which the collapse of the Russian armed force might occasion.

Furthermore, if such a policy is adopted, I wonder if it is not a good idea for Japan to have the pending understanding between Japan and the U.S.A. reached as quickly as possible and push on the negotiations on the pending issue of self-defense as a reciprocal matter.

And again, if you are resolved to use armed force against the Southern Regions at this time, there seems to be no room at all for adjusting Japanese-American relations.

My judgment of the existing situation being as stated above, no matter what national policy you may adopt, I think it necessary to try some means or other toward the U.S.A. So I await your instructions in return.

At noon, the Rev. Drought called on me.
At night the Postmaster General called me up on the phone.

*Nomura sent a message similar in content to Tokyo, No. 463, on 3 July 1941.

Friday, July 4, 1941

At 6 P.M. sent for Counselor Ballantine and asked him to communicate to Secretary of State Hull the purpose* of the Tokyo dispatch ("we have no objection to your stating positively that there is no objection in the Government circles to the fundamental principle for adjusting Japanese-American relations on a fair and just basis").

This was written in a note addressed to Secretary of State Hull, who was recuperating.

Saturday, July 5, 1941

The gist of the telegram (dispatched, July 6)†

> Yesterday, on the 4th, I sent for Ballantine and through him communicated to Secretary of State Hull that our Government had no objection to the fundamental principle for adjusting the relations between Japan and the U.S.A. under a fair and just basis. On the night of the 5th Hamilton called on me with Ballantine to inform me that they had communicated it to the Secretary of State.
>
> They told me that, as stated in the oral statement of June 21st, the maintenance of peace in the Pacific was the foundation of a Japanese-American understanding. However, they had obtained information that Japan was, at last, going to wage [war?] against the Soviet Union. This was reported to the President (a military conference was held as soon as he returned home yesterday) and a telegraphic instruction was sent to Grew‡ to ascertain the Japanese Government's intentions.
>
> Then, taking out a newspaper clipping which he had brought with him, he talked of its contents (Japan will start within two weeks her advance to the south. First she will occupy Saigon and its vicinities and seek air bases in Thailand; on the one hand she will bomb the Burma route and on the other hand she will make preparations to advance southward to Singapore and the Netherlands Indies. She will endeavor to avoid a conflict with Britain and the U.S.A. until the preparations are finished. By so doing she will hold in check the U.S. Navy in the Pacific Ocean, in return for the recognition of Nanking Regime by Germany and Italy.)
>
> To this I replied that I had read the paper once, but that I had received no information; that, however, so long as the U.S.A. helped Chiang Kai-shek, giving financial support, sending airplanes and munitions and moreover dispatching pilots, it was only natural for Japan to take a countermeasure; that

---

*An erasure on the copy leaves a question as to whether this word is "purpose" or "purport."

†Telegram No. 470. *The Magic Background of Pearl Harbor*, Vol. II, "Appendix," prints only a portion of paragraph 4 of this message, indicating that out of three parts, parts 1 and 3 were not available.

‡Joseph C. Grew, U.S. Ambassador to Japan.

as I had already told the Secretary of State, an American fleet had gone on a cruise of Australia; that the U.S.A. had stationed military and naval attachés in various districts; that there was information purporting to be the nature of the conversations between the military authorities of the U.S.A. and the Netherlands Indies and the British territories; that, besides, there appeared to be military reinforcements in those districts; that moreover, there was afloat even the report that they were about to arrange for reciprocal support with the Soviet Union by strengthening the defense of the Aleutians and its vicinities; that this was tantamount to an encirclement of Japan from a strategic point of view; that furthermore, we had obtained information that the U.S.A. was about to place an embargo on oil; that if such a situation should develop, the maintenance of peace would become difficult; and that is why I was endeavoring to bring about the Japanese-American understanding. I further stated that the Japanese were exceedingly prudent toward war, and none, with the exception of a few, desired a Japanese-American war; that the Americans, on the contrary, were apt to treat war lightly and some blindly believed that they could beat Japan in a few months; that I knew that the responsible authorities did not cherish such an idea, but still the situation, as seen from Japan's side, did not warrant optimism; and that, hence, I felt keenly the necessity of our arriving at a point of understanding somehow or other.

Hamilton said that he had come to me as a messenger of the Secretary of State.

According to the press, the Government will make it its principle not to publish its policies, but to make them known to the people through its future activities. However, when we read the papers here, we cannot but feel that this statement alone would make the countries surrounding Japan very cautious, leading them gradually to build up political and strategic citadels. Besides, the atmosphere here does not warrant optimism at all. (Reported by telegram on July 6.)

Tuesday, July 8, 1941

The gist of the telegram (dispatched on July 8)*

Many a day has passed since I asked for instructions, but still I have not received them. The other side, as seen clearly in their oral statement of June 21st, has doubts about our true intentions. Though they appreciated our intentions to a certain extent as the result of my explanation, in which I had clarified our Government's intentions in accordance with your telegraphic instructions, I have not succeeded yet in clearing away their doubts. On the contrary, the postponement of our reply, together with other circumstances, is giving them the impression that it substantiates their doubts, thereby

*No. 478.

causing them to lose gradually hope for the adjustment of diplomatic relations and making the future of the negotiations harder.

A certain cabinet secretary is said to have confided to a person connected with our embassy that, unless the negotiations are promptly resumed, the circumstances surrounding the American side are developing very unfavorably for the negotiations. He said he was greatly worried over the situation.

It is a matter for regret that, the negotiations having come to such a standstill, I am unable to carry your instructions through.

Upon careful consideration of the situation in this country, I find that since the outbreak of the Soviet-German War the people have been paying particular attention to Japan's movements, [sic] some observe that Japan will carry out at this juncture her long-cherished policy of northward advance and, consequently, will not think much of the Soviet-Japanese treaty; others think that Japan, at this juncture, will make great strides southward, which will coincide with Germany's eager desire. In either case, they assert that it is mere illusion to promise peace in the Pacific and the nonexpansion of the war situation under such circumstances. Besides, we even find people who depreciate Japan's international faith.

The Secretary of State, however, has attached from the beginning much importance to the Japanese-American problem, and he has already conducted seventeen conversations with me. Even after he was confined to bed, he repeated to me twice that he attached great importance to the problems.

The same impression has been gained by those who have been conducting flanking movements in close contact with cabinet secretaries with whom they are on intimate terms. The President also is said to be of the same opinion. And naval circles seem to favor this view as a whole.

This, I think, is quite natural for this country from a political standpoint, as well as from that of national defense. For all that, I cannot believe at all that they will by any possibility finally become conciliatory if we keep up our resolute attitude toward them. Judging from the tone of argument seen in the newspapers and magazines, I should think that the United States Government will be unable to assume such an attitude. On the contrary, there is a considerable fear that the United States Government would take advantage of this opportunity to suspend negotiations. In this connection, I at this end will tax my ingenuity further in regard to the three pending points (self-defense, the question of stationing troops, the principle of nondiscrimination in commercial opportunity) and try to keep up contact with the other party by some means or other so as not to break it off. In case we succeed in thinking of a concrete plan, I shall report to you, but in the meantime please favor me with your early instructions in regard to the disposition of the American proposal which I have already reported to you. (Dispatched, July 9.)

Thursday, July 10, 1941

On the morning of the 10th I sent telegrams to the Navy Minister and the Chief of the Naval General Staff reporting the particulars of the adjustment of the Japanese-American diplomatic relations. In response to that, I *received on the 15th a telegram from the Navy Minister and the Chief of the Naval General Staff dissuading me from resigning.*

On this very day, I received a telegram from the (Japanese) authorities, ordering Wakasugi to return to Japan because they wished to receive directly from him report concerning the questions pending between Japan and the U.S.A. So I wired the following in return:

Gist of the telegram*

I acknowledge receipt of your telegram No. 350 (ordering Wakasugi home).

Just after the outbreak of the Soviet-German War, the American side seemed to have thought that it was to their advantage if they completed beforehand the adjustment of the Japanese-American diplomatic relations, but it seems that subsequently they began to cast a considerable doubt upon the Japanese attitude on account of the information they had obtained. Accordingly, although there is still a ray of hope if our side should push on the negotiations swiftly, but if you intend to decide one way or the other after receiving the report on the situation from a person to be called back from here (it takes three weeks or so), there is no hope of arriving at an understanding, and the diplomatic relations between Japan and the U.S.A. will come very near to the rupture.

(Request for permission to return to Japan)

Since under such circumstances my stay here would be meaningless and since I believe it more appropriate for me to report on the situation to you (than to make another do it), I request your permission to return to Japan.

Friday, July 11, 1941

(Disapproval)

On the afternoon of the 11th, I received an instruction disapproving my request for permission to return to Japan. The telegram read in part as follows: "*Aside from His Majesty's opinion, the feelings of our people will never acknowledge your leaving the place of your appointment at this time . . .*"

Saturday, July 12, 1941

Together with Mr. Obata, I went to the Homestead, Hot Springs, Va., and stayed there overnight.

Sunday, July 13, 1941

Arrived at the Greenbrier, White Sulphur Springs, West Virginia, at 11:30 A.M.

*No. 495.

Paid a visit of inquiry to Secretary of State Hull, who has been recuperating here since the 23rd (Mon.) of June. His private secretary, Mr. [Cecil] Gray, received me on behalf of the Secretary of State. According to him, Mr. Hull is getting better and will probably be able to go back in ten days or fortnight. Though the Secretary of State is declining to see his visitors under his doctor's advice, he expressed thanks for my kindness. Although he wished to resume the conversations, he had not yet thoroughly read the documents which had been relayed through Mr. Walker.*

I requested Mr. Hull's private secretary to convey to Mr. Hull that, according to a dispatch from Tokyo, /Japanese/ Premier, Foreign Minister, War and Navy Ministers, and other Cabinet ministers are all hoping for the adjustment of the diplomatic relations between Japan and the United States.

Monday, July 14, 1941

Telegram Informing My Remaining in Office for the Present†

I acknowledge receipt of your telegram No. 356. I am deeply moved by your favor. In accordance with your kind instructions, I will remain in office for the time being to exert myself until the pending problems are decided some way or other. Being an amateur, I fear I have given you so much trouble that I do not know how to apologize for it. But, on my side, things have gone contrary to my expectations and we have constantly lost our prestige to a great extent at home and abroad as the result of your successive telegraphic instructions. I will try my best not to make gross mistakes in future by attending to my duties with scrupulous care but no matter how much I may try, I am afraid I may again cause troubles to you and our country, since I come from circles where a certain amount of free rein is allowed under instructions and this has become my second nature. And at the same time, viewing from every angle, I keenly feel that [it] is necessary for me to resign from my post as early as possible for the benefit of the country.

In this connection, I earnestly desire that you would, from a long-range view of things, immediately replace me with a skilled person acceptable to you. I know perfectly well that I am not qualified for the post, and besides, from the very beginning, I have been a time-serving existence [sic]. Moreover, I have had no intention to remain long in this post, as I told you before my departure. So I make an earnest appeal for your favorable consideration. (Dispatched on the afternoon of the 14th.)

On Monday afternoon Hamilton and Ballantine came to me to return a courtesy visit at the Secretary of State's order.

*Postmaster General Frank C. Walker
†The "Magic" Background of Pearl Harbor indicates "no number" on this message.

Tuesday, July 15, 1941

The instructions asked for (in our telegram No. 424 sent on the 23rd of June) finally arrived.

At night Hamilton and Ballantine called on me. After saying that they had come at the order of the Secretary of State, who is now recuperating, they said that, whereas the conversations centering around the problem of maintaining peace in the Pacific were now in progress, information had kept pouring in that Japan was establishing naval and aerial bases [in] French Indochina. So they asked to know the actual facts of the case.

To this I replied that I only knew what had been reported in the press, but I was not surprised in the least by such a rumor at this time when Japan was being gradually sieged by the increased British and American support of Chungking, by the cooperation among the United States, Great Britain and the Netherlands Indies, and by the cooperation between the United States and the Soviet Union. I pointed out that, when compared with the fact that the U.S.A. had actually occupied Iceland and that there were rumors that she would take over the Azores and Dakar, it was not at all strange even if Japan should carry out what the rumors said. I told them that anyway, I would give an answer after inquiring of our Government about it.

Then they asked me if there was, besides the Pact of Alliance, any special agreement with Germany and Italy that would place Japan under obligation to wage war against the U.S.A. in the event of the latter's participation in war.

I replied that I didn't think there was any, but that the obligations provided for in Article III of the pact would arise under such circumstances. As to the particulars of the obligations, I told them that there was no need to inquire of Tokyo, for they were just as they were written in the treaty. Then I repeated what I had told the Secretary of State before, namely, that the Japanese Government could not acknowledge in advance that all future actions of the United States would be based solely on self-defense. There would be no way to judge them except by investigating each case minutely. I added that the U.S.A. was in the safest condition as far as national defense was concerned, for there was no fear at all of she [sic] being attacked by other countries. Moreover, pointing out that the United States was on especially friendly terms with Canada, that Mexico was just like what Manchukuo was to Japan, that the countries south of Panama, not to speak of north of it, were gradually coming within the sphere of American influence, I declared that there was no comparison between the United States and Japan in point of national security.

To this, they advanced the Secretary of State's own arguments. (Dispatched on the afternoon of July 16th).*

*No. 520.

Wednesday, July 16, 1941

Return of the Oral Statement

On that occasion (T.N. when Ambassador Nomura had a talk with Hamilton and Ballantine on the 15th), I conveyed to them the complaint of the Foreign Minister to the oral statement of June 21st. To this they replied that they had no intention at all of interfering in the internal affairs of Japan. On the 16th and the 17th Wakasugi called on the Secretary of State and returned the oral statement, with the consent of the Secretary of State. I telegraphed the particulars of the case to Tokyo.

Friday, July 18, 1941

At 6 P.M. I called on Under Secretary of State Welles and asked for friendly arrangement for the passage through the Panama Canal of the /Japanese/ merchantmen lying at anchor at Panama. He said that the /prohibition of passage/ was for an indefinite period from the standpoint of national defense, but that he would give me an answer after making a minute inquiry.

I also talked of the cabinet change in Tokyo and of Japan's position from the standpoint of national defense. The Under Secretary of State, on the other hand, wished to maintain peaceful relations between Japan and the U.S.A., which he said had extended for some 90 years.

Saturday, July 19, 1941

Today new /Foreign/ Minister VADM Teijiro Toyoda sent me his compliments, asking for my cooperation. Accordingly, I made a representation with an introductory remark acknowledging receipt of his telegram and pledging to exert my utmost.

I also *asked for instructions again concerning the pending problems.* The latter part of the telegram ran as follows:

> In short, according to my view, it may not be quite impossible to find some means to come to terms on the question of the right of self-defense, but there is probably no room for compromise in respect to the stationing of troops for anti-Communist purposes. Therefore, we must find some wording which is acceptable to both sides and contrive to obtain the substance to our side, but this is the most difficult problem in my opinion.*

Sunday, July 20, 1941

Called on Admiral Stark (he was out), and dropped in at Rear Admiral Turner's home and talked over with him the /Japanese/ advance into French Indochina, Japanese-American understanding, etc.†

*A similar paragraph appears in message No. 540.

†Adm. Harold R. Stark, Chief of Naval Operations; RADM Richmond K. Turner, Director of War Plans, a close adviser of Stark's.

Monday, July 21, 1941

Went to New [York] and stayed at the "Plaza." At night received an urgent telephone call from Wakasugi and decided to leave here early next morning by air.

Wednesday, July 23, 1941

Wired the following telegram dated the 23rd.*
The gist

In my telegrams of July 3 and 19 I reported on the effect of our southward advance on Japanese-American relations. This effect is now developing with considerable speed, and there is a great fear that it will come very near to the critical point of severing diplomatic relations. Feeling the tenseness of the situation from the talk on Monday between Wakasugi and the Under Secretary of State, I asked for an interview with the Under Secretary on Tuesday, but received an appointment at 3 P.M. on Wednesday.

I met a certain cabinet secretary who hastily returned from a tour last night. He intimated to me that nothing could be done as Secretary of State Hull was recuperating, while Welles was much embarrassed. As he asked my view, I told him that I would do my utmost according to my conviction, without losing hope. Anyway, it is my observation that the situation will come very near to the severance of diplomatic relations.

This rapid change of the sentiment here toward Japan is due to our southward advance. It is the observation here that this southward advance is the initial step in the eventual advance to Singapore and the Netherlands Indies. The Navy here seems to make the same observation. There appears to be the criticism that Japan is on the one hand proposing Japanese-American understanding, but on the other hand mapping out the policy of southward advance, thus duping the Secretary of State. This, together with the state of his health, has given rise to the rumor that the Secretary of State might resign.

Moreover, information which is likely to cause the people here to doubt our true intentions is pouring in from Tokyo. The most striking one says that (a) my negotiations here will be "torpedoed" in Tokyo, and (b) Japan has given to the Axis side the explanation that the adjustment of Japanese-American diplomatic relations is a stratagem employed to gain time until the completion of preparations for the southward advance. Even the highest responsible persons are said to have gradually begun to lend their ears to such reports. In short, there is no doubt that, while the negotiations were in progress, third parties have made slanderous reports to estrange Japan from the U.S.A. and opposition movements have occurred on both sides. We are now in a delicate situation indeed.

In this connection, I wish you would take this opportunity to express to the American Ambassador the /Japanese/ Government's sincere wishes for the

*This important telegram does not appear in *The "Magic" Background of Pearl Harbor*.

adjustment of the Japanese-American diplomatic relations and explain our true intentions in respect to the advance into French Indochina. I also request that you indicate to me privately the policies of the new cabinet. I, on my part, am determined to do my very best as if I had revived from death.

(Dispatched at noon on the 23rd).

Wednesday, July 23rd, 1941

At 1 P.M. was invited by Admiral Stark and dined with him.

At 3 P.M. called on Acting Secretary of State Welles.

In my talk with Admiral Stark on the 23rd of July I remarked that it seemed to me that the heads of the American Navy here were made up of outstanding first-rate figures. Thereupon the Admiral said that Ingersoll was "very able," Turner "especially good" and so was Tower of the Air Bureau. As for the fleets, he said that both Kimmel and King, whom he had recommended, were fitted for their posts. He also explained that Hart, though already beyond the age limit, was being retained in service because he was an able man.*

TELEGRAPHIC REPORT (9 P.M., the 23RD)

Interview with Welles

In view of the nature of the interview between Wakasugi and Welles, I had a talk with Welles on the afternoon of the 23rd and expatiated on the fact that our southward advance was based on an indispensable necessity for national security and economy, especially that Japan alone could not assume an attitude of remaining idle, only to be destroyed, in an economic war in which every other country was carrying out an "embargo." And then as to the problem of French Indochina, I told him that, since there was prospect, according to the press, of a peaceful negotiation between Vichy and the Japanese Government, it would be desirable for the United States Government to watch the situation for a while and refrain from making a "hasty conclusion." I also told him that if an embargo was placed on oil too, I feared this would greatly excite the feelings of our people. As to the conclusion of a Japanese-American understanding, I informed him that the new cabinet was as eager as the former cabinet to arrive at an understanding.

The Under Secretary of State, though he did not repeat what he had told Wakasugi, said to the following effect:

In brief, the spirit which has guided the conversations between Hull and me is incompatible with the Japanese policy toward French Indochina. Nei-

---

*RADM John H. Towers, Chief of Naval Aeronautics; Adm. Husband E. Kimmel, CinC US; Adm. Ernest J. King, CinClant [Commander in Chief Atlantic]; Adm. Thomas C. Hart, CinC Asiatic Fleet. RADM Royal E. Ingersoll, Deputy CNO. Nomura sent [sic] a telegraphic account of this talk to Tokyo on 25 July by No. 571.

ther the U.S.A., nor Great Britain, will ever attack French Indochina. Vichy's submission is due to Hitler's pressure. *It is obvious that Japan will further advance southward making French Indochina her foothold.*

Then he added that the U.S. Government had never made a hasty conclusion for ma[n]y years in the past, and that, in short, the United States was being influenced by Japan's policies.

Though he did not refer to the future, he told me on parting that the Secretary of State would come back soon and would probably be pleased to resume the conversations with me.

(9 P.M., 23rd)*

Thursday, July 24, 1941

TELEGRAPHIC REPORT (8 P.M., 24th)†

INTERVIEW WITH THE PRESIDENT

Feeling keenly the urgency of the situation, I had asked the Chief of Naval Operations, during the course of a luncheon with him alone yesterday, the 23rd, to convey to the President my desire to have a talk with the President. At five this afternoon I met the President privately.

In accordance with your successive instructions, I explained to the President in detail the unavoidable circumstances which necessitated Japan's advance into French Indochina from the standpoint of national economy and stabilization of that area. I also explained Japan's respect for the territorial integrity and the sovereignty of French Indochina. Next, after informing him that the new cabinet also was very eager to arrive at a Japanese-American understanding, I urged him to give a political consideration based on a broad point of view to the maintenance of peace in the Pacific.

The President replied that, though public opinion had advocated strongly an embargo on oil export to Japan, he had so far persuaded the public as to the necessity (of exporting oil) in order to maintain peace in the Pacific. Saying that he had now lost the basis of this argument, he hinted that an embargo on oil export might be enforced. And as to the advance into French Indochina, he clarified the views of the U.S. Government by stating the main points of the statement issued by the State Department today, the 24th.

Then the President, with the introductory remark that it was probably too late and that he had made no previous arrangements with the State Department in regard to this point, said to the following effect:

If Japan should withdraw her troops from French Indochina, if all countries guaranteed her neutrality (as was done in the case of Switzerland), and then if some means could be found whereby all countries could obtain goods and materials freely and fairly from French Indochina, he would do all he can for it. He himself had deep sympathy for Japan's efforts to procure materials.

*No. 555.
†No. 565.

The long and short of it was that I received the impression that some kind of an economic pressure will be enforced in the near future. The Chief of Naval Operations, who was specially called in, sat beside Under Secretary of State Welles. (8 P.M. the 24th).

INTERVIEW WITH THE PRESIDENT*

In my interview with the President I explained the following, besides the problem of French Indochina:

That the proposal for a Japanese-American understanding should aim to maintain peace in the Pacific; that it is a matter for regret that there are some indications that the U.S. Government suspects the true intentions of the Japanese Government; that the Japanese Government has become much more enthusiastic since the present cabinet was formed; and that, in my opinion, there are means for settling the three difficult points: *namely, the right of self-defense, the stationing of our troops in Inner Mongolia and in North China, which is not permanent, and nondiscrimination in trade.*

In our conversation, the President declared that Hitler was scheming the conquest of the world (He said the same thing during my interview with him on the 14th of March. When asked for his view by the President, the Secretary of State, who sat in company with him then, stated that he, too was of the same opinion); that after Europe, Africa would be the next victim, and so on—there would be no end; that in ten years it might so happen that Japan will fight on the side of the U.S.A.

I refuted his view by saying that since ancient times it was proverbially said in Japan that "when the people become warlike, the state will surely be in danger" and "swords are for refuting false doctrines and bringing out the truth."

As the President seemed to regard that our advance into French Indochina would extend further southward under Germany's pressure, I refuted him by saying that there was no German pressure upon us and that Japan was acting from her own independent standpoint. The President accepted my explanation, at least in words. However, as you already know, public opinion in the U.S.A. believes that Japan, either in concert with Germany or independently, will advance either southward or northward when a favorable opportunity offers. (Dispatched at noon on the 25th.)

Friday, July 25, 1941

At night the White House published a directive for "freezing" Japanese assets.

---

*No. 566. Nomura's paragraph one does not appear in this message as printed in *The "Magic" Background of Pearl Harbor.* In that work appears a five-part telegram, No. 589, in which Nomura amplifies both Nos. 565 and 566, which is not in the Nomura diary.

Saturday, July 26, 1941

Went to New York by plane and stayed at the Hotel Plaza overnight. Returned on Sunday.

Monday, July 28, 1941

The M.S. *Tatsuta-Maru*, not /being permitted/ to enter port, anchored outside San Francisco Harbor. Accordingly I called on Welles (at 5 P.M.) to find out the connection between the "freezing" and shipping movements.

TELEGRAPHIC REPORT (DISPATCHED, 29TH)*

In my interview with Welles on the 28th, I reminded him, as the sequence of my talk, that some time ago he had told me that for the past ninety years peaceful relations had been maintained in unbroken succession between Japan and the United States. I then said that it was a matter of grave concern that the two countries were moving more and more in the direction of a dangerous course, unless some harmonizing measure could be found against the policies which the two countries were now adopting. If there was no "statesmanship" to avoid this, it would be a great sin against humanity, I said.

As he told me that it seemed that at the time of Your Excellency's conversation with Ambassador Grew, you had not yet been informed of the President's proposal which was made the other day, in spite of its importance, I replied that I had submitted only the main points to you at that time, but that I had reported it to you in detail today.

What Welles said to me contained the same meaning as the President's; that is, he made it clear that, so long as Japan did not resort to armed occupation, the /United States/ had no intention of preventing us from obtaining goods and materials under the principle of equal opportunity and there would be no fear of threat against the security of French Indochina.

Now, under the present situation, we are proceeding single-handed toward the worst in East Asia, against America, Britain, the Netherlands Indies, China and the Soviet Union. While Japan is performing her duty of checking the United States for the sake of Germany, Germany is facing the United States with the greatest possible care and prudence, contriving to moderate the American people's sentiment and also doing their best to avoid a German-American War, by bringing out peace terms as a flanking operation. It looks as if Japan were unwittingly venturing to plunge headlong single-handed into a war against Britain and the U.S.A.

It is my earnest desire that you would exercise the utmost prudence and cope with the situation for the benefit of a far-sighted state policy by politically taking a long view of the whole situation, even if quick decision is necessary from a military point of view.

(Dispatched 19th).

*No. 600.

Wednesday, July 30, 1941*

At 11:45 A.M. called on Acting Secretary of State Welles at his request. He handed to me a note regarding the bombing of the gunboat *Tutuila* and, remarking that it was the President's order, stressed the following three points:

(a) The Japanese Government had given a guarantee /for not repeating the mistake/ at the time of the Panay Case; (b) Are the Army and Navy invested with the power of doing such a thing? (c) The *Tutuila* and the American Embassy were located in the "safety zone," which is on the opposite bank.

I replied that such an incident was likely to happen in the battlefield and that there was no way of absolutely avoiding such a mistake other than by giving up the bombing of Chungking or by moving away the embassy and the gunboat. However, I promised to report it to the Government.

Thursday, July 31, 1941

At 6:45 P.M. called on Acting Secretary of State Welles and elucidated the viewpoint of the Imperial Japanese Government on the *Tutuila* Case. Took my leave after asking him to arrange for me a direct interview with the President should my explanation fail to settle the question.

Mr. Welles, after consulting with the President, announced to the press the settlement of the incident. (In my interview with him on Saturday, Welles told me that he had wired to the above effect to Grew.)

In the afternoon Takeo Iwakuro (Colonel) and Tadao Nakagawa started for San Francisco by airplane. I am very grateful for the cooperation they have given me. I also did my best for them.

Further, Mr. Welles requested me to add Thailand, besides French Indochina, in the President's proposal of the other day.

Friday, August 1, 1941

Tonight the embargo on oil was proclaimed (it is published in the newspapers of the 2nd, Saturday).

Saturday, August 2, 1914

At 1:45 P.M. called on Acting Secretary of State Welles and asked him to use his influence for enabling the M.S. *Atsuta-Maru* to leave port. In view of the guarantees he had given me several times, he felt very sorry for it and said that he would do something to cope with the litigation of private par-

---

*Although the diary does not indicate that this was the gist of a telegram, such was sent to Tokyo on 30 July, No. 608.

ties. He further asked me to call him up in case I wanted to see him as he would report for duty tomorrow, Sunday, too.

On this occasion I explained to him that in regard to the President's proposal, though I had not yet received instructions, it had become clearer and clearer that Tokyo was desirous of reaching a Japanese-American understanding. I added that it must be remembered that in Tokyo important problems are submitted to Cabinet conference, and so things cannot be handled as expeditiously as in the U.S.A., where the President decides things himself with great authority.

Sunday, August 3, 1941*

At 10 A.M. yesterday, Sat., I called on Postmaster General Walker. After asking him about the recent state of affairs, I told him the reasons for the advance of Japanese troops into French Indochina, explaining that the Franco-Japanese Treaty regarding French Indochina had made it clear that the advance of Japanese troops was an unavoidable measure under the present state of affairs, and that this measure was not a permanent one by any means. Then I asked him if it was not a good idea to pledge nonaggression against the neighboring states—the Straits Settlements, the Netherlands Indies and so on—and to provide for the free exchange of goods and materials, thus going a step further from the past negotiations. But he showed little interest in it and asked me in return whether it was not true that Japan had been making preparations for an advance into Siberia.

He also said that, as we already knew, the President did not want war. However, as I see it, the U.S.A. is, first of all, trying to check the Japanese advance by economic war. All the authorities maintain that this is a countermeasure to the Japanese policies. And at the same time she is preparing for an armed clash and seems to be endeavoring to make China and the Soviet Union, not to speak of Britain and the Netherlands Indies, act in concert with her.

The fact that Germany's war against the Soviet Union is being prolonged more than it was expected is, indeed, a good news for the U.S.A., but Walker did not talk so optimistically as the President had done at the press conference yesterday, or as Harry Hopkins, a trusted follower of the President, is reported to have said in Moscow.

However, he believed that Germany would not be able to undertake great operations for some time even if the eastern front is cleared off, because of the heavy loss in personnel and goods and materials sustained by the German forces, and also because of the shortage of oil. Predicting that during this period production in the U.S.A. would make a great stride and thereby make the situation favorable to her, he believed that a protracted war of several years in duration would take place.

*Although the diary does not so indicate, the gist of this day's entry was sent as No. 649.

Monday, August 4, 1941

Request for the dispatch of a Veteran Diplomat (Dispatched, Monday August 4).*

All the papers on Sunday (yesterday) devoted large spaces to comments on the Japanese-American problems, supporting in general the strong attitude of the U.S. Government. The Gallup Poll also showed that there were many people who favored a strong attitude. But they hinted that not all the doors have yet been closed. As affairs now stand, public opinion is focusing its attention more on the relations between Japan and the U.S.A. than on the problems between the U.S.A. and Germany. As the days pass, some degree of moderation may be expected, but we cannot predict the future as it also depends on the war situation in Europe. Although Wakasugi and Iwakuro will report to you the situation upon their return to Japan, the situation is developing so fast every moment that time is an important factor. *As I will have no excuse to offer if I commit mistakes at this time, and besides, as there is a limit to my humble ability, I wish that you would be good enough to arrange to send some veteran diplomat who is well informed on the state of things at home and abroad (say, Ambassador Saburo Kurusu) by the first available ship in order to cooperate with me for the present.*

Inasmuch as I have no means of knowing the delicate phase of the Government's policies, and since I can do nothing about it here, I ask you carry out promptly my recommendation after special consideration.

(Dispatched on the afternoon of the 4th)

Wednesday, August 6, 1941

Visit to Secretary of State Hull.†

At 6 P.M. called on Secretary of State Hull at his private residence (accompanied by Okumuro;‡ Ballantine sat in company). In compliance with your instructions, I submitted the proposal written in English, as per attached, after explaining it in detail.

The Secretary of State showed little interest in our proposal, saying that he would examine it afterward. With an apology that he would state his own ideas, apart from the proposal, he expatiated on the relations between Japan and the U.S.A.

In brief, he said that apart from the relations between him and me, he could not but be deeply disappointed on observing Japan's successive actions; that so long as Japan did not stop her conquest by force, there was no room for reaching an understanding; that so long as the Japanese Government authorities termed the United States actions as an "encircling" policy, there was

*No. 646.
†No. 659.
‡Katsuzo Okamura was Secretary of the Embassy.

nothing to be expected from Japan; that, whereas they, the Americans, wish to lead a peaceful life, it is Hitler's way of acting to smash up in the name of "self-defense" everything that lies in his way. The Secretary of State apparently used a satire against Japan in saying so.

No matter how much we may explain, it is now difficult to make the other side understand our country's intentions, and besides, we can unmistakably notice that the U.S. Government has made up its mind to cope with whatever situation might arise.

Friday, August 8, 1941

Visit to Secretary of State Hull on the 8th

NO. 671

At 12:45 P.M. the Secretary of State handed to me the reply to our proposal of the 6th. The reply, just as the President had told me, did not yield a single step.

Further, I stated strongly the substance of your telegraphic instructions and the proposed holding of a meeting of the leaders of both countries in Hawaii.

Thereupon the Secretary of State pointed out that, while recuperating at White Sulphur Springs, he had received information that the Japanese Government had decided to use armed force and that since then Japan had been carrying out steadily her decision. As /t/his was inconsistent with what he had been talking over with me, he said that so long as there was no change in this policy there was no basis for our talks.

Then, to make sure, I sounded out Ballantine, who sat in company with the Secretary of State, on this point. Repeating what the Secretary of State had said, Ballantine declared with dissatisfaction that the use of armed force and the policy of maintaining peace in the Pacific were incompatible with each other, and that Japan was mistaken in regard to the "encircling policy" of which she mentioned so often. (The Secretary of State had already repeated that twice, while Welles had once said that the turn of expression was similar to that used by Germany).

Thereupon I pointed out that, notwithstanding the fact that the U.S.A. was in a very safe position from the standpoint of national defense, she was speaking of various dangers and explaining the necessity of strengthening her national defense, of lengthening the term of military and naval service, and of increasing taxes. Saying that it was the same with Japan, I declared that what Japan had done or was doing was necessary to warn and awake the people.

In short, what the other party insists on is that America will resume the conversations only if Japan suspends the use of armed force. In this respect, the other side will never retreat and so long as there is no change in our policy, there is no longer any room for proceeding with the talks. Accordingly, please take into consideration the matter of conveying your intentions through Grew as occasion demands.

(Dispatched 6 P.M., 8th.)

Saturday, August 9, 1941

NO. 673*

Though it is not yet possible to find out the actual nature of the interview between Roosevelt and Churchill, of which I reported to you yesterday, rumors have it that the brains of the Army and the Navy here are participating in it. And there is also a rumor that they will issue a joint statement concerning the Far Eastern problem. Also in consideration of the fact that the relations between America and Britain on the one side and the Soviet Union on the other side are becoming closer and closer, the Far Eastern problem, whether in the north or south, has become the common problem of the aforesaid states and there is no doubt that they will carry out concerted action or parallel operations on every occasion. Besides, China and the Netherlands Indies will follow their example. Therefore I make this report even if it be a duplication.

(Dispatched in the afternoon of Saturday, August 9.)

NO. 674 (DISPATCHED AUGUST 9)

Upon the President's return I will endeavor to convince him of the point of your telegram; however, as I have reported in my previous successive telegrams, so long as Japan proceeds with the present policy, the U.S.A., too, will stick consistently to her own policy. In view of the U.S. Government's attitude with regards that our advance into the southern part of French Indochina has made the trend of our country's policy definite (on this point, both the President and the Secretary of State are of the same mind), I think it is difficult to move the other party by merely having the Premier come out in person to carry on the negotiations (this is clear from my interviews on the 6th and the 8th). Almost no hope should be placed on my coming interview with the President. Accordingly, I believe that we cannot find a way out of the situation unless our Government takes some measure that would bring about a change in the U.S. policy.

(Dispatched, 4 P.M., August 9)

Wednesday, August 13, 1941

VISIT TO WALKER ON THE 13TH.

Today (Wednesday, the 14th) I had a talk with Walker. He judged that the advance into French Indochina had been carried out, after all, in concert with Hitler, and that Hitler had brought considerable pressure to bear upon the puppet French Government. As he said that he was of the same opinion as the President and the Secretary of State on the question of maintaining peace in the Pacific, I retorted that, while it was impossible to withdraw our troops at

*This message, No. 673, does not appear in *The "Magic" Background of Pearl Harbor*.

once from French Indochina, I thought it would be realized at a certain opportune time, as declared by the Japanese Government.

Then, referring to the meeting of the heads of both countries, I told him that, if such a meeting is held, we might be able to find out some measure which would be tolerably acceptable to both sides from a broad point of view, even if it might not be satisfactory. Although he did not seem to be much interested in it, he said that he would talk it over with Hull. Next I pointed out that accounts in the press indicated that the U.S. fleets would be assigned to and concentrated in the Pacific, and that the British and American Navies would pool their strength and post necessary forces in the Pacific. I further pointed out that not a few persons had declared that American attention of late had been focused on Japan rather than on Germany, and that in congressional quarters agreement of opinion was easily possible in respect to the policy against Japan.

Though he did not venture to deny this, he stated that since the Japanese Navy was highly trained it would be able to cause a great "trouble" should it act in concert with Germany. Next he said that it was not because the U.S.A. favored the Soviet Union or because she did not anticipate an annoying situation in the future, but that she could not but cooperate with the Soviet Union now in order to beat Hitler before everything.

I told him that the pressure upon Japan was harmful because it would only invite reaction and complicate the situation. If dealt with, with a great political consideration, the common sense of the Japanese people would make them naturally adjust themselves, I said.

(Dispatched, 9 P.M., 13th.)*

VISIT TO HULL ON THE 13TH

At 4 P.M. today, Wednesday, I called on Secretary of State Hull at his request. He handed to me a note on the infringement of American rights and interests, explaining that this had no connection with the freezing of funds but concerned only individuals.

To this I said that it was becoming a reciprocal matter to say disagreeable things against individuals, and since such a "pinpricking" had no influence on the general situation but was unsavory from the moral point of view, both sides had better stop doing so.

As he next talked about our resumption "saiko" of the bombing of Chungking, and so forth, I explained our standpoint.

Further, he asked me whether I would be in Washington at the weekend, which gave me the impression that they will propose something at that time.

(Dispatched, 9 P.M., 13th.)†

Friday, August 15, 1941

As I had telephoned to Father James M. Drought last night to obtain his assistance, he took the trouble to call on me at 3 P.M. today.

*No. 684.
†No. 689.

Saturday, August 16, 1941

INTERVIEW WITH SECRETARY OF STATE HULL ON THE 16TH (SAT.)

Dispatched at midnight of the 16th (Sat.)*

In regard to the conference of the "Big Two" of Britain and America, I obtained the information that Britain tried to drag the United States into the war and to cope with her insecurity in the Far East from Japan by utilizing the United States mainly, while the United States, on the other hand, made Britain clarify her war aims and also tried to check British ambitions. Thus, the information said, the joint statement contained just what America wanted, which would place Britain at a disadvantage. After careful consultation, I considered it necessary to try some sort of measure toward the United States before the President's return to Washington. Accordingly, I called on the Secretary of State this afternoon and explained the necessity of adjusting diplomatic relations, laying to heart your successive instructions.

The Secretary of State repeated what he had told me previously and said that, whereas he had intended to settle the problem by peaceful means between him and me, a "military domination" had been carried out.

To this I replied that the future was not difficult to predict if we left the matter as it was, that the Pacific War would not be such a simple matter as people in general presumed, but that it would present a scene unprecedented in history; that success or failure would not be decided merely by the fact that America was rich and Japan poor, that it was destined to be a war of attrition extending over several years; that both countries would profit nothing by it; that the statesmen of both countries should not follow blindly what their "hotheads" advocate; and that they should not be off their guard since the war was very likely to be instigated by third countries.

Affirming the instigatory [sic] movement of third powers, the Secretary of State said with a sympathetic attitude that there was such a movement in Japan and also in the United States, adding that some said that Hitler had started the war after spying into Stalin's intentions.

As to "military domination," I strongly refuted his view, explaining that Japan was an everlasting country led by the Imperial family and possessing a history of two thousand six hundred years; that she was quite different in her origin from countries where revolutionists of the age staked the existence of the state and nation at a stroke; and that when we talked to the East Asia Coprosperity Sphere we meant not conquest, but neighborly friendship, coexistence and coprosperity, which was little different from the American policy of good neighborly relations.

The Secretary of State seemed to concur with me to some extent and said that the United States recognized the equal position of every country and that she would never use armed force.

Then I explained that should outward pressure be brought to bear on Japan she would repel it and stiffen her attitude, but otherwise the common

*No. 705.

sense of the Japanese people would enable them to find out a way for adjusting themselves. The Secretary of State seemed to agree with me on this point.

Then I said that, as to the conference of the leaders of both countries, there were, among the light points taken up this time, several points which, in my personal opinion, coincided with those published in the Konoye statement and others, such that I felt rather encouraged; that I felt there would be a way somehow or other for the adjustment of diplomatic relations; and that I considered Japan's determination to send her leader for the negotiations to be an indication of her confidence in, and determination to achieve, success. Finally, I asked the Secretary of State if the U.S. Government still thought it impossible.

Thereupon the Secretary of State replied that the matter was still in his hand and that he had not yet submitted it to his superior. He added, however, that if I was confident that it stood a good chance of success, he would be glad to convey it to the White House. Thus, I found his answer to be different from previous ones.

Then he further asked me what I thought of the existing situation. I replied that I felt it very dangerous to leave it as it was.

Incidentally, I have already been informed of the limit of the southward advance, but I hope you would kindly let me know confidentially Japan's intentions toward the north, because here we hear many "alarming news" [sic] regarding Japan's attitude toward Siberia.

(Dispatched at midnight on the 16th.)

Sunday, August 17, 1941

At 4:30 P.M., 17th (Sunday) had an interview with the President, who had just returned to Washington. (The Secretary of State sat in company). Wired home by an urgent telegram the necessary part of the interview, and also wired home on the 18th the details of the conversation and my personal opinion about it (see the accompanying papers Nos. 709 and 713.)*

Monday, August 18, 1941

Father Drought came to Washington.

Tuesday, August 19, 1941

NO. 719 (DISPATCHED, TUESDAY, AUGUST 19)

The fact that the President received me last Sunday before anybody as soon as he had returned home and talked a few hours with the Secretary of State attests fully to the importance of Japanese-American relations. What I reported to you in telegram No. 707 seems to have been prepared beforehand

*No. 713 does not appear in *The "Magic" Background of Pearl Harbor.*

by the State Department. As I told you already, the President took the utmost care in every way in reading it out to me. And it seems that much of the President's opinion was woven into what I reported in telegram No. 708. It looks that he has the intention of responding to our proposal and carrying it out, depending upon the conditions. When I said that the point depended on the President's statesmanship, he stated that it was not his desire to close the doors, but that it was our turn now to take means for opening the door.

Judging by his cordiality throughout the interview, there is no doubt that he still cherishes some hopes and wishes that the situation would turn for the better. According to the press today, the President seems to feel that there is a great danger of the United States being dragged into a war in the Far East and considers the "chances" of Japan's starting a new aggression almost fifty-fifty.

Although it is clear that the present proposal for a meeting has been effective in softening the intention of the U.S. Government, the matter requires strict secrecy. Should it leak out, it must surely cause movements for wrecking it from every quarter. I feel keenly the necessity of guarding its secrecy to Tokyo, too.

Since I too am studying it here, I shall submit it to you for your reference in case I succeed in drawing up a definite program.

(Dispatched, 6 P.M., August 19.)

Wednesday, August 20, 1941

VISIT TO WALKER ON 20TH (WEDNESDAY)

NO. 722 (DISPATCHED, AUGUST 20 [WED])

During my interview with Walker, he said that the President held a wide view of the world; that he was not anti-Japanese in the least; that in his speeches and the present statement the President did not refer to Japan; and that it was unprecedented for the President to take up soon after returning to Washington the Japanese proposal for a Japanese-American conversion from the State Department and reply direct to me. Under such circumstance, Walker declared, the Japanese Government should reciprocate.

Thereupon I said that it was a decisive measure on the part of the Japanese Government to go as far as this point on this problem.

Walker replied that it was so with the President, too. In the first place, he said, if this should transpire at a time when anti-Japanese sentiment was prevailing and the atmosphere in Congress [was] also anti-Japanese, even if there were no grounds for it, there would be opposition all at once. But if we should succeed in it and as a result peace in the Pacific should be maintained, the people would be satisfied with the result for the first time. He, too, would be satisfied that he had lived to some purpose for having made some efforts on this problem. Saying that it would be absolutely impossible to expect again from the President anything beyond this "wholehearted" attitude, he expressed the wish that success would be achieved somehow or other.

(Dispatched, 6 P.M., 20th.)

NO. 723 (DISPATCHED, AUGUST 20)

The President seems to have an idea that he might see Premier Konoye if circumstances require (my telegram No. 722). It is not difficult to see that he has the intention of taking up the matter himself and settle it quickly from a long-range viewpoint. I consider that the President made this proposal in order to display his final political ability at this time when anti-Japanese atmosphere is especially growing worse.

Accordingly, it is desirably that the Japanese side, too, give a resolute reply *kakan naru oahu* to this. I believe that it is the most urgent matter at the present time to clarify our position, show the other side that our position is not inconsistent with the American policy, and resume this spring's unofficial conversations which have been since suspended, reserving the settlement of each concrete item to future negotiations. From this point of view I drew up a tentative plan as per telegram No. 724. The tentative plan [does not] fully convey our meaning as it was done in haste, and we shall inform you by telegram anything which may come to our mind, respects on the whole American intentions and policy, and at the same time explains Japan's firm national policy, and corrects misunderstanding concerning it, on the basis of the Konoye statement and other important statements made by the Ministers [Baron Kiichino] Hiranuma, [Hachiro] Arita, and Matsuoka. I should imagine that this plan can be taken up for consideration by the United States as a satisfactory statement insofar as the points contained in the American proposal are concerned. No doubt it is unwise to refer at this time to the other points and touched upon by the President [sic]. The plan is merely an expediency for starting Japanese-American conversations, and is not a matter to be elucidated at home and abroad. I hope you would use the plan for reference, bearing in mind the foregoing points.

Now that the Government has decided to adjust the diplomatic relations between Japan and the U.S.A., I don't think there will be another good chance if you should miss this one now.

If, as the President says, the meeting is to be held in the middle part of October, we shall have only a month for completing preliminary talks. And if the meeting is to materialize, we shall have to arrange for a ship, select the suite, and make other preparations. So I wish you would kindly give me your instructions as early as possible.

(Dispatched, at midnight of August 20.)

Thursday, August 21, 1941

In the afternoon went to the Blue Ridge Summit and stayed there overnight.

NO. 725 (DISPATCHED, AUGUST 21 [THURS.])

According to information from the same source as that of my telegram No. 722, it seems that the President at last intends to embark himself upon the resumption of the negotiations for adjusting Japanese-American relations. It is reported that the latter half of my telegram No. 706 was drafted by the President himself. Furthermore, there is a rumor that he is expecting to receive directly from me the Japanese reply to this. In this connection, I think it would be appropriate to draw up the reply as courteously and briefly as possible, omitting all argumentative matters (passages omitted).*

Besides, I should think that rhetorical considerations should be given and that it is necessary to point out that Japan has a great concern over the guarantee of her security in the Far East.

(Dispatched, 1 P.M., Wednesday August 21.)†

Saturday, August 23, 1941

NO. 735

This morning, Saturday, I called on the Secretary of State and thanked him for his good offices in arranging the interview at the White House last Sunday. When I told him that I expected to receive instructions from Tokyo in a few days, he expressed his doubt as to whether the Japanese Government could control those who advocated expansionism. Furthermore, he said that, whereas he and the President were of the same opinion in regard to the unofficial conversations between the U.S.A. and Japan and it was at the President's instruction to push on that the conversations had come to the present stage, it would be necessary to modify them so as to make them fit in with the present situation. He spoke of his pains in trying to make people at home and abroad agree to the conception embodied in the conversations.

In reply I told him that it was the same with the Japanese side and that it was necessary for responsible persons to be ready to make martyrs of themselves, in order to strive for the sake of peace in the Pacific.

Then I stated that the transportation of planes to Vladivostok and the passage of munitions cargo ships through Japanese home waters excited our people's susceptibilities. Since he referred to the Soviet-Japanese treaty and gave a "noncommittal" answer, I told him that we had also warned the Soviet Union about this. To this he listened intently.

And besides, during our conversation, I explained the meaning of additional dispatch of our troops to Manchuria. And on my referring to the release of the blocked funds for oil, he explained that this was under the jurisdiction of the Treasury Department and that it was to be decided after taking into consideration the British attitude. He therefore inquired of me about the progress of the negotiations between Japan and Britain.

(Dispatched, 5 P.M., August 23.)

---

*These passages were transmitted and appear in the published version of this telegram in *The "Magic" Background of Pearl Harbor*.
†August 21, 1941, was actually a Thursday.

NO. 739

At five P.M. this Saturday, I had a talk with the Secretary of State again. Regarding your telegram No. 495, I informed him that the Japanese Government was taking measures with the attitude of mind to give its reply as early as possible and to bring about an early meeting of the leaders.

On my referring, in compliance with your instructions, to the Moscow conference and to our demand for the suspension of the transportation of goods and material for the support of the Soviet Union, he pointed out with a smile the Soviet-Japanese Neutrality Treaty, as he had done this morning, but failed to reply to the former. He added, however, that he would report to the President what I had requested. I understand that the President, last Thursday, before he went to Hyde Park, asked about the Japanese answer. He seems to be the most zealous of all.

(Dispatched, 7 P.M., August 23.)

Sunday, August 24, 1941

At 7 P.M. talked with the Foreign Minster by telephone. (When shall I have his answer? Has my telegram reached him? etc. etc.)

Monday, August 25, 1941

NO. 740 (DISPATCHED, 1 P.M., AUGUST 25)*

By the British Premier's radio address the attention of all quarters has been directed more and more to Japanese-American relations. Hereafter every sort of intrigue for interfering with the adjustment of diplomatic relations will be undertaken not only in the two countries, but also in third countries. I feel that we should pay the greatest care and speedily effect the adjustment of diplomatic relations.

Though the President says that Britain does not want disorder in the Far East, Britain, as I have already wired you, is reported to be maneuvering to make the U.S.A. fight against Japan and thus drag her into the European war. Moreover, Britain and America seem to have the mind to refuse peace with Germany to the last.

Tuesday, August 26, 1941

Received telegrams Nos. 501, 502, 503 and 504. (Official proposal for a meeting of the leaders of the two countries, Premier's message, etc.)

Wednesday, August 27, 1941

NO 748. (AUGUST 27 [WED.])

With reference to your telegram No. 501, I called on the Secretary of State at noon, Wednesday, and in accordance with your instructions, handed a copy

*This message does not appear in *The "Magic" Background of Pearl Harbor*.

of the Premier's message, stated orally the points of your telegram No. 503 (its English translation being unfinished), and, after stressing the great significance of this meeting, asked for a direct interview with the President.

He answered that it would be difficult to reply today, but that he would reply tomorrow morning.

In the course of the conversation I told him that Churchill's speech was harmful. Thereupon the Secretary of State referred to my reply to the reporters that I did not answer the detailed questions put to me by the reporters, but only talked about Churchill's elegance, etc. And as he also talked of his apprehension that, judging from the trend of the press opinion in Tokyo, those who advocated expansionism would win out. I rejoined with appropriate remarks and tried my best to enlighten him.

(Dispatched, 6 P.M.)

Second visit to the State Secretary. Calling on the Secretary of State at 8 P.M., I handed to him the translation of telegram No. 503, and talked with him for twenty minutes.

Thursday, August 28, 1941

INTERVIEW WITH THE PRESIDENT

No. 752 (Dispatched 1:40 p.m., August 28)

With reference to my telegram No. 748, I had an interview with the President (the Secretary of State sat in company) at 11 A.M. today (Thur., 28th) and handed to him the message and the English translation of No. 503, explaining the points of your instructions. *On reading the message, the President highly commended it as very splendid.*

As he read the part of No. 503 which stated that it was difficult to distinguish the cause from the effect, he smiled as if to nod assent to it.

As to French Indochina, he cynically remarked in a very light vein whether Japan was not going to advance into Thailand during the course of the conversation between Prince Konoye and himself, just as Japan had advanced into French Indochina during the progress of conversations between Hull and myself.

The President, however, seemed to be satisfied as a whole.

As to the conversation, he hoped for a meeting of about three days and appeared to sympathize with Japan's intention to save the situation by means of this meeting.

As to Hawaii, he said that he would not be able to go there as it would take him three weeks to go and return from the meeting, pointing out that the President was required by the Constitution to sign or veto within ten days bills passed by Congress one after another, adding that this function could not be performed by the Vice President as proxy. He explained that in this respect the President's position was quite different from the Japanese Premier, who may be represented by Acting Premier protempore. But if it was Juneau, the President said, he would be able to realize his purpose in a fortnight, that is two days as far as Seattle and two days more from there on, or ten days for a return trip. I replied that, since our objective was in the meeting itself and that the place was of secondary importance, I would report to Tokyo in detail the circumstances and as to the date, I expressed my wish that the meeting would be held as early as possible. The President, though he did not seem to be opposed to an early date, did not give a ready answer about the date. And concerning the meeting with Churchill, he said that it had been proposed some time in February but postponed on account of the Balkan war. *He told me that this also was carried out after obtaining the approval of Congress.*

Such was our talk and this is to be continued.

(Dispatched 1:40 P.M., 28th.)

NO. 753

With reference to my telegram No. 752, it was mutually agreed between the Secretary of State and me that, in view of the fact that the White House had announced the appointed hour of the interview, an announcement should be made stating simply that I had transmitted the message of Premier Konoye without any reference to the contents of the message.

(Dispatched 1:40 P.M., 28th.)

Friday, August 29, 1941

NO. 756 (DISPATCHED 6 P.M., AUGUST 29)

INTERVIEW WITH SECRETARY OF STATE HULL ON THE 28TH

Concerning my telegram No. 752, I had a long talk with Hull on the night of the 28th. He talked of the subjects of the coming meeting and others, which may be summarized as follows:

a. Since a grave consequence would arise in case the leaders of the two countries should fail to come to an agreement because one side stuck to its own opinion, it is the desire of the American side to have the questions discussed beforehand so that, when the two leaders meet together, the form of making final notification (the word "ratification" was really used) could be adopted. (Regarding this, see the latter part of my telegram No. 703.)

b. He repeatedly stated that, although it was necessary to bring our past talks "up to date," the American side would find it difficult to adjust to Japanese-American diplomatic relations if the China question was separated, because the China problem was an important one to the American side.

c. He stated that, whereas Japan talked of the United States acting merely as an intermediary between Japan and China, the American side, as had been repeated so often, did not wish to jeopardize Sino-American relations by improving Japanese-American relations; that the United States Government did not wish to "explode" China through its own acts; and that, consequently, it was necessary for the American Government to be well informed of the principles underlying Sino-Japanese negotiations and to make China convinced. He declared that, after all, this was a very difficult task for the U.S. Government because it must "placate" Japan and China and then make Britain, the Soviet Union and the Netherlands act in concert with her.

d. Regarding the withdrawal of our troops from China, I answered that I had nothing to add to what I had told him in the past. As to the right of self-defense, I also repeated the usual reply. However, I explained that since Prince Konoye had decided to come in person, he must be confident of success with regard to these points. Thereupon he said that he wished to know the definite intentions of the Imperial Government because it was futile to proceed under the past understanding only.

Accordingly, I request that you give definite instructions of the Government regarding the question of troop evacuation and of the right of self-defense after referring to my telegram No. 540. Furthermore, please hear from Colonel Iwakuro in regard to the particulars of this case.

e. And next, as to the routine side of the meeting of the leaders in case it is agreed to hold the meeting, I told him my private ideas as follows:

1. Since the President considered it difficult to choose Hawaii as the place of the meeting, which was preferred by the Japanese side, because of geographical and also constitutional considerations, and proposed Juneau, which lies halfway between Tokyo and Washington, it was my conjecture that Tokyo would also agree to it.

2. As to the date, I suggested between September 21 and the 25th.

3. As to the number of personnel, I figured that five persons would be selected each from the Foreign Office, the Army, the Navy and the embassy— twenty or so in all, but it might be less.

4. I thought Prince Konoye had better come on board a warship as this would take him about ten days.

5. As to the time of its announcement, I considered it necessary to make mutual arrangements and that, in my opinion, sometime after the departure of Prince Konoye would be proper.

The Secretary of State said that he would talk over with the President with regard to the points mentioned above. Generally speaking, he is very careful and cautious in handling this question and he seems to have been giving it careful consideration from every angle. So it is my *observation that the meeting of the leaders will not materialize unless both parties reach an agreement on the main points.* (Dispatched 6 P.M., August 29th.)

Saturday, August 30, 1941

NO. 761

On the 30th the Italian Ambassador called on me and inquired about Japanese-American relations. Accordingly, within the bounds of your telegram No. 517 and your announcement, I explained that, since the relations had become so extremely tense, such that the most influential senator had dared to declare that the chances of a war were fifty-fifty, we had sent a message with a view to alleviating the situation.

As he asked me very inquisitively, I said that from a humanitarian point of view, I wished the European war would end soon (he said emphatically that he, too, felt the same); that Japan did not wish the U.S.A. to enter the war; that, needless to say, Japan was faithful to the alliance; that the U.S.A. was very cautious about participating in the war because she knew Japan's faithfulness to the alliance; and that Pacific War, if it should ever come about, would be a protracted war.

Then I remarked that the Americans, far from harboring ill-feeling toward Italy, were rather sympathetic toward her, which I attributed to the fact that there are several million Americans of Italian extraction.

He replied that socially there was nothing wrong and the Americans were kind to them, though politically things were going difficult. (Dispatched 8 P.M., August 30.)

Monday, September 1, 1941

Called on the Secretary of State at 8 P.M.

Tuesday, September 2, 1941

NO. 762 (DISPATCHED 5 P.M., SEPT. 2)

INTERVIEW WITH SECRETARY OF STATE HULL ON SEPT. 1

On the night of the 1st, I called on the Secretary of State and made a proposal for maintaining secrecy and making previous arrangements for publication, as per your telegram No. 518. It seems that the President himself is taking charge of matters concerning the meeting. Since I understand that he has gone to Hyde Park and will return to Washington tomorrow and lunch with the Secretary of State, I expect to have an answer before long. The two seem to take a keen interest in the meeting, but I should judge that the Secretary of State is acting very cautiously in view of his official responsibility and also his own personality.

It appears that the Secretary of State considers that, though the maintenance of peace in the Pacific is desirable, there is the fear that adverse public opinion would force the Konoye Cabinet to resign if it should all at once revert to peaceful policies from militaristic policies. As I understand that he is being warned against this fear by people at home and abroad, I explained that such a fear was absolutely unnecessary, in view of Prince Konoye's position and also his determination to carry out a meeting which was an unprecedented one for a Japanese premier. It seemed that the Secretary of State had been informed by Grew of all the editorials of the Japanese press, for he expressed the desire that the Japanese Government, through its own ingenuity, would so guide public opinion, influential politicians, and the military men as to make them concur in peaceful policies. (I presume that he wanted to avoid the criticism of interfering in the internal affairs of our country. He said that this would make it easier for the American side.)

As he said then that China did not wish peace and that the Chinese observed that there would appear in Japan a military cabinet before long, I replied that China was a spoilt child of America and said what she wished. The Secretary of State, as usual, said that it would be difficult for Japan and China to improve their friendly relations without provoking China to anger. He also stated the necessity of convincing Britain and other countries of this.

I then stated that, of the three existing questions, the right of self-defense was not so difficult; that there was a way to settle the principle of nondiscrimination, as it was acknowledged in outline in the present statement and also contained in the Konoye message; and that the stationing of troops in Inner Mongolia and North China could be settled, depending upon the circumstances of the time, inasmuch as the stationing of troops was not for an indefinite period of time. So I said that the Japanese Government would have some kind of a plan of her own for it.

In short, I made it clear that, when judged from a long-range political viewpoint, even the U.S.A. had no cause to wish for a two-front "trouble" and that there was not the slightest doubt that Japan cherished the maintenance of peace and tranquility in the Far East, as was clearly indicated in the successive Imperial rescripts [sic]. So I urged a quick realization of the meeting.

The Secretary of State, too, said that it would be a matter for rejoicing if peace in the Pacific could be maintained.

Though our talk did not go so far as to discuss the place of the meeting, it was 3,400 miles to Honolulu and 3,800 miles to Juneau. The weather at Juneau is said to be good even in October. In any case, I think that when we make the announcement, we had better state that the meeting is to be held at a certain place in the Pacific (halfway between Tokyo and Washington).

Wednesday, September 3, 1941

At 5 P.M. had a secret interview with the President and the Secretary of State at the White House.

NO. 776

INTERVIEW WITH THE PRESIDENT ON THE 3RD

At 5 P.M. on the 3rd (Wed.) I had an interview with the President. On reading what I had informed you of in my telegrams Nos. 776 and 777, the President stated that he and Prince Konoye and the Secretary of State and I, all of us would strive for peace in the Pacific, but that both Japan and the U.S.A. had their respective public opinions. Saying that he had received frequently telegrams demanding no change in American policies in order to compromise with Japan, he stated that he sympathized with Prince Konoye very, very sincerely.

And then the Secretary of State, who sat beside him, inquired about the present state of affairs in Japan. I replied that the Premier would proceed resolutely.

Regarding the three pending questions, I explained that we had already come to an agreement in principle on two of them, and that, as to the evacuation of troops, the Premier's personal participation in the forthcoming conference showed that the Premier was confident of reaching an American-Japanese agreement on this point also.

The Secretary of State said that there were still some points on wording that he wished to discuss and again repeated the necessity of convincing Britain, the Netherlands Indies and China when an agreement is reached between the U.S.A. and Japan.

The President stated that he did not touch on the details of the adjustment of Japanese-American diplomatic relations in the course of his talks with Churchill, because of the difficulty of keeping things secret as it was customary in Britain to let all things [be] known to the cabinet ministers, who in turn revealed the matters to the Parliament.

And as to the date of its meeting, the President seems to have no engagement for the present, except one at the end of September.

On parting, I told the President that the maintenance of peace in the Pacific depended much on his high statesmanship. The President concurred in this remark, but the Secretary of State asked a few more questions, worrying about the tone of the press comments in Tokyo.

The President had no objection to the statement of our standpoint, but the Secretary of State made no answer. As I am to meet the latter tomorrow morning, I shall confirm it then and inform you of his opinion. (Dispatched 8:30 P.M., Sept. 3.)

Thursday, September 4, 1941

At 9 A.M., I (accompanied by Obata) called on the Secretary of State at his private residence.

The Foreign Minister made a proposal to Grew in Tokyo.

NO. 782 (DISPATCHED 8 P.M., 4TH.)

INTERVIEW WITH HULL ON THE 4TH

At 9 A.M., on the 4th, I called on Secretary of State Hull. Taking up the four principles of the oral statement, especially the principle of equal opportunity, Hull repeated his usual contentions. I expressed our desire to dispose of the unsettled questions first because the Japanese Government had no objection to them in principle, as was stated in our reply of the 26th.

To this, Hull replied that it was necessary to dispose of the fundamental principles first, for the U.S.A. did not wish to give the impression that she was trading off the third powers, such as Britain, China, and the Netherlands Indies. He added that it was necessary for Japan, too, to clarify that she stood for the same principles and thereby convince the third powers. When I referred to the

American proposal of June 21 and asked for the elimination of the proposal for exchanging official notes on the European war, Hull showed disapproval. I also gathered from what he said that he was opposed to the station of troops for anti-Comintern purposes and that he desired a complete evacuation. I noticed that the attitude of the other party had considerably stiffened.

Saturday, September 6, 1941

At 9 A.M. called on the Secretary of State and submitted the proposal of our Government. (It was the same as the one made on the 4th by the Foreign Minister in Tokyo.)

NO. 788 (DISPATCHED 3 P.M., SEPT. 6)

INTERVIEW WITH HULL ON SEPT. 6

At 9 A.M. on the 6th I called on Secretary of State Hull. Saying that the views of the Imperial Government were as clarified in the proposals of August 6th and 28th, and in the Premier's message and documents annexed thereto, I explained that the present proposal, especially items B and C, should meet with the wishes of the American side; adding that, in my opinion, this was the maximum which the Japanese Government could do. Next I expressed the hope that the American side, with insight into the situation, would cooperate to bring about the swift materialization of the meeting of the leaders of both sides. (*The telegram regarding the proposal came to hand on the afternoon of the 4th.*)

Hull replied that he had only read a part of Grew's report, but that he would thoroughly study it at the weekend. Moreover, showing great concern as to the reliability of the present cabinet, he expressed the wish that, since arguments for adjusting diplomatic relations had arisen in the United States, Japan, too, would endeavor to guide her public opinion into this direction.

On my emphasizing the necessity of maintaining peace in the Pacific, he seemed to be very prudent in setting forth his opinion, though he endorsed my view.

Sunday, September 7, 1941

The President's mother passed away. I went to Virginia Beach yesterday and came back today.

Monday, September 8, 1941

TELEGRAPHIC REPORT (DISPATCHED 3 P.M., SEPT. 8)*

According to today's Gallup Poll report, the number of people favoring the checking of Japan's development at the risk of a war has suddenly increased from 51% in July to 70% today.

*Not in *The "Magic" Background of Pearl Harbor.*

At 9 A.M. called on the Secretary of State.

At 3 P.M., Hamilton, Ballantine and Max W. Schmidt called on me and asked me questions regarding the documentary proposal submitted on the 6th. (Though I had "discouraged" the Secretary of State from asking questions about the business side of this case, they came to me under his instructions on the ground that they found it difficult to understand the papers because the wording in the documents tendered by our side in the past varied.)

Tokyo

On the night of the 10th the American Ambassador handed an American note to the Foreign Minister. The telegram informing that the answer to this note will be given in Tokyo came to hand on the 12th [sic].

NO. 798 (DISPATCHED 4 P.M., 10TH)

At 9 P.M., on the 10th (Wed.), I called on Secretary of State Hull and according to your instructions, requested that the President refrain from referring to matters concerning Japan in his radio speech tomorrow, the 11th.

On my asking when I shall have a reply to the proposal (made on the 6th) of the Japanese Government regarding the adjustment of diplomatic relations, he replied that it would be after he had had a talk with the President, which he expected to have when the President had finished his broadcasting on the 11th (tomorrow), because so far he had had no chance to meet the President, who left Washington last Friday.

Then betraying his dissatisfaction in a measure, he said that the Japanese Government's reply had "narrowed down" a great deal the points discussed in the past. I explained that, as written down in our reply, we had specially picked out difficult points, omitting those upon which both sides were in agreement.

In short, the American side seemed to be consulting the views of Britain, China, and the Netherlands Indies.

He severely criticized Germany's faithlessness regarding the destroyer *Greer*.

Thursday, September 11, 1941

The President spoke on the radio.

My Opinion on the Stationing of Troops in China

The gist of telegram No. 810 (Dispatched 8 P.M., Sept. 11)

The difficult point in adjusting the diplomatic relations, as you have seen in my successive telegrams, lies in the stationing of troops for anti-Comintern purposes. I feel that the U.S.A. is not greatly opposed to other points, but she seems to be strongly opposed to the stationing of troops. To effect a break in the deadlock, I wish you would consider a compromise to a proposal providing for the withdrawal of troops within two years after the restoration of peace, without touching on the question of stationing of troops. And I hereby ask you to decide your final attitude as quickly as possible, as it is necessary for me to proceed with the negotiations. As this is primarily a question between China and Japan, and since America is obliged to comment upon it out of duty as intermediary, it may perhaps take a year or more under this proposal to bring about the meeting of the leaders of the two countries, conclude a detailed agreement, and then armistice and a peace conference. Therefore, even if we promise now to evacuate within two years, we may be able to negotiate with China for the postponement of the evacuation according to the changing situation, or we may perhaps be able to keep our troops in order to protect the lives and property of Japanese residents. I don't think that this will necessarily lead to a result contrary to our past national policies. No doubt, I admit, it is a truly difficult question as a domestic issue, but it is my earnest desire that you would give me reply instructions some way or other as soon as possible. Regarding this, I think it might be a good idea to insert a clause for joint Sino-Japanese cooperation (nonmilitary) for the purpose of checking activities harmful to their national well-being in place of a clause for the stationing of troops for anti-Comintern purposes.

Saturday, September 13, 1941

The reply to the American note, which the Foreign Minister had explained to Grew, came to hand on Sept. 13. (Nos. 561, 562, 563, and 564.)

In Tokyo, in the evening of the 13th the American Ambassador was requested to bring our proposal to the President's knowledge as quickly as possible and to give an expression of intention thereto. (Telegram came to hand on the 13th.)

Sunday, September 14, 1941

Visited Philadelphia, stayed overnight on the way and came back on Monday.

NO. 819 (DISPATCHED 7 P.M., 14TH)

Regarding your telegrams Nos. 561–563, I wish to tell you below, for your information, what has come to my mind:

1. You may understand that any proposal made to Secretary of State Hull will be immediately brought to the President's knowledge if the President is in Washington. It appears that all preliminary talks are entrusted entirely to Hull. The President, for instance, once went so far as to say to me that what cannot be settled between Hull and me cannot be settled even

if it is tackled by other persons. Hull himself once said to me that the President and he had always agreed with each other on foreign policies during the past eight years.

2. The words "communistic and subversive activities" in the article on the stationing of troops may first draw their attention. Also the term "common defense in China" is likely to become a subject of discussion. Their doubt as to what the "agreements" definitely mean may still remain.

3. With regard to the intermediation between China and Japan, I believe it certain that so long as the American side makes it a prerequisite to be apprised unofficially of fair and square conditions, the U.S.A. will not comply with our request for intermediation even if we refrain from specifying our conditions.

4. The plan to leave politically the interpretation of the Tripartite Treaty [until] when the leaders meet will be unavailing in view of the state of affairs in this country, and the President's position.

At any rate, I feel that there is no hope for a meeting of the leaders unless we come to an agreement in our preliminary talks.

5. I will convey at once to Hull your intention to confine the present understanding to that between American and Japan only.

6. I will do my utmost in accordance with the purpose of your instructions. However, in respect to the points which you are negotiating at present in Tokyo, please note that I shall watch developments for a while, because of the fear of causing misunderstanding and of complicating the negotiations if I should deal with them at this end.

Wednesday, September 17, 1941

NO. 822 (DISPATCHED ON SEPT. 17TH)*

I acknowledge receipt of your telegram No. 554. Everything that you say therein is right, and I feel a deep responsibility for the few omissions contained in the translation.

NO. 823 (DISPATCHED SEPT. 17 [WED.])

On August 6 (subsequently corrected as a mistake for Sept. 3) I explained at the White House that we had already come to an agreement in principle on two of the three pending questions, while, as to the evacuation of troops, the Premier's decision to personally conduct the negotiations showed that the Premier was confident of reaching an American-Japanese agreement. Thereupon the Secretary of State said that there were still some points the wording of which he wished to discuss and bring them "up to date." This was based on the June 21st proposal for understanding.

As to your instructions of July 15, though I received further instructions No. 397 dated July 24, I could do nothing and so left them unproposed [sic]

*Not in *The "Magic" Background of Pearl Harbor.*

because the negotiations had been suspended then. The talks were resumed through the new message. In accordance with your instructions of May 11, I had negotiated more than ten times with the Secretary of State and had also conducted flanking operations in various ways during that time. The June 21st proposal for understanding contained developments of the negotiations up to the time of the Secretary of State's departure for a change of air. It is natural for Hull to be excessively attached to the draft which he had succeeded in making up so far after negotiating with me for several months. So I think it will be more acceptable to the American Government and convenient for expediting the preliminary negotiations if we take in the forms and contents of the former negotiations as much as possible, and I add here that Hull once said that the negotiations were to be conducted here.

Such being the circumstances, I doubt whether we can conclude the preliminary talks by means of our proposal of September 4th alone. In any case, it is the most important matter to find out a measure acceptable to both America and Japan on three pending problems, especially the question of stationing troops.

According to information from the usual source, a tendency favorable for Japanese-American negotiations developed among the cabinet secretaries at the Cabinet Conference last Friday, and there is no doubt that the President has a mind to personally appear at the meeting if the preliminary talks are concluded. However, according to the information Nishiyama* obtained from a friend of his, *Hull told this friend that the President had gone too far during my interview with him.* (Dispatched, Sept. 17.)

Thursday, September 18, 1941

NO. 829 (DISPATCHED SEPT. 18 [THURS.])

According to what Nishiyama heard from Desburnin (?),† Hull told him that the prospect for Japanese-American negotiations were not so good as they had been two weeks ago; that it was very difficult to predict the future because opinion in the Japanese Government was divided; that for the present no consideration would be given to the question of bartering silk for oil; and that for the coming one or two weeks they could do nothing but watch developments in the situation.

However, Hornbeck, who had been on leave for a fortnight since the last weekend, is said to have told an Associated Press correspondent that no developments would occur in the adjustment of Japanese-American relations during his furlough. I add this for your information.

---

*A financial attaché at the Japanese Embassy.

†The name of Nishiyama's source does not appear in the version of this message in *The "Magic" Background of Pearl Harbor.*

Friday, September 19, 1941

At 9 P.M., called on Secretary of State Hull.

Saturday, September 20, 1941

NO. 838 (DISPATCHED SEPTEMBER 20)

INTERVIEW WITH SECRETARY OF STATE HULL ON FRIDAY

For the first time in nine days I visited Hull on the night of the 19th and asked his opinion on our proposal of September 4th. He gave me no substantial answer, but only said that he had expected that he might be handed some proposal that night as Grew had told him by wire that Japan would make, in a few days, a proposal which would be acceptable to the United States. He said that he was awaiting Japan's proposal. And to my question, he answered that the United States had not yet made any further suggestion concerning the interpretation of the Tripartite Treaty.

The following were what I understood to be his thoughts during the course of my conversation with him, and I submit them for your information.

1. Though he said that the United States, like Japan, had no intention of prolonging the conversation and that it was her wish to complete it as soon as possible, I think it advisable for us to take this as a reply for form's sake.

2. Repeating what he had told me before, he said that the United States was opposed to the policy of advocating peace on one hand, and of using armed force on the other hand; that Japan was sure to make good progress through peaceful policies during the period of peace in the whole Pacific, and this would be advantageous to Japan also.

He had once told me that the existence of a strong Japan was necessary for peace in the Far East and at the same time had said that, whereas it would not be acceptable to America if we adopted a policy of partly peace and partly conquest, American-Japanese problems would be settled in a single night if Japan would adopt a thoroughly peaceful policy, and that then the question of wording would be of no importance.

3. He recognized that the internal affairs of Japan were more difficult than those of the United States. He seemed to have received a report on the functions for commemorating the first anniversary of the Tripartite Alliance to be held on September 27th, but he recognized that those who favored peace outnumbered those who wish to wage war on the side of Germany.

4. He agreed to the proposal, contained in your telegram No. 560, to confine the talk to that between America and Japan only, but he said that it was necessary to keep in touch with the other interested powers in the Pacific.

In short, I think that what I told you in my telegraphic reports Nos. 822 (it might have been No. 823) and 829 has come true as a whole.

(Further, Vice President Henry A. Wallace is said to have confidentially told Desburnin (?) during the course of a talk between them the other day that it was the policy of the U.S. Government not to effect any "appeasement" toward Japan). It is a patent fact that the United States is skeptical of Japan. Frankly speaking, the United States recognizes that Japan will adopt an armed force policy, while trying "to appease" the United States.

Such being the case, I think the settlement of the problems lies not in the wording but is connected with their substance.

Your telegram No. 584 has duly come to hand. As to the attitude of the other party, please understand it from the aforesaid Hull's talk and my telegrams Nos. 822 and 829. (Dispatched Sat. 20th.)

Sunday, September 21, 1941

At 6 P.M., had a six-minute telephone talk with my family at home (cost over $30).

Monday, September 22, 1941

NO. 839 (DISPATCHED ON MONDAY)

THE RECENT STATE OF AFFAIRS IN AMERICA

As for the recent state of affairs in this country, America is still endeavoring to defeat Germany by supporting her own friendly powers. Though she was satisfied with the fight put up by the Soviet Union, which was better than she had expected, she is not* wishing, in view of the undeniably unfavorable tide of war against the Soviet Union, to assist that country jointly with Britain as much as possible in order to prevent her from making a separate peace or from surrendering, and thus make her tide over the winter and maintain her fighting power up to next spring. At this juncture the U.S.A. has further set up in the budget the sum of six billion dollars for assisting other countries, and by this she intends to bolster the fighting spirit of the British people.

The landing operations against England have become extremely difficult, and besides, the U.S. Navy has undertaken an active convoy of shipping in the Atlantic. Moreover, she is planning to build six million tons of ships in deadweight during the next year. She thinks that when this is completed she will be able to tide over the crisis in the Atlantic and thereby make Britain safe. America, however, knows that she will not succeed by such a passive policy because the fighting spirit of the Germans is still strong. On the other hand, she is hoping against hope that Italy would fall out of the line of battle on account of the growing disaffection among the Italian people and that, taking an exaggerated view of the unrest of the people's minds in the occupied areas, German endurance would also break down before long. And that is why there are some who think that the war will continue one or two years at the shortest, and even, for five or ten years if it becomes protracted. The peo-

*We believe "not" is a misprint for "now."

ple in general are self-composed and easy-going as is peculiar to a great nation; we may safely say that none of them think that they will ever be defeated in a war. As to war operations, they think that it will be sufficient to make the Navy participate in the war, and apart from the preparations made by the Army authorities, it seems that the people are in no mood to send expeditionary forces on a large scale. But isolationism is gradually losing popularity in political circles and public option is nearing step by step toward that of supporting the Government's foreign policies. As to the Far Eastern question, the people in general are taking it in a further easy-going manner, thinking that it cannot be helped if a war should break out between Japan and America. There are many comments on the comparative strength of the navies of both countries, but, in short, they claim that the United States will win in the end on the ground that in the (coming) Japanese-American war the Navy will have a clear field, that a protracted war will be too strong a strain on Japan's economic strength, and also that American capacity for replenishing lost warships is greater than that of Japan. So we find very little sign that they feel danger from Japan. Hence the opinion most prevails that, in respect to diplomatic problems, they should firmly maintain the past Far Eastern policy and that it is wrong to compromise at this juncture at the expense of China. The Hyde Park news in the *New York Times' Sunday Edition*, for instance, reports to the following effect: The adjustment of diplomatic relations between Japan and the U.S.A. *is at present in a deadlock*. Prince Konoye is now wishing for a direct negotiation with the President as the Japanese demand for the recognition of her special position in China disagrees with Hull's denial of such a position. The President, however, is constantly consulting with Hull. The greater part of the U.S. Navy still remains in the Pacific, but Japan is likely to move to the south or to the north, depending upon the situation of the Soviet Union. Consequently the U.S.A. is in danger of being obliged to fight in the two oceans at the same time. The President is especially giving this point careful consideration.

The paper further reported a rumor that, as the terms of peace, Japan will hold several treaty ports and the four provinces in North China, and may also station small units for guarding other places.

In conclusion the report said that, although the U.S. Government was unwilling to compromise with Japan at the expense of China, she would be ready to revive commercial relations between Japan and the United States and give economic support to Japan if she would stop her armed aggression.

The foregoing commentary was written by Crackhorn and is most to the point. (Dispatched Sept. 22nd.)

Tuesday, September 23, 1941

Visited the old battlefield at Gettysburg (for the third time). Stayed overnight at Blue Ridge Summit.

At 9 A.M., called on Secretary of State Hull.

NO. 842 (SEPT. 23RD [TUES.])

At 9 A.M. on the 23rd (Tues.), I called on Hull and handed to him the English versions of your telegrams Nos. 562 and 564 and also our terms of peace between Japan and China, No. 590. On the basis of your successive instruc-tions, I explained that we had already said all that we had to say, that we had nothing further to tell Ambassador Grew, that further matters concerning the Tripartite Alliance must be reserved for discussion in the meeting of the leaders of the two countries, and that the proposal made in Tokyo on the 4th did not "narrow down" the American proposal but rather expanded it. At the same time I stated the state of affairs in Tokyo on the basis of your telegraphic instruction No. 589 and then told him that our Government earnestly wished the swift realization of the meeting of the leaders of both countries.

To this, Hull said that they were taking much time to hasten the meeting of the leaders and then he asked how the guidance of Japanese public opinion, which he had requested in the past, was getting on. I replied that, as I had repeatedly told him, our Government had been paying much attention to that, and that consequently the situation was gradually improving. Further, as he asked for my personal opinion, I told him that our Government considered the Tripartite Alliance could be compatible with the adjustment of diplomatic relations between Japan and the United States, and that we were sure that the meeting of the leaders of the two countries would strengthen peace in the Pacific.

Hull stated that, as to the conversation between Minister Toyoda and Ambassador Grew, he had received Grew's report and was studying it carefully in a friendly spirit, and that it was his desire to reply as soon as possible. I asked for his agreement to the meeting of the leaders in principle, but I could not get any definite reply.

Hull then referred to the situation of the world, saying that it would not be too early for Japan and the U.S.A. to think of reconstructing world peace at this time, and that, as for him, he thought Japan and the United States had a golden opportunity to take the "leadership" of the world, but that he doubted whether the "statesmanship" of both countries would be competent to meet the situation. Then I explained that for that very purpose the meeting of the leaders of both countries would be necessary, and thus ended our talk. (Dispatched 23rd).

Wednesday, September 24, 1941

At 7 P.M. called up Minister Toyoda on the telephone (for ten minutes).

NO. 847 (DISPATCHED SEPT. 24)

Though I could grasp the general idea of your opinion through the telephone talk between us just now, there are still some points which I cannot understand thoroughly. As I reported to you in my telegram No. 842 of the 23rd, I told the Secretary of State, in compliance with your instructions, that we had already said our say and had nothing further to tell Ambassador Grew in Tokyo. To this, he replied that he would endeavor to give an answer as early as possible. In short, I am now awaiting their attitude. At this juncture your telegraphic instructions No. 591 arrived. There being many points in it which I myself can hardly understand, I should be unable to reply to the other side if I should present it now to the other side. Not only that, I fear that the other side might interpret it to mean that we shall be able to station troops at any point throughout China. So please let me know as soon as possible, for my own confidential information, by return telegram, the explanatory statement to which you referred in our telephone talk. As you say, we have now come to the last five minutes. It is my intention to do my best so far as my side is concerned in compliance with your instructions. (10:30 P.M.)

Saturday, September 27, 1941

Secretary Matsudaira called on Ballantine and handed him (with the request that it be delivered to the Secretary of State) No. 595 (a proposal for an understanding which had been drawn up in Tokyo, based on the proposal of June 21).

Monday, September 29, 1941

At 9 A.M. called on Secretary of State Hull, and in the afternoon visited Admiral Stark.

NO. 867

INTERVIEW WITH SECRETARY OF STATE HULL

On the morning of the 29th (Monday) I visited the Secretary of State and asked for a secret interview with the President in compliance with the purpose of your instructions. He said that, as the President had been staying in Hyde Park since Thursday on account of the death of a relative, he would see the President as soon as the latter returned to Washington, and give us a memorandum of the American Government in one or two days. He said that he had read yesterday the report from Grew and seemed to know everything about the matter.

During our conversation, Hull agreed to the opinion that we should submerge minor differences for greater common interest by taking a long-range view of things, but he asked me about the public opinion of entire Japan. I replied to the following effect:

Our Government, the Army and the Navy are for reaching an understanding between Japan and the U.S.A., but it will take much time for the whole nation to understand it. There are some people who wonder why the U.S.A., advocating as she does the Monroe Doctrine and holding as a matter of fact the leadership of the American continent, should interfere so much in Asiatic affairs. Japanese public opinion cannot be expected to be changed overnight to what the United States desires. To wait for this change would be like wait-ing one hundred years for the waters of the Huang-Ho (Yellow River) to be-come clear. (Dispatched on the afternoon of the 29th.)

Tuesday, September 30, 1941

NO. 881

On the 29th (Monday) I called on Admiral Stark after a long interval and had a talk with him (Rear Admiral Turner participated from the middle part of our talk). The Admiral acknowledged that the problem of stationing troops in China would be the stumbling block to the negotiations and that it was difficult to effect Japanese-American understanding unless the China Affair was settled. Apparently judging that Japan would not readily consent to the withdrawal of troops, Turner seemed to regard that it would be dangerous to hold the meeting of the leaders of the two countries before arriving at a pre-liminary agreement. While we were talking about the Tripartite Alliance, Ad-miral Stark said that the U.S.A. would never attack Japan on her own initiative. I should judge that when it comes to two-ocean operations, the U.S.A. will naturally take a defensive or a passive-offensive position in the Pacific.

Admiral Stark is one of those persons who consider that a Japanese-Ameri-can war will bring no benefit whatever to the two countries and that economic questions cannot be solved by force. As he has been always kind and good to me, I told him that I was overwhelmed with shame for my failure to bring about satisfactory results since my arrival here. To this, he stated that all those who knew me appreciated my efforts. And then he showed and urged me to read an article on the Far Eastern question appearing in the *Business Condi-tion Weekly* (the article said that a "show-down" between Japan and the U.S.A. was drawing near, but that there was no need for war to both Japan and the U.S.A. for the U.S.A. wished prosperity for Japan would so change her policies as to make possible the adjustment of diplomatic relations. He himself promised to do what he can. Please convey this to the Navy Minister [sic]. (Dispatched Sept. 30.)

Thursday, October 2, 1941

NO. 889

VISIT TO SECRETARY OF STATE HULL

At 9 A.M. on October 2 (Thursday) I called on Secretary of State Hull at the other party's request. Hull handed to me a document, as per telegram No. 890, and stated that *the U.S. Government considered it dangerous to hold the meeting of the leaders without reaching a preliminary understanding,* that "a patched-up understanding" would be unsatisfactory, and that "*a clear-cut agreement*" would be necessary for maintaining peace in the whole Pacific. After replying that, though I knew very well Tokyo would be disappointed with this reply, I would transmit it anyway, I withdrew. (Dispatched 2 P.M., the 2nd.)

Friday, October 3, 1941

Called on the Secretary of State and made representations on matters relating to the docking of incoming vessels and the use of funds in South America for purchasing oil. (Wired home today as per 898.)

Saturday, October 4, 1941

NO. 901

REPRESENTATION OF OPINION (DISPATCHED OCTOBER 4)

Ever since my appointment, I have worked day and night but I regret to say that things have not gone on as I had expected.

Now, I must apologize for sending you my imperfect opinion yesterday in a hurry and beg you will be kind enough to excuse me and consider it as an act motivated by patriotism in view of the pressing emergencies.

Further, I think it quite necessary for Japan to effect a drastic reform in her economic life if she is to achieve self-sufficiency within the present coprosperity sphere. I imagine that this is really a very difficult problem. I do not know to what extent we shall be able to surmount the difficulties when we advance northward, but I am sure that when we advance southward, there is a great possibility of our obtaining a certain advantage after the advance.* However, if we do so, we must be prepared to fight against Britain and America in the Pacific while further expanding our battle line during the China Affair and we should expect nothing less than a protracted war. Such being the case, it is not a question that can be readily solved, I suppose.

Since my observation [is] based on the limited information that I have obtained here, I cannot but hope that you would decide by degrees the questions of readjustment of international relations and of national development, *after considering the advantages and disadvantages, without making a hasty conclusion in regard to war or peace.* (In regard to the question of China, for example, you might try to direct negotiations with Chungking, if you want to obtain conditions to which America would agree.) I hereby wire you my foregoing opinion again for your information. (Dispatched Saturday, Oct. 4th, 1:00 P.M.)

*From this point, this telegram does not appear in The *"Magic" Background of Pearl Harbor*, in accordance with [the] notation that Part 2 was not available.

[Thursday, October 9, 1941]

NO. 915

INTERVIEW WITH HULL

Accompanied by Obata, I called on Hull at 9:00 today, Oct. 9. In accordance with your successive instructions, I referred to the conversations at the White House on September 3 and tried to confirm his opinion. He repeatedly said that the nondiscrimination principle should be applied to the whole Pacific area and that geographical adjacence [sic], etc. could be interpreted in various ways. Anyhow, he said that he would reply in detail through Ballantine and others, after studying the document. (In the afternoon, Hamilton, Ballantine and Schmidt called on me.)

And again, I urged him to reconsider the matter, giving him a detailed description of China in respect to her administration, finance, and military affairs, and added that it was necessary for us to station our forces at certain points. Further, when I told him that the Premier had simply agreed to the four principles in principle, he seemed to have been already aware of it.

(Dispatched 9th, 1:00 P.M.)

Friday, October 10, 1941

Your telegram No. 650 has been received. Regarding the maintenance of peace in the Pacific, the other side, though they wish it, maintain that it would be absolutely impossible for them to arrange for the preliminary conversation, because they consider our policy to be partly peaceful and partly aggressive, and further that it seems to them that our proposal of September 6 had further "narrowed down" the talks we have had so far. They seem to have some objections also to the points other than the three points indicated by you, but they won't give me an exact answer even though I questioned them closely. However, I can at least see that they are requiring us to make a concession along the "line" of the note handed to me on Oct. 2nd. It is my observation that there is absolutely no prospect for holding a meeting of the leaders of the two countries so long as we do not make this concession. In short, sticking to their reply of Oct. 2nd, they show no further conciliatory attitude. They seem to take the attitude that they are ready to take up Japan's proposal only when and if it agrees with that contained in their above reply. . . .

(Dispatched, 10th).*

Tuesday, October 14, 1941

NO. 943

I met Rear Admiral Turner and what he said may be put together as follows:

What the U.S.A. wants is not a "show" but a reliable promise. Supposing that a conference of the two leaders is held before reliable preliminary conversa-

*The number of this telegram is not given in the diary. It is No. 923.

tions are completed, and if it should so happen that the advance into Siberia is carried out during that time, the President would get into a predicament. Insofar as Japan says she desires peace in the Pacific, and insofar as she says that she will decide it from her own standpoint, her obligations under the Tripartite Alliance can be understood on the whole. As to the question of withdrawing or stationing troops, the former cannot be carried out at one time. So Japan had better do it gradually after laying down the details by agreement between Japan and China.

He seemed to imagine that there are various difficulties in the way from the viewpoint of domestic questions.

This opinion of his seems to have been communicated to the Secretary of State also. Further, according to him, even if the Soviet-German War comes to a close and Germany takes the initiative toward Britain for the restoration of peace, Britain would never respond to it because it would be a peace imposed by Germany.

Since Rear Admiral Turner is an able man who holds an important post, we may regard this opinion as the Navy's opinion. However, according to the Castle, J. Edgar Hoover, who seems to have obtained information of separate peace between the Soviet Union and Germany, is of the opinion that peace may come about unexpectedly early, if Germany should offer Britain lenient terms. He added that Hugh Gibson, also, views the matter in that light, and hence it would be advisable for Japan to exercise a judicious caution. The foregoing opinion, however, is the opinion held by a few isolationists.

According to Moore's* report, Secretary of State Hull stated in his reply to Senator Thomas† that, though he would continue the Japanese-American negotiations with patience, he hoped that Japan would not mistake it for an American weak point and that the reply to the note of October 2nd had not yet arrived.

I add for your information that, according to Kipplinger, the rumor of the truce between Germany and the Soviet Union appears to be well grounded and that the prospects for a Japanese-American war are fifty-fifty. (Dispatched Oct. 14.)

Thursday, October 16, 1941

INTERVIEW WITH LORD HALIFAX

I called on Lord Halifax at 5 P.M. and had an hour's talk with him. Starting the conversation, I stated to him to the following effect:

Japan and the United States hope for the stabilization of peace in the Pacific and, as he had once declared, Britain also entertained the same desire. The U.S. maintains that the settlement of the China Affair is a prerequisite for the stabilization of peace in the Pacific.

*Possibly R. Walton Moore, Counselor of the State Department.
†Probably Senator Elbert D. Thomas, Democrat of Utah.

Now, there are three difficult points in the Japanese-American parley. Two of them have the chance of being settled somehow or other, but the question of stationing Japanese troops in China has always been a "stumbling block." Japan has proceeded on the principle of "no annexation and no indemnity" after four years' fighting. Now, in view of the present state of affairs in China, Japan feels it necessary to station troops at certain points for some time and make this her minimum demand. If even this should be rejected as impossible, it would be tantamount to Japan's acknowledgement of "surrender" in spite of her minimum demand. If even this should be rejected as impossible, it would be tantamount to Japan's acknowledgement of "surrender" in spite of her victory in war. This the Japanese people's sentiment will not permit acknowledgement [sic]. Moreover, it is true that Japan concluded the Tripartite Alliance, but the Japanese people have been told that it was an inevitable measure under the international circumstances in which Japan was placed. The oppression by the Anglo-Saxon nations, indeed, was one of its causes. And recently economic oppression has been added. Under these circumstances, Japan is placed in the fate of being obliged to find a way out of it even against her will, for the protection of her own economic life.

Since Great Britain has great "interest" in East Asia and since the question of stationing troops in China is not to be settled by force between Britain and America on the one hand and Japan on the other, I have been wondering if there isn't a capital idea of finding a "modus vivendi" for preventing war in the Pacific Area.

Then I told him that the Japanese Navy, in view of its tradition, could not be "pushed over" so easily as the Americans say, and moreover, the Japanese people could stand a plain diet.

Lastly I added that, since such a war would be useless, there should be a "statesmanship" for preventing it. He expressed his wholehearted agreement to what I had said and even intimated his wish to talk with Secretary of State Hull. He was very courteous to me all throughout the conversations.

Saturday, October 18, 1941

EXPRESSION OF RESIGNATION TO THE FOREIGN MINISTER

DISPATCHED, OCT. 18, 1941 (SAT.)*

It is a matter for regret that I have been of no service though I have tried my utmost in compliance with the previous cabinet's policies and I feel myself greatly responsible for it. Indeed, I am burning with shame because things

*This telegram is unnumbered.

have not gone according to my wishes since my assumption of the present post. As to the future, it can be easily foretold what I shall be able to do with my little ability. I fear that I should prove to be a harmful existence [sic], to say nothing of being a useless person, but I have decided to think it over at the ex-Minister's earnest encouragement. Now it is my desire to return to Japan at the first opportunity and report to you the state of affairs here and also to ask for your proper instructions. I hope you would give your consent to this request as early as possible. As Wakasugi and Sabao Iguchi,* who are capable men, will look after affairs while I am away, there will be no inconvenience.

Monday, October 20, 1941

Expression of Resignation to the Navy Minister
  Dispatched Monday, Oct. 20†
  Kindly communicate this to the Navy Minister, keeping it for Your Excellency's private information:

To the Navy Minister:
I congratulate you on your appointment.
  I am burning with shame because things have gone contrary to my wishes since my arrival here, though I was honored with the enthusiastic support of the ex–Minister of the Navy on the occasion of my assumption of the present post. I don't think I should remain a sinecurist [sic] when there are no prospects of any success for me.
  America is confronted with the European war on one hand, and the Pacific question on the other, but she has yet many strategically weak points. So I had expected that this would make her more or less cooperative, but, contrary to my expectations, she has stuck on to her own policy up to now, showing no conciliatory attitude. This may be because she has gone too deep into China.
  Therefore, I had once thought of establishing a "modus vivendi" for the Far East, putting aside the question of China, and had hinted at it to the Secretary of State, but he rigidly maintained the indivisibility of the Chinese question and the stabilization of the Pacific.
  A few days ago, I had an hour's talk with Lord Halifax. I told him that Great Britain had great concern over the acute state of things and asked him whether there was any "modus vivendi" for avoiding the crisis and maintaining the present state of things. In reply he intimated his wish to have a talk with Hull, but he has not yet advised me anything about it.
  Next, before my departure (for the U.S.A.) I had several talks with the then cabinet ministers and thoroughly understood the trend of the Government (policy). But since then there have been two cabinet changes, with the result that I am now in the dark, and know not what to do. In view of the fact that

---

*A counselor at the embassy.
†Both of these telegrams are unnumbered.

I have already [had] scores of talks with the Secretary of State, my continuance in the present post would doubtless be disadvantageous to Japan in case she reopened the negotiations from a new angle.

From this viewpoint, I wired home yesterday asking for permission to return temporarily. If the Foreign Minister asks for your opinion, I earnestly hope that you would kindly take the trouble of helping me in realizing my object. (Dispatched 20th.)

Saturday, Oct. 21, 1941

A SECOND TELEGRAPH TO THE FOREIGN MINISTER (DISPATCHED WEDNESDAY, OCT. 22)

Some time ago I wired home about my personal affairs. I am firmly convinced that I should retire from office along with the resignation of the previous cabinet.

From the first, the Secretary of State has recognized my sincerity, but it has been his judgment that I have no influence over Tokyo. So is the President's opinion, I hear.

There are some Americans who put hopes on my existence, saying that I am a preventive medium against the rupture of the present situation, but this is a mere compliment to me and not worth taking notice of. Among the Japanese residents in the United States, also, there are some who hold the same idea, but really this is only a superstitious misunderstanding.

As to the instructions from you, Wakasugi will be able to carry them out satisfactorily, and I don't think there are any objections to it in the Foreign Office. I am now, so to speak, a skeleton of a dead horse. It is too much for me to be a sham existence, cheating others as well as myself. I do not mean to run away from the battlefield, but I believe that this is the course I should take as a public man.

I entreat you appreciate my true feelings and speedily grant my request. (Dispatched Oct. 22.)

Saturday, October 25, 1941

Converses with Admiral Pratt. Stayed overnight at the Hotel Plaza.

Monday, October 27, 1941

NO. 1004 (DISPATCHED 6:00 P.M., OCT. 27)

I had a talk with Admiral Pratt on the 25th. He is one of those men who admit that economic blockade and armed war have the same end, after all. He told me that there would be no war between Japan and America so long as the spheres of the Japanese activities were limited to the China Affair, but that he feared the consequences in case Japan should advance northward or southward. However, he said that the last hope lay in His Majesty and the President. Moreover, expressing his regret over Knox's* speech, he said that he made it a rule to be very careful not to hurt Japanese feelings in writing for journals or in broadcasting on the radio.

According to Admiral Pratt, Stark is no doubt the Chief of Naval General Staff to the President and the two are of the same opinion, but Stark cannot be said to [be] the "strongest" man. Admiral Hart is a man of strong character, though he has some enemies in naval circles, according to Pratt.

I also heard from other sources that the President, though desirous of maintaining stability in the Pacific, is wavering because of various advice given to him.

Pratt said that [W. Averell] Harriman, American envoy to the Soviet Union, is an able man, who holds the view that Stalin is not in a position to effect a separate peace, nor is Hitler able to do the same.

And against the argument that Italy should be induced to conclude a separate peace, Pratt stated that Italy would then get into the same scrape as France did and consequently there was no prospect of peace.

In short, he expressed the optimistic point of view, which is peculiar to Americans, that the war would be protracted, during which time one side would be more and more exhausted. Making the observation that the Atlantic War would be safe for Britain, he said that it was his opinion that if Japan would preserve her naval power, she would be able to have a big voice in the peace conference, but that it would be very disadvantageous for Japan to diminish that power. (Dispatched Oct. 27.)

Tuesday, October 28, 1941

Called on Lord Halifax. (Refreshments served.)

Wednesday, October 29, 1941

NO. 1010 (DISPATCHED 7:00 P.M., 29TH, WED.)

I submit to you the following report for your information:

1. Reserve Admiral Standley† told Mr. Kasai, member of Diet, who called on him, that an influential senator from the Middle West (many German-Americans are found there) had informed him that many persons in that part of the country were opposed to a German-American war, but favored a Japanese-American war. Admiral Standley, however, thought it to be a mere propaganda on the part of Germany. I heard a similar story before from O'Laughlin, who is closely connected with that part of the country.

2. Secretary of State Hull declared in Congress that, according to the American Government's view, the aims of the Tripartite Treaty were to

---

*Secretary of the Navy Frank Knox.
†Adm. William H. Standley, USN (Ret.) was a former Chief of Naval Operations.

"intimidate" America so that she would be unable to support Britain and also force her to retreat to her shores so as to make it impossible for her to exercise the right of self-defense til she had lost naval supremacy in the Atlantic.

Then he said that *America naturally desired peace but that there would be a greater possibility of ensuring peace if she demonstrated power*; and that the axis powers would rapidly push forward according to their policies if America should concede too much or betray her weakness. Now relating mainly to the situation in Tokyo, he continued that there were signs of Japan's "temperature" rising or falling according to the progress of the Soviet-German war and that the whole situation was "very delicate and very changeable" (*New York Times*, 28th).

Secretary of State Hull once said to me that since the Americans and the Japanese were both "proud peoples," they would not be moved by "bluff."

3. Assistant Secretary of State Breckenridge Long is said to have stated to a certain Japanese visitor that it would be impossible to arrive at a Japanese-American understanding by the 15th of October. This Japanese visitor had stressed the advantages of quick consummation of Japanese-American understanding, referring to press dispatches from Tokyo.

4. Recently I have had talks with Lord Halifax twice and tried to feel out the British attitude toward a Japanese-American understanding. Britain seems to follow [in] the wake of America after all, as would be seen in Churchill's speech.

Lord Halifax hoped that *Japan would bear patiently after mature consideration* because both Britain and the U.S.A. did not want any complications in the Pacific. He avoided going deep into the "embargo" now being enforced by Britain and the U.S.A.

(Dispatched 29th.)

Tuesday, November 4, 1941

NO. 1034* (DISPATCHED NOV. 4)

General Situation in the U.S.A.

Observing the recent situation in this country, I find that there are no signs of indignation in the people's sentiment toward Germany in spite of the frequent damages to American destroyers and merchantmen. The people here think that America will never break off relations with Germany, nor will she declare war. They think that Germany knows too well the disadvantages of waging war against America. This country has yet made no preparation for participating in the European war. For the present, this country is helping the countries siding with this country to the extent of supplying goods, defending and patrolling the seas and giving technical support.

As the country proper is not in imminent danger, the people in general are easygoing and they are more interested in questions of livelihood, such as the rising of prices, the increase of taxes, and inflation, than in war. The Govern-

*Not in *The "Magic" Background of Pearl Harbor*.

ment authorities, too, seem to be trying to make a cat's paw of other countries as much as possible and, if unavoidable, to appear on the final scene to win victory. Consequently they assume the attitude of not minding the continuation of war for five or ten years. Though they are supporting the Soviet Union at present, it is only to make a cat's paw of her, and not because they are friendly to Communist Russia.

The severance of economic relations with Japan is supported by the whole nation. As to the imminent danger of war, they seem to be of the opinion that they need not worry much, since the forces on the Pacific will be able to secure national defense, and in the southwestern Pacific, Britain, America and the Netherlands have gradually repleted [sic] their forces. They are not afraid at all of Japan's strong attitude toward America and are hinting that the ABCD powers' conference has arrived at an agreement on the distribution of materials and goods needed for war. They show an attitude of proceeding along the prearranged policies to the end.

The Army and Naval authorities, however, are not so consistently optimistic: (1) some admit that the British "morale" is not as high as is reported by the newspapers and that there is a possibility of a British-German peace, if the Soviet Union should drop out of the ranks; (2) they think that the Mediterranean Sea will face danger before long and, therefore, some make the observation that Churchill, in view of the American tendency to direct its attention to the Pacific, spoke directly to the President and succeeded in making the latter assume a cautious attitude in the Pacific; and (3) I should judge that the American authorities are well aware of the fact that the Pacific war will be very burdensome and difficult. Commentaries and newspaper reports indicate that once war breaks out, they will concentrate their power and watch for the chance of a decisive battle on the basis of a thorough examination of the whole war situation.

I hereby submit the above report for your information.

(Dispatched Nov. 4th, 4 P.M.)

Thursday, November 6, 1941

Called on Postmaster General Walker in the afternoon.

Friday, November 7, 1941

NO. 1055 (DISPATCHED 2:00 P.M. NOV. 7 [FRIDAY])

Called on Secretary Hull at 9 A.M. (Wakasugi accompanied me.) Attended reception in commemoration of Soviet Unions' Revolution at 5 P.M.

Re: Interview with Hull on the 7th.

At 9 A.M. on the 7th, I, accompanied by Wakasugi, met Hull (Ballantine sat in company with him), and told him that in accordance with the instructions of the Japanese Government, it was our desire to settle Japanese-American relations as soon as possible. Hull replied that there were in the world at present two influences fighting each other, that since neither side could win over the other swiftly, there would be a danger of steadily entering into a chaotic state of "anarchy," and that if Japan and America should adopt peaceful policies in the Pacific at such a time, this chaotic condition could be prevented.

I explained to him as follows on the basis of your instructions: (1) Of the three pending problems, two are likely to be solved somehow or other. In respect to the stationing and withdrawing of our troops, we are ready to make the maximum concession permissible under the state of our home affairs. (2) We earnestly desire that America would cooperate with us in settling our relations with her by taking a long-range view of the present situation from the standpoint of friendship between Japan and America. (3) Our Government instructed me to settle the question as soon as possible after fully explaining Japan's resolution and standpoint to the President and the Secretary of State. (4) We ardently desire the speedy consummation of our negotiations, because Japan's state of affairs has become so "impatient" after six months' negotiations that the situation is serious. (5) In view of the seriousness of the current situation, a parley will be started in Tokyo also, parallel with that conducted here. Thus explaining, I submitted the proposals instructed by you, saying that we proposed the above in the most friendly and conciliatory spirit, and asked him to agree to them from a long-range view of the situation.

After reading them carefully, Hull, nodding assent to the principle of non-discriminatory treatment, said that this would be advantageous to Japan too. Regarding the stationing and withdrawing of our troops, he simply inquired about the proportion of the troops to be stationed to those to be withdrawn. To this, I explained that the greater part would be withdrawn, stationing only a portion. I also gave explanation, based on your instructions, on the right of self-defense. To this he replied that he would answer afterwards after studying the subject. I decided to give detailed explanation and obtain a reply in my next interview with the President.

Further, Hull revealed to me that, as he had told me before, it was necessary to hold a conference among Britain, China, the Netherlands and other countries concerned in regard to the maintenance of peace in the Pacific and that the United States was consulting with China in respect to the Chinese question. Then he asked me as his own idea what would be Japan's opinion if the supreme authorities of China should declare to the Japanese Government and people China's sincere friendship for and trust in Japan and express the desire to restore friendly relations between Japan and China. To this, Wakasugi asked Hull in return whether this question was made after he had ascertained China's intention. Hull said that it was entirely his own personal idea, and *that it would set a very good example and influence to the world.* However, it seems to me that he probably put this question *after he had obtained China's opinion beforehand.*

Hull wished me to refer the aforesaid idea of his to the Japanese Government for its opinion. I simply replied that I would take it into consideration.

(7th, 2 P.M., No. 1055.)

Sunday, November 9, 1941

At night I called on Walker. Ordering the room cleared, he told me substantially as follows, with extremely earnest attitude:

"I tell this only to you, swearing to God. Both our 'boss' and the Secretary of State have received authentic report that Japan has decided a policy of taking action. So the interview with the President tomorrow, the 10th, will be, in a word, a perfunctory one and almost no hope is placed on Kurusu's coming to Washington."

I told him that he was wrong and explained that although Japan was becoming impatient on account of the economic oppression against her and was longing for a swift settlement, she was sincere in her wish to reach an understanding with America.

His talk, in brief, seemed to disclose the substance of the Cabinet conference yesterday, the 8th. He informed me that, although the President and Hull placed unshakable confidence in me, they possessed authentic report on the situation in Tokyo.

Monday, November 10, 1941

NO. 1066 (DISPATCHED 10TH)

1. We had more contact with Thomas (member of the Senate Committee on Foreign Relations who is intimate with Hull).

The gist of his report is as follows:

America is not "bluffing," but will fight Japan, if Japan dares undertake further invasion. The Americans are spiritually prepared for the worst and the Navy is "ready for action."

2. Yesterday (Sunday) evening, a cabinet secretary, ordering the room cleared, told me in earnest with an introductory remark that he was disclosing the matter only to me, swearing to God, in view of my intimacy with him, that the U.S. Government had obtained an authentic information [sic] that Japan would start action very soon and hence considered that neither my visit to the President on Monday nor Kurusu's coming to America would have any important effect on the general situation. Therefore, I explained to the minutest detail that, although the Japanese people had become especially "impatient" since the "freezing" and had been longing for the swift consummation of Japanese-American understanding, neither the Government nor the people wanted a Japanese-American war but desired friendly relations to the last. To this he replied that their "boss" (the President) believed the aforesaid information and so did the Secretary of State.

As for the comments seen in the newspapers and magazines here, excepting the *Daily News* and the Hearst papers, a Japanese-American war seems to be far more popular than a German-American war and there are some among Englishmen who even try to avail themselves of this popularity. As to military and naval cooperation between Britain and the U.S.A., a preliminary understanding is reported to have been reached and some urge the necessity of dispatching a part of the British fleet to Singapore. We cannot be sure that the President will not be influenced by domestic political considerations to move toward this direction. *Anyhow, the abovementioned cabinet secretary stated that the U.S.A. would never take the initiative of starting action, but once Japan starts action, she would surely do the same to keep her honor by force of past circumstances.*

3. In my interview with the President today, the 10th, I will do my utmost to carry out the purpose of your instructions.

November 10, 1941

INTERVIEW WITH THE PRESIDENT (THE SECRETARY OF STATE AND WAKASUGI BEING PRESENT ALSO).*

I had an hour's talk with the President from 11:30 A.M. I read our so-called "final proposal" from my prepared "statement." The President's answer to this may be summarized as follows:

(a) The whole world was in danger because of disturbances caused by the "forces of aggression." He earnestly desired that the world would return to the regular course of peace. From the spirit of "fair play," he would do his best to contribute to the establishment of peace and stability all over the Pacific. To this end, we should give practical efficacious results to the welfare of humanity. He wished the preliminary parley would produce such good results as to form the basis for our negotiations and promised to endeavor to expedite this parley.

He wished Japan would take "peaceful courses" and make clear that she would never resort to opposite measures. This, he believed, was the way to achieve our mutual[ly] desired end.

(b) The United States desired to prevent the war from extending farther and to establish everlasting peace.

(c) He hoped the principle of nondiscrimination would be carried out throughout the world, which was just the contrary of what Germany had generally been adopting in Europe.

In view of the failure of the American high-handed policy in the past, he adopted a good neighbor policy which brought about friendly relations between the U.S.A. and the other countries of America. Thus he stressed the need of new policies to cope with the new situations.

(d) When I pointed out that the economic oppression had made the Japanese people "impatient," he annotated the term "modus vivendi" by saying

*Nomura dispatched two messages to Tokyo convering this conversation. One, No. 1069, was a brief summary; No. 1070 was a detailed account.

that sometimes a "modus vivendi" was necessary in order to live, but I could not understand clearly what he really meant.

At our parting, I said that even though I knew there was a limit to what an ambassador could do, I could not help feeling keenly my responsibility to the present and coming generations of the Japanese people and that it was not my wish to be the last ambassador. To this, the President listened intently, and so did Hull.

Wednesday, November 12, 1941

INTERVIEW WITH HULL ON THE 12TH*

I had a talk for an hour and a half with Secretary of State Hull (Wakasugi accompanied me; Ballantine sat with Hull). Hull inquired of me whether the new cabinet also would confirm the note dated August 28th (taking out the note) and he also handed to me a note, explaining the "suggestion" concerning peace between Japan and China, which he had made to me in our last interview.

As to our proposal on three questions, he replied that the United States, too, recognizing the acute state of the present situation, was hastily deliberating on them, but that it was difficult to settle overnight questions that had been pending for ten years. According to him, we shall have an answer the day after tomorrow.

(a) Asking him the connection between the aforesaid "suggestion" and the consummation of the Japanese-American negotiations, I inquired whether it could be construed that China held the key to the solution of Japanese-American relations, if it was his opinion that the Japanese-American negotiations would not be consummated in case mutual agreement between Japan and China is not reached. Hull, however, referred only to the application of the general principle to China and so on, but failed to give a clear answer to the above inquiry.

Further, he told me that the U.S.A. had already apprised in a general way Britain and the Netherlands on this matter and that he believed they were ready to sign simultaneously with the U.S.A. as soon as the basis of negotiations are agreed upon. To this Ballantine added that, as had been stated in the proposal of June 21, Japan could not participate "*kanyo*" in the affairs of other countries with the conditions contrary to the principles the United States advocated.

(b) When I clarified that the period of stationing troops was not indefinite, he hinted that it was difficult to admit the indefinite stationing of troops under the policy of no interference in other countries' internal affairs.

---

*While this is not indicated as a telegram in the diary, Nomura sent a very detailed account of this conversation to Tokyo as No. 1087.

(c) Referring to the Tripartite Alliance, he said that he found it very difficult to fully explain it to politicians and others, because some said it was peaceful, while others maintained that Japan had an indivisible relation with Germany. He declared that, since Hitler would not remain long in power, he thought it necessary to devise a postwar program. He expressed the opinion that, if Japan would cooperate with the United States as "leaders" in a peaceful program, it would be necessary for Japan to remain in the Tripartite Alliance in case an agreement for general peace in the Pacific is reached. Thereupon, I strongly explained to him the compatibility of the Tripartite Alliance and a peaceful plan, citing the Anglo-Japanese Alliance as an example.

(d) I added that Japan naturally did not desire to resort to force and that she would have no need of force as long as she could obtain oil and other raw materials from the U.S.A. and the Dutch Indies.

Saturday, November 15, 1941

Accompanied by Wakasugi, I called on Secretary Hull at 9:00 A.M. (Ballantine was in company with Hull.)

Ambassador Kurusu arrived here at 1:30 P.M.

INTERVIEW WITH HULL ON THE 15TH*

(1) The proposals (including a proposal for a joint Japanese-American statement) for nondiscrimination in trade and commerce were made.

(2) When I insisted that the conversations had reached the stage of "negotiations," he declared that it would be very improper for us to assume that Japan and the U.S.A. had initiated negotiations between themselves only, before the United States had negotiated with Britain and the Netherlands, because (as Japan, too, had hoped) it was necessary to negotiate with them, too, in order to settle this issue. He was very much dissatisfied, saying that the Japanese demand was "peremptory.")

(3) As to the Tripartite Alliance, Hull said that, in view of the fact that Japan was attempting to arrive at a peaceful agreement with the U.S.A. on the one hand and stressing the military alliance with Germany on the other, he found it rather difficult to explain this contradiction to the American public and the world, though he himself understood my explanations. Such being the case, he wanted to confirm the intentions of the new cabinet toward peaceful policies; namely, *he would like to have the new cabinet confirm the Japanese Government's statement which was presented last time and the Japanese Government's intention in regard to the American*

---

*Nomura dispatched two messages covering this conversation, the gist in No. 1095, the details in No. 1106.

proposal of June 21 for political stability throughout the whole Pacific (though Japan wished to limit it to the southwestern Pacific). He further stated that *the U.S.A. would reply* on the other two problems *after receiving answers to today's proposals.*

Hull further said that, although a neutrality treaty had been concluded between Japan and the Soviet Union, the United States did not desire to see large forces set up in opposition on the frontier and that she also wished that the Tripartite Alliance Treaty would prove to be a scrap of paper when a Japanese-American understanding is reached. To this, I strongly elucidated the compatibility of the Tripartite Alliance and Japanese-American peace, giving him various explanations.

Upon my telling him at parting that Tokyo would be disappointed over our conversation today, he replied in such a manner as to give the impression that there was still room for negotiation.

Monday, November 17, 1941

I called on Secretary of State Hull at 10:30 A.M., accompanied by Kurusu.

Hull said that the absence of far-sighted statesmen after World War I caused the present situation of the world. He stressed the necessity of taking measures for preventing such a situation from reemerging.

Kurusu said that the responsibility resting upon both Japan and the United States was great and that before everything there were things that needed swift disposition between Japan and America, etc.

INTERVIEW WITH THE PRESIDENT*

I called on the President at the White House at 11 A.M.

The President said in substance as follows:

(1) "There is no last word between friends."

(2) Many of the nonaggression pacts are now "out of date," but the establishment of a "general understanding" may save the situation.

(3) In regard to the Chinese question he had heard of the difficulty of withdrawing troops, but the U.S.A. has no intention to "intervene" or "mediate" in the Sino-Japanese question. She is simply trying to be an "introducer," though he doesn't know whether this term is used in diplomatic phraseology.

(4) Kurusu explained that if a great understanding regarding the Pacific should be arrived at, it would "outshine" the Tripartite Alliance and automatically dispel all suspicions as to the application of the alliance.

Hull stressed the necessity of self-defense against the danger of Germany

---

*Nomura sent a very detailed account of this meeting to Tokyo by No. 1118.

coming on as far as South America after conquering Britain and gaining possession of the British fleet.

(5) The President said that he would see us again if we so desired after a talk with Secretary of State Hull.

Secretary Hull handed us a note on the two problems of confirming to the Konoye Cabinet's statement and expanding the southwestern Pacific question into the whole Pacific question.

Tuesday, November 18, 1941

Called on Secretary of State Hull at 10 A.M. and had a talk (for three hours) with him. Called on Walker at 9 P.M.

INTERVIEW WITH HULL*

Hull expatiated on the incompatibility between the American peaceful policy and Hitler's "conquest" policy and on the difficulty of readjusting Japanese-American diplomatic relations so long as Japan was tied up with Hitler by the Tripartite Alliance. He further commented on the impossibility of effacing from the American people's mind the idea that Germany would carry out a "conquest" policy in Europe and that Japan, too, would do the same in East Asia. He feared that there might be some Americans who would even argue that the U.S.A. was supporting Hitlerism through Japan. Hull insisted that even if an agreement is reached between Japan and America, such an agreement would be of no use, if the relations between the two countries were similar to those now existing between Japan and the Soviet Union.

Against Kurusu's explanation that the aim of the Tripartite Alliance is not to expand [by] force of arms, Hull insisted on the necessity of carrying it into effect actually.

Seeing that the situation had come to an impasse, I explained in detail the crisis in [the] southwestern Pacific and proposed a tentative plan to return to the status existing before the "freezing." After making various refutations, he promised to take the proposal into consideration.

Wednesday, November 19, 1941

At 5 P.M. called on Secretary of State Hull at his private residence. Engaged in chats only.

NO. 1136

Representation of Opinion (Dispatched 10:20 A.M. on the 19th)
    At a time when Japanese-American relations have become acute and we

*This diary item is a very brief synopsis of a long telegram, No. 1131, sent on 18 November. Nomura also sent a synopsis by No. 1127.

are at the crossroads, it is beyond my imagination to judge how worried you ministers are who occupy seats in the Cabinet and bear the great responsibility of saving our country and people.

Now, the courses which our Empire should take on this occasion are as follows:

1. To maintain the status quo.
2. To break the deadlock by military advance.
3. To establish a state of mutual inviolability by some means or other.

Course 1 will cause both sides to strengthen preparedness and dispatch additional fleets which will bring about a situation full of dynamite and finally lead to an armed clash, though there may be some difference of time when compared with course 2. Course 3 is a makeshift to settle the situation for the present by a modus vivendi and to make every effort to achieve our objectives during the interval of peace. In fact, yesterday's telegram No. 1134 was intended to give this opinion. I know quite well that our Government will be discontented with that idea, but *I do not think it opportune to wage a great protracted war* when the country is in an exhausted condition after the Manchurian Incident and the succeeding four years of the China Affair. In my opinion, a temporary truce based on a "give-and-take" principle at present will be a stepping-stone for future great achievement.

I hereby express the foregoing view as a supplementary explanation of my telegram of yesterday. *Kindly communicate this to the Premier.*

Thursday, November 20, 1941

At noon, I called on Secretary of State Hull at the Department of State and had a talk with him for an hour and a half.

NO. 1147

INTERVIEW WITH HULL

To Kurusu's explanation on the various items of our proposal "B," Hull asked no important questions on items other than the particular item promising that no measures or acts shall be taken as will obstruct the efforts toward a general peace between Japan and China. He showed great disapproval of this item and repeated his past contentions against the Tripartite Alliance. Hull explained that it would be difficult for the U.S.A. to discontinue her support of Chiang Kai-shek so long as there was an ineffaceable doubt in the American people's minds; that in opposition to Germany's "conquest" policy, the United States was supporting Britain on the one hand and Chiang Kai-shek on the other and hence so long as Japan's policy did not definitely become a peaceful policy, the support of Chiang Kai-shek would be tantamount to the support of Britain; and that American rights and interests had been infringed upon before the situation had come to what it was at present.

Thereupon Kurusu asked him if it was not quite proper for the U.S.A. to suspend the support of Chiang since the President had declared he would act as an "introducer."

To this Hull explained that the President had said so on the assumption that Japan's policy would be peaceful. Then I explained to him that since no progress had been made in regard to two or three points in our proposal "A," and since in the meantime the situation had become acute, today's proposal aimed to bring about a speedy compromise in order to alleviate the tense situation between Japan and America, especially in the southwestern Pacific, and to restore a friendly atmosphere even a little, and thereafter expedite the negotiations.

Hull replied in a sad tone that he understood what I had said, but that there was the aforesaid difficulty, adding that he and I bore a great responsibility toward the American and Japanese peoples, respectively, and also to all of humanity. However, he promised to sympathetically study our proposal.

Saturday, November 22, 1941

Accompanied by Kurusu, I called on the Secretary of State at 8:00 P.M. and had a three hours' talk. (Ballantine sat with Hull).

CONVERSATION WITH SECRETARY OF STATE HULL

To sum up the talk we had on the night of the 22nd, Hull stated that the U.S.A. would gradually restore Japanese-American trade and commerce, if Japan would adopt a peaceful policy. Regarding the cooperation among the countries concerned, Hull said he had fully discussed it with the representatives of these countries, and that they would hold a second talk by Monday, after consulting with their respective home governments. This was the best he could do, as there was a limit to his ability, Hull added. While recognizing the reason for the pressing demand from Tokyo, he seems to believe that there is no reason why Japan cannot wait for a few days more.

I hear that Hu Shih,* who had been ill in bed, also came in haste on the 22nd to participate in the later stage of the conference. The Secretary of State has no intention of acting as a go-between for Japan and China at present, and he maintains that the discontinuation of the support of Chiang is very difficult. However, he betrays the attitude that the present extent of support does not seem so great and that there is the possibility of developing the above problems depending upon the progress of the peaceful policy. For the present, America appears to be trying to put off the China problem, but according to authentic information from other sources, she seems to take the view that if the period necessary for stationing Japanese troops is, even under "indefinite period of stationing troops," limited to four or five years as the first period and then set another date depending upon the subsequent developments, there will be no special objection against it, but if it is for an indefinite period of

*Chinese Ambassador to Washington.

time, it will run counter to the principles of *nonannexation* and of respecting *sovereignty*.

(Hull said again that he was very sorry that the preliminary conversations had to be suspended in July because Japan had advanced her troops to French Indochina while the conversations were still in progress. He is indirectly warning us not to duplicate such a thing again.)

Hull pointed out that the transfer of troops from the southern part of French Indochina to the northern part would be of no avail in alleviating the situation in the southwestern Pacific, because the countries concerned would still be held in check and find it necessary to "freeze" their forces, thus making the situation not much different from what it is at present. Thereupon I explained that, as I look at it from a strategic point of view, it was a great concession and would greatly contribute to the peace of that area. To this the Secretary assumed an attitude of not being able to understand strategic affairs, saying that the nature of the conversations was kept to himself only, allowing no participation by others (but he admitted that he had spoken to a few influential senators).

Showing him the preamble of our proposal "B," I tried to ask him article by article if he accepted or rejected it. Apparently viewing proposal "B" as a "demand" toward the U.S.A., he stated in a very displeased tone that he saw no reason why we should make such a demand, and that he was "discouraged" by the fact that we had forcibly demanded acceptance or rejection in spite of the fact that he had done his utmost so far. We parlayed with a presence of mind and remained unexcited, and so did he.

The Secretary hoped that Japan would keep in step with the American peaceful policy, as the United States was negotiating with Japan on the assumption that we were taking the golden mean of peace. (Dispatched the 23rd, 1 p.m., No. 1161.)*

Tuesday, November 25, 1941

In the afternoon I called on Walker and learned the difficulty of accepting our proposal "B."

Wednesday, November 26, 1941

At 5 p.m., I called on the Secretary of State (accompanied by Kurusu) and had an hour's talk with him, who handed to me three documents.

MOST IMPORTANT

INTERVIEW WITH SECRETARY OF STATE HULL†

The Secretary of State said to the following effect:

(1) He is very sorry to say that he cannot agree to our proposal "B"

---

*Nomura dispatched further details in No. 1159.

†No. 1189 covers this conversation.

(excepting Nos. 6 and 7), which was submitted to him on the 20th, though he has studied it for five days (he discussed it with the countries concerned, too).

(2) This proposal is one which is made up of the American proposal of June 21 and the Japanese proposal of September 25. He is obliged to make this proposal in view of the demand of American public opinion that China should not be left to her fate and also in view of the unpeaceful discussions carried on by Japanese high officials.

(3) The U.S.A. is not demanding the immediate application of the principle of discrimination in China. It is a general principle.

(4) To Japan's opposition to the revival of the nine power machinery, the Secretary of State made no refutation.

(5) By the withdrawal of troops stipulated in No. 3, the U.S.A. does not mean to ask the immediate withdrawal of troops, he said. To our contention that we cannot leave the Nanking Regime to its fate, Hull said that the Nanking Regime had no power to rule over China. Then I said that I never dreamt the President had meant such a thing when he told us that he would be an "introducer" and so forth, but Hull gave no particular answer to this.

(6) Kurusu told Hull that, since this proposal included items absolutely unacceptable to the Japanese, because they were tantamount to pressing Japan to make as much concession as possible in respect to the Tripartite Alliance on the one hand and urging her to beg China's forgiveness on the other, we wondered whether or not we should transmit it as it was to our home government. He added that we would decide after talking it over between us two.

(7) I asked whether the U.S. considered there was no room for consideration other than this proposal. Pointing out that the President had told me some time ago that there are no last words between friends, I requested Hull to arrange for an interview with the President. Saying that this was one plan, he agreed to do so.

Wednesday, November 26, 1941

NO. 1180 (DISPATCHED THE 26TH)

MY OPINION (THE GIST ONLY)

I believe it advisable at this juncture to have the President wire to His Majesty the Emperor his desire for Japanese-American cooperation with the object of maintaining peace in the Pacific and in reply to it have His Majesty send a telegram to the President, thereby clearing the present atmosphere and providing sufficient time for Japan to propose the establishment of a neutral zone comprising French Indochina and Thailand, taking into consideration the possibility of protective occupation of the Netherlands Indies by Britain and the U.S.A. on our side.

According to my observation, the rupture of the negotiations will not necessarily bring about a Japanese-American war, but since the advance of British and American troops into the Netherlands Indies is expected, there will eventually occur a clash between Japan and Britain and the U.S.A. as the result of an attack by our side. Furthermore, it is doubtful whether Germany would respond to the demand for the fulfillment of treaty obligations. The China Affair also will be protracted.

Thursday, November 27, 1941

At 2:30 P.M. called at the White House (accompanied by Kurusu) and had an hour's talk with the President.

INTERVIEW WITH THE PRESIDENT (27TH)*

The President said to the following effect:

(1) In World War I, Japan and the U.S. took sides with the Allies. Germany then could not grasp the other nations' mind.

(2) It is a pleasure to learn that there are in Japan many lovers of peace who are exerting their utmost for peace. A great majority of the Americans are doing the same. *He still places great hope in them.*

(3) On my saying that the new proposal would disappoint Japan, he said that he was also disappointed that things had come to such a pass. *Japan poured over the U.S.A. her first cold water when she advanced into French Indochina and now there is the danger of a second cold water.* (He means our advance into Thailand.)

(4) The fact that no peaceful words were uttered by the leaders of Japan during my negotiations with Secretary of State Hull had made the negotiations very difficult, he said.

(5) In his opinion *a temporary solution would be after all of no effect if we could not agree on fundamental principles.*

(6) To my question concerning China he stated that he had not given up his idea of introducing the two countries, but that it was necessary for both Japan and China to hope for it simultaneously. From his experience in domestic administration, he thought there was some way for it.

(7) When I expressed the hope that, though I had not yet received from Tokyo any instructions, some measure for breaking the deadlock would be found through the statesmanship of the President, whom I held in great esteem through thirty years' friendship, he stated that he wanted to see me again next Wednesday when he comes back to Washington. He should be very glad if developments which would contribute to finding a way out of the deadlock would occur in the meantime.

To the above explanations of the President, Secretary of State Hull added the following as the reasons why he thought a modus vivendi would be unsuccessful:

Japan is dispatching additional troops to French Indochina, thereby holding in check the troops of other countries, and furthermore, she is flinging up the Tripartite Alliance and the Anti-Comintern Treaty on the one hand and

*Nomura dispatched an account of this conversation by No. 1206.

demanding oil from the United States on the other. To this, American public opinion cannot agree. And then he pointed out the following contradiction:

When we are endeavoring to arrive at a peaceful settlement, the high officials in Tokyo are, on the contrary, advocating the establishment of a new order.

Friday, November 28, 1941

GIST OF TELEGRAM NO. 1209 (DISPATCHED ON NOV. 28TH)

Regarding the attitudes of Britain, Australia, the Netherlands and China as well as the U.S.A., there may be various arguments, in view of the President's "oral" statement on the 17th of August that the United States would take appropriate action in such an event and in view of the press comments, it is my observation that even if Britain and the U.S.A. do not oppose us by military action in Thailand, there is no small possibility that the United States will gather together the countries concerned and take the step of reinforcing their joint defense in the southwestern Pacific area.

Sunday, November 30, 1941

Tokyo is naturally dissatisfied with the proposal made by the Secretary of State last Wednesday (I met with the President on Thursday); there has been as yet no detailed instructions. As an interim measure, I promised to see the Secretary of State tomorrow, Monday. The U.S.A. has not yet declared that the negotiations have broken off, and the President started for Warm Springs last Friday, announcing that it all depends on what attitude Tokyo will assume.

This morning, the Australian Minister called on me and stated that it was necessary for Japan to stop her military movements in order to save the situation.

The newspapers utilized and played up the report that the Premier declared in a speech last night that Britain and American should be "purged" with a "vengeance." The President is reported to leave Warm Springs tomorrow, Monday (his return to Washington was scheduled for Wednesday) in order to cope with the situation in the Far East.

Monday, December 1, 1941

Called on Secretary Hull at 10:15 A.M.

INTERVIEW WITH THE SECRETARY OF STATE*

Calling on Hull, I communicated to him our Government's instructions. The Secretary, *referring to the trend of our Government's attitude and pub-*

---

*Nomura sent an account of this conversation to Tokyo by No. 1225.

lic opinion and the reinforcement of Japanese troops in French Indochina, said that the President's return to Washington was partly due to these factors. To this I offered various explanations and refutations to remove his misunderstanding, whereupon Hull expressed the wish that Japan, too, would state that she desires to establish peace in the Pacific through the consummation of the present negotiations and also supports the efforts of the Secretary of State and myself.

Regarding the reinforcement of the troops in French Indochina, he said that the U.S.A. was in possession of various intelligence reports and that the destinations of the reinforcements were unknown. *Since not only Thailand but all other areas in the southwestern Pacific were feeling the danger, the U.S.A. would naturally be forced to take counteraction,* he declared. Japanese public opinion and actions being such as described above, he said that there was no way of finding a way out of the situation. While he and the President fully agreed that a Japanese-American war would be not constructive but destructive, they were placed in a difficult position, he explained. He further referred to the circumstances which obliged him to propose last Wednesday's proposal in view of the situation in Japan and American opinion. And finally he expressed the wish that, in view of the present situation, Japan would take some measure for improving first of all public opinion, etc.

Tuesday, December 2, 1941

At 10:15 A.M. called on Acting Secretary of State Welles (at his request).

INTERVIEW WITH WELLES*

The Acting Secretary of State made several inquires through documents regarding our advance into French Indochina, saying that the inquiries were made under order from the President. I promised to transmit them to Tokyo. I explained that economic oppression was more poignant than force of arms and the Japanese people were now driven to an impasse of being obliged to choose between submission and breakthrough. I said that Tokyo was now giving careful consideration to the recent American proposal, but that I thought that this proposal was a great backward step as compared with the proposal of June 21 (Sept. 25th). I asked him if it was [sic] not true that, in view of the fact [that] withdrawal of troops from French Indochina was under proposal, the problem proposed by the American side would also be settled as a matter of course when the fundamental problems are settled.

The Acting Secretary of State paid much attention to my remarks and

*Nomura sent an account of this conversation to Tokyo by No. 1232.

said that the proposal of November 26th had been made under the necessity of clarifying first of all the American standpoint.

Anyhow, I observed that both Hull and Welles desired a peaceful solution.

OPINION

On the 1st of December (yesterday), I proposed a conference of the most trustworthy of the leaders of the two countries, the American side by Wallace and Hopkins, our side by Prince Konoye or Viscount Kikujiro Ishii, to be held in Honolulu. To this they replied on the 3rd that it was improper for Japan to propose this at this juncture.

Secretary of State Hull at a press conference made an important statement regarding the adjustment of Japanese-American relations. (For particulars see the accompanying clipping from the *New York Times*.)

Wednesday, December 3, 1941

OPINION*

To the Navy Minister and the Chief of the Naval General Staff:

It is true the other side is taking a firm attitude, but on the other hand, they desire peace and wish to resume the negotiations on receipt of a favorable (*"iro aru"*) Japanese reply.

Such being the situation, I earnestly wish to receive such replies to an American proposal of the 26th and to the inquires of the 2nd of December as will save the critical situation.

Thursday, December 4, 1941

In the documents handed to us on the 2nd by the Acting Secretary of State inquiring about the reinforcement of the Japanese troops in French Indochina, reference was made to the danger to the Philippine Islands, the Netherlands Indies, Burma and Malaya. The President gave detailed explanations of the above to the reporters. (See the annexed clipping from the *New York Times*.)

Received the following telegram from Sugi on Dec. 4:

"I can clearly picture your strenuous efforts. I withdraw my request. Your family at home are all well." Masato Sugi

Friday, December 5, 1941

At 11 A.M Dec. 5, I called on Secretary of State Hull† and submitted a written reply. I explained to him the reinforcement of our troops in French

---

*Nomura sent this request in amplified form to Tokyo by No. 1256.
†Nomura reported this conversation to Tokyo by No. 1261.

Indochina. Then I told him that lest such misunderstandings as the inquiries made by the President should arise, I believed it best to try to break the deadlock by adopting my proposal of November 20. As to the repeated reference to the sending of Japanese troops to French Indochina, I said this was a matter of "power politics." Pointing out that even in America it is held that the best defense line is attack, which idea is cherished especially by Army and Navy circles, I told him that our Army and Navy also could not remain indifferent to the reinforcement of the troops and fleets of the "ABCD" powers.

Then, saying that he had been severely criticized for having permitted the export of oil to Japan from the time the negotiations were started down to the end of July, when Japan advanced into French Indochina, Hull stated that it was very difficult to resume the supply of oil to Japan under the present circumstances.

Thereupon, I insisted on the necessity of breaking up the deadlock by taking up my proposal of November 20, as the aforesaid problem would be automatically solved when a general understanding for the improvement of Japanese-American relations is reached.

Our written reply was made public afterward by the White House.

Sunday, December 7, 1941

The day on which diplomatic relations between Japan and American were severed.

At 2 P.M., called on the Secretary of State and handed to him our reply (though it was instructed to be handed at 1 P.M., we could not make preparations in time).

After reading it through once, the Secretary of State said that he had told only the truth during the past nine months, but that he had never seen a public document more crowded with "distortions" than this one. (See accompanying clipping.)

The report of our surprise attack against Hawaii reached my ears when I returned home from the State Department; *this might have reached Hull's ears during our conversation.*

F.B.I. began strict surveillance from today and we began a life of confinement.

Monday, December 8, 1941

The President read his message to Congress. Congress, excepting Miss Jeanette Rankin, passed the declaration of war against Japan. (The President signed it at 4:10 P.M.) Britain declared war against Japan a little before America did.

The Imperial Headquarters in Tokyo made public the existence of a state of war at 6:00 A.M. on the 8th (Tokyo time; i.e., 4 P.M., Sunday, by Washington time).

Churchill, in his speech in the Parliament stated that "some of the finest ships" were reaching their destination at "the very convenient moment."

Saturday, December 13, 1941

Swiss Minister Charles Bruggman called on me. Making an introductory remark that he came to me in a private capacity, the Minister told me that he had received a report informing that Switzerland was to represent the American rights and interest in Japan and the Japanese rights and interests in the Philippine Islands and the Samoan Islands. *He was afraid that, if I should commit suicide in indignation over the treatment accorded by the American officials, it would immediately affect greatly the American officials in Japan.*

Toward evening Spanish Ambassador Don Juan Francisco de Cardenas called on me and told me that he had immediately come to me to inform me that, according to a telegram he had received at 4 P.M., Spain was to represent Japanese rights and interests in America. (Counselor and concurrently Minister Molina was with him [sic]).

According to this morning's papers, *Pravda* is reported to have predicted that Japan would be defeated, as she has to face the allied forces of Britain, America and China, but it did not refer to the attitude of the Soviet Union. The Russian authorities are reported to be taking a silent attitude.

Sunday, December 14, 1941

According to this morning's papers Litvinov* held a press interview yesterday (Saturday) and issued a statement concerning the policies of the Soviet Union. In response to reporters' questions he is said to have stated that *though Japan was the common enemy of the Soviet Union, Britain and America, the Soviet Union would concentrate her energies on the annihilation of Hitler and could not relax her efforts in the least for the consummation of this object.*

Judging from the reports in the various papers, it appears that, though serious damage was suffered in the Japanese attack against Hawaii, the public has calmed down a little owing to the measures taken by the authorities to quiet down the "panic" by holding back the disclosure of the actual state of things and the official announcement of the number of the killed.

They seem to have awakened from their dream of underestimating Japan's real power. Especially in regard to the real power of our Navy, partic-

*Maxim Litvinov, Soviet Ambassador to the U.S.

ularly its air wing, we come across comments which say that it was *"grossly underestimated"* or that *our bombings have "fiendish accuracy."*

Monday, December 15, 1941

Had a visit from the Spanish Ambassador and the Counselor.

In the afternoon, called on the Spanish Ambassador and the Swiss Minister to return courtesies (accompanied by the F.B.I.).

Tuesday, December 16, 1941

Today is my birthday. I am now fully sixty-four years old.

This morning's papers carried the President's report to Congress yesterday concerning Japanese-American relations. They hinted that His Majesty the Emperor's implication in this treacherous act would become a serious problem in Japan's national structure.

They are endeavoring to calm down public opinion by publishing yesterday's statement of Secretary of Navy Knox. The paragraph which disclosed that *the responsible officers were "not on the alert against a surprise attack"* is arresting public attention. It appears that the Navy and Army will start investigations first of all. And it seems that dissatisfaction still prevails in congressional quarters; Chairman Connally* of the Committee on Foreign Relations, for instance, is reported to have said, "I am pained and grieved at its seeming failure of its high duty."

Wednesday, December 17, 1941

According to a London dispatch in this morning's paper, Britain and Australia are beginning to feel uneasy about the ability of the Commander of the Far Eastern Forces in view of the situation in the Far East, especially in the sinking of the two battleships, the loss of the Kota Bharu airdrome, the destruction of oil fields in Sarawak and the imminent threat against Singapore. Criticisms are leveled against Duff Cooper's incompetency as First Lord of the Admiralty, [Air Chief Marshal Sir Robert] Brooke-Popham's failure to provide sufficient number of fighters for land and sea operations, and [Admiral Sir] Tom Phillip's† lack of many years' experience in sea service.

Under date of Dec. 16th, the Pearl Harbor Investigation Commission was officially created. (It consists of five members: Admiral [William H.] Standley, [Rear Admiral Joseph M.] Reeves, [Major] General [Frank B.] McCoy,

*Senator Thomas T. Connally.
†Commander of the British Far Eastern Fleet.

Brigadier General [Joseph T.] McNarney, and Justice [Owen J.] Roberts of the Supreme Court, who is chairman of the Commission.

According to the *New York Times* of the 17th, Secretary of State Hull is reported to have sent on November 27th a warning to every department (including the Army and the Navy Departments, of course) of the U.S. Government just after handing over his "final proposals)" to Japan. (The same paper carried on the 18th an article confirming this.)

Thursday, December 18, 1941

Under date of December 17th, [Adm. Chester W.] Nimitz appointed Commander in Chief of the U.S. Fleet in the Pacific; [Lt. Gen., Delos C.] Emmons, of Air Force origin, Supreme Commander of the Army in Hawaii; and Brig. General [Clarence L.] Tinker, Commander of the Air Force.

Though it is generally argued that Hawaii and Singapore should be defended "at all costs" as two important bases, and the Philippine Islands are of second rate, the difficulty of defending Singapore is acknowledged by well-informed circles. Mr. [Hanson W.] Baldwin of the *New York Times* wrote in his paper on the 17th that the situation of the Pacific was "bleak." Citing the Japanese surprise attack on Hawaii, the sinking of the two British battleships, and the Soviet Union's unwillingness to allow the use of her territory in the Far East to the United States, he declared that the United States' ability to participate in [the] western Pacific had been reduced and the chance of launching operations greatly delayed.

Friday, December 19, 1941

The competency and boldness of our naval officers and sailors as demonstrated in the surprise attack on Hawaii and the sinking of the two British battleships have startled the world. The *Washington Post* of the 18th had the following account: When an A.P. reporter interviewed a British officer who was a veteran of many a battle, the officer stated that the Japanese never feared death, that bullets failed to prevent the Japanese from advancing, and that because of this, Japan had achieved such a triumphant success, which would not be expected from the German or Italian forces.

In his address at the commencement exercises of the Naval Academy on the 19th, Knox said to the following effect with reference to Japan: At present Japan has the "largest naval force" in the west Pacific and the bravery of her officers and sailors is characteristic of the "bravery of fanaticism." The commanders are skilled in their leadership and defy everything in the battlefield in order to achieve victory. However, the United States will surely win the final victory.

Under date of December 20th, [Adm. Ernest J.] King was appointed

Commander in Chief of the Combined Fleets and Ingersoll Commander in Chief of the Atlantic Fleet. King is highly spoken of as the man most fitted for the post.

Saturday, December 20, 1941

Through the defeat in Hawaii the Americans have come to acknowledge their past mistake in underestimating Japan's real power. Even those commentators or editorial writers who swaggered that Japan could be "pushed over" in a short time have changed their tune and now admit the impossibility of saving the critical situation of the Philippine Islands and Singapore by dispatching fleets. They simply urge the dispatching of planes from the Near East via Rangoon for the defense of the important base of Singapore. *Our overwhelming victory at the outset of the war really gave a great shock to the people at large.*

Mr. Baldwin of the *New York Times* pointed out the following defects (in the Sunday [31st] edition) [sic]:

1. The Army and the Navy, especially the Navy, had looked down on Japan and had indulged in self-confidence to such an extent that they might be called easygoing.

2. Lack of "unity of command" in Hawaii among the Commander in Chief of the Fleet, the Commander of the Harbor, and the Army Commander.

3. Too many warships were assembled in Pearl Harbor.

4. No torpedo nets had been laid at the entrance of the harbor.

5. Oil storage tanks, etc., were not placed underground.

6. Army and Naval planes were assembled in small areas.

Monday, December 22, 1941

British Prime Minister Churchill arrived at Washington and entered the White House on Dec. 22. Lord Beaverbrook [Minister of Supply], [Admiral of the Fleet Sir Dudley] Pound, Chief of the Naval General Staff [i.e., First Sea Lord], [Field Marshal Sir John] Dill, Chief of the Army General Staff, and [Air Chief Marshal Sir Charles] Portal, Chief of the Air Forces General Staff, comprised the important persons of his suite.

The President had interviews with Livinov, Hu Shih and Lauden, in that order, before Churchill's arrival.

The White House statements are given in the accompanying clipping.

Tuesday, December 23, 1941

The President signed the "draft bill" on the 23rd. Those between twenty-two and forty-four years of age will be subject to military service, the number of which will total 7,000,000.

The Senate carried the bill for increasing the naval personnel from 300,000 to 500,000 and the number of marines from 60,000 to 104,000.

The President and Prime Minister Churchill had an interview with the reporters. Churchill's consummate tact in meeting reporters testifies vividly to his fame as a veteran parliamentary statesman.

As to Singapore, he hinted that it would be defended to the last and later used as a starting point for [an] offensive.

According to an editorial in the *New York Times* (Dec. 24) the shortage of air force will prevent them from fully assisting Singapore and the Philippines Islands; the loss of Singapore will naturally lead to the loss of the Netherlands Indies; this is indeed a matter of national honor, but for all that, the detailing of air force to that part should be judged from the whole war situation.

Thursday, December 25, 1941

Today is Christmas.

Wake Island has fallen; landings of large forces said to have been carried out at Lingayen and Atimonan in the Philippine Islands; and the landings on Manban and Nasughu are also reported. The American Army has really got into a scrape. The experts here, recognizing the difficulty of holding out, seem to anticipate receipt of bad news unexpectedly earlier. Consequently the desperate defense of Singapore for the sake of Britain, America and the Netherlands is being vigorously urged.

The problem has been discussed at the White House, too, and the Prime Minister of Australia is reported to have demanded the defense of Singapore to the last.

Now, when seen from the American viewpoint, the war situation is very pessimistic and there is no possibility of its retrieval for a long time. For instance, the President, who possesses keen military insight, realized from the first the difficulty of two-front operations, as well as that of the Pacific operations. I remember his dwelling on this point once. Chief of Naval Operations Stark once declared that a Japanese-American war would exhaust both countries, only to benefit a third country. The opinions of Admiral Pratt, former Chief of Naval Operations, and of Admiral Standley and also Rear Admiral Sterling's comments in the press all predicted the present state of affairs. I have heard that even Secretary of War Henry L. Stimson had favored a Japanese-American understanding, since Chief of the General Staff George C. Marshall thought a Japanese-American war could be disadvantageous.

Secretary of State Hull, responding to my opinion that, if the war is extended to the Pacific, it would be "Armageddon," and the greatest misery of mankind, declared to me at the White House that we should actually cooperate to achieve our common objectives. Nevertheless, apparently influenced by the contentions of the officials of the State Department (this is disclosed in the "Merry-Go-Round")* and moved by crude public opinion and the strong opinion of Secretaries [Henry] Morgenthau [Jr.] and [Harold L.] Ickes,† he put out the so-called "final proposals" on November 26. Such is my observation. This may be considered as an evil caused by the lack of military insight on the part of American statesmen.

The high-handedness of the militarists is indeed annoying, but the lack of military insight on the part of statesmen and, moreover, the almighty authority of civil officials, as seen in America, must be said to be dangerous, too.

Friday, December 26, 1941

Hong Kong is reported to have fallen yesterday, Christmas Day.

The press is trying to make the people prepare themselves for the worst news, reporting that the Japanese forces had landed at various parts of the Philippine Islands and that, the air force strength being insufficient, it might be almost impossible to hold out.

The press is arguing that since the important base of Singapore is more important than the Philippine Islands, it is necessary for the U.S.A. to support its defense from the standpoint of "grand strategy." That is, it is said that the war will become harder and longer if this base is lost.

It may be imagined that they will undertake operations of sending submarines or airplanes either from the Near East or by aircraft carriers.

Saturday, December 27, 1941

Yesterday, the 26th, at the Anglo-American joint addresses in Congress, Churchill condemned Japan's participation in war, which address met with approval from all quarters.

Churchill appears to be a man of iron nerves. He went to church with the President on Christmas Day. Whereas the President looked very tired owing [to] the great burden of state affairs, Churchill maintained an imposing figure, despite his age of sixty-seven. He looks to be a man of high caliber.

According to the press, since Churchill is concentrating his attention to the Atlantic too much and putting off the Pacific Ocean, Australia and her neighboring countries are feeling uneasy about it, calling in question

*Nomura referred to Drew Pearson's widely read column, "The Washington Merry-Go-Round."

†Secretaries respectively of the Treasury and Interior.

whether they will be able to maintain the present situation if Singapore should fall.

According to the newspapers, the question as to whether or not energies should be concentrated for the defense of Singapore seems to be much discussed in America, too.

Sunday, December 28, 1941

The President wired today a message to the Philippines, saying "their freedom will be redeemed and their independence established and protected."

The *New York Times* (Dec. 29) said that, whereas the people were wondering why the American Air Force in the Philippine Islands was not active, this was so because the airdromes at Nichols, Clark and other places had been destroyed at the outset of the war and have not been restored since. Experts stressed the indispensability of "underground hangars," the paper reported.

Monday, December 29, 1941

Left Washington for Hot Springs, Va. My heart was full of emotion. Made an address [sic] to the inmates to the following effect:

(1) Generally speaking, it is when the national existence is at stake that we have recourse to arms. It has been my mission to strive for national development in obedience to the Imperial command, without appealing to arms, but I am sorry to say that things have gone wrong, contrary to my intentions. Time and again I laid my wish before the President that I would not like to be the last ambassador. But alas, my words came true! I am full of deep emotion indeed. I will never forget the wholehearted cooperation of the Minister, Counselor, and others of the staff members and the military and naval attachés Iwakuro and others. And I pay high tribute to the patriotic spirit of Envoy Kurusu and Secretary Yuki, who came from afar by air at the supreme hour, without any time to think about success or failure, advantage or disadvantage.

(2) Our operations are progressing favorably. The ingenuity and minuteness of our operational planning and our boldness and scrupulousness in putting them into practice have really made the enemy's blood run cold. But this we must remember; that a rich man is spoiled by his wealth, a tactician by his tactics, a wise man by his wisdom, and a brave man by his bravery. And so we must be prudent to the end[;] as the proverb runs, "Let the victor look to the laces of his helmet." And we must be prepared for a "long and hard war." In everything, danger comes soonest when it is despised.

(3) Since we are the representatives of the government and the people, we must really maintain our dignity in advance or retreat, whether we stand

or fall. Now, I wish to add that this is the best chance for training our minds and bodies, especially for improving our minds. I wish you young people would not miss this opportunity.

Tuesday, December 30, 1941

The *New York Times* gave a full account of the departure of the Ambassador and his followers, with a photographic insertion.

Australia and the Netherlands Indies have pointedly emphasized to the U.S. Government that the west Pacific is "equal in importance to Europe." Minister London* had a talk with the President.

Majority Leader Senator Alben W. Barkley† stated that "eventually" bombing raids against Tokyo might be carried out as "a terrible retribution."

Senator [Elbert D.] Thomas (of Utah) is reported to have said that the Japanese Ambassador and others in America, foreseeing the worst coming, had endeavored "in good faith" to prevent it. (the *Times*, 30th.)

Wednesday, December 31, 1941

In today's *New York Times*, Mr. Baldwin (retired Lt. Commander) said to the following effect in response to the criticism, "What's the Navy doing?"

The U.S. Navy was equally divided on both oceans from the beginning of this year. There might have been some changes in this detailment [sic] after the outbreak of war, but this takes much time, as the oceans are vast. In order to defend Singapore and the Philippine Islands, it is necessary to send arms, above all airplanes. But to this end we are forced to depend on vessels, excepting the transportation of bombers. [sic]

The Pacific fleet is being reorganized since the 7th of December, but in the Far East, we have no base except Singapore. Under the circumstances, we cannot carry out any large-scale operations against Japan at present. In the course of time it may be "possible and probable" to surprise attack Japan by means of [a] "carrier striking group" (by this he probably means "*koku sentai*") and by submarines. However, for the advance of large forces, the command over sea and air is essential, and "months or years of preparations" may be needed for it.

*i.e., Lauden.
†Senate Majority Leader.

Part III

Post–Pearl Harbor

Introduction

In the main, this section covers Japanese activities following the attack on Pearl Harbor although, as mentioned before, a certain amount of overlapping in time occurs. When Prange was collecting these studies, his prime interest was Pearl Harbor, so the material in this section is much less extensive than that contained in the other sections of this book. What is here, however, is valuable and interesting. We know of no better account of Japan's submarine warfare than that contained in the Shibuya monograph. As always, Chihaya's studies are informative and thought provoking. From Adm. Nobutake Kondo comes an excellent account of certain engagements in which he was involved.

Japanese Monograph No. 102: Submarine Operations December 1941–April 1942

Introduction

This is another of the many studies prepared in the Military History Section, Headquarters, USAFFE, in Tokyo during the occupation. As mentioned in our foreword, this study, like other such monographs, was prepared from memory and fragments of other documents. For details, see this study's foreword and preface. The principal compiler of this monograph was Capt. Tatsuwaka Shibuya. This officer, a submarine expert, was assigned to the staff of the 1st Air Fleet on 9 November 1941.* Prange knew Shibuya well and interviewed him a number of times.

Of particular interest is the account of the submarines' part in the Pearl Harbor attack. An example of the high regard in which the Japanese Navy held the submariners of that operation versus the taking for granted of the airmen is found on p. 18. The compilers could seriously believe that "the confusion in Pearl Harbor" was caused by the six midget subs, not the attacking aircraft, and that these subs, rather than the air raid, occasioned the American message "giving general warning."

A notable feature of Japanese submarine operations was the failure to exploit fully the submarine's capability against Allied commercial shipping, in sharp contrast to Germany's U-boat warfare in the Atlantic.

*Dates given are one day ahead in accordance with the Japanese calendar.

SUBMARINE OPERATIONS, DECEMBER 1941–APRIL 1942

Military History Section, Headquarters, Army Forces Far East

Distributed by Office of the Chief of Military History Department of the Army

1953

Foreword

This monograph was compiled by Capt. Tatsuwaka Shibuya, former staff officer of the Combined Fleet. Due to the lack of official documents this record was compiled partially from the recollections and personal papers of Capt. Shibuya and Comdr. Yasuo Fujimori, former staff officer (operations), Imperial General Headquarters, and partially from fragmentary battle reports of the Submarine Force. Additional material was obtained by interrogation of former Japanese officers of the Submarine Force.

Additional monographs covering the operations of Japanese submarines during World War II are as follows:

Title	Period	Mono No.
Submarine Operations in the Second Phase Operations, Part I	Apr. 42–Aug. 42	110
Submarine Operations in the Second Phase Operations, Part II	Aug. 42–Mar. 43	111
Submarine Operations in the Third Phase Operations, Part I	Mar. 43–Nov. 43	163
Submarine Operations in the Third Phase Operations, Part II	Nov. 43–Mar. 44	171
Submarine Operations in the Third Phase Operations, Part III	Mar. 44–Aug. 45	184
Imperial Japanese Navy in World War II	Nov. 41–Aug. 45	116
	14 January 1952	

Preface

Through Instructions No. 126 to the Japanese Government, 12 October 1945, subject: Institution for War Records Investigation, steps were initiated to exploit military historical records and official reports of the Japanese War Ministry and Japanese General Staff. Upon dissolution of the War Ministry and the Japanese General Staff, and the transfer of their former functions to the Demobilization Bureau, research and compilation continued and developed into a series of historical monographs.

The paucity of original orders, plans and unit journals, which are normally essential in the preparation of this type of record, most of which were lost or destroyed during field operations or bombing raids, rendered the task of compilation most difficult; particularly distressing has been the complete lack of official strength reports, normal in AG or G3 records. However, while many of the important orders, plans and estimates have been reconstructed from memory and therefore are not textually identical with the originals, they are believed to be generally accurate and reliable

Under the supervision of the Demobilization Bureau, the basic material contained in this monograph was compiled and written in Japanese by former officers, on duty in command and staff units within major units during the period of operations. Translation was effected through the facilities of Allied Translators and Interpreters Service, G2, General Headquarters, Far East Command.

This Japanese Operational Monograph was rewritten in English by the Japanese Research Division, Military History Section, General Headquarters, Far East Command, and is based on the translation of the Japanese original. Editorial corrections were limited to those necessary for coherence and accuracy.

Table of Contents

Charts

In November 1941, the submarines of the Japanese Navy suitable for use as first line strength consisted of 30 submarines of the newest type and 18 submarines of older types of almost equal efficiency. The second line strength consisted of 12 very old submarines which could only be used in the coastal waters of Japan or for training. In addition to these 60 submarines the Japanese Navy had under construction at the time 18 submarines to be completed by the end of 1942 and 11 to be completed by the end of 1943. Approval had been granted for the construction of an additional 38 submarines after the end of 1942 (Chart 1).

Operational Policy for Submarine Warfare

The fundamental operational policy for submarine warfare was formulated by the Japanese Navy in November 1941 at the time when it became neces-sary to prepare for the war with the States, Britain and the Netherlands. This policy called for the early annihilation of the enemy fleet by the coordi-nated efforts of submarine units, the surface fleet and the air force.

The United States Fleet in the eastern Pacific was the principal target of

Chart 1   Approved Submarine Construction (November 1941)

	Under Construction To Be Completed by the End of 1942	
Type I-15	*I-27, I-28, I-29, I-30, I-31, I-32, I-33, I-34, I-35* and *I-36*	10
Type I-176	*I-176, I-177* and *I-178*	3
Type RO-100	*RO-100, RO-101, RO-102* and *RO-103*	4
Type I-9	I-11	1
Total		18
	Under Construction To Be Completed by the End of 1943	
Type I-15	*I-37, I-38* and *I-39*	3
Type I-176	*I-179, I-180, I-181* and *I-182*	4
Type RO-100	*RO-104* and *RO-105*	2
Type RO-35	*RO-35* and *RO-37*	2
Total		11
	Approved for Construction To Be Started by the End of 1942	
Type I-18		6
Type I-52		3
Type I -54		3
Type I-9		1
Type I-176		3
Type RO-100		10
Type RO-35		12
Total		38
Grand Total		67

submarine operations and the United States, British and Netherlands Fleets in the Far East were classified as secondary targets. Disruption of enemy commerce on the key sea routes by submarine warfare was to be conducted against the United States, Britain and the Netherlands. These operations were to be conducted only in such a manner as not to interfere with the objectives of the main operation which would vary in accordance with the progress of the Fleet operation.

The distribution of submarines Japan had at the outbreak of the war and the assignment of duties thereof naturally had to be decided in accordance with the mission to be performed and the ability of particular submarines to perform the task. The organization of fleets was also decided with the same purpose in mind.

The 1st, 2d [sic] and 3d Submarine Squadrons which had the greatest operational ability and consisted chiefly of the newest type submarines made up the 6th Fleet (Chart 2). The 6th Fleet was organized under a single commander with the aim of destroying the United States fleets in the eastern Pacific. The 4th and 5th Submarine Squadrons, which were next to the first line strength but included old type vessels and those somewhat inferior in operational ability were attached to the Combined Fleet. The principal mission of those squadrons was the destruction of surface strength in the southern area and support of the invasion operations in the Philippines, British Malaya and the American Fleet after the outbreak of war[;] it was intended that two submarine squadrons, along with the 6th Fleet, were to engage in interception operations by shifting quickly to operations in the western Pacific.

The 6th Submarine Squadron, which was nearly equal in efficiency to the first line strength and consisted of submarines with mine-laying facilities, was attached to the 3d Fleet and was assigned chiefly as support for the invasion of the Philippines, Dutch East Indies and British Malaya. The remaining submarines capable of frontline operations were selected from the submarines of second line strength and were organized as the 7th Submarine Squadron. This squadron was attached to the 4th Fleet, with the assignment as a defense force to operate chiefly in the inner South Sea and Japanese waters. Those vessels of second line strength which were unsuitable for operations in the open sea were attached to the Kure Navy District Force as a component of the Homeland defense force and were assigned to the training of submarine crews.

Submarine Operational Plans

The Commander in Chief of the Combined Fleet, assuming that war with the United States, Great Britain and Netherlands would break out while

Chart 2   Assignment of Submarine Units (Beginning of the War)

Combined Fleet

4th Submarine Squadron	5th Submarine Squadron
Kinu (Lt. Cruiser-Flagship)	*Yura* (Lt. Cruiser-Flagship)
18th Submarine Division	28th Submarine Division
I-53, I-54, I-55	*I-59, I-60*
19th Submarine Division	29th Submarine Division
I-55, I-57, I-58	*I-62, I-64*
21st Submarine Division	30th Submarine Division
RO-33, RO-34	*I-65, I-66*
Nagoya Maru (Tender)	*Rio de Janeiro Maru* (Tender)

Sixth Fleet (Submarine Fleet)
(Flagship-Lt. Cruiser *Katori*)

1st Submarine Squadron	3rd Submarine Squadron
I-9 (Flagship)	*I-8* (Flagship)
1st Submarine Division	11th Submarine Division
I-15, I-16, I-17	*I-74, I-75*
2nd Submarine Division	12th Submarine Division
I-18, I-19, I-20	*I-68, I-69, I-70*
3rd Submarine Division	20th Submarine Division
I-21, I-22, I-23	*I-71, I-72, I-73*
4th Submarine Division	*Taigai* (Tender)
I-24, I-25, I-26	
Yasukuri Maru (Tender)	

2nd Submarine Squadron
I-7 (Flagship) *I-10*
7th Submarine Division
I-1, I-2, I-3
8th Submarine Division
I-4, I-5, I-6
Santos Maru (Tender)

Third Fleet	*Fourth Fleet*
6th Submarine Squadron	7th Submarine Squadron
Chokai (Lt. Cruiser-Flagship)	*Jingai* (Lt. Cruiser-Flagship)
9th Submarine Division	26th Submarine Division
I-123, I-124	*RO-61, RO-62, RO-63*
13th Submarine Division	27th Submarine Division
I-121, I-122	*RO-65, RO-66, RO-67*
	33rd Submarine Division
	RO-63, RO-64, RO-68

Kure Navy District Force
I-52, RO-31 (training only)
6th Submarine Division
RO-57, RO-58, RO-59

Japan was still at war with China, issued on 5 November 1941 the following fundamental operational policy:

(a) In the eastern Pacific, the American fleet would be destroyed and her supply route and line of operation to the Orient severed.

(b) In the Western Pacific, the campaign in Malaya shall be conducted to sever the British line of operation and supply to the Orient as well as the Burma Route.

(c) The enemy forces in the Orient shall be destroyed, their strategic bases captured, and important areas endowed with natural resources shall be occupied.

(d) Strategically important points shall be captured, expended in area and strengthened in defensive forces in order to prepare for a prolonged war.

(e) Enemy invading forces shall be intercepted and annihilated.

(f) Successful operations shall be exploited to crush the enemy's will to fight.

Based on this operational policy, the operational plans of the Combined Fleet in the first stage of the war were prepared. The Submarine Force (6th Fleet), the Carrier Striking Force, the South Seas Force, the Northern Force and the Main Force were to engage the United States Fleet. The Carrier Striking Force was to commence hostilities with a surprise attack on the enemy fleet in the Hawaiian Islands. The Submarine Force was to advance secretly to the Hawaiian Area prior to the opening of hostilities and support the Carrier Striking Force by observing and attacking the enemy fleet stationed in that area. A unit of the Submarine Force was also to attack the enemy fleet berthed in Pearl Harbor with midget submarines. These midgets, manned by a crew of two men, had a 46-ton displacement submerged. They were 23.9 meters in length and 1.85 meters in breadth and depth each. After release from the deck of the mother submarine, they were propelled by batteries and motor power at a speed of 19 knots and were capable of running for 50 minutes underwater. They were armed with two 45-cm torpedoes.*

*In 1934 two midget submarines were built by Capt. Kishimoto Kaneji at Kure Navy Yard for experimentation. It was intended that they be used as auxiliary weapons carried on board fast surface vessels. The two experimental models without conning towers had [the] shape of a torpedo. As the result of further experiments a small conning tower was fitted to each of them. They were called "A-targets" for confidential purposes.

Again in 1936, another two were built and were launched successfully from the *Chitose* (Seaplane Tender) in 1937. Mass production of this type was started in Kure under strict secrecy. In the summer of 1941 the Seaplane Tender *Chiyoda* was converted to a midget submarine carrier capable of carrying 12 midgets in her hanger and launching them through a hinged door at her stern. Necessary training was started of personnel to operate the midgets.

The South Sea Force, while carrying out the campaign against the enemy's strategic points in the South Sea, was to be prepared to engage the enemy fleet around Australia, while the Northern Force was to be prepared for possible Soviet intervention. The Main Force was to stand by in the western area of the Inland Sea, and take action when occasion demands [sic], in order to support the entire operation.

The Southern Force was to destroy and sweep away the enemy fleet in the Philippines, British Malaya and the Dutch East Indies and, in cooperation with the Army, gradually take over these areas.

In the event the United States Fleet assumed the offensive and appeared in the Western Pacific, the Southern Detachment Fleet and the 3d Fleet were to temporarily assume operational duties in the southern area, while the bulk of the Combined Fleet was to intercept and engage the invading United States Fleet.

Plans for the Hawaiian Operation

The Pearl Harbor attack was to be a surprise attack, initiated by an air attack, which would be sudden and complete. The submarine attack was necessary to obtain subsequent cumulative effects. The first priority was given to an air attack by the Carrier Striking Force. The principal aim of the Submarine Force therefore, was to render the result of air-attack more effective. Its principal operational duties were the secret preliminary reconnaissance of Lahaina Anchorage and of strategical points in the Aleutians and the South Pacific Areas; the tracking down and destruction of the enemy fleet, which might run out of Pearl Harbor escaping the air attack, and the interception of any counterattack against the Carrier Striking Force by the enemy fleet; participation of the Submarine Force in the attack calling for an attack by midget submarines against the enemy fleet in the harbor and the rescue of crews of aircraft of the Carrier Striking Force which might be forced down.

In the event the attack by the Carrier Striking Force on Pearl Harbor succeeded, the Submarine Force was to maintain submarine patrol and reconnaissance of Pearl Harbor for a long period of time after the Carrier Striking Force had withdrawn to home base. The disruption of enemy surface traffic between [the] West Coast of North America and Hawaii and submarine attacks on enemy air bases lying between Hawaii and Samoa Islands were to be carried out.

In compliance with the above operational duties, the commander of the Submarine Force formulated the Task Organization of his forces for the

---

At the end of October 1941, [the] Commander in Chief of the Combined Fleet decided to use midgets in the Pearl Harbor operation.

opening of hostilities. For command of the overall operation the commander of the 6th Fleet, Vice Admiral Shimizu Mitsoyoshi, was to be aboard the flagship *Katori* stationed in the Kwajalein atoll. The commander of the 1st Submarine Squadron, Rear Admiral Sato Tsutomu, was to command the 1st Submarine Group consisting of the *I-9, I-15, I-17* and *I-25*. The mission of this group was to patrol the sea northeast of Oahu, tracking down and annihilating any escaping vessels and in readiness for intercepting any counterattacks against the Carrier Striking Force. Assigned the same mission was the 2nd Submarine Group under the command of Rear Admiral Yamazaki Shigeteru, commander of the 2nd Submarine Squadron. The 2nd Submarine Group, composed of the *I-1, I-2, I-3, I-4, I-5, I-6* and *I-7* was to patrol the area between Oahu and Molokai. The commander of the 3rd Submarine Squadron, Rear Admiral Miwa Shigeyoshi, was to command the 3rd Submarine Group composed of the *I-8, I-68, I-69, I-70, I-71, I-72, I-73, I-74* and *I-75*. This group was to patrol the area south of Oahu and in addition to the mission assigned the 1st and 2nd Groups, the 3rd Group was to make prior reconnaissance of the Lahaina anchorage and during the attack was to rescue the crews of downed aircraft from the Carrier Striking Force. Also the Submarine *I-74* was to be in the vicinity of Niihau on the day of the attack. The Special Attack Unit, composed of the *I-16, I-18, I-20, I-22* and *I-24* under the command of Capt. Sasaki Hankyu, commander of the 3rd Submarine Division, was to attack the enemy fleet in the harbor with midget submarines. The submarines *I-10* and *I-26* under their respective commanders was [sic] to scout the Aleutian and South Pacific area. The Submarine Force was to be supplied by the supply ships *Ondo, Toamaru, Aratama-Maru* and *No. 2 Tenyo-Maru* which would be in the vicinity of Kwajalein or off the Homeland.

Besides the above forces, attached to the Carrier Striking Force from the 6th Fleet to perform patrol duties, were the submarines *I-19, I-21* and *I-23*. In addition to acting as the Patrol Unit in front of the Carrier Striking Force, this unit was to rescue the crews of downed aircraft and be prepared to resist counterattack.

Immediately after the air raid the Carrier Task Force commander was to assume command of the Submarine Force for a three-day period, for it was anticipated that the two forces would be operating in the same area.

The Patrol Unit attached to the Carrier Task Force naturally was to be under the direct control of the task force commander when the latter advanced or withdrew after the air raid. However, in the event the unit was found unnecessary in checking counterattacks of the enemy fleet, it was scheduled to return to the command of the Submarine Force as early as possible.

After the attack had been completed and submarines had returned to the control of the 6th Fleet the plan called for the 1st and 2nd Submarine

Squadrons to remain in the area for patrol and observation and to attack enemy vessels. The 3rd Submarine Squadron was to destroy surface traffic between the United States and Hawaii.

In advancing to Hawaiian waters, secrecy was of the utmost importance. The Submarine Force was to proceed on the surface by night and under water by day within a radius of 600 nautical miles of the Aleutians, Midway, Johnston, and Palmyra Islands. Taking into consideration the secrecy of advance, the time of starting the war, the speed of each submarine, and the time of completing preparations for war, the time to commence action and the routes were selected. The 1st and 2nd Submarine Groups were to depart Yokosuka around 20 Nov. 41, pass between the Aleutians and Midway north of Oahu and be within 300 miles of Oahu around 3 December 41. The 3rd Submarine Group was to depart Saeki around the middle of Nov. 41 and Kwajalein around 25 Nov. 41, proceed eastward from Kwajalein, passing south of Johnston and north of Howland and Palmyra reaching their station south of Oahu around 2 Dec. 41. The Special Attack Unit was to depart Kure around 20 Nov. 41, pass south of Midway and north of Johnston arriving off Oahu around 2 Dec. 41.

Although the secrecy of movement of the Special Attack Unit with midget submarines aboard was threatened thereby, the unit had to take the shortest route by passing between Midway and Johnston Islands because it was impossible to move forward the departure date of the mother submarines due to the delay in the preparation of the midgets.

On the assumption that the Carrier Striking Task Force would carry out the air raid on 8 December, it was planned that all submarines of the Submarine Force except the reconnaissance unit for strategic points were to arrive within 300 nautical miles of Oahu on 3 December and thereafter gradually tighten their dispositions arriving at close position for observation by the day before the attack.

The *I-72* and *I-73* were in charge of the secret preattack reconnaissance of Lahaina Anchorage and it was decided that both submarines should report their observation results by the 7th at the latest. In the event any enemy fleet was found in the Lahaina Anchorage, disposition of submarine groups with Oahu as its nucleus was expected to be changed so that its center would be transferred to Lahaina. Furthermore, it was decided that in this case the submarines of the Submarine Force should penetrate into the anchorage from three mouths, Pailele, Kalehi and Auau Channels, after the air raid of the Carrier Striking Task Force and carry out attacks on the fleet.

The mother submarines for the midget submarines were to be within 100 nautical miles of Pearl Harbor after sunset on 6 December, and there, all preparations for launching the midget submarines were to be completed. The mother submarines were to approach within 10 nautical miles of the mouth of the harbor secretly and launch the midget submarines after locating the harbor entrance. The attack was to be delivered between the first and the second waves of air attacks by the Carrier Striking Task Force, but the scheduled attack could be postponed until after sundown of the same day if circumstances required it. Each midget submarine, after launching attacks on the enemy fleet, was to sail counterclockwise around Ford Island, get out [of] the harbor and proceed to the rendezvous. The mother submarines were to surface some seven nautical miles west of Lanai Island on the night of the attack to pick up midget submarine crews. However, if the rescue was not possible on the first night, another attempt was to be made on the following night.

It was decided that the *I-10* would execute the reconnaissance of Fuji, Samoa and Tutiila and the *I-26* of the Aleutian Islands by 5 December. Furthermore, it was decided that, if they found a powerful enemy force, the submarines would keep the force under observation. If there was no such force, the submarines were to advance to a point halfway between Hawaii and the west coast of North America by the time of the outbreak of war.

It was prearranged that, in the event war was not to be commenced because of a favorable turn in the diplomatic situation while the Submarine Force was under way, it would turn back home without further orders.

The Hawaiian Operations

About the middle of November 1941, the 3rd Submarine Group, initiating the move on Hawaii, left Saeki for Kwajalein and the others followed almost as prearranged. The *I-10*, on strategic reconnaissance, set out from Yokosuka toward Fiji* and Samoa on 16 November, and the *I-26* toward Kiska and Adak on 19 November. The submarine of the Patrol Unit of the Striking Force left Yokosuka on 20 November for Hitokappu Bay, there joined the Carrier Striking Force and set out toward Hawaii on the 25th.

The Commander in Chief of the 6th Fleet who commanded the Submarine Force went on board the flagship *Katori* and arrived at Kwajalein on 5 December by way of Truk. The commanders of the 1st, 2nd and 3rd Submarine Squadrons who respectively commanded the 1st, 2nd and 3rd Submarine Groups proceeded to Hawaii on board the flag submarines, *I-9*, *I-7* and *I-8* respectively.

The 1st, 2nd and 3rd Submarine Groups and Special Attack Unit bound for Hawaii steered east as scheduled and from about 3 December gradually closed in on Hawaii. On the day before the attack, they completed the planned disposition. The strategic reconnaissance unit sighted no enemy

---

*Ed. note: After reporting no enemy in Suva Bay, Fiji Islands, *I-10*'s patrol plane was lost, whether to British gunfire or accident is not known. *I-10* searched for it fruitlessly for three days.

vessels or planes either at Kiska, Adak, Dutch Harbor or Suva except for an Astoria-type cruiser which was witnessed by the *I-10* off Pago Pago Harbor on 4 December. The *I-20* and *I-26* were halfway between the Hawaiian Islands and the American Mainland on the eve of the war. The Patrol Unit which had accomplished the Striking Force separated from the Main Force on 7 December and proceeded ahead at full speed. By the time of the attack on the following day, it had moved forward between the Striking Force and Oahu and completed its deployment.

Thus each submarine took up a position to watch over Pearl Harbor. Prior to this the *I-71, I-72* and *I-73* carried out secret reconnaissance missions around Lahaina Anchorage and reported to the Striking Force that no major unit of the United States Fleet was stationed there.

Security of secrecy was the supreme watchword among the submarines of the Submarine Force in the Hawaii Area and this was carried out so well that it is believed today that there was no chance of being discovered by the enemy till the day of the attack.

The Special Attack Unit approached the mouth of Pearl Harbor about 2300 on 7 December, and from there dispatched their midget submarines. The operation could be carried on without any interference due to the lack of enemy surveillance. It was presumed that the midget submarines penetrated deep into Pearl Harbor and, after sunset, attacked unguarded ships anchored in the harbor.

Each submarine which had dispatched its midget submarine kept on watching enemy forces around the mouth of the bay until sunset of the day of the attack and, returning to the rendezvous points after sunset, they carried on a search all through the night, but could not find a single one of their midget submarines. On the night of the 9th the search was again carried out, but it too was unsuccessful[;] therefore, the commander of the attack unit, deviating from the schedule, kept up the search again on the following day but it too was in vain.

Reliable information on the effectiveness of the midget submarine attack could not be obtained. It was believed that they caused a certain amount of damage to the enemy fleet considering the confusion in Pearl Harbor as witnessed by one or two submarines. A radio message of success from one of the midget submarines and an intercepted plain message dispatched from the United States forces giving general warning supports this belief.

When the air attack of the Carrier Striking Force commenced on 0330, 8 December, the Submarine Force commander, preparing for the possible sortie of the enemy fleet from Pearl Harbor, ordered all submarines except the Special Attack Unit to exercise strict surveillance.

The next day, it was found that the enemy had taken strict precautionary measures in southern Oahu and it was confirmed that antisubmarine nets were laid between Diamond Head and Barbers Point. The commander of the Submarine Force therefore ordered the 3rd Submarine Group, which had been stationed south of Oahu, to move further south.

After completing the air attack on Hawaii, the Carrier Striking Force withdrew northward of Hawaii and on 9 December 1941, the Carrier Striking Force commanding officer released the three submarines, which had been accompanying his force as the Patrol Unit, and directed them to return to the command of the Submarine Force. Thereafter, the Patrol Unit was assigned to the direct command of the 1st Submarine Group commander. Also on the 9th, the Commander in Chief of the Combined Fleet issued orders to the commander of the Carrier Striking Force to release the submarine force from his command. All submarines in the area of Hawaii were under the direct command of the Submarine Force.

At about 0400 on the 10th, the *I-6* stationed in Kauai Channel reported that two heavy cruisers and a Lexington class aircraft carrier were heading northeast. The Submarine Force commander ordered the 1st Submarine Group, located north of Oahu, and the *I-10* and *I-26* to track down the aircraft carrier which evidently was moving toward the United States.

On 11 December, the Submarine Force Commander made a slight change in the operational plan, which had been drawn up before the outbreak of the war, in the disposition and operational duties of the Submarine Force. The Special Attack Unit was not assigned to the 1st Submarine Group, but was placed under the direct command of the Submarine Force and was to discontinue the search for the midget submarines and return to Kwajalein. The 2nd and 3rd Submarine Group was to continue observation of Hawaii. The 3rd Submarine Group was to return to Kwajalein on or about [the] 18th and the 2nd Submarine Group was to continue to observe the whole island of Oahu alone after that date. The 1st Submarine Group and the *I-10* and *I-26* were to continue to track the enemy fleet toward the United States mainland.

During the period 8–11 December only a few of the submarines, including the *I-6*, had discovered the enemy aircraft carrier, cruiser, and destroyer and none of these achieved any direct attack results. The *I-70* was the only submarine lost, having been missing in the area south of Oahu since 9 December.

Subsequent Operations of the Submarine Groups

Upon receipt of orders, the 1st Submarine Group, with the *I-10* and *I-26* attached, took up the chase of the Lexington class aircraft carrier and the two heavy cruisers reported by the *I-6*. However, this chase was of no avail[;] therefore the units participating in this action were designated the Submarine Force Detachment and were directed to commence operations against shipping off the west coast of the United States. The disposition of submarines was as follows: *I-26* off Cape Flattery; *I-25* off Cape Disappointment; *I-9* off Cape Blanco; *I-17* off Cape Mendocino; *I-15* off San Francisco; *I-23* off Monterey Bay; *I-21* off Estero Bay; *I-19* off Los Angeles and *I-10* off San Diego. The submarines took up their positions and engaged in operations from the middle to the latter part of December. It is believed that the enemy losses as a result of this operation were about ten tankers and transports.

In the latter part of December the antisubmarine measures taken by the United States became very severe and the Submarine Force Detachment withdrew as planned. The Submarine Force Detachment had been scheduled to shell the coastal cities of the United States on Christmas Eve, just before their withdrawal[;] however, the detachment was ordered by the Combined Fleet Headquarters to abandon the plan. On the way home an element of the detachment carried out air reconnaissance of Pearl Harbor and on 28 January 1942, the *I-25* sank a seaplane tender about 600 nautical miles southwest of Johnston Island. By the middle of January all submarines had returned to Kwajalein and the Submarine Force Detachment was dissolved. The *I-10* and *I-26* were ordered to return to Japan for equipping and training.

Meanwhile, the 3rd Submarine Group, which had been engaged in observing the Hawaii Area with the 2nd Submarine Group, in mid-December completed its patrol and started for Kwajalein. On about 22 December, while en route, three submarines of the group shelled Johnston and Palmyra Islands as previously ordered. In the latter part of December, all the submarines returned to Kwajalein.

The 2nd Submarine Group patrolled about 60 miles off the entrance to Pearl Harbor and on 17 December, a seaplane from the *I-7* carried out a dawn reconnaissance over Pearl Harbor, obtaining valuable information regarding the results of the attack. In late December submarines of the group shelled points on Hawaii, Maui and Kauai.

On 10 Jan. 1942, a submarine attached to the Special Attack Unit, which at that time was heading toward Hawaii to relieve the 2nd Submarine Group, reported a Lexington class aircraft carrier sighted northeast of Johnston Island. The commander of the Submarine Force ordered the 2nd Submarine Group to cease the patrol of Hawaii and to search for and attack the carrier. The 2nd Submarine Group, [sic] passed north of Johnston Island and searched for the enemy in the vicinity of the Marshall Islands. At 1440, 12 January, two Lexington class aircraft carriers were sighted 60 degrees 270 nautical miles from Johnston Island and were hit by two torpedoes released from the *I-6*.

The group was then ordered to return directly to Kwajalein, and all submarines returned there by the end of January. After arriving at Kwajalein, it was decided to send the group to Japan for maintenance and it returned to Yokosuka in early February and began repairs.

The Special Attack Unit was ordered to return to Kwajalein after its midget submarine attack on Hawaii and en route (about 16 December) a part of the unit shelled Johnston Island. On or about 20 December, the entire unit returned to Kwajalein and prepared for the next operation. Although the next operation planned for this unit, relief of the 2nd Submarine Squadron, required no midget submarines the name Special Attack Unit remained unchanged.

The Special Attack Unit completed its preparation by the beginning of January 1942 and left Kwajalein to relieve the 2nd Submarine Group off Hawaii. En route, as previously mentioned, they sighted a carrier but the attack on this carrier was ordered to be made by the 2nd Submarine Group[;] therefore, the Special Attack Unit took up the patrol of Hawaii. The unit patrolled off Hawaii until about 20 January, when it was ordered to return to Yokosuka by the commander of the Submarine Force. En route a part of the unit reconnoitered [at] French Frigate Shoal and shelled Midway. After the successful completion of the Hawaiian operations [the] strength of the Submarine Force (6th Fleet) was reduced by the return to Japan of the 2nd Submarine Group, the Special Attack Unit and the *I-10* and *I-21*. The 2nd Submarine Group, after maintenance and resupply, was to be dispatched to the Indian Ocean Area to strengthen the submarine forces there. The Special Attack Unit, the *I-10* and the *I-21*, returned for reequipping for future operations using midget submarines. Based on the estimate that the United States Fleet had been so severely hit at Pearl Harbor that it lacked offensive power, it was expected that the submarines of the 1st and 3rd Submarine Group would be sufficient for subsequent operation. In late January, the 3rd Submarine Group composed of the Flagship *I-8*, and the 11th, 12th and 20th Submarine Divisions, was committed to various operations in the field.

In early February, the submarine *I-8* reached the water west of San Francisco on the mission of disrupting coastal communications. It patrolled north as far as Seattle and returned to Japan in early March without encountering any enemy vessels. The 11th Submarine Division, composed of the *I-74* and *I-75*, reached the Aleutian Area around the end of January and patrolled the water off Unalaska, Amukta, Atka and Kiska, returning to Japan in mid-February. During the period of their patrol they did not participate in any action and observed no unusual enemy movements.

In the latter part of January, the 20th Submarine Division, composed of the *I-71*, *I-72* and the *I-73*, patrolled the waters off Hawaii without any noteworthy result. However, around the end of January there was no further contact with the *I-73* and it was presumed lost. Early on the morning of 1 February, word was received from the commander of the Submarine

Force to cease patrol and to stand by for interception of an enemy force. This force, with a carrier as a nucleus, had been sighted near the Marshall Islands. Although all submarines were alerted, no enemy vessels were encountered and the two remaining submarines of the division returned to their base at Kwajalein in mid-February.

The 12th Submarine Division, consisting of only the *I-69* (the *I-68* having returned to Japan and the *I-70* having been lost), reconnoitered Midway in late January. In early February the *I-69* shelled the military installations on Sand Island and returned to Kwajalein in mid-February.

Meanwhile the remainder of the Submarine Force was at Kwajalein preparing for further operations. In late January the ships at the Kwajalein base were the Submarine Force flagship *Katori*, the *Yasukuri Maru* (the tender for the 3rd Submarine Group), the three supply ships of the force and the reorganized 1st Submarine Squadron (Group). The 1st Submarine Squadron was now composed of the flag submarine *I-9*, the 2nd Submarine Division (*I-15, I-17, I-19*), and 4th Submarine Division (*I-23, I-25, I-26*) and the tender *Haian Maru*. Also at the Kwajalein base at that time were the submarines *RO-61* and *RO-62* of the 7th Submarine Squadron.

In late January, communication traffic among the Allied Forces became noticeably more active, an indication of imminent enemy action. Suddenly, at 0400 hours on the 1st of February, an attack was launched against the Marshall and Gilbert Islands by a strong carrier task force and the submarines based at Kwajalein were forced to submerge to avoid damage. Only the *I-23* suffered minor damage to its deck[;] however, the *Katori, Haian Maru* and the *Yasukuni Maru* sustained some damage and had to return to Japan "on repair."

Although plans had been made for submarines of the 1st Submarine Squadron to engage in the "K" Operation (Surprise air raid on Hawaiian Island [sic] by flying boats) and patrol, all submarines of the 1st Submarine Squadron promptly set out on a sweeping formation east of Kwajalein in an effort to locate the invading enemy task force. They were unsuccessful and on the morning of the 3rd the *I-15, I-19, I-26* and *I-25* were ordered to return to Kwajalein and *I-9, I-23* and *I-17* to continue to search towards Hawaii. The latter three submarines searched for the enemy south of Oahu but the enemy could not be located. The commander of the Submarine Force, according to the schedule, therefore ordered the *I-17* to advance to the west coast of United States and the *I-9* and *I-23* to continue observations of Hawaii.

The *I-9* and *I-23* continued observation of the Hawaii Area, with little results, until the end of February. Contact having been lost with the *I-23*, it was reported missing about the middle of February. Meanwhile, the *I-17* reached the waters off San Diego about 20 February. It succeeded in penetrating the Santa Barbara Channel on the 24th and successfully shelled the

Elewood oil fields after sunset of that day[;] later, the *I-17*, operating off San Francisco to Medocino Cape, sank two enemy vessels. The *I-17* left the west coast of North America and returned to Japan at the end of March.

The *I-25* left Kwajalein on 8 February for the eastern coast of Australia, and the duty of reconnoitering the important ports on the eastern coast of Australia and New Zealand. During February and March, she completed the following air reconnaissance missions: Dawn, 17 February 42, Sydney; Dawn, 26 February, Melbourne; Dawn, 1 March, Hobart; Dawn, 8 March, Wellington; Night, 13 March, Auckland; Dawn, 18 March, Suva; and at Dawn, 21 March, completed a submerged reconnaissance of Pango Pango.

The *I-15*, *I-19* and *I-26*, which since early February were being equipped with refuelling apparatus for the "K" Operation, finished their remodelling works in the middle of February. The commander of the Submarine Force made preparation for initiating the "K" Operation. The "K" Operation was a plan for an air attack on Pearl Harbor by flying boats. The planes were to leave Jaluit Island before dawn on the day of the attack and reach French Frigate Shoal about sunset. There they were to be refueled by submarines and leave there for Pearl Harbor. Seven hours after sunset they were to make a surprise attack on Pearl Harbor and return straight to Jaluit. Three refuelling submarines, *I-15*, *I-19* and *I-23* assumed their position at French Frigate Shoal on the day of the attack to act as a radio beacon. The first "K" Operation was placed into effect on 4 March and the operation went off as planned.

As the second "K" Operation scheduled for 7 March was called off, the commander of the Submarine Force recalled these submarines to Japan. While en route an American carrier task force attacked Marcus Island and these submarines made attempts to intercept the task force but could not locate the enemy. All the submarines returned to Japan, arriving there in late March.

As previously stated, certain submarines had returned to Japan for re-equipping in preparation for an operation using midget submarines. On 10 March 1942, these submarines and the newly built submarines, *I-27*, *I-28*, *I-29* and *I-30*, were assigned to the newly organized 8th Submarine Squadron, a component of the 6th Fleet.

Operations of the 7th Submarine Squadron

The South Seas Force had been organized for the attack on strategic points in the South Seas and for the invasion of the Bismarck Archipelago. The 7th Submarine Squadron (26th, 27th, 33rd Submarine Divisions) was assigned to this force to participate in these operations, as well as to patrol and defend these areas. The South Seas Force was scheduled to take action immediately upon the outbreak of war. The bulk of the force was assigned the

Chart 3 Changes in Organization of the Sixth Fleet
(Dec. 1941)

(Flagship Lt. Cruiser *Katori*)

1st Submarine Squadron
 I-9 (Flagship)
 1st Submarine Division
  I-15, 1-16, I-17
 2nd Submarine Division
  I-18, I-19, I-20
 3rd Submarine Division
  I-21, I-22, I-23
 4th Submarine Division
  1-24, I-25, I-26
 Yasukuri Maru (Tender)

3rd Submarine Squadron
 I-8 Flagship
 11th Submarine Division
  I-74, I-75
 12th Submarine-Division
  I-68, I-69, I-70
 20th Submarine Division
  I-71, I-72, I-73
 Taigai (Tender)

2nd Submarine Squadron
 I-7 (Flagship)
 7th Submarine Division
  I-1, I-2, I-3
 8th Submarine Division
  I-4, I-5, I-6
 I-10
 Santos Maru (Tender)

Sixth Fleet
(Mar. 1942)
(Flagship Lt. Cruiser *Katori*)

1st Submarine Squadron
 I-9 (Flagship)
 2nd Submarine Division
  I-15, I-17, I-19
 4th Submarine Division
  I-23, I-25, I-26
 Haian Maru (Tender)

2nd Submarine Squadron
 I-7 (Flagship)
 7th Submarine Division
  I-1, I-2, I-3
 8th Submarine Division
  I-4, I-5, I-6
 Santos Maru (Tender)

3rd Submarine Squadron
 1-8 (Flagship)
 11th Submarine Division
  I-74, I-75
 125th [sic] Submarine Division
  I-68, I-69
 20th Submarine Division
  I-71, I-72
 Yasukuri Maru (Tender)

8th Submarine Squadron
 I-10 (Flagship)
 1st Submarine Division
  I-16, I-18, I-20
 3rd Submarine Division
  I-21, I-22, I-24
 14th Submarine Division
  I-27, I-28, I-29, I-30
 Rio Maru (Tender)

task of invading Wake Island, scheduled for 11 December 1941. The rest of the force was scheduled to carry out mopping-up operations on Howland and Gilbert Islands, on 10 December.

The 27th Submarine Division (*RO-65, RO-66, RO-67*) of the South Seas Force, which was assigned to the invasion forces of Wake Island, departed Kwajalein on 6 December 41 and reached the waters near Wake on the 10th. One of the submarines, after reconnoitering the island, acted as a pilot and led the invasion forces to the landing point. On the day of the landing, the submarines patrolled the outer waters of Wake and remained in the vicinity after the landing failed and the invasion forces withdrew to make another attempt. On 12 December, the 27th Submarine Division was released from the invasion force of Wake Island and ordered back to Kwajalein. However, the *RO-66* failed to receive the returning order, due to failure of radio communication, and only the *RO-65* and *RO-67* returned to Kwajalein.

The 33rd Submarine Division (*RO-63, RO-64, RO-68*) which was temporarily assigned to the mopping-up operation around Howland Island, departed Kwajalein several days before the outbreak of hostilities and on 10 and 11 December shelled Howland and Baker Islands and destroyed military installations. These submarines patrolled the vicinity of the island until about the 15th and then returned to Kwajalein.

The 26th Submarine Division (*RO-60, RO-61, RO-62*) was standing by Kwajalein during the outbreak of hostilities. On 12 December, it was incorporated into the invasion forces which were to make the second attack on Wake Island and left Kwajalein on the same day to patrol around Wake. On the night of 17 December the *RO-62* collided with the *RO-66*, which had remained on patrol near Wake due to failing to receive [the] recall order. The *RO-66* sank instantly but no damage was incurred by the *RO-62* which continued the patrol.

After 19 December the submarines of the 26th Division took positions east of Wake Island as a supporting force for the invasion forces. The other submarine acted as a pilot for the invading forces in their second attempt on the 23rd. After the invasion forces had succeeded in effecting a landing on Wake the submarines returned to Kwajalein. En route, the *RO-60* lost her position due to stormy weather and sank on 29 December after running aground off Kwajalein.

After returning from the operation around Howland, the 33rd Submarine Division was ordered to replace the 26th Submarine Division on patrol of the waters around Wake. Taking up the assignment in the latter part of December the division was ordered to Truk in early January 1942. The 27th Submarine Division (the *RO-65* and *RO-67*) which returned to Kwajalein in mid-December after the first landing attempt on Wake, was ordered to patrol the vicinity of Howland Island late in December. However, it was ordered to Truk at the end of the same month and with the 33rd Submarine Division, made preparation for the Rabaul invasion operation which was scheduled after mid-January.

In an attempt to capture Rabaul early in January 1942, the South Seas Force assembled its invasion forces at Guam and its supporting forces at Truk. As part of the supporting force in this invasion the submarines of the 27th and 33rd Submarine Division made intense preparation for the operations in the St. George Channel.

As the invasion of Rabaul was scheduled for 23 January, the Submarine Group patrolled the water south of St. George Channel for several days starting on 21 January in order to cover the landing operation against the possible interference of the enemy surface forces. No counterattack was made by the enemy, however, and as the landing operation was successful, the submarines returned to Truk in the latter part of January. The 26th Submarine Division remained around Kwajalein and Wotje as a part of the naval forces defending the Marshalls Area.

Within the two months after the operation commenced in December 1941, the Gilbert Islands and Wake Island were mopped up and occupied, while the landing on Rabaul was successful. Therefore, the duty of the Submarine Group of the South Seas Force was mainly defensive. The 26th Submarine Division was based at Kwajalein for defense of that area. While the 27th and 33rd Submarine Divisions did the same at Truk, they were to be prepared to move against any possible enemy counterattack on strategic areas and to prevent the attack of the enemy in cooperation with the defense forces stationed therein.

From early February to the middle of March, the commander of the South Seas Force ordered each submarine division to patrol and search against any possible enemy counterattack, in connection with the enemy carrier striking task force invasion of the Marshalls Area.

The 26th Submarine Division was at Kwajalein when the United States carrier task force raided the island on 1 February 42. The division patrolled the eastern coast of the Marshall Islands for counteraction against the enemy carrier task force, but could not locate the enemy. As an attack on Wake by the United States carrier task force was expected in the middle of February, the division advanced to the waters off Wake and waited [for] an opportunity together with a part of the 3rd Submarine Group of the Submarine Force. However, it could not contact the enemy by the end of February and so returned to Japan proper for repairs at the end of March. After the occupation of Rabaul, the 27th and the 33rd Submarine Divisions completed their maintenance at Truk and in the middle of February, both Divisions left Truk for defensive duty in the area of Makin. As a United States carrier task force was sighted east-northeast of Rabaul on 20 February, the disposition of the two divisions was changed to Greenwich Island (approximate position 1 deg. 5 min. N. 153 deg. 45 min. ENE). However, as the location of the enemy was unknown, the following day, both divisions moved to the waters of the Marshalls and patrolled the area from the end of February to the middle of March. They returned to Japan in early April.

The Southern Operations

The 4th, 5th and 6th Submarine Squadrons were assigned to the Southern Force to participate in the invasion of Malaya, the Philippines and the Dutch East Indies. These three submarine squadrons, with a combined strength of 18 submarines, were to support the invasion operations by patrol of the invasion areas, protection of the transports of the invasion forces and the laying of mines at key points in the invasion area. The 4th Submarine Squadron, with the 13th Submarine Division of the 6th Submarine Squadron attached, and the 5th Submarine Squadron were assigned to the Malay Force, while the remainder of the 6th Submarine Squadron was assigned to the forces invading the Philippines.

The Philippine Force

In December 1941, the 9th Submarine Division (*I-123, I-124*), the part of the 6th Submarine Squadron assigned as the Philippine Submarine Group, left Samah on Hainan Island for operations in the Philippine Area. The *I-123* proceeded to Balabas Strait and the *I-124* to Manila Bay and, as per prearranged schedule, on 8 December the two submarines secretly laid about 40 mines at the western entrance to the Balabas Strait and at the mouth of the Manila Bay. Later that day, the *I-124* proceeded to the area southwest of Lubang Island where she engaged in reporting the weather conditions in the Manila district and stood by as a service boat to the air force attacking Manila. Later she was charged with the duty of patroling the neighborhood of the bay to keep guard, and about the middle of the month, returned to Camranh Bay after sinking a ship on the 10th. The *I-123,* due to a defect in her hull, returned to Camranh Bay, French Indochina, immediately after laying mines in the Balabas Strait, and arrived at the bay around the 10th.

In the middle of December 1941, the 13th Submarine Division (*I-121* and *I-122*), part of the 6th Submarine Squadron, under the command of the Malaya Force, was ordered to rejoin the Philippine Submarine Group. The *I-121, I-122, I-123* and *I-124* left Camranh Bay in the middle of December. The *I-121* and *I-124,* after patrolling the entrance of Manila Bay around 22 December, proceeded into the Sulu Sea via the Mindoro Strait, then arrived at Davao via the Pilas Channel. Though the *I-121* was scheduled to lay mines outside Manila Bay, the plan was given up because of the strict antisubmarine measures of the enemy. The *I-122* arrived at Puerto Princesa through the Balabas Strait and then patrolled the western entrance of the Pilas Channel. The *I-123* sailed south to the South China Sea and moved to the Java Sea through the Karimata Strait. After laying mines in the northern entrance of the Soerabaja (Madiera) Strait she proceeded to Davao via Makassar Strait. By the end of the month all the submarines had arrived at Davao and with the arrival of the *Chokai,* flagship of the 6th Submarine Squadron, the squadron was again intact. The squadron immediately began preparations for further operations.

The Malaya Force

On 1 December 1941, the 18th Submarine Division (*I-53, I-54, I-55*) and the 19th Submarine Division (*I-56, I-57, I-58*) of the 4th Submarine Squadron left Samah Harbor on Hainan Island and by 8 December had reached their battle positions northwest of Anambas Islands in the South China Sea. The 13th Submarine Division (*I-121, I-122*) left Samah on the same date and on 8 December reached the waters off Singapore Strait, where the division proceeded to sow mines in the eastern entrance to Singapore Strait. Of the remainder of the 4th Submarine Squadron, the 21st Submarine Division (*RO-33, RO-34*) was standing by ready for action at Sasebo and the flagship *Kinu* was in the South China Sea off Cape Camau, having also departed Samah on 1 December.

The 29th Submarine Division (*I-62, I-64*) and the 30th Submarine Division (*I-65, I-66*) of the 5th Submarine Squadron departed Samah on the 5th of December and were deployed in the waters north of Anambas Islands on 8 December. The 28th Submarine Division (*I-59, I-60*) was standing by at Kobe. The *Yura* flagship of the squadron left Samah on the 5th and on the 8th was in position south of Cape Camau. Units of both squadrons, which had been placed under the operational command of the commander of the 4th Submarine Squadron, were now in position to support and protect the invasion forces as planned.

On 8 December the invasions along the west coast of Malaya began and were generally successful. Planes reconnoitering Singapore Harbor sighted a British fleet which included two battleships[;] however, it was reported that they were not taking any action.

At 1515 hours on 9 December, the submarine *I-65* reported that it suddenly came across two British battleships proceeding northward at the point roughly 5° North Lat., and 105°31′ East Long. This report of the sighting of enemy vessels started the Battle of Malaya and all the submarines turned to tracking down and intercepting the enemy battleships. About 2100 hours of the same day, the submarine groups changed the line of deployment in anticipation of the turning back of the enemy. At about 0340 hours of the

10th, and 20 nautical miles west of the spot where they were first sighted by the *I-65*, the *I-58* sighted the two British battleships proceeding south. That afternoon, however, the naval battle came to an end with the attack of our planes.

The invasion of British Borneo was started on 12 December [on] which the Malaya Campaign was still being carried out. Submarines of the 18th and 19th Submarine Divisions took positions in the waters north of the Anambas Islands and the 29th and 30th Submarine Divisions were deployed in the waters southeast of Great Natuna Island. From these positions they were able to support the invasion forces by covering the forces from possible enemy attack in the South China Sea and by reconnoitering landing points. On the 15th, the 13th Submarine Division was ordered to return to the Philippine Force and they departed for Camranh. At the end of December, the 4th and 5th Submarine Squadrons returned to Camranh Bay after the completion of this operation. During the return movement, the *I-66* sank one enemy submarine in the area north of Api Passage.

When the 5th Submarine Squadron arrived at Camranh Bay, it was transferred from the Malaya Force to direct control of the Southern Force and was assigned to operations in the Indian Ocean. Thus only the 4th Submarine Squadron remained in the Malaya Force, which was to operate in the South China Sea and in the waters around Java from its base in Camranh Bay. From the end of December 41 to the latter part of January 42, the submarines *I-55*, *I-56*, *I-57* and *I-58* were in the Java Sea and the waters south of Java on the mission of disrupting the enemy line of communications. The submarines of this force sank several enemy ships around Java in early January. Meanwhile, the submarines *I-54* and *I-55*, together with *RO-33* and *RO-34*, which had left Japan after the war began, deployed in waters extending from the south of Anambas Islands to Karimata Strait. They were to support the third landing on Malaya and make reconnaissance of the landing points.

The 4th Submarine Squadron which returned to Camranh Bay late in January after completing the above missions, dispatched a part of its force submarines (*I-55*, *I-56* and *RO-34*) to the Sunda and Bombac Straits to cut the enemy line of retreat in support of the Malaya Force's invasion of Banka and Palombang. These submarines were also assigned to the task of disrupting enemy sea communications. Banka and Palombang were captured about the middle of February and up to that time the above-mentioned three submarines sank one enemy light cruiser and some other vessels. Later, the *RO-34* returned to Camranh Bay and the *I-55* and *I-56* went to Sterling Bay.

While the above-mentioned three submarines were engaged in these operations, the other five submarines of the 4th Submarine Squadron (*I-53*, *I-54*, *I-57*, *I-58* and *RO-33*) remained in Camranh Bay and made preparations for the invasion of Java which was scheduled to start about the middle of February.

Operations North of Australia and the Indian Ocean Area (Early January 1942 to mid-February 1942)

In an attempt to directly command the operations of the area north of Australia and the Indian Ocean, the Southern Force Commander, around the end of December 1941, organized Submarine Group "A" (6th Submarine Squadron) and Submarine Group "B" (5th Submarine Squadron). Submarine Groups "A" and "B" were to start operations in the first part of January 1942, and the commander of the Southern Force gave operational orders to the submarine groups under his command, the main points of which were as follows:

(a) Since the United States Asiatic Fleet in cooperation with the remaining British Far Eastern Fleet and the Dutch East Indies Fleet is expected to carry out joint defensive operations in the area of the Dutch East Indies and Australia, the submarine groups will be deployed in the Dutch East Indies and northwest of Australia. They will cooperate with the Invasion Forces in the Dutch East Indies by patrolling, observing and intercepting of enemy counteraction. Concurrently, elements of the submarine groups will engage in the disruption of the enemy communication lines.

(b) Allotment of duties, areas and bases for operations of each submarine group shall be classified as follows:

(1) Operational area of Group "A" shall be the area of the Dutch East Indies and Australia east of the 117 degrees East longitude, with Davao as its operational base. Its main duties are to patrol, observe and intercept the Allied Fleet and to lay mines around Australia.

(2) The operational area of Group "B" shall be the Indian Ocean west of 106 degrees East longitude. It will promptly proceed from Camranh Bay to its base at Penang, and will destroy communications in the Malacca Strait and the Indian Ocean.

(3) The commander of the Malaya Force will command the operation of his submarine group. Their zone of operation will be the Java Sea and the Indian Ocean between 117 degrees and 106 degrees East longitude. This group shall cooperate directly with the Invasion Forces to the Dutch East [Indies] destroying communication lines when [the] situation permits.

Submarine Group "A" proceeded to Davao in the latter part of December 1941 and prepared for operations around Australia. In the first part of

January of the following year, it completed preparations for mine laying and left Davao for the coast of Port Darwin and Torres Strait. After laying their mines according to plan, the submarines *I-121* and *I-122* on 15 January started on their return to the base. On 10 January, all submarines were notified [that] radio intelligence indicated that the main force of the United States Far Eastern Fleet might be in the Flores Sea[;] therefore, each submarine took precautionary measures. On 14 January, the *I-124* sighted the *Houston* and two destroyers in the southwest Banda Sea. The *I-123* and *I-124* tracked them toward Darwin, but missed the opportunity for an attack. On the 17th, while en route home the *I-121* sighted an enemy cruiser and four destroyers in the northeast Flores Sea. The *I-121* and *I-122* were ordered to reverse their courses and participate in the patrol of the area off Port Darwin with the *I-123* and *I-124*. There, the patrol was carried out until the end of January but information could not be obtained on the enemy's location and the order to return to Davao was issued.

Besides the enemy cruisers sighted by the *I-121* and *I-124* during this operation, a number of destroyers and transports were also sighted. There were opportunities of attacking some of them, but only one transport was sunk. The *I-121* and *I-124* succeeded in laying mines around the western entrance of the Clarence Strait, the *I-123* in the northern entrance of Torres Strait. During this operation, the *I-124* disappeared in the Darwin area on 20 January and failed to return.

Meanwhile, Submarine Group "B" left Camranh Bay and Davao for operations in the Indian Ocean. According to the plan formulated by the commander of the group, all submarines were to proceed to Penang after performing various operations in the Indian Ocean. The *I-59* and *I-60*, after departing from Davao, sailed south of the Sunda Islands through the Banda Sea. The *I-59* was instructed to head for Penang passing near Christmas Island while the *I-60* was to head for Penang along the west coast of Sumatra, after patrolling around the southern entrance of Sunda Strait. However, on 17 January, the *I-60* was attacked by the British destroyer *Jupiter* and sank in the southern entrance of the Sunda Strait. The *I-59* entered Penang at the end of January, having sunk two ships while en route. The *I-62* and *I-64* passed south of the Sunda Islands and headed straight toward Ceylon. They operated along the coast of India between Madras and Cochin from the end of January to the beginning of February. During this period, they sank several ships, and both submarines entered Penang early in February. The *I-65* and *I-66*, leaving Camranh Bay, sailed through the Java Sea, passed south of the Sunda Islands, then proceeded north along the west coast of Sumatra to the northern entrance of [the] Malacca Strait. With the receipt of the information that one British battleship had been sighted in Singapore Harbor and there was a chance that she would sortie, the two submarines were ordered to remain in position in the north entrance of [the]

Malacca Strait for possible ambush of the British battleship. Later it was found that the information was erroneous and the *I-66* was ordered to proceed to the Rangoon Area and the *I-65* to Penang. The two submarines entered Penang after sinking several ships during the operation.

Judging that minesweeping operations in the Malacca Strait would require a considerable amount of time, the commander of Submarine Group "B," who had commanded operations from the flagship *Yura* since the beginning of the war, went ashore at Singora (Songkhla) on the east coast of the Malaya Peninsula in mid-January, and moving overland, transferred his headquarters to Penang. At Penang construction of necessary facilities had been started to make it a submarine base for operations in the Indian Ocean. During this period, the *Yura* took part in various operations under the direct command of the Malaya force.

Operations North of Australia and the Dutch East Indies (mid-February 1942 to early March 1943)

As stated above, the two submarine groups which were engaged in operations in the waters north of Australia and around the Dutch East Indies in the early part of February 1942 were Submarine Group "A" (the 6th Submarine Squadron) and the submarine group of the Malaya Force (the 4th Submarine Squadron). However, as the campaign in the Southern Area progressed as scheduled, and the time was ripe for the invasion of Java scheduled for mid-February, it became advisable to place these two submarine groups under a single command. Therefore, the commander of the Southern Force placed the submarine group of the Malaya Force directly under his command and incorporated it into Submarine Group "A."

Although the British Forces at Singapore laid down their arms on 15 February 1942, and the operations of the Malaya Java Force came to a close, the time came for the Dutch East Indies Invasion Force to begin its operation. The commander of the Southern Force ordered his Submarine Group "A" to support the Dutch Indies Force in the Java campaign after mid-February as follows:

(a) The submarines shall be mainly deployed in the waters around Java and off the north coast of Australia in order to disrupt and sever the enemy line of reinforcement and to capture enemy forces escaping from the Dutch East Indies;

(b) Patrol the strategic areas east of Java along the southern coast of the Dutch East Indies, Torres Strait and around Port Darwin.

Conforming with this plan, the commander of Submarine Group "A" deployed the bulk of the 4th Submarine Squadron in the waters around Java and the entire 6th Submarine Squadron around the north of Australia to support the invasion campaign. Mine-laying activity in the Torres Strait was to be increased. The commander of Submarine Group "A" assigned the submarines *I-53, I-54, I-57, I-58, RO-33* and *RO-34* to participate in the campaign which started around the middle of February and ordered the submarines *I-55* and *I-56* to remain in the Sterling Bay for repair and supply. The *I-57*, however, did not participate in the operation because of an outbreak of dysentery in the crew.

The *I-53, I-54, I-58, RO-33* and *RO-34* left the Camranh Base, and passing through the Lombok Strait about 20 February, took positions in the waters ranging from the southern entrance of the Sunda Strait through the waters off Tjilatjap to the southern entrance of the Lombok Strait. From the end of February to early March they supported the Java invading operations by destroying the retreating enemy. The *I-56*, having completed its resupply at Sterling Bay, started early in March for the sea off Tjilatjap to participate in the operation. In this operation, most of the submarines encountered a fairly large number of combat vessels as well as other types of ships and sank several of them. The submarines returned to the base at Sterling Bay during the first half of March. The *I-57*, in which an epidemic of dysentery occurred, also moved to Sterling Bay early in March.

The 6th Submarine Squadron of Submarine Group "A" was at Davao early in February 1942, making preparations for the next operation, when the commander of Submarine Group "S" ordered the *I-121, I-122* and the *I-123* to leave Davao and advance to the Timor Sea, Arafura Sea, and Torres Strait respectively. The submarines were ordered on guard duty through February in cooperation with the occupation of Java. The *I-123* was engaged in laying mines at the western mouth of the Torres Strait late in February. These submarines returned to Sterling Bay early in March without encountering any enemy ships.

Operations in the Indian Ocean (February–April 1942)

The 2nd Submarine Squadron of the Submarine Force returned to Japan early in February 1942 after carrying out its mission in the east Pacific Ocean and was assigned to the Southern Forces. The squadron, under the command of Rear Admiral Ichioka Hisashi set about making preparations for operations in the Indian Ocean, and in early February, it was ordered by the commander of the Southern Force to advance to Sterling Bay. Early in February 1942, the commander of the Southern Forces modified the task organization of his submarine groups following the entry of the 2nd Submarine Squadron into his command. The 2nd Submarine Squadron was designated Submarine Group "C" and placed under his direct command, together with Submarine Groups "A" and "B."

In February 1942, the Carrier Striking Force was assigned to the Southern Force to carry out carrier operations in the Southern Areas. It was planned to carry out carrier attacks on the Tjilatjap area and, in support of the operations for the occupation of Java, intercept and annihilate the enemy combat vessels and other ships in the Java area. In the latter part of February, Submarine Group "C" was ordered to cooperate with the Carrier Force in this operation.

When it was decided that Submarine Group "C" was to operate in the Indian Ocean in concert with the Carrier Force, the commander, aboard the *I-7*, ordered all submarines of his command to leave Sterling Bay around 22 February for the new mission. They sailed south of Sunda Island through the Flores Sea and on 25 February they had formed a line of deployment about 300 miles south of Soemba Island, from where they proceeded westward in search of the enemy. The *I-5*, however, went aground in the north passage of Sterling Bay and did not participate in the operations. The remaining submarines provided the vanguard for the Carrier Force till the end of February.

With the successful completion of the vanguard action, 11 submarines began the attacks on the enemy lines of communication. The *I-4*, *I-6* and *I-7* began operations around 400 miles southwest of Christmas Island and sweeping northwest all submarines returned to Penang. During this period two enemy ships were sunk and in early March the *I-4* shelled Cocos Island. At the end of February, the *I-1*, *I-2* and *I-3* arrived at a point 300 miles northwest of Northwest Cape in Australia. The *I-2* and *I-3* sailed south along the west coast of Australia and operated off Freemantle and around Shark Bay. In early March, they left the area for Penang, arriving there in mid-March. The *I-1* had engine trouble at the beginning of March and returned to Sterling Bay, arriving there early in the month. During this time, these submarines sank a total of three enemy vessels. Because of the lack of repair facilities of the submarines' tender, which had been anchored in Sterling Bay, the *I-1* returned to Yokosuka at the end of March. The work of salvaging the *I-5* off the reef was successful in the latter part of March and her preparations for the next operation were completed.

Submarine Group "B," having finished its first mission of disrupting enemy communications in the Indian Ocean, returned to Penang late in January and early February. Submarine Group "B" started a second similar mission early in February. The *I-65* and *I-66*, operating mainly in the [vicinity] of Ceylon, sank four vessels during February. The *I-59*, operating near the southwest coast of Sumatra from the end of February to the middle of March, sank one vessel. The *I-62* and *I-64*, operating in the waters extending from Madras (the east coast of India) to Cochin (southwest coast) from the end of February till the middle of March, sank several vessels. In addition, as the result of these operations it was ascertained that the enemy ships in the Bay of Bengal were navigating close to the coast, and this finding contributed to the Third Operation of the Carrier Force.

The greater part of Submarine Group "C" (*I-7, I-2, I-3, I-4, I-6*) in support of the Third Operation of the Carrier Force, began operations in the Indian Ocean around 26 March, after repairs and supply had been completed at Penang. The *I-5* which had been under repair in Sterling Bay also commenced operations in the Indian Ocean at about the same time. The disposition and the mission of each submarine, ordered by the commander of Submarine Group "C" to participate in the Third Operation of the Carrier Force, was generally as follows: the *I-7*, operating north of Chagos Archipelago, so as to make an air reconnaissance over Colombo in the beginning of April, and in the first ten days of April, was to be responsible for patrol and disruption of enemy communications north of Chagos; the *I-2* and *I-3*, operating around Ceylon, was [sic] in early April, to reconnoiter the enemy situations in Trincomalee and Colombo and, thereafter, were to disrupt enemy communications; the *I-4*, operating in the Eight and Nine Degree Channels, was to patrol and disrupt enemy communications in the vicinities of [the] Eight and Nine Degree Channels during the first ten days of April; the *I-5*, operating in the One and Half Degree Channel, was to patrol and disrupt enemy communications in the vicinity of the One and Half Degree Channel during the first ten days of April; the *I-6*, operating west of Bombay, was to patrol and disrupt enemy communications in this area during the first ten days of April.

The submarines conducted operations generally according to the plan. However, the *I-7* gave up the air reconnaissance over Colombo because of intensified enemy security measures in Ceylon and the difficulty in handling seaplanes in rough seas. Due to the heavy patrols, the *I-2* and *I-3* were able to report only on the situations in regard to the enemy patrols in the waters near Trincomalee and Colombo, though they did attempt to make a general reconnaissance in those areas. All of the submarines arrived at the port of Singapore, having passed through the Strait of Malacca in mid-April, without sighting any of the main enemy combat vessels during the period of the Carrier Forces Operation. In this operation the submarine group sank approximately seven enemy vessels.

Submarine Activities of the Southern Force (March–April 1942)

The 4th Submarine Squadron of Submarine Group "A" assembled at Sterling Bay in early March and with the reshuffles in Wartime Fleet Organization, this squadron was disbanded on 10 March. The *I-53, I-54* and *I-55* were transferred to the Kure Naval District Force, the *I-56, I-57* and *I-58* to the 5th Submarine Squadron and the *RO-33* and *RO-34* to the 6th Submarine Squadron. All submarines except *RO-33* and *RO-34* left for

Japan in the middle of March and the *RO-33* and *RO-34* started for Truk late in March for temporary duty with the South Seas Force. It had been decided that the 6th Submarine Squadron of Submarine Group "A" would be repaired and resupplied in the Homeland after operations were completed in early March. Therefore, by order of the Southern Force Commander, the *I-121, I-122, I-123* and the *Chokai* started for Japan in the middle of March. It had also been decided that the 5th Submarine Squadron (Submarine Group "B") would return to Japan for a period of one month, when the second operation for the disruption of enemy communications in the Indian Ocean was over. The submarines, therefore, sailed successively for Japan in late March and early April. The 2nd Submarine Squadron (Submarine Group "C") was ordered by the Combined Fleet commander to rejoin the Submarine Force after the termination of the Third Carrier Force operation in the Indian Ocean. This Submarine Squadron left Singapore for Japan in the middle of April. Under these circumstances, submarine operations in the Indian Ocean, the seas off North Australia and the Dutch East Indies were temporarily suspended in mid-April.

Other Chihaya Studies

Introduction

By this time, the reader of this book is well acquainted with Chihaya. Here we find an illuminating account of the Main Body's sortie on 8 December (Japan time) and subsequent discussions on board *Nagato* concerning a possible second attack on Pearl Harbor.

His second essay is in effect a book report on a well-known American account of the war from Pearl Harbor to the Coral Sea. It is especially noteworthy because Chihaya was in a position to answer some of the questions raised in the book.

Next comes a detailed account of the Battle of the Java Sea (27 February–1 March 1942). Although a Japanese victory, it involved an example of failure to pursue—a Japanese tendency Chihaya deplored.

His account of the air raid on Truk on 27 February 1944 is a no-holds-barred indictment of Japanese blunders, although the main fleet element stationed there had been removed earlier in the month.

All military organizations experience periodic shakeups, and the Imperial Japanese Navy was no exception. Chihaya points out that the lst Air Fleet was organized in April 1941 "from such administrative demands as training and replenishment of aircraft rather than from operational demands." It was not yet a true task force, and in maneuvers of the time the carriers performed the customary support functions. Oddly enough no major reformation of the fleet to emphasize the role of the air arm took place after Pearl Harbor. It took the defeat at Midway to prod the Japanese into "a drastic reform" of the fleet organization. Throughout the war, other reorganization took place, dictated by the necessities of the moment.

The three-part report of 20 August 1947 relates the fate of the ships participating in the Pearl Harbor attack. All but one, the DD *Ushio*, were sunk in the course of the war. Chihaya also tells something of the background of major participants in Operation Hawaii.

The two-part report of 5 September 1947 explains how Japanese warships were named, and also contains some information about the skippers of the Pearl Harbor tankers.

The Movement of the Japanese Battleship Group at the Outbreak of the War

Masataka Chihaya

13 September 1947

When I told you on 8 September that the Japanese battleship group sortied as far as north off Midway Island at the outbreak of the war, it was the first time, you said, that you heard of the movement of the battleship group. Also you asked me to make an investigation into the matter.

It was not, however, the first time that you had heard of it. In my C Information No. 14 dated 16 March, Subject: "Some features concerning changes of Japanese fleet organizations during the war," I included how the Japanese Navy intended to launch "One Big Battle" at the time of the Pearl Harbor attack as follows:

> When the 1st Air Fleet attacked Pearl Harbor, the battleship group under the direct control of Admiral Yamamoto sortied northwest off Midway Island. The mission of this battleship group did not lie in expanding the achievement following the attack of the 1st Air Fleet, but to take the 1st Air Fleet under its cover in case the air attack should fall.

Accordingly I made a further investigation and discovered my misapprehension about it, for which I must tender my fullest apology.

It is not, however, that they did not sortie from the Inland Sea at all. They did sortie in fact, but just after the Pearl Harbor attack and as far as, believe me, some 300 miles east off Japan proper.

They were commanded by Admiral Yamamoto and consisted of:

1st Sqd.   *Nagato* and *Mutsu*

1st Fleet under the command of VADM Shiro Takasu:

2nd Sqd.   *Ise, Hyuga,Yamashiro* and *Fuso*
21st Des. Div.   *Hatsushimo, Wakaba, Hatsuharu* and *Nenohi*
27th Des. Div.   *Shigure, Ariake, Yugure* and *Shiratsuyu*
Hosho (CVL), *Mikazuki* and *Yukaze* (both DDs)

Their mission was to offer a cover for the withdrawal of the Nagumo force after leaving the Inland Sea on "X" day viz. 8 December 1941. How funny it was! How it contradicted itself! It would not be so difficult even for me to point out its contradictions, if I were not so wise as Mr. Genda.

Because it was quite apparent that whether the Nagumo force would successfully withdraw from the Hawaiian Island area, after launching an air raid on the islands, it would be brought to an end in a few days after the air raid, more likely on the very day of the attack. How far was the distance between the Nagumo force and the Yamamoto force, whose mission was to tender a cover for the former's force on "X" day? It was just as far as from Japan to Hawaii. Even if the Yamamoto force exclusively consisted of B-29s or the forthcoming B-36s long-distance bombers, the distance would be too far to be covered. I have recalled that ever at that time not a few officers had considerable doubts about the intention of the Yamamoto force, which was called the "Main Force."

The Yamamoto force sortied [to] the Inland Sea on 8 December 1941 and passed south of Hachijo-Jima, the Izu Archipelago. When they reached about 300 miles east off the Izu Archipelago, on 11 December, they were ordered to make a return trip to Japan where they arrived on 13 December.

Additionally, I got a very interesting story about Admiral Yamamoto from a former Japanese captain who was a staff officer of the Combined Fleet* at the outbreak of the war, when I was gathering information for this report. He said to me:

> I remembered that there was a heated discussion in the headquarters on board the *Nagato*, as to whether an order to launch a second blow on Pearl Harbor should be issued to Vice Admiral Nagumo. At that time Admiral Yamamoto told me privately to the effect that Vice Admiral Nagumo would not dare to make a second attack on that island after all, he supposed. However, it was finally decided not to send any order to Vice Admiral Nagumo about it, placing all matters in Nagumo's hand. This decision might come from an old saying: "Don't interfere with generals on the battlefields." By the way, Admiral Yamamoto had some sense of inspiration which were [sic] revealed sometimes as well as on this occasion!

*Capt. Shigeru Fuji.

Supplement A: The Leaders of the Japanese Battleship Group at the Outbreak of the War, and the Approximate Track Chart of That Force
12 September 1947

The skippers of each of the Japanese battleship groups at the outbreak of the war, under the direct control of Admiral Yamamoto, were as follows:

BB	*Nagato:*	Capt. Hideo Yano
BB	*Mutsu:*	Capt. Gunji Kokure
BB	*Ise:*	Capt. Isamu Takeda
BB	*Hiyuga:*	Capt. Noboru Ishizaki
BB	*Yamashiro:*	Capt. Chozaemon Obata
BB	*Fuso:*	Capt. Mitsuo Kinoshita
DD	*Hatsushimo:*	Lt. Cmdr. Satoru Furuhama
DD	*Wakabe:*	Lt. Cmdr. Masakichi Kuroki
DD	*Hatsuharu:*	Lt. Cmdr. Tan Makino
DD	*Nenohi:*	Lt. Cmdr. Tosoji Senbongi
DD	*Shigure:*	Lt. Cmdr. Noboru Seo
DD	*Ariake:*	Lt. Cmdr. Syoichi Yoshida
DD	*Yugure:*	Lt. Cmdr. Kiyoshi Kamo
DD	*Shiratsuyu:*	Lt. Cmdr. Nagahide Shugitani
CVL	*Hosho:*	Capt. Noboru Umetani
DD	*Mikazuki:*	Lt. Cmdr. Saneho Maeda
DD	*Yukaze:*	Lt. Cmdr. Tsuyoshi Kajimoto

Generally speaking, none among them later influenced the war, as did Mr. Ohmae and Mr. Genda.

Supplement B
26 October 1947

1. The principal characteristics of Japanese ships which belonged to the Main Force as of December 1941:

Names of Ships	Tonnage	Breadth (m)	Length (m)	Main Guns, etc.	Radius of Action
Nagato & Mutsu	43,581	34.6	201.1	40 cm × 8 14 cm × 16	16 knots— 7,000'

Fuso & *Yamashiro*	39,154	33.0	212	36 cm × 12	12 knots—
				15 cm × 14	12,670'
Hyuga & *Ise*	38,687	33.8	195	36 cm × 12	16 knots—
				14 cm × 16	8,000'
Hosho	10,500	18.0	155	14 cm × 4	Unknown
				21 planes	
Hatsushimo	2,060	10	103	12.7 cm × 4	18 knots—
				61 cm tube × 6	4,000'
Mikazuki	1,270	9.1	99.8	12 cm × 3	14 knots—
				53 cm tube × 4	4,000'

2. The names of the chief members of the Combined Fleet who were aboard the *Nagato*:

Admiral	Isoroku Yamamoto
Rear Admiral	Matome Ugaki
Capt.	Kameto Kuroshima
Capt.	Yoshiyuki Miwa
Capt.	Shigeru Fuji
Cmdr.	Yasuji Watanabe
Cmdr.	Akira Sasaki
Cmdr.	Takayasu Arima
Cmdr.	Shigeru Nagata
Cmdr.	Yuushiro Wada
Cmdr.	Taro Isobe

3. On 20 October I called on Mr. Watanabe to find out the following information: First, I asked him the movement of the Main Force under the direct control of Admiral Yamamoto. He said:

It was sometime around ten o'clock in the morning of 8 December 1941 that the Main Force left Hashirajima anchorage in Hiroshima Bay. There were 6 BBs, one CVL, and 9DDs. By that time we had vague but not detailed information to the effect that the Pearl Harbor attack had been successfully completed, due to the successful receiving of wireless communications directly from planes that attacked the island.

The purpose of that movement was to receive the Nagumo force in case of the latter being chased by the American Fleet. It might seem to be a little funny now, but it was seriously considered necessary at that time to give some cover to the Nagumo force in order to receive them safely. Although we had received the information saying that the surprise air attack on the island was successful when we left the Inland Sea, we had not yet had any information from Vice Admiral Nagumo concerning whether they met any encounter or not. In other words, the sortie of the Main Force on December the 8th was entirely due to the scheduled plan, but not due to the circumstance that happened.

It was not until December the 11th that Admiral Yamamoto was given comparatively detailed information about the attack, especially the fact that the Nagumo force met no serious encounter from the enemy and they were returning very safely. In consequence, it became apparent that there was no need to prepare to give them some cover for their retreat. Immediately the fleet was ordered to return to the homeland.

Then I asked him, "If the purpose of the Main Force was to give some cover for the Nagumo force's safe retreat, the Main Force ought to have left the Inland Sea, just following the Nagumo force or ought to have been in the Marshall Islands. Why did they stay in the Inland Sea until December the 8th?"

To this question, he replied:

Three things were considered the reasons for it. One thing referred to communications between the General Headquarters in Tokyo and his headquarters. The *Nagato*, Admiral Yamamoto's flagship, used to moor at a buoy in Hashirajima which had a phone connected directly to Headquarters in Tokyo. Through this phone Admiral Yamamoto could make close connections to the General Headquarters in Tokyo. So important was this connection, especially in the very grave moments before the war, that Admiral Yamamoto could not leave this buoy until the very moment the war started at last.

The next was the problem of sufficient tankers for the long voyage and sufficient numbers of destroyers for escort. Japan had not a sufficient number of tankers, particularly oceangoing ones, at that time. The tankers that accompanied Nagumo's force were all we had at that time capable of accompanying the fleet.

The last reason came somewhat from oriental leadership. In oriental leadership it was considered very important that the supreme commander take the risk of conducting campaigns at the foremost battlefront. From this point of view, a movement of the Main Force at the very moment of the outbreak of the war was considered deserving to encourage all the men of the Combined Fleet.

I asked him for further information concerning the said heated discussion about the second attack on Pearl Harbor in the headquarters aboard the *Nagato*. He said:

I do not remember whether there was a heated discussion in the headquarters about the second attack on Pearl Harbor. On the contrary it seems to me that the problem of the second attack on the island was at that time out of the question. I thought we had not yet had sufficient information to decide whether an order for the second attack would be issued to the Vice Admiral or not.

We had, however, a heated discussion whether an order should be issued for the Nagumo force to launch an air raid on Midway Island on their way to the homeland or not. Although some staff officers strongly stressed an air raid on Midway Island, the problem was at last settled in not sending an order to Vice Admiral Nagumo for an air raid on Midway Island. This decision was based upon the opinion that there was not sufficient information on board the *Nagato* to judge the situation, and the matter would be better placed into the hands of the Vice Admiral who must have known the situation better than anyone.*

In connection with the Pearl Harbor attack, he disclosed his impression which he got at the time of the attack. He said, "Hearing of the great success of the Nagumo force, nothing was more regretful to me than my having committed a great blunder in planning the Pearl Harbor attack. The fact is that I and my company staff officer never had the slightest plan nor ever dreamed of a second attack on the island when we planned the Pearl Harbor attack."

He added:

What impressed me most at that time was that we planners had to keep always in our minds three phases of every situation—they were cases of great success, of expected results, and of failure. When we planned the Pearl Harbor attack we considered a situation of expected results and even thought in our minds of an unsuccessful case, but never dreamed of such a great success as was achieved by the Nagumo force in reality. Because such a case would be entirely out of the question, we thought.

If we had the slightest idea of launching a second attack in case of a great success—even dreamed of it—we would not have failed to indicate such an idea or a hint to Vice Admiral Nagumo which would have been some help for him to make a second attack on the island just following the first attack. The subsequent proceeding of the war might have changed somewhat, had there been some indication for a second attack revealed to Vice Admiral Nagumo.

He revealed this story confirming some notes which he had written during the war.

4. The wireless communications between the Combined Fleet and the Task Force as of the outbreak of the war.

It is my great regret that so far I have failed to get satisfactory information concerning the above-mentioned subject. What I got about it are only

*Translator's note: As to this information, I got a different one. It said that on 10 December the Nagumo force was ordered by Admiral Yamamoto to make an air raid on Midway Island. Owing to bad weather they failed.

Ed. Note: Nagumo's orders contained the qualifying phrase, "If the situation permits . . ." Neither he nor his chief advisers approved of the Midway idea, so he took advantage of the bad weather and his "out" to call it off.

some telegrams which were sent by Japanese airplanes that sortied from the Nagumo force during the attack. They were received aboard the *Nagato* directly, without being relayed by the task force. They were, however, considered nearly all the information Admiral Yamamoto received on board the *Nagato*, because the task force kept very strict radio silence after the attack being carried out as well as before the attack. On 8 December, Admiral Nagumo sent only one message, saying that the surprise attack on Pearl Harbor had been made successfully.

It was likely on 10 December that Admiral Nagumo sent a relatively detailed message to Admiral Yamamoto. I hope you refer to Mr. Watanabe the following wireless messages which are expected to renew his memory:

From	To	Time	Message
Plane from *Chikuma*		0305	Enemy fleet form in anchorage: so and so. Direction of wind: 80° and speed of wind: 14 meters.
Plane from *Chikuma*		0312	Enemy fleet is not in Lahaina Anchorage
Plane from *Chikuma*		0308	Enemy fleet is in Pearl Harbor.
Plane from *Chikuma*		0308	Overhead clearance over enemy fleet is 1,700 meters and mounts of cloud: 7 degrees.
Commanding plane of all air force		0318	All force: Make dash attack.
Commanding plane of all air force		0322	A surprise attack made successfully.
Commanding officer of task force	CinC of Combined Fleet	0337	A surprise attack made successfully.
Commanding plane of *Zuikaku* dive bombers		0348	3 hangars and 50 planes on ground were set on fire.
Commanding plane of *Shokaku* dive bombers		0339	Direction of wind: 70° and speed of wind: 10 meters.
Commanding plane of *Shokaku* dive bombers		0342	Bombed Ford and Hickam with good results.
Commanding plane of *Zuikaku* force		0413	Make formation ready to launch dash attack.
Commanding plane of *Zuikaku* force		0425	All force: Make dash attack.

Commanding plane of *Zuikaku* force	0427	Direction of wind: 55° and speed of wind: 10 meters.
Commanding plane of *Shokaku* force	0500	Bombed Ford with little result.
Commanding plane of *Zuikaku* force	0447	Bombed Hickam with good result.
Commanding plane of *Shokaku* force	0458	Bombed Kaneohe with result.
Commanding plane of *Zuikaku* force	0445	22 BBs are leaving Pearl Harbor.
Dive bomber of *Hiryu*	0635	Enemy flying boat is likely tracking us.

Essay Concerning the Book Battle Report

Masataka Chihaya

14 February 1947

I have been given the favor of reading the book entitled "Battle Report," covering the period from Pearl Harbor to the Coral Sea. It is my great pleasure to report to you that I have found much of interest in that book.

As was written in the book, it is quite true that there were many achievements incidental to the battle. Also it is true that there were many achievements for each opponent to be still obscure, doubtful and even unknown until the very moment of the veil of the war being completely taken off. Indeed, in reading through the book I found many events of the Allied side which had since been unknown to the Japanese side. And at the same time I was not slightly astonished to learn how difficult work it was even for the thorough Americans to get the whole objective picture of the Japanese side of the war.

Now, I want to touch my pen at first to several achievements of the Allied side which had since been unknown to the Japanese side. From page 128 to page 132 it was released that just three days before the outbreak of the war Admiral Sir Tom Phillips of the Royal Navy flew to Manila in order to negotiate with Admiral Hart of the United States Navy. The immediate purpose of his flying trip to Manila was to request at least four American destroyers as part of the screen for the *Prince of Wales* and the *Repulse*. This was a very interesting fact and also had since been unknown to our Japanese.

On page 173 the reason why the *Boise* and the *Marblehead* were out of the Java Sea Campaign was also uncovered, to our utmost interest. The

*Walter Karig and Welbourn Kelly, *Battle Report: Pearl Harbor to Coral Sea* (New York, 1944).

Boise hit the jagged point of an uncharted pinnacle rock. The *Marblehead* limped from a turbine casualty which reduced her speed to 15 knots. This fact, together with the DD *Peary*'s misfortune of being bombed by very friendly planes, were some [sic] of the unavoidable achievements in the battle. When things turn smooth with God, everything turns out well even though it seems to run against it at the first glance. On the contrary, everything does not turn out well in spite of every minute care when things turn rough with the Devil. We, the Japanese Navy, had a lot of experiences of them: in the first quarter part of the war with good luck and in the remaining period against luck.

On page 107 a surprising fact to our Japanese, though maybe so only to Japanese, was also revealed. It was the very fact that the U.S. aircraft carrier *Langley*, which met her doom a few weeks later south off Tjilatjap, was carrying out the mission of ferrying P-40s from Port Darwin to Timor at the time of the Japanese invasion of the Netherlands East Indies, because the distance between those places was too near the limit of action of P-40s at that period. Never did the Japanese Navy imagine it at all at that time, because the Zero fighter of the Japanese Navy did not find difficulties in carrying out strafing operations to Port Darwin from Timor. Indeed, on 3 March 1942, 9 Zero fighters even at Broome succeeded in strafing a dozen flying boats and a dozen other planes to blow out. The distance from Koepang to Broome [is] at least not less than 500 miles.

I have also found some mistakes committed by the American Navy in the field of naval strategy. In February and March of 1942 the U.S. task forces commanded by either Admiral Halsey or Fletcher took the risk of making air raids upon the Marshalls, Wake and Marcus Island. They consisted of a carrier as their nucleus, 2 or 3 cruisers and several destroyers as their screens. These operations were very dangerous risks indeed, because, when the American task force came to attack the Marshalls on 1 February 1942 the Japanese task force happened to be in Truk—the very task force which succeeded in attacking Pearl Harbor about two months before and was in the pink of condition, their blood fired with the firmest confidence.

Immediately responding to the warning saying "air raid" from the Marshalls, the Japanese task force left Truk at 1100[;] less than twelve hours later came the attack on the islands. It made its way to the Marshalls to be there in 48 hours. On 3 February, however, it was decided that it would return to Truk and resume the original operational plan—participation in the Netherlands East Indies invasion. Then it went westward to Palau Island and Kendari, Celebes.

If the Japanese task force had successively remained in the Truk area and had made some effort to take on an American task force, what would be the result of it? Although to take on an American force when it came to attack [the] Wake and Marcus Islands would be very difficult, it would not be impossible for the Japanese, especially in the event that Japan would make such further chase as to threaten the Australian-American lifeline. What would come of it, if an engagement between both carrier forces happened? It would be out of the question.

Then, would attacks on the Marshalls and other islands be worth such risks? It is undeniable that such daring actions of the American did much to contribute to stirring up the morale of not only Americans but all Allied people when the situation in the Far East was getting worse day by day. It is also evident that in these operations the American Navy learned a lot of lessons in equipment and techniques as well as in tactics and strategy to which great successes of subsequent powerful carrier groups' operations undoubtedly attributed the utmost degree.

The first mission of the American Fleet, however, was to destroy Japanese bases on those islands. Then, what was the result of it? About this I have gotten some information from copies of telegrams which were received from those islands after the enemy air raid. They read:

At Marshalls:	2 transport ships and a small craft sunk. A transport ship and a small craft damaged. About 90 dead including the commanding officer of the naval base. (On page 269, it said 73,000 tons of enemy ships including 2 submarines and 35 aircraft destroyed.)
At Wake:	A patrol vessel sunk and a four-engine flying boat destroyed. 150 drums of gasoline blown up. About 10 dead and wounded. (On page 278, it said 3 four-engine aircraft destroyed and 2 patrol vessels sunk and many other installations destroyed.)
At Marcus:	The radio transmitter equipment went silent about half a day. 5 dead

Were these results worth such dangerous risks? I wonder if they were. If there had been an urgent need to do so chiefly from the political point of view as well as for a laboratory experiment that was to develop into a new kind of war at sea, only the air raid upon the Marshalls of 1 February 1942 should have sufficed. It was in this that I think the United States Navy committed a mistake in the first stage of the war.

A Japanese chart of Pearl Harbor found in a captured Japanese midget submarine[. . .] was one of the items that surprised me very much. Undoubtedly that chart indicated that the two-man midget submarine went around Ford Island during the period from 0430 to 0530 of 8 December 1941. It also showed that he made a torpedo attack on the first ship in Battleship Row at 0450. Additionally the author of that book presumed that the same two-man submarine communicated their knowledge of the ships based inside Pearl Harbor to their fleet, though no message was heard from those midget submarines, except at night of that day a short message saying "TORA TORA," which meant "Tiger" in Japanese, was heard from one of those submarines. That message was decoded as "Attacks succeeded."

It goes without saying that to get objective pictures of the opponent in war is very difficult, if not impossible. So that it is unavoidable not to get rid of some mistakes in that book as far as Japan is concerned.

As to the Pearl Harbor attack by the Japanese Navy, a report to be made by the Historical Section of the 2nd Demobilization Bureau is expected to be submitted to your section in the not far future, so that I want you to prefer that report. Here, I only point out some of them, chiefly both in the Philippines and the Netherlands East Indies invasions.

1. On pages 137–38 it argued that they could not find out the exact reason why the Japanese so delayed in launching their first air attack on Luzon on the very morning of 8 December 1941. However, it was very simple. According to the Japanese original Philippine Invasion Plan, top priority was given in launching initial air attacks on Luzon by naval land-air forces operated from Formosa. This was because the success of the Philippine Invasion, which was deadlined [sic] to be finished in less than a month, exclusively depended upon whether the initial air attacks on Luzon mainland succeeded or not. But this was not an easy task, nay, a very difficult problem, for the distance from Formosa to the Manila Area where the main American air forces were suspected to be was about 500 miles. This was almost the limit of action of even the Zero fighters, at that time when Allied P-40s found many difficulties in even flying from Port Darwin to Timor, less than 500 miles.

Accordingly the Japanese Navy at first intended to use carrier groups in order to launch an initial air raid on the Manila Area most effectively. But, as training for practice reached its peak just [a] few months before the outbreak of the war, the Zero fighter began to prove its effectiveness, capable of launching about 500-miles sortie from Formosa to the Manila Area. So that the plan of using carriers for the initial blow to the Luzon area was given up and the light carrier *Ryujo* was assigned to complement air raids on southern Mindanao which was beyond the reach of the Japanese air raid operated from Formosa.

The initial air attack of the 11th Air Fleet under the command of VADM Nishizo Tsukahara was to be launched in the early morning of 8 December just after the time of the Pearl Harbor attack. In the early morning of 8 December, however, the southern Formosa area had unfortunately such thick fog that the sortie of the Japanese naval air forces had to be held up for a while against all the men's fiery wishes. It was apparent that more delay would mean more disadvantage, for a warning message "Air Raid on Pearl Harbor" was undoubtedly received in the Philippines. The thick fog that had used to clear [up] in daytime did not clear up completely until at least at 0930. The sortie was decided upon in spite of the fog still remaining in the air. Eighty-four Zero fighters and 108 land-based bombers roared up into the air. When they returned to Formosa, having achieved remarkable successes, it was already in the twilight darkness and some fog still remained. Not a few planes could not find their mother bases and managed to land at other bases. The Japanese losses, however, were only 7 fighters including the missing. It was well-nigh a miracle.

2. On page 140 there was a famous "Kelly bombing." But we Japanese had no record of a hit on the *Haruna* class battleship at that time.

3. On page 146 the aircraft carrier *Langley* and the oilers *Trinity* and *Pecos* managed to escape from two Japanese warships in the Sulu Sea. But, according to our records, no Japanese warship was in that area at that time.

4. On page 178, the reason why the first Japanese ship which the Allied Fleet sighted in the Battle of the Makassar Strait had not fired on them was considered to be because the Japanese ship perhaps mistook Allied ships for their own forces. That exactly hits the nail on the head. The commanding officer of the Japanese naval force of the Balikpapan Invasion hoisted his flag on the *Naka*, one of two Japanese four-stack light cruisers. Naturally the first Japanese patrol ship sighting American four-pipers in the darkness mistook them for their flagship, the *Naka*.

5. On page 215 the Japanese force which engaged in the Badoeng Strait engagement was estimated as a powerful task force including 8-inch cruisers, and two destroyers were believed to be sunk. In reality, however, the Japanese force in Badoeng Strait consisted of four destroyers of which two destroyers only engaged in the latter part of that engagement at the eastern part of the strait. And no ship was lost, although a destroyer was severely damaged and was towed to Makassar.

6. On page 224 it was said that a Japanese force landed on Bawean Island on 25 February as a preparatory operation to Java, but neither the Japanese Army nor Navy landed there.

As to the Battle of the Java Sea, I have made some survey to prepare a report by the requisition of Lieutenant Commander Salomon who came here to investigate war records last spring. That report was considered helpful in making clear the account of that battle from the Japanese point of view, so that I want to add a copy of it as my next report.

After all, what impressed me most in reading through the book was the fact that in order to make the whole picture of the war objectively, a one-sided account of the war, no matter how thorough it may be, would not suffice, but accounts of the war from both sides would be badly needed.

Account of the Battle of the Java Sea

Masataka Chihaya
15 February 1947

1. The Outline of the Battle

Having secured Celebes, Borneo and Sumatra as springboards to Java, and also having covered almost the whole air of Java under her control, towards the end of February 1942 Japan intended to invade Java which was the final destination of Japan's preliminary operation.

Japan's invasion forces under the command of General K. Imamura planned to penetrate Java from two points—the eastern part and the western part of the island. The eastern group which intended to land on Kragan, 90 miles west of Soerabaja, consisted of 41 convoy ships. In order to land on the designated spot on 28 February, the convoy, under escort consisting of several destroyers, minesweepers and submarine chasers, left Jolo on 19 February and on the way touched Balikpapan for a while, whence it departed on 23 February.

The western group, which was the main force, consisting of 56 convoy ships, left Camranh Bay, French Indochina, on 18 February to land its forces at P. Marak, Banten and Patrol which is situated about 70 miles east of Batavia on 28 February.

VADM Ibo Takahashi, who was then Commander in Chief of the Third Fleet, took the responsibility of cooperating with General Imamura and divided his commanding force into two groups in accordance with the Army's invasion plan.

RADM Takeo Takagi, who was the commanding officer of the 5th Cruiser Sqd., took the task of escorting the eastern convoy group and reached the area about 60 miles northwest of Soerabaja in the afternoon of 27 February, commanding the 5th Cruiser Sqd., the 4th Destroyer Sqd. and the 2nd Destroyer Sqd. There he met the Allied Naval Forces which had been in Soerabaja since the engagement off Bali Island on 19–20 February and took the risk of encountering the Japanese forces. For the first time since the beginning of the war, a large-scale engagement occurred, not far from Soerabaja and was fought during the afternoon of the 27th which we may call the *Day Action of 27 February* and continued until night, which we may call the *Night Action of 27 February*. Having received heavy damages during the Day and Night Action of 27 February, the Allied Naval Forces withdrew to Soerabaja. Owing to these actions, the date of the landing was postponed to the day following the scheduled date, this is, on 1 March.

About one hour before noon, two days after the action of the 27th, a cruiser accompanied by two destroyers was caught at the spot about 100 miles northwest off Bawean Island and all were sunk by the Japanese forces which were covering the landing operation. We may call this engagement the *Action of 1 March*.

In another theater, RADM Takeo Kurita, who was the commanding officer of the 7th Cruiser Sqd., escorted the western landing group, commanding his 7th Cruiser Sqd., the 5th Destroyer Sqd. and several small vessels. Except for the date of the landing being postponed to the day after the scheduled plan, due to the Action of 27 February off Soerabaja, the invasion forces successfully proceeded without any counterattack by the enemy to the designated place, which they reached in the night of 28 February. Soon after midnight of the 28th, two enemy cruisers penetrated the anchorage of the invasion group off Banten Bay and a night action occurred which we may call the *Night Action of 1 March off Batavia*. During this engagement they received small damages, but not to the extent of preventing their landing operation at all. Two enemy ships were sunk.

In spite of these actions, Japan's landing operation succeeded as scheduled.

Throughout the actions, the Japanese Army and Navy air forces, which took the responsibility of cooperating with the invasion operation, did much to neutralize the remaining Allied air forces in Java, but made little direct contribution to these actions.

2. The Day Action of 27 February

(a) General proceedings.

The 4th Destroyer Sqd., commanded by RADM Nishimura, consisted of the CL *Naka*, the 9th Destroyer Div. (*Asagumo, Minegumo*), and the 2nd Destroyer Div. (*Murasame, Samidare, Harusame, Yudachi*). The 4th Destroyer Sqd. took the job of escorting the eastern group of the invasion forces, composed of 41 transport ships, and left Jolo, Soeloe Archipelago, in the morning of 19 February and touched Balikpapan whence they departed 23 February. On 24 February they were tracked by an enemy flying boat which was shot down by Japanese fighters.

In the morning of the 28th, on the southern sea off Laoet Island, the southeastern tip of Borneo, they rendezvoused with the 5th Cruiser Sqd., consisting of the *Nachi* and *Haguro,* screened by four destroyers (*Ushio, Sazanami, Yamakaze, Kawakaze*) and the 2nd Destroyer Sqd. consisting of the *Jintsu,* the 16th Destroyer Div. *(Yukikaze, Tokitsukaze, Amatsukaze, Hatsukaze).*

At about noon of the 27th, when the convoy reached about 150 miles northwest of Soerabaja, a warning message saying that five enemy cruisers and six destroyers were sighted at 63 miles in the direction of 310 degrees from Soerabaja, coursing 110 degrees at speed of 12 knots was received from a reconnaissance plane of the 11th Air Fleet that was [Takeo] teamworking with them. Rear Admiral Takagi turned the course to southeast to come up to the enemy fleet and also ordered the 4th Destroyer Sqd. to lead the convoy to the westward.

At about 1600 it was found from a reconnaissance plane that the enemy had converted their composition into a single column and turned their course to 20 degrees. At about 1700 Rear Admiral Takagi predicted their command to be deployed to the south, finding the distance between both fleets about 60 miles at that time. Soon later [sic], at 1830, enemy masts were sighted in the direction of 170 degrees.

About five minutes later, after enemy masts were sighted, the *Nachi* and the *Haguro* opened fire on the head of the enemy fleet at about 22,000 meters for about one hour. During this engagement the enemy were observed to return their fire, frequently changing their courses to avoid Japanese salvoes. At the same time, other duels were also engaged between light vessels of both sides.

At about 1830, sighting a cruiser dropping out of their ranks, and other vessels receiving several hits, Rear Admiral Takagi ordered his command to rush upon the enemy. Many Japanese vessels torpedoed their fishes, but almost in vain. Observing the Japanese Fleet rushing upon them, the Allied Fleet did a nine-point turn to the left simultaneously into the southeast course and expanded [sic] smoke screen.

At about 1900 the Japanese Fleet changed its course to eastward to make a further approach to the enemy and torpedoed other fishes. At about 1915 the Allied Fleet changed their course to northward and began to return fierce encountering gunfire which inflicted some hits on the *Asagumo,* forcing her to stop for about 40 minutes. From 1930 to 1945 Japanese torpedoes reached the Allied Fleet and two or perhaps three destroyers were observed to be sunk.

At about 1930, in spite of observing the enemy's damage and confusion inflicted by his fleet, Rear Admiral Takagi, however, decided to give up his further chase and ordered his command to change their course to the north.

The reason why Rear Admiral Takagi gave up his further chase at that precious moment was said to be as follows:

(1) At about 1800 some explosions were observed in the engaged area which seemed to be those of enemy mines. But it was learned that those explosions were those of our oxygen torpedoes due to some deficiencies which were discovered through the investigation which was made after the battle.

(2) They observed a light of the lighthouse at Soerabaja which indicated that they had reached within 30 miles of Soerabaja, so that there was fear of enemy mines.

(3) For fear of enemy submarines.

(b) Damages received and damages inflicted:

Damages received: DD *Asagumo* slightly damaged but able to sail.

Damages inflicted: Two, perhaps three, DDs sunk. A cruiser severely damaged.

* * *

3. The Night Action of 27 February

(a) General proceedings.

At about 2000 of the 27th toward the evening, for sunset of that day was about 1950, the Japanese Fleet continued to withdraw to the north, while on the other hand the Allied Fleet changed its course to northward after the preceding half an hour's withdrawal to the south.

Soon before 2100 the Allied Fleet was observed approaching in the direction of 150 degrees, and not long passed before the Japanese Fleet was illuminated by blinker lights overhead. And about five minutes later, the Allied Fleet's gunfire was observed flashing through the darkness. Then the Japanese withdrew to the northwest at an increased speed, laying a smoke screen behind.

And it followed from that time to about 2330 that the Japanese Fleet reciprocated almost a north or south course to keep pace with the movement of the Allied Fleet, over which there were two watchful planes tracking, catapulted from the *Jintsu* and the *Naka*. After the tracking planes withdrew at about 2330, however, no further information was received.

Just after half past midnight, when the Japanese Fleet took the southward course, suddenly the enemy fleet was sighted at about 15,000 meters to the left ahead of the Japanese Fleet. Immediately the Japanese Fleet turned to north to make a parallel course with the Allied Fleet, and at the same time heightened its speed to 33 knots. Also at this time blinker lights were observed overhead, which caused too much of an obstacle to see the enemy.

About a quarter of an hour later after the Allied Fleet was sighted, the *Nachi* and the *Haguro* began to fire several salvoes against the enemy without [a] searchlight and discharged their torpedoes (*Nachi*, 8 and *Haguro*, 4 fishes) against the enemy fleet sighted at about 10,000 meters almost the beam. About ten or fifteen minutes passed which was considered necessary for the fishes to reach the enemy, before two huge columns of flame were observed to the eastward so that two cruisers, perhaps the Dutch cruisers *DeRuyter* and *Java*, were sighted sinking at once.

Later, exact time unknown, Rear Admiral Takagi ordered his commanding fleet to chase the enemy, but he could not discover the remaining enemy fleet owing to the squall that happened to come. Although he continued searching until about 0315 he ordered his command to withdraw to the northwest to be in the convoy patrolling position.

And before the dawn of the 28th, the order was issued saying that the Date of Invasion would be postponed twenty-four hours.

(b) Damages received and damages inflicted:

Damages received: None.

Damages inflicted: Two cruisers, probably *DeRuyter* and *Java*, sunk.

* * *

4. The Action of 1 March

(a) General proceeding.

Throughout the whole day immediately after the Day and Night Actions of the 27th, the Japanese Fleet had to stay north off Java to wait for the time, because of the Date of Landing being postponed 24 hours. Any counterattack of the Allied Forces which could be expected was not met. In the night of the 28th, the convoy proceeded successfully to Kragan, 90 miles west of Soerabaja and just prior to reaching the anchorage received a night attack of about ten dive bombers, so that one transport ship went ashore damaged and another ship was also damaged, with the result of about 150 dead and wounded. The Japanese landing, nevertheless, was carried out successfully, although a dawn attack of about 15 enemy fighters was made without effect to the Japanese convoy in the morning.

Throughout this landing operation, the Japanese Fleet stayed north off Java covering the operation and in the morning of 1 March they reached the area about 100 miles northwest off Bawean Island.

At about 1100 the 5th Cruiser Sqd., commanded by Rear Admiral Takagi, suddenly sighted a mast of a cruiser at a distance of less than 30,000 meters to the north of it and signaled to all the Japanese Fleet nearby [the] warning "enemy sighted." The Japanese cruisers *Ashigara* and *Myoko*, escorted by two destroyers (*Akebono, Ikazuchi*) under the direct control of Vice Admiral Takahashi that were sailing about 30 miles northwest of the

5th Cruiser Sqd., hurried to the sighted enemy cruiser, receiving a warning message. In less than one hour since sighting the enemy, the Japanese Fleet took the very advantageous position to put the enemy cruiser, accompanied by two destroyers, into the midst of the 5th Cruiser Squadron and Vice Admiral Takahashi's. At this moment, about noon, the enemy was observed to endeavor to escape at top speed to the eastward, changing its course to avoid Japanese salvoes and also laying a smoke screen. The Japanese Fleet attacked the enemy from both the north and south sides with fierce gunfire and torpedoes, so that after more than one hour's duel a cruiser, perhaps the *Exeter*, and a destroyer were seen to be sunk and another destroyer to be burning fiercely. Against a burning destroyer Vice Admiral Takahashi successfully made such a further chase that at last, time unknown, he caught it and sank it at the point of 30 miles in the direction of 160 degrees from Tg. Poeting, Borneo, although the prey had already been devoured by the attack of Japanese naval air forces previously.

(b) Damages received and damages inflicted:

Damages received: None.

Damges inflicted: One cruiser, perhaps *Exeter*, sunk.

Two destroyers also sunk.

* * *

5. The Night Action of 1 March off Batavia

(a) General proceeding.

In another theater, the western landing groups successfully proceeded to their destination without any counterattack of the enemy, under the escort of RADM T. Kurita. On the night of the 28th, Japanese invasion forces reached the planned landing anchorage of P. Marak, Banten and Patrol as scheduled.

A few minutes past midnight of the 29th, the Japanese Destroyer *Hubuki*, which was patroling the north waters off Toenda Island, about 12 miles off the Java mainland, discovered two enemy ships penetrating Banten Bay from the east of Toenda Island and signaled "enemy sighted" and further information, following the rear of the enemy.

At about 0030 the Japanese destroyer *Harukaze* expanded an effective smoke screen between the enemy and the convoy.

Meanwhile, two enemy ships began to fire and to torpedo the convoy with the success of a transport ship sunk and three others severely damaged. The Japanese Fleet which was charged with the responsibility for guarding the convoy, concentrated at the enemy's northern area. Those forces were composed as follows:

Light cruiser	*Natori* and *Yura*
Destroyer	5th Des. Div. (*Harukaze, Hatakaze* and *Asakaze*)
	11th Des. Div. (*Hubuki, Hatsuyuki* and *Shirayuki*)
	12th Des. Div. (*Shirakumo* and *Murakumo*)
Minesweeper	*Shirataka*

At about 0100 the Japanese Fleet began to encounter the enemy fiercely, enforced by the 2nd division of the 7th Cruiser Squadron (*Mikuma* and *Mogami*) with a destroyer (*Shikinami*) from the north. Severe damages inflicted upon the enemy were observed all the while the enemy began to circle, remarkably reducing its speed and finally stopping. A cruiser, perhaps the *Perth*, was observed to be sunk at about 0140 and about half an hour later another one, perhaps the *Houston*, also to be sunk.

(b) Damages received and damages inflicted:

Damges received: One transport ship sunk.

Three others severely damaged.

Damages inflicted: Two cruisers, perhaps *Perth* and *Houston*, sunk.

Account of the Fiasco of Truk on 27 February 1944

Masataka Chihaya

3 February 1947

Until the beginning of February 1944, Truk Island was the center of the Japanese naval operation in the Southwest Pacific Area. Almost all of the Japanese naval forces gathered there under the command of Admiral Mineichi Koga, the Commander in Chief of the Combined Fleet, who succeeded Admiral Isoroku Yamamoto after his death in April 1943. Truk Island was also a powerful air base situated behind New Britain and Bougainville where, in the air, desperate duels had heretofore been fought between the Allied Powers and Japan, though resulting in gradually losing the balance against the Japanese side.

Active planes for defense of that island were not so many, though in the Takeshima airstrip there were more than 100 planes which were being equipped and fitted for use, overhauls and repairs. In fact, on 15 February 1944, two days before the powerful American task forces came to attack Truk Island for the first time, there were about 50 Zero fighters on Takeshima, 24 *Tenzan* carrier-borne torpedo planes on Kaedeshima and 8 twin-engined land-based bombers on Harushima as well as about 250 planes on Takeshima which were under repair, and also happened to be there en route to Rabaul.

Such being the case, it must have been the natural conclusion for the Japanese Navy that even Truk Island would be subjected in the very near future to revengeful attacks of more-powerful American task forces, at the time after the barrier of the Gilberts and the Marshalls line had been broken and also the fate of the once-strong base of Rabaul was already doomed. Besides, there were several ominous indications of it from the early beginning of February 1944. Around 6–7 February, Truk Island suffered enemy

279

reconnaissance planes overhead. Aerial observation through wireless instruments indicated that American fleets were in action not far at sea from there.

Thereupon, towards 10 February the main striking forces of the Japanese Navy then in Truk began to withdraw to the westward, leaving there only the CL *Naka,* a training cruiser, the *Katori,* about 4 destroyers in action, about 4 other destroyers under repair, and smaller vessels. It was at large only less than a week before the American fleet came on to attack there at last. The Japanese Fleet might literally be said to have managed to escape annihilation by a hair's breadth.

Then, was the Japanese Navy that had its fleets withdrawn successfully from Truk, though by a hair's-breadth escape, also alert to take every necessary measure to minimize supposed damages? Did it still continue the strictest preparations for coming air raids? No, it wasn't, nor did it at all. Maybe it is beyond your imagination, but quite true. Then, why?

A repatriated ex–naval commander, who had been returned from Truk recently and since December 1943 had been a staff officer of the 4th Fleet then stationed in Truk, revealed some reason for it though not perfectly. His narrative release in mid-December of last year read:

> Almost at the same time when the main forces of the Japanese Navy left Truk towards 10 February 1944, the highest order of preparation for air raid was ordered throughout the island, requesting everybody to attend his quarter at any time when requested by the Commander in Chief of the 4th Fleet, who took the responsibility of defending that island after the departures of the Commander in Chief of the Combined Fleet, the 2nd Fleet and the 3rd Fleet.

Moreover, there were lacking such air-defense facilities as air raid shelters, underground storage and AA guns as mentioned in my previous report. In fact, there was no underground storage available.

Then followed several comparatively dull days, with the exception of 15 February. The headquarters of the 4th Fleet, however, was not too patient to continue the first degrees of alertness for air raid without permitting his men shore leaves. In the midst of this most critical period, on 16 February he committed a great blunder of relaxing the alertness against air raid for a somewhat lower degree, also permitting his men shore leaves. When American planes began their attacks in the morning of 17 February, some persons were observed to hurry to their quarters from the small town in Natsushima. But it was too far for them to be in time to counterattack and also too late. And the worst case was for the pilots. There was a narrow slit between Natsushima, where there was a small town, and Takeshima, where the majority of fighters assembled. This worse situation became the worst when the ferry point to Takeshima, situated unfortunately very near to oil tanks, was bombed.

In order to make clear why such a great blunder was committed, it seems necessary to add some explanations about the circumstances under which the decision was made.

On 15 February 1944, aerial observation through wireless instruments caught loud voices suspected to be from American task forces. In the morning of that day, air reconnaissance made by 6 land-based bombers and 3 Tenzans covered the eastern sea area off Truk Island, resulting in two land-based bombers being lost. They were suspected of being shot down by American task forces.

The following morning, the same air reconnaissance cover was made, except for two reconnaissance lines, because two land-based bombers to be used were engaged in searching for the missing planes. With still more obscure reasons, important gaps were not supplemented after all.

On the same day, a message was received to the effect that the *Agano*, which several weeks ago had received severe damage north of Rabaul and had left Truk for repairs in the homeland on 15 February, was torpedoed by a submarine northwest off Truk Island. Accordingly, the *Naka* was ordered to take on the job of rescuing the *Agano*. Thus, the headquarters of the 4th Fleet had been very busy for the preceding several days. Everybody then in Truk was the same, too. They wanted relaxation more or less.

There is a saying in Japan to the effect that "incidentally tempted by some evil, he committed a blunder." This was the case of the 4th Fleet, too. Under these circumstances the Commander in Chief of the 4th Fleet issued the order to lower alertness. Maybe this is far beyond the imagination of persons who are not familiar with these circumstances. But thus it happened.

In the morning of 17 February, the very day when American carrier-borne planes at last began attacks on Truk, the Japanese radar caught echoes of some groups of aircraft at a distance of some half an hour's plane flight. Almost at the same time, the air reconnaissance net made by 6 Tenzans discovered the enemy task forces. But for the relaxation of alertness which was issued on the very day before the attack, there might have been enough time to counterattack the enemy effectively. Under the circumstances mentioned, however, it had to be termed too late. Japanese fighters that succeeded in taking off into the air failed to make systematized counterattacks when coming upon enemy planes. They had to fight separately.

Besides, they had some defects in the organization of the intercepting operation. Also they lacked experience in the Truk intercepting operation. This needs further explanation. Airplanes based on Truk at that time belonged as follows:

Eight land-based bombers and four flying boats: 22nd Air Sqdn., whose headquarters was stationed on Tinian Island.

Twelve seaplanes: 4th Naval Base in Truk.
About 50 fighters and about 24 Tenzans: 26th Air Sqd., whose headquarters was stationed on Truk Island.

While the 22nd Air Sqd. and the 4th Naval Base were under the command of the Commander in Chief of the 4th Fleet, who took the responsibility of defending Truk, the 26th Air Sqd., originally belonging to the 11th Air Fleet in Rabaul, was to be temporarily under the command of the 4th Fleet only for such emergency period as when the enemy attacked Truk. This very fact that the would-be main striking forces against the enemy were not under the direct control of the Commander in Chief of the 4th Fleet until the very moment hostilities occurred was undoubtedly one of the major factors that at last resulted in the fiasco of Truk.

It was, therefore, natural that the punishment for this blunder by the Japanese Navy was great. They lost:

Aircraft:	About 325 planes of which about 270 were caught on the ground.*
Naval vessels:	The CL *Naka,* a training cruiser *Katori,* and 4 destroyers.
Other vessels:	26 merchant ships
2,000 tons of food	
17,000 tons of fuel	

Sources of this information:

1. Narrative of ex-commander who was a staff officer of the 4th Fleet since December 1943.
2. Answer to the Questionnaire NAV No. 10 of the United States Strategical Bombing Survey dated 15 October 1945.

---

*According to copies of telegrams which were received after that fiasco, the number of planes destroyed on the ground were reported as about 100, though the narrative of a former staff officer of the 4th Fleet and also the Answer to the Questionnaire NAV No. 10 showed the number of them at about 270. Then, it is desired to correct the figure of Japanese planes lost in my previous memorandum.

Some Features Concerning Changes in the Japanese Fleet Organization during the War

Masataka Chihaya

17 March 1947

It goes without saying that naval fleets are organized so as to display their powers most effectively in the hour of need, because in their proper organizations elements of their organizations are so closely combined not only technically but mentally. So that one can easily discover the intentions of that navy by looking over the organizations of that navy; that is, of what fleets the whole naval forces are composed, and of what elements each fleet is composed. At the same time, by so doing one can easily recognize what influence a reaction can bring upon that navy in reality, for changes of fleet organizations are usually immediate and the easiest responsive [sic] to reactions.

The other day you asked me the Japanese reaction to the report of the Pearl Harbor attack. As to personal opinions, Mr. Ohmae is expected to submit sufficient reports. So that I intended to make an investigation into that matter from another angle; that is, as to what changes the reaction to the Pearl Harbor attack brought upon the Japanese naval fleet organizations. I think this one of the most important angles in order to get the objective picture of the Japanese reaction to the Pearl Harbor attack.

Prior to the main discourse, it is considered necessary to add a supplemental account about some features of the Japanese fleets before the war. Evidently it was a common feature in all navies of the world that fleets were organized with battleships as their nuclei, until the surprise attack on Pearl Harbor. Even the Japanese Navy, which achieved the honor of revolutionizing naval tactics and strategies by the surprise attack on Pearl Harbor, and

283

also by the subsequent success of sinking two British battleships east off Kuantan, Malay, could not be free from being without exception.

It was a long-cherished policy of the Japanese Navy to organize fleets with battleships as their nuclei, following the great success of the Battle of Tsushima in 1905. The Japanese Fleet which won that battle comprised six battleships and six armed cruisers. In 1917, the Japanese Navy established the naval policy of eight battleships and four battle cruisers as their nuclei, which was called the "8 to 4" fleet plan. In the next year, 1918, that plan was expanded to be the "8 to 6" fleet plan, which meant eight battleships and six battle cruisers. In 1920, the Japanese Navy succeeded in establishing the so-called "8 to 8" fleet plan, which was the final goal of the Japanese Navy of that date. This naval policy of the so-called "8 to 8" fleet plan was revised drastically in accordance with the Naval Treaty which was agreed to in Washington two years later in 1922, though, of eight battleships and eight battle cruisers under the program, six battleships (the *Nagato, Mutsu, Hyuga, Ise, Fuso* and *Yamashiro*) and four battle cruisers (the *Hiei, Kirishima, Kongo* and *Haruna*) were built and all of them retained their power as nuclei of the Japanese Navy.

* * *

Now, let us take a glance at the fleet organization of the Japanese Navy as of 15 November 1940, just one year before the outbreak of the war. Generally speaking, the main striking force of the Japanese Navy was apparently divided into four groups:

1st Fleet which was a battleship group:

1st BB Sqd.	*Nagato, Mutsu*
2nd BB Sqd.	*Ise, Hyuga*
6th CA Sqd.	*Aoba, Furutaka, Kako*
1st Des. Sqd.	
3rd Des. Sqd.	
3rd Air Sqd. (CVL)	*Hosho, Ryuho*
7th Air Sqd. (Seaplane tender)	*Mizuho, Chitose*

2nd Fleet which was a cruiser and destroyer group:

4th CA Sqd.	*Takao, Atago, Maya, Chokai*
5th CA Sqd.	*Haguro, Nachi*
7th CA Sqd.	*Mogami, Mikuma, Suzuya, Kumano*
8th CA Sqd.	*Tone, Chikuma*

2nd Des. Sqd.
4th Des. Sqd.
1st Air Sqd. (CV)   *Kaga*
2nd Air Sqd. (CV)   *Soryu, Hiryu*
1st Naval Base

6th Fleet which was a submarine group.

Land-based naval air forces which were not yet organized into an air fleet.

Taking this table of the Japanese fleets organization into consideration, it would not be so difficult to discover the main intentions of the Japanese Navy of that date which was [sic] as follows:

(1) The main striking force of the Japanese Navy was undoubtedly the battleship group, as it had been for a long time.

(2) The principal missions of the 2nd Fleet were, first, to launch a preceding attack, chiefly by means of long-range oxygen torpedoes, upon enemies prior to a main duel being fought between the battleships of both sides, and second, to attempt a night engagement upon the enemy fleets.

(3) The mission of both the 1st and the 2nd Air Sqds. was to make a forestalling attack upon enemy carriers as well as to take the responsibility of air scouting of fleets, while the mission of the 3rd Air Sqd. was to provide air cover over the main battleship force against air and underwater enemies.

*   *   *

On 15 January, 1941, the 11th Air Fleet was newly organized, comprising the 21st, 22nd and 23rd Air Sqds.

*   *   *

Four months later, on 10 April 1941, the 1st Air Fleet was organized for the first time, comprising the 1st, 2nd and 4th Air Sqds. This was the origin of the very air fleet which just eight months later succeeded in launching a decisive blow on Pearl Harbor. However, each air sqd. composing that fleet was organized exclusively of carriers and several attached destroyers. This drastic change in the Japanese Fleet organization seemed to have come from such administrative demands as training and replenishment of aircraft, rather than from operational demands. In naval maneuvers of that date, the newly organized 1st Air Fleet used to have been assigned almost the same missions as before. It had scarcely been formed into a task force, with an air group as a nucleus, even in a tactical field, much less in a strategical field.*

Also on the same day, 10 April 1941, the 3rd Fleet, which later took the responsibility of invading the Philippine Islands, was organized.

On 31 July 1941 the Southern Expedition Fleet, which later invaded Malay, was organized.

* * *

It was a task force consisting of six carriers, two battleships, two cruisers, a light cruiser and about a dozen destroyers that surprised all the navies of the earth with the remarkable success inflicted upon Pearl Harbor. Of those ships, only six carriers belonged originally to the 1st Air Fleet, the remainder being temporarily assigned missions. Compared with later-developed task forces, this task force had a comparatively thin guard screen. Why this insufficient number of screen vessels? Is it because the Japanese Navy had an insufficient number of vessels? No, not at all! It is because the Japanese Navy had no intention of carrying out the launching of a decisive clash upon Pearl Harbor, so far as facing a serious encounter with the enemy.

The origin of the idea of attacking Pearl Harbor never came from such a great strategy as taking a decisive standpoint in a war by an initial attack. The immediate purpose of Japan's operation at the time of the outbreak of the war was apparently to secure the necessary southern area in our hands as soon as possible. In the achievement of this purpose, there was a fear of encountering American fleets from the east which were considered most urgent to check by all means. The most reliable method in achieving this aim was undoubtedly to catch American fleets at their base, Pearl Harbor, before they tried to sortie, although it would be very dangerous and also gambling, in all probability.

In determining such a grave decision, did not some of our great leaders seek the merit of such popular sayings as follows:

"Let us seek life in death itself!"

"Before a supreme decision, even a demon shrinks."

"Desperate rats will bite attacking cats."

To attack Pearl Harbor as the setting up of this war was the only alternative which had finally been concluded under such circumstances. The real

---

*Translator's note. I think this very important to take an objective picture of the mental attitudes of the responsible men of the 1st Air Fleet who failed to continue decisive blows, following the great success of the initial attack, instead of attempting a "hit and run" policy. In fact, the staff members of the 1st Air Fleet could not be free from some criticism that they did not have necessarily sufficient abilities in dealing with such a great tactic as the Pearl Harbor attack, although they demonstrated their extraordinary abilities in bringing their fleet to top efficiency.

intention of the Japanese Navy in attacking Pearl Harbor was to launch a surprise attack upon there, in order to achieve enough time to carry out the invasion into the southern area without any intervention by American fleets from the east, by destroying enemy ships at Pearl Harbor at most. It was evident that the basic tactical thought of the Japanese Navy of that date lay in the "One Big Battle" chiefly to be fought between battleships of both sides. The reason is this: When the 1st Air Fleet attacked Pearl Harbor, the battleship group under the direct control of Admiral Yamamoto sortied northwest off Midway Island. The mission of this battleship group did not lie in expanding the effect of attacks following the attack of the 1st Air Fleet, but to take the 1st Air Fleet into its cover in case the air attack on Pearl Harbor should fail.

※　※　※

Then, what changes were made in the fleet organization of the Japanese Navy as a reaction to the great success of the Pearl Harbor attack? Was the task force that attacked Pearl Harbor organized into a proper fleet? No, none of these. Of course, in some quarters, especially air circles, there were not a few loud voices which claimed drastic reforms of the fleet organization so as to concentrate powers into carrier groups. However, the Japanese naval authorities, who had long taken a comparatively conservative attitude, lacked enough courage to take the daring action of reforming the fleet organization. Maybe it would be hard to believe that any reform of the fleet organization was not taken except that on 10 April 1942, screen destroyers were newly attached to the 1st Air Fleet, until the very fiasco of the Battle of Midway Island. For this, somebody would propose a pretext to the effect that at that time the Japanese Navy was too busy engaging the designated southern area invasion to reform the fleet organization, but after having finished the initial stage of the designated operation in April 1942, there would have been enough time to take the reform of the fleet organization into consideration.

The complete defeat at Midway Island, however, sufficed to have the conservative Japanese naval authorities make a drastic reform of the fleet organization. This was undertaken on 14 July 1942. The Third Fleet was newly organized, comprising the 1st Air Sqd. (*Zuikaku, Shokaku*), the 2nd Air Sqd. (*Junyo, Hiyo*), 11th BB Sqd. (*Hiei, Kirishima*), 7th CA Sqd. (4 CAS), 8th CA Sqd. (2 CAs) and 10th Sqd. (one CL and more than 15 DDs). But the other two fleets, the 1st and 2nd, remained as they had been before. About three months later, on 26 October 1942, the said 3rd Fleet, together with the 2nd Fleet, engaged in the Battle of Santa Cruz. As Admiral Kondo, the then Commander in Chief of the 2nd Fleet, opined in his report [of] which a translation was forwarded to you the other day, in that engagement he was in a very strange position, being given the responsibility of charging an air operation, which was the main operation, into the hand of the Commander in Chief of the 3rd Fleet, who was then junior to him. This strange situation had continued successively until in July 1943 Admiral Kondo was relieved of this post by Vice Admiral Kurita.

* * *

On 1 April 1943 another reform of the fleet organization was taken so as to reduce the position of the 1st Fleet, which had long been assumed to be the main striking force of the Japanese Navy, although somewhat overshadowed by the brilliant successes of the air forces, to a training fleet.* No doubt this was a marked progress in naval thought. In the relation between the 2nd and 3rd Fleet, however, which it had been considered necessary to be improved, no attempt was conducted after all.

It was as late as on 1 March 1944 that the 1st Task Force Fleet, comprising the 2nd and 3rd Fleets, was organized for the first time, and the 2nd Fleet came under the command of the Commander in Chief of the 3rd Fleet in the proper fleet organization. Japan endeavored to strengthen this 1st Task Force Fleet, and employed three regular carriers, four light carriers and two converted carriers in the engagement far east off the Philippines in July 1944, in which engagement Japan intended to launch a long-cherished "One Big Battle" against American fleets, and lost the battle.

As a result of that battle, the Japanese Navy lost hundreds of skilled fliers as well as several carriers, so that the Japanese Navy could no longer rely upon carrier-borne air forces as its main striking force. Consequently, on 15 August 1944, the reform of the fleet organization was made again so as to concentrate as many as possible of such surface vessels as battleships and cruisers in the 2nd Fleet, while the 3rd Fleet consisted of remnants of carriers and screen destroyers. Nevertheless, the relationship between the 2nd and 3rd fleets remained unchanged. In this fact, again we can easily discover a conservative attitude of the Japanese Navy.

* * *

About two months later, in October 1944, when American fleets came to land on the Philippines, this 2nd Fleet, commanded by Vice Admiral Kurita, as you know well, made the once-and-for-all dash into Leyte Gulf, with the result of grave losses received, including the *Musashi* and two other battleships being sunk. At the same time, the 3rd Fleet, consisting of chiefly a regular carrier and three light carriers, headed south for northeast off Samar

*Translator's note: On 25 February 1944 the 1st Fleet was dissolved.

Island with the aim of diverting to them the attention of American carrier groups, which otherwise would be a grave menace to Vice Admiral Kurita's forces. In these engagements, the Japanese Navy received fatal damages and became nothing but remnants of unbalanced forces.

On 15 November 1944, the 3rd and the 1st Task Force Fleets were dissolved, while the majority of the remaining vessels were formed into the 2nd Fleet.

*   *   *

Of those remaining ships, the *Yamato* and the CL *Kahari* accompanied by several destroyers made the last one-way sortie to Okinawa, when the Americans came to assault there in April 1945, and they met their dooms without making any contact with the enemy. This was literally the funeral of the once-famed Japanese fleets because, after the dissolution of the 2nd Fleet on 20 April 1945, no longer did the Japanese Navy have any surface-craft fleet.

Three-Part Report

Masataka Chihaya

20 August 1947

Subject No. 1. Fates of the *Hiei* and other vessels that participated in the Pearl Harbor attack.

In my previous report I mentioned about the fate of Japanese carriers that participated in the Pearl Harbor attack. Without exception they met their catastrophes in fighting duals between two carrier groups. Having some interest about their fates, I tried to find out the fates of other Japanese vessels that participated in the Pearl Harbor attack. It was some sort of surprise even to men who ought to have been accustomed to such bad news. Except for a destroyer, they were all sunk during the war. I think you will have some interest too. Their fates are as follows:

Two battleships, the *Hiei* and the *Kirishima*, were sunk at the time of the Guadalcanal campaign in the fall of 1942. On 12 November 1942, the Japanese Navy intended to bombard Henderson airfield on Guadalcanal Island. Both ships, the *Hiei* and the *Kirishima*, were then the nucleus of the Japanese Fleet, of which I was a staff officer in charge of gunnery. Thus the Guadalcanal Battle occurred. In the late afternoon of the following day, the *Hiei* was sunk. In the night of 14 November, the *Kirishima* went down, having suffered heavy damages during the gunfire duel.

The *Chikuma*, one of the two heavy cruisers that participated in the Pearl Harbor attack, was sunk off the east coast of Leyte on 25 October 1944. Her sister ship, the *Tone*, escaped from being sunk for a long time, until she was finally bottomed in the Bay of Etajima on 26 July 1945.

The only light cruiser, the *Abukuma*, was sunk by American task forces near Mindoro Island on 26 October 1945.

Of eleven destroyers that engaged in the Pearl Harbor attack, the *Kasumi*, *Arare* and *Shiranuhi* were torpedoed by American submarines near Kiska Island in the Aleutian Islands, in the summer of 1942, with the result of the *Arare* being sunk and the remaining ships being badly damaged but managing to return to the homeland. The *Kagero* was lost in the sea near Kolombangara, New Georgia, on 8 May 1943. Five destroyers were lost in 1944. They were:

Akikumo	Zamboanga	11 April 1944	Submarine
Tanikaze	Celebes	9 June 1944	Submarine
Shiranuhi	Panay	27 October 1944	Airplane
Oboro	Cavite	30 November 1944	Airplane
Urakaze	Formosa	21 November 1944	Submarine

Of the remaining four, the *Kasumi*, *Isokaze* and *Hamakaze* were sunk in the southwest off Kyushu on 7 April 1945, by American task forces. The *Ushio* was the only ship that remained until the surrender.

Of the three submarines, the *I-23* went to the sea near Hawaii Island in February 1942 and was never heard of since. The other two submarines were sunk around Gilbert Island in December 1943.

Seven tankers that engaged in the Pearl Harbor attack were all sunk by the fall of 1944. Of seven tankers, five were sunk by submarines and the remaining two were sunk by enemy air forces.

Subject No. 2.   Characteristics of I-type submarines.

Name	*I-19*	*I-21*	*I-23*
Place of construction	Kobe	Kawasaki	Yokosuka
Laid keel	1938	1939	1938
Launched	1939	1940	1939
Completed	1941	1941	1941
Standard displacement	2,212	2212	2212
Speed on surface	23.6 kt	23.6 kt	23.6 kt
Speed under water	8 kt	8 kt	8 kt
Radius of action	16 kt–14,000'	16 kt–14,000'	16 kt–14,000'
Length	108.7m	108.7m	108.7m
Width	9.3m	9.3m	9.3m
Ordnance	14 c/moxl	14 c/moxl	14 c/moxl
	25 m/mo MGxl		
	53 c/m tube × 6		
	Small seaplane 1		
Complement	97	97	97

They were all the newest type submarines in the Japanese navy at that time.

Subject No. 3. Some stories about Japanese skippers who engaged in the Pearl Harbor attack.

VADM Chuichi Nagumo, who made his name as commanding officer of the Japanese task force that succeeded in attacking Pearl Harbor at the outbreak of the war, was not a flier. He was a so-called "torpedo man" to the core. (In the once–Japanese Navy, officers were called gunnery men, torpedo men and airmen respectively according to their professions).

His naval career was as follows:

His naval life began when he entered the Naval College in 1906. His original profession was torpedo, and also he finished the course of the Naval Staff Academy. He spent most of his time in the General Staff in Tokyo except for being abroad about nine months in 1924. Although he had had no experience in the naval air forces, he was appointed Commander in Chief of the newly organized 1st Air Fleet on 10 April 1941.

He was born in Yamagata Prefecture in 1887. He was a comparatively small man even for a Japanese, but had very sharp eyes. He was known as a strong-spirited and indomitable man. It is not that this does not remind me of a story told by Mr. Genda this spring to the effect that he was not as strong as expected, but rather too thoughtful at the time of the Pearl Harbor attack as it proved. However, he was said to be a little timid and doubtful about the plan of the Pearl Harbor attack when he was shown the plan for the first time.

The success of the Pearl Harbor attack, however, made him the "Number 1" leader of air carrier task forces in the Japanese Navy. So that even after the fiasco of Midway Island, he and his Chief of Staff, RADM Ryunosuke Kusaka, who you know, remained in their positions. As I told previously, the 3rd Fleet was newly organized with the *Zuikaku* and the *Shokaku* as the nucleus after the defeat of Midway Island. Vice Admiral Nagumo was reassigned as the Commander in Chief of that fleet.

During the tenure of his position he fought twice against American task forces. One was a battle fought northeast off Isabel Island, the Solomon Islands, in August of 1942. Another was the so-called Santa Cruz battle in which he achieved some success by sinking the *Lexington* and inflicting some damage upon the enemy. After this battle, he was relieved of his important position of commanding the main striking forces of the Japanese Navy. He was assigned the position of Commander in Chief of Sasebo Naval Base and later Commander in Chief of the Kure Naval Base and the 1st Fleet.

The gradually worsening situation of Japan, however, did not allow him to rest long. Toward the end of January 1941 when the Allied Powers invaded the Marshall Islands, following the invasion of the Gilbert Islands in the fall of 1943, Japan faced the immediate menace of a break through her most important defense line—the chain of islands stretching south from Japan proper to the mid-Pacific. To cope with this worse situation, Japan made desperate efforts in fortifying islands, reinforcing defense forces, deploying air forces and organizing higher command organizations—which afterward proved too late for the prompt advance of daily increasing American forces. On 4 March 1944, the Mid-Pacific Area Fleet was newly organized under the command of Vice Admiral Nagumo. He made desperate efforts to accomplish this grave mission, but he failed, and died on Saipan Island with his men when the Allied Forces made a landing there in June of 1944.

The commanding officer of the 3rd Sqd., consisting of the *Hiei* and the *Kirishima,* was VADM Gunichi Mikawa. He was a "navigation man" and his naval career was as follows:

He was born in Hiroshima Prefecture in 1888 and entered the Naval College in 1907. He also finished the course at the Naval Staff Academy. He had been long in France as a naval attaché and an attendant of Japanese delegations to the League of Nations and to the London Naval Conference. On 6 September 1941 he was appointed commanding officer of the 3rd Sqd.

On 14 July 1942 he was appointed Commander in Chief of the 8th Fleet which was then newly organized to take charge of naval operations [in] the Southwestern Area, viz. the Solomon Islands and the New Britain Area. He was the same man who commanded the fleet that dashed into the Guadalcanal Area with great success, almost annihilating the Allied Fleet there, when the Allied Powers made a landing there as a first step of the offensive in August 1942. On April 1943 he was relieved of his position and returned to Japan.

On 3 September 1943 he was appointed Commander in Chief of the 2nd Expeditionary Fleet which was stationed at Soerabaja, Java. On 18 July 1944 he took the position of Commander in Chief of the Southwestern Area Fleet, taking charge of all Japanese-occupied south areas, until he was relieved of his office on 1 November 1944 just after the American landing on Leyte Island. After returning to Japan, he did not occupy any responsible post. Now he is in the custody of the Allied Powers in Sugamo Prison, under the charge of violating international law.

RADM Hiroaki Abe, later Vice Admiral, commanded the 8th Sqd. consisting of the *Tone* and the *Chikuma.* He was a "torpedo man." He was born in Osaka in 1889 and entered the Japanese Navy in 1908. After graduation from the Naval Staff Academy, he served most of his life at sea as a torpedo man.

He took the post of commanding the newly organized 11th Sqd., consisting of the *Hiei* and the *Kirishima,* on 14 July 1942. The 11th Sqd. was the main covering force of the Japanese carrier forces at the time of the Pearl

Harbor attack. During his tenure he engaged in the sea battle of Isabel Island, the sea battle of Santa Cruz and the sea battle of Guadalcanal Island. Vice Admiral Abe commanded the Japanese Fleet to bombard Henderson airfield with the *Hiei* and the *Kirishima* as I have written previously. Both ships were sunk during the engagement. Immediately after that sea battle he was relieved of his post, and soon later [sic] retired. He is still alive in Kamakura.

RADM Sentaro Omori commanded the destroyer group. It goes without saying that he was a "torpedo man." He was born in Kumamoto Prefecture in 1892 and entered the Naval College in 1910. He spent most of his naval life in torpedo circles and got the post of commanding the 1st Des. Sqd. in the fall of 1940. In the fall of 1942, he was relieved of his post and was appointed commanding officer of the 5th Sqd., consisting of *Nachi* class cruisers. He remained active in the Japanese Navy until the surrender of Japan.

As written in my previous letter, the commanding officer of the 2nd Air Sqd. was RADM Tamon Yamaguchi. He was born in Tokyo in 1892. His naval life began in 1909. He received education in the Torpedo School and also in the Naval Staff Academy. He had been in America twice, totaling about four years. In 1940 he got the post of commanding [the] 1st Combined Air Sqd., although he had no previous experience in the naval air forces. On 1 November 1940 he became the commanding officer of the 2nd Air Sqd. As I have written in my previous letter, he died with his ship and his men in the sea near Midway Island in June 1942.

Another air sqd., consisting of the *Zuikaku* and the *Shokaku,* was commanded by RADM Chuichi Hara. He was a torpedo man, too. He was born in Shimane Prefecture in 1889. His naval life began in 1908 when he entered the Naval College. He graduated from the Naval Torpedo School in Yokosuka and also from the Naval Staff Academy in Tokyo. He was abroad about nine months in 1933. Having served as skipper of several ships, he got the name of a good skipper. This was one of the reasons why he was appointed to the important position of commanding the 5th Air Sqd. in the fall of 1941, although he had no experience in the air service. In July 1942 he got the position of commanding the 8th Sqd. In February 1944 he was assigned as Commander in Chief of the 4th Fleet in Truk and remained there until the surrender of Japan. He is still in Guam under suspicion of violating international law.

Thus far, I have mentioned biographical stories of Japanese commanding officers who took part in the Pearl Harbor attack. Now, I would like to tell you some stories about Japanese skippers who engaged in the Pearl Harbor attack.

As I have written in my previous letter, the captain of the *Akagi* was Capt. Kiichi Hasegawa. He was born in Saitama Prefecture in 1894. He entered the Japanese Navy in 1911. First he began his naval life as a torpedo man, but in 1922 he became an airman and since then he served most of his life in the Japanese naval air service. On 25 March 1941 he became skipper of the *Akagi*. After the fiasco of the Midway battle, he was relieved of his post. On 20 March 1944 he died in a battle as the commanding officer of the 22nd Air Sqd.

The skipper of the *Kaga* was Capt. Jisaku Okada, who was born in Ishikawa Prefecture in 1893. He entered the Navy in 1911. The same as Captain Hasegawa, he went into the air service in 1922 after having begun his naval career as a gunnery man. After having served most of his life in the air service, he became the skipper of the *Kaga* on 15 September 1941. He died in the Battle of Midway Island.

The captain of the *Soryu* was Capt. Ryusaku Yanagimoto, who was born in Nagasaki Prefecture in 1894. He entered the Japanese Navy in 1913. After graduation from the Naval Gunnery School and the Naval Staff Academy, he served his time as a member of the General Staff in Tokyo and also a member of the Personnel Bureau. He had been in England as a naval attaché. He became skipper of the *Soryu* on 6 October 1941. He died in the Midway battle, too.

The boss of the *Hiryu* was Capt. Tomeo Kaku, who was born in Kumanoto Prefecture in 1893. He received education in the Naval Gunnery and the Naval Staff Academy, though in 1927 he entered the air force. After having served several posts in the Japanese naval air force, on 8 September 1941 he was appointed boss of the *Hiryu,* in which he went under the surface in June 1942.

The captain of the *Shokaku* was Capt. Takatsugu Jyojima, later Rear Admiral. He was born in Saga Prefecture in 1890. He entered the Japanese Navy in 1909 and later became a navigation man. His naval career was not so brilliant, but luck turned in his favor when he was appointed captain of the Kure Naval Air Corps in 1939. So excellently did he prove his ability to command units that he got the important post of commanding the *Shokaku,* the newest type regular carrier in the Japanese Navy, when she was completed in the fall of 1941. After the Coral Sea battle he was appointed commanding officer of the 11th Air Sqd., consisting mostly of seaplanes based at Rakata, Isabel Island. His force accomplished such a brilliant achievement during [a] most fierce engamement in the fall of 1942 that it received a letter of appreciation from the Commander in Chief of the Combined Fleet. Later he had taken several posts commanding air forces until the surrender of Japan. He is alive now.

Capt. Ichihei Yokokawa was the captain of the *Zuikaku.* He was a very lucky man, too. He was born in Okayama Prefecture in 1893 and entered the Japanese Navy in 1912. He was a so-called gunnery man, and was known as a gunnery expert. When the Japanese Navy expanded its air forces largely around 1938, there was a problem of [a] shortage of responsible officers able to command newly organized air corps, so that a good many officers outside the air forces were employed as commanding officers of those air forces. The traditional conservative attitude of the Japanese Navy could be seen in solving this problem, for the majority of the newly assigned commanding officers of those units [were] rather ordinary men. Captain Yokokawa was one of them, and Captain Jyojima was also in that category. Captain Yokokawa's luck began with his assignment as skipper of the *Kamikawa-Maru,* a seaplane tender, in the fall of 1938. One year later, in 1939, he got the post of commanding the *Hiryu.* In September 1941 he was finally appointed captain of the *Zuikaku.* Just after the Coral Sea battle he was relieved of his post and since then occupied posts mostly on land until the surrender of Japan. He is now alive.

Capt. Masao Nishida, who was boss of the *Hiei,* was born in Hyogo Prefecture in 1895. In 1913 he entered the Naval College and later received education in the Torpedo School and the Naval Staff Academy. He spent most of his time in Tokyo as an important member of the General Staff and also of the Naval Department. He had been in England as a navel attaché and an attendant of the Japanese delegation to the London Naval Treaty. On 10 September 1941 he got the post of skipper of the *Hiei.* But luck turned against him when he lost his ship, the *Hiei,* in the engagement of Guadalcanal Island in the fall of 1942. In March of the next year, 1943, he retired from the Japanese Navy. He is alive now.

The skipper of the *Kirishima* was Capt. Jihei Yamaguchi. He was born in Kanagawa Prefecture in 1891 and entered the Navy in 1911. Later he became a gunnery man. On 15 August 1941 he was appointed captain of the *Kirishima.* On 20 April 1942 he was transferred to the post of Chief of Staff of the newly organized 1st Convoy Sqd. He is alive now.

The captain of the *Tone* was Capt. Tametsugu Okada, later Rear Admiral. He was born in Nara Prefecture in 1895, and entered the Naval College in 1914. He was originally a gunnery man. He finished the course of the Naval Staff Academy and had been in Germany as a naval attaché. Spending most of his naval life in the Naval General Staff, he was appointed captain of the *Tone* in September of 1941. Later he got the posts of skippers of such ships as the *Junyo* (converted carrier) and the *Shokaku.* He remained in the Japanese Navy until the surrender. He is now in Rabaul as a war crime criminal. [sic]

The captain of the *Chikuma,* the sister ship of the *Tone,* was Capt. Keizo Komura, later Rear Admiral. He was born in Nagano Prefecture in 1896, and began his naval life in 1912. Originally he made his profession as a torpedo man, but later graduated from the Naval Staff Academy. He had been in England as a naval attaché. In August of 1941 he was appointed captain of the *Chikuma.* In December of 1943 he got the post of Chief of

Staff of the Third Fleet, which was then the main striking force of the Japanese Navy. He fought the sea battle of the Marianas in June 1944 and lost the battle as you know well. He is still alive in Tokyo.

The captain of the *Abukuma*, the only light cruiser, was Capt. Seiroku Murayama. He was born in Kagoshima in 1893. He entered the Navy in 1911. He was a man of navigation. His naval career in the Japanese Navy was not so brilliant as other skippers who took part in the Pearl Harbor attack. He got his post in November 1940. He is alive now.

The skipper of the *Oboro* was Cmdr. Minoru Nakagawa, who was the youngest skipper among Nagumo's forces. He was born in Chiba Prefecture in 1907. He entered the Navy in 1924 and became a torpedo man. After finishing the course of the Naval Staff Academy, he was appointed boss of the *Oboro*. He died in Saipan Island in May of 1944.

Cmdr. Yoshio Uesugi was skipper of the *Ushio*. He was born in Hiroshima Prefecture in 1900 and entered the Naval College in 1919. Later he became a torpedo man. He got the post of commanding the *Ushio* in October 1941. He died in March 1943 on board the *Minegumo*, a destroyer.

Cmdr. Terumichi Arimoto and Cmdr. Nagoyoshi Shiraishi were skippers of the *Akikumo* and the *Urakaze* respectively. Arimoto was born in Tottori Prefecture, and Shiraishi in Toyko in 1900. They were both torpedo men. Arimoto was assigned as skipper of his ship on 27 September 1941. They are both alive.

Cmdr. Tsuneo Orita was born in Kagoshima Prefecture in 1900 and entered the Naval College in 1918. He was also a torpedo man. On 30 June 1941 he became skipper of the *Hamakaze*. He died on 7 June 1944 in an engagement.

Skippers of the *Isokaze*, *Kasumi*, *Arare* and *Tanikaze* were as follows:

	Isokaze	*Kasumi*	*Arare*	*Tanikaze*
Skipper	Shunichi Toyoshima	Kiyoshi Tomura	Yukei Ogata	Moto Katsumi
Born	1902	1898	1902	1899
Entered Navy	1920	1918	1919	1917
Date assigned	1941	1940	1941	1941
	Alive	Alive	Alive	Died in the sea

Skippers of the remaining two destroyers, the *Kagero* and the *Shiranuhi*, could not be [made] clear so far, to my great regret.

Skipper of the *I-19* submarine was Cmdr. Syogo Narahara, who was born in Koochi Prefecture in 1889 and entered the Navy in 1919. On 26

April 1941 he was appointed skipper of that ship. In July 1942 he died in battle.

Skippers of the other two submarines were Cmdr. Genichi Shibata of the *I-23* and Cmdr. Tatsu Irie of the *I-21*. Commander Shibata died in an engagement in February 1942 and Commander Irie died in an engagement in January 1943.

Skippers of tankers that took part in the Pearl Harbor attack are not clear, to my regret. But it was the custom of the once Japanese Navy that skippers of tankers were complemented by such men as retired officers and ordinary officers.

Two-Part Report

Masataka Chihaya

5 September 1947

1. A story about the naming of Japanese warships.

In the once Japanese Navy there was a certain formula for naming warships. Following this formula, even ordinary Japanese people could distinguish the type of any Japanese warship without too much effort.

Traditionally, Japanese battleships were named after the old names of provinces in this country. The old names of provinces in this country were quite different from the names of prefectures now in use, for the present names of prefectures were newly designated at the time of the Meiji Restoration, quite independent of the old names of provinces. At present those old names of provinces are not used either formally or in business, but they are so often used in literature and art that their influence on the Japanese people is not yet neglected.

It is not clear when the old names of provinces were designated, but it seems that they became quite popular among the Japanese people after the Tokugawa Shogunate. For in the era of the Tokugawa Shogunate, *daimyos* (feudal lords) who governed their lands were called by their names along with the names of the provinces where they governed. For example, a famous Japanese fencer who was of *daimyo* descent was called Yagui Tajima-no-kami Shigenori. Shigenori Yagui was his full name and Tajima-no-kami meant the landlord of Tajima which was a small part of the Tottori Prefecture.

Well then, what provinces were Japanese battleships named after? The Japanese "Number 1" battleships, the *Musashi* and the *Yamato*, were named after Musashi and Yamato provinces respectively. Musashi province was a part of the Kanto, near Tokyo. The western part of a suburb of Tokyo is often called the Musashi-no which means Musashi Plain.

Yamato province was a vicinity of Nara, but sometimes it represents Japan proper. The Japanese race is sometimes called the Yamato race. Six other battleships represented the following names of old provinces in this country:

Nagato: Yamaguchi Prefecture, in the western part of Japan proper
Mutsu: Amori Prefecture, in the northern part of Japan proper
Ise: Mie Prefecture, south of Nagoya
Hyuga: Miyazaki Prefecture, south of Kyushu
Yamashiro: A part of the Osaka Prefecture
Fuso: This is not a proper name for an old province, but it sometimes means a name for Japan

As written in my previous letter, the *Kaga* was originally designed as a battleship, although she was later converted into a carrier. She was named after Kaga province which represents Fukui Prefecture of today.

Names of Japanese battle cruisers were traditionally taken from the names of mountains in this country. The *Hiei* type four battleships were originally battle cruisers, though they were later converted into battleships. Their names were taken from the following mountains:

Hiei: Mt. Hiei east of Kyoto, being a very famous place in both Japanese history and Buddhism.
Kirishima: Mt. Kirishima in Kagoshima Prefecture, being very famous for its beautiful scenery.
Kongo: Mt. Kongo in Wakayama Prefecture, being famous in Japanese history.
Haruna: Mt. Haruna in Tochigi Prefecture, noted for its beautiful scenery

The *Akagi* was also converted into a carrier from an original battle cruiser, so that her name was taken from Mt. Akagi which is in Gumma Prefecture.

Names of Japanese carriers were taken from flying creatures that are imaginary, but not in existence, except cranes and hawks, which symbolized flying over the sky. The first carrier built in this country was the *Hosho,* which means a monster bird believed to be in existence, flying the sky. Four other carriers besides the *Akagi* and the *Kaga* were named as follows:

Soryu: Dark blue dragon
Hiryu: Flying dragon
Shokaku: Flying crane
Zuikaku: Glorious crane

Names of rivers were used as the names of Japanese cruisers. The *Tone* was named after the Tone River which runs through the Kanto Plain, finally into the Pacific. The *Chikuma* was taken from the Chikuma River which runs north in the Shinano Plain in Niigata Prefecture, into the Japan Sea. The light cruiser *Abukuma* was named after the river which runs into the Japan Sea in Akita Prefecture.

First-class destroyers of the Japanese Navy were named after astronomical phenomena such as the moon, wind and clouds. The eleven destroyers that took part in the Pearl Harbor attack were named as follows:

Ushio:	Tide	*Kasumi:*	Mist
Oboro:	Hazy	*Arare:*	Hail
Akikumo:	Autumn cloud	*Urakaze:*	Wind of the bay
Kagero:	Summer vapor	*Isokaze:*	Wind of the seashore
Shiranuhi:	Will-o-the-wisp	*Tanikaze:*	Wind of the valley
		Hamakaze	Wind of the beach

Second-class destroyers were named after vegetation such as pine tree, cherry tree and bamboo, while light destroyers less than 1,000 tons took the names of light birds such as pheasants and plovers.

Japanese submarines were named only by numbers.

The seven tankers that took part in the Pearl Harbor attack were originally merchant ships. They were recruited into the Navy before the war. And their names were still used in the Navy as before. You can find them, seeing their *Maru* names. In the Japanese Navy *Maru* names were not used at all. The meaning of "*Maru*" is not clear, but it seems to have some meaning of affection. Sometimes it was used in boys' names but at present it is only used in ships' names and sometimes in "geisha" girls' names.

In naming merchant ships, some forms could be seen in a certain company. Sometimes common Chinese characteristics such as rivers and mountains could be seen in those ships, sometimes common capital letters were used throughout their ships. In such cases, there might be no peculiar meaning in their names. Of the seven tankers, both *Toho-Maru* and the *Toei-Maru* have common Chinese characteristics of "To" which means "east." *Toho* meant "east country" while *Toei* mean "east glory." The other five tankers' names meant—if they meant anything—as follows:

Kenyo-Maru:	Sound sea	*Kokuyo-Maru:*	State ocean
Kyokuto-Maru:	Far east	*Shinkoku-Maru:*	Divine country
		Nihon-Maru:	Japan

2. Some stories about Japanese skippers of the *Kagero* and other ships whom I failed to make clear in my previous report.

What I failed to do in my previous report was to make clear some stories about Japanese skippers of the *Kagero,* the *Shiranuhi* and the seven tankers.

The skipper of the *Kagero* was Cmdr. Minoru Yokoi, who was born in Koochi Prefecture in 1899. In 1917 he entered the Naval College and later made his profession in torpedoing. He took his post of commanding the *Kagero* in October 1939. After the Pearl Harbor attack he got sick and died in 1943.

The skipper of the *Shiranuhi* was Cmdr. Shijuo Akazawa. He was born in 1899 in Kanagawa Prefecture. He graduated from the Naval College in 1921, and did not get further education, though he got his job in the torpedo circle. He was appointed boss of the *Shiranuhi* in 1939. During the remaining time of the war, he spent most of his time as skipper of a destroyer and commanding officer of a destroyer squadron. He died in an engagement in June of 1944.

In my previous report I mentioned that skippers of Japanese tankers were usually complemented by rather ordinary officers such as retired officers and plain officers. However, this was not necessarily true in the case of Japanese tankers at the time of the Pearl Harbor attack. I must apologize for my carelessness in making an investigation. Because of seven skippers of the Japanese tankers, five were in active service the time of the battle. They were the skippers of the *Shinkoku-Maru, Nihon-Maru, Toho-Maru, Kenyo-Maru,* and *Kyokuto-Maru.* Judging from the conservative attitude of the Japanese Navy, the fact that five of seven skippers were appointed from active service officers deserved to be noted, although they were all rather plain career naval officers. At the time of the battle their classmates of the Naval College were getting posts of commanding squadrons in the rank of Rear Admiral.

Capt. Yasutaka Ito was skipper of the *Shinkoku-Maru.* He was born in Aichi Prefecture in 1889. He was a man of navigation. He was assigned his post in the fall of 1941. In the fall of the next year, he retired from the Navy and is still alive.

The skipper of the *Nihon-Maru* was Capt. Hironosuke Ueda, who was born in Ibaraki Prefecture in 1892. He entered the Navy in 1911 and got work with torpedoes. He was appointed to the post of skipper in the fall of 1941. He is still alive.

The *Toho-Maru* was commanded by Capt. Yasutaka Niimi, who was born in Kumamoto Prefecture in 1889. He entered the Navy in 1909. He got his post on board the ship in the fall of 1941. He died in the Marshall Islands in February 1944.

Capt. Yoshio Kanamasu, who commanded the *Kenyo-Maru* at the time of the battle, was born in Hiroshima Prefecture in 1890. He entered the Navy in 1909 and got his post in torpedoing. In the fall of 1941 he obtained his post on board the *Kenyo-Maru*. In February 1944 he died in an engagement.

The skipper of the *Kyokuto-Maru* was Capt. Masanao Goto, who was born in Yamaguchi Prefecture in 1888. He was appointed to his post in the fall of 1941. He is still alive.

The other two tankers were commanded by retired officers. Capt. Kiyoshi Kusakawa was skipper of the *Toei-Maru*. He was born in Mie Prefecture in 1890 and entered the Navy in 1907. Although he retired from the Japanese Navy in the beginning of 1941, he was recalled in the fall of 1941 and was appointed skipper of the ship. He died on board the battleship *Hyuga* in July 1945 when she was bombed by a powerful air raid launched from crack American forces.

Capt. Toraji Hidai commanded the *Kokuyo-Maru*. He was born in Nagano Prefecture in 1886, and entered the Navy in 1906. In 1934 he retired from the Japanese Navy, but three years later he was recalled into the navy. In the fall of 1941 he got his post of commanding the ship. He died of sickness in 1942.

Some Opinions Concerning the War

Admiral Nobutake Kondo
28 February 1947

Introduction

As Commander in Chief of Japan's Second Fleet, Kondo played a major role in many engagements of the Pacific War.* Prange had two very valuable interviews with him in December 1948. This study gives a revealing glimpse into the thinking of one of Japan's top admirals. Kondo realized that he had made mistakes, and did not spare himself in analyzing them.

Kondo believed that Japan's only possible chance for winning the war was to achieve a signal victory at the beginning while the enemy forces were "considerably unprepared." However, he foresaw "a lot of ominous probabilities" that the conflict would become a long war, a development he feared "to the utmost degree." He gives an account of one of Japan's successes— the sinking of the British battleships *Prince of Wales* and *Repulse*.

His summary of the preliminary South Area Invasion reveals that a number of factors plagued the Japanese, which is particularly interesting as one sometimes has the impression that Japan's early march was a triumphant, problemless procession. Also noteworthy is his analysis of the sea action around Guadalcanal, in which Kondo was quite severe on himself.

This translation is one of a number of studies that Masataka Chihaya prepared for Prange during the latter's service in Tokyo.

(Translator's note: Admiral Kondo was the Commander in Chief of the Second Fleet from December 1941 to August 1943. During his tenure of that post, he engaged in Japan's Southern Area Invasion of 1941, the Midway battle and battles around the Solomon Islands, in which on 14 Novem-

---

*More about Kondo appears on p.1.

Adm. Nobutake Kondo. *U.S. Navy*

ber 1942 he himself dashed into the Guadalcanal Area commanding the Japanese Fleet. Very recently he released some of his opinions about the war, which I believe would interest you very much. He added in his note that he did not have adequate figure information at hand, so that he failed to clarify his arguments concretely, to his great regret. But he stressed in the same note that these opinions though written very recently were based upon some notes now in his hand, which he had written during the war.)

1. My impressions when I was informed officially that the decision for war was being made by the Government at last.

a. It was the opinion unanimously agreed to by almost all of the high-ranking officers of the Japanese Navy that war against America should be avoided by all means. So that the grave decision which was made when the negotiations with America had not yet deadlocked seemed to me very strange, and I hoped sincerely that the negotiations would reach settlement after all.

However, as to the strategy of the forthcoming war which was decided after all, I thought as follows: Japan should win the war in a short period. (Translator's note: He expressed this conviction in the Japanese motto "Fast progress in a war to win it immediately.") Comparing strengths of both sides, especially in such a war, materials like iron and fuel, manufacturing facilities and supply abilities including ship-repair and harbor facilities, it was apparent that a long war would be disadvantageous to us. In particular, a most important factor was fuel storages. It therefore should be under constant, careful consideration of the responsible men in Tokyo, how and when the end of this war would be achieved. I wondered whether they took it into their considerations or not.

b. I was convinced of winning the victory in the early stage of the war, because we, Japan, with forces carefully prepared, would easily knock down enemy forces which seemed to be considerably unprepared under the support of powerful air cover. As to the remaining stages of the war, however, there seemed to be a lot of ominous probabilities that it would become a long war, which I feared to the utmost degree. It seemed to me very urgent, therefore, that the political and economical structure of Japan should be quickly reorganized so as to enable her to concentrate her efforts in the war. Above all, the thoughts of the Japanese Army concerning Russia should be revised.

c. Judging from our forces at hand and supply facilities, it was most important that our Japanese operations be conducted so as not to spread out too much. According to my opinion, the principle of our operation should be conducted along the following line: Japan at first would secure concretely a minimum area necessary to maintain the Japanese defense line, then, when the chance came, active attacks with concentrated necessary forces should be launched on the enemy's vital points. Otherwise, gap areas would arise which could not be maintained with our insufficient vessels and aircraft. Had we failed to conduct satisfactory operations in one theater in such a case, we could have had no sufficient reserve forces to cope with that situation, which might have resulted in losing the balance of all other theaters. My plan for this, therefore, was:

The Army should assume the responsibility for charging the air operation of at least one flank; for instance, the Malay area.

Production of aircraft, prompt training of airmen and prompt production of submarines should be spurred further.

The outset of the Southern Invasion should be launched on the Philippines and on Malay simultaneously, then the Dutch East Indies Invasion should follow. In case we did not have enough forces for such simultaneous landings on both places, there would be no alternative but to make a landing on the Philippines at first, then on Malay.

2. My impressions when I was appointed commanding [officer] of the Naval Southern Expedition Forces.

a. In case the Allied Powers would come to the Far East en masse to encounter us during our invasion operation, when and how many forces should be drawn from the invasion operation in order to take a position to encounter the enemy fleets, should be a matter under my constant consideration. In consequence, it would necessitate that the invasion operation could not be conducted without giving careful consideration to developments in other theaters.

b. Such being my judgment about the circumstances, I planned in my preliminary operation plan that the covering forces for the invasion under my direct control would be in Bako, Formosa, so as to take the position not only for the invasion, but for an Allied fleet which might be expected to come. (Translator's note: He said this in Japanese "an unbiased position.")

However, just prior to the outbreak of the war, towards the end of November, when our fleets were to leave the homeland for the initial deployment of the war, I was informed to the effect that two British battleships, the *Prince of Wales* and the *Repulse,* had arrived at Singapore very recently, so that I changed the initial position of my covering forces to Camranh Bay, French Indochina. (Translator's note: He added in his note that about this decision he consulted with the headquarters of the Combined Fleet.)

c. Before the war, we had some information which indicated our superiority to the potential enemy in skillfulness of operations, though obscure in mental abilities. So that, judging from the differences in both sides' strengths, in particular war materials and industrial abilities, it was apparent that the enemy would seek their superiority in quantities. Our measure for this situation, therefore, should be to strike a blow against separated enemies with our concentrated forces, thus summing up damages inflicted upon enemies to their final vital losses, and also at the same time to preserve our forces as long as possible.

There was a fear, however, of weakening fighting spirit, one of the most important factors in battle, if the need to preserve our fleets would be too much stressed. It would suffice that only the commanding officer of that theater would take it into consideration, so as to take an adequate measure of the situation. For instance, when we attempted to launch a fatal blow upon an enemy in a night engagement, dashing into an area under enemy air control, it was apparent that we should be apt to remain in that area until at the following dawn, we would be so subjected to powerful enemy land-air forces that we might receive severe damages. In such a case, the commanding officer of the force should give up the engagement to withdraw at the proper time.

3. My impressions about the Battle of Malay (the sinking of the *Prince of Wales* and the *Repulse*).

a. This battle was the most important achievement during the Japanese Southern Area Invasion in which I took the responsibility of commanding the Japanese naval expeditionary forces.

b. My observation of the situation:

At 1700 of 9 December 1941, a warning message saying that two enemy battleships, accompanied by several destroyers, headed north at 1515 on that day, position so-and-so, was received on board the *Atago,* my flagship, from the submarine *I-58* which was patrolling the area between Singapore and the Japanese landing beaches. What impressed me instinctively and concerned me most, receiving that warning, was whether or not the enemy main fleet aimed to divert our fleet in the South China Sea so as to make an attack with their other light vessel group upon our landing forces then under the landing operation. According to the scheduled plan, our army landing operations on Malay would take three or four days after the first step of the landing was set at about 0130 of 8 Dec. 1941.

Against this sighted British fleet, I decided to decoy them up north in the area within the reach of our land-based air forces in French Indochina, in order to launch a decisive blow upon them with all our air and surface forces. The submarine force was assigned to continue their original missions at their present positions.

c. My conduct of the operation:

Its principle was: All convoys would immediately stop their landing operations and head north into Siam Bay as far as possible.

The 22nd Air Sqd. (a land-based air force) would make searching attacks upon the suspected enemy fleet with all its forces from dawn of 10 Dec.

The lst Southern Expeditionary Fleet, including the 7th CA Sqd. and the 3rd Des. Sqd. temporarily assigned under its control, would join in the covering forces under my direct control.

Meanwhile, radio activities would frequently be discharged so as to divert enemy attention to us.

At that time, the 3rd Des. Sqd., that was directly covering the landing operation, needed refueling, so they were being refueled one by one from an oiler which had previously been at Poulo Condore Island. In consequence, those ships of the 3rd Des. Sqd. were under such circumstances that they could not but join the fleet one after another.

This problem of refueling the 3rd Des. Sqd. was one of the factors which made me give up a night engagement, together with the fact that those of the lst Expeditionary Fleet lacked enough training in night engagements and also that there was little hope of making contact with the enemy fleet by midnight, even if the enemy fleet had continued to head north at the speed observed in that afternoon, so that we would not have enough time to make a systematized night attack against the enemy. Therefore, I gave up a night attack and attempted a day attack after dawn of 10 Dec.

In order to achieve this aim, I fixed our rendezvous point at about 40 miles southwest of Poulo Condore Island (position is not sure because it is based upon my memory) at 1000 on 10 Dec.

d. General proceeding of the engagement.

At 0400 10 Dec. all forces except destroyers of the 3rd Des. Sqd. rendez-voused as scheduled at the designated point, thence we headed south [sic]. However, having received a message radioed at about 1300 from submarine *I-58* saying that the enemy fleet [was] headed south at high speed, I ordered the fleet to increase speed and at the same time ordered the air force to make every effort to catch the enemy fleet.

In the morning of that day, there were such low, thick clouds over the South China Sea that it hampered our air operations not a little. No message had been heard from our planes. It was not until 0800 that at last I gave up the chase and ordered my fleet to withdraw to the north for a while, finding little hope of making contact with the enemy.

On the other hand, however, since the early dawn of that day our land-based air force did their utmost to reconnoiter the enemy fleet despite the bad weather. Visibility was bad and no message was heard of, although the air searching net had been already reaching its end. Scarcely before reaching its turning point, our planes succeeded in catching the enemy fleet in sight off Kuantan just through a slit in the clouds. And they succeeded in sinking them!

The success of this operation, I believe, can be attributed to the following factors:

(1) We were favored by such good luck as to catch the enemy in sight through the slit in the clouds.

(2) Crews of the naval air forces were fired up with fierce fighting spirit and firm confidence in the battle. It would deserve to be cited as one of good examples that some planes showed no hesitation in making attacks upon the enemy, even at the moment when so doing would have caused a shortage of fuel necessary to return to their bases.

(3) Good conduct of the leaders of the air force.

(4) Japanese air forces did not meet any enemy interceptors.

(5) The enemy fleet not only lacked sufficient screen but did not make an efficient avoiding movement.

4. My impression after having finished the preliminary Southern Area Invasion (I proposed this to the Commander in Chief of the Combined Fleet).

a. The most important factor which had hampered the development of the Southern Area Invasion Operation was the fact that refitting of newly occupied airstrips was difficult to finish sufficiently in the scheduled time, so that advances of our air forces to these strips were apt to be obliged to delay. The most critical moment for attackers in the landing operation lay obviously in the period from the landing until our planes were advanced to newly occupied and refitted strips.

Apparently our damages to transports and escort vessels were mostly inflicted in that period. Our landing force on Kota Bharu seemed to have suffered considerably from enemy planes, until they were relieved by activities of our friendly planes which had leaped on Songkhla and Pattani.

b. Generally speaking, most of the air fields in the southern area were so narrow and soft-surfaced that such planes as the Zero fighters and naval land-based bombers found it difficult to use these fields.

c. For refitting those fields there was a need for 8-to-10-ton rollers, but even the most powerful rollers we had brought from our homeland were little more than 5 tons.

d. It was in the rainy season, so air fields were too muddy owing to insufficient drainage management.

e. Organization, equipment, and transportation methods of a construction corps were not adequate and much remained to be done.

f. Transport ships which were assigned the mission of advancing the Air Corps were too slow in speed as well as insufficient in number. Landing craft were also badly short in number.

g. Air fields on the west coast of the Malay Peninsula were in comparatively good condition, but the Army forces which had occupied those fields showed reluctance for the Navy to use those fields. The General Headquarters of the Army well realized the necessity of advancing naval air forces there, though it seemed that it failed to order or instruct the 3rd Army Wing to do so.

h. Enemy submarines were the most troublesome problem to our surface vessels. Accordingly, the need for effective high-speed small craft for chasing enemy submarines was badly realized.

i. It impressed me much that removals and advances of our naval air forces were not done alertly. Much effort, I thought, had to be made to improve its effectiveness in its organization and its equipment.

j. In order to keep our transportation routes safe from enemy submarines, the following measures had to be taken at once:

Shipping traffic under the control of the unified organization.

Convoy system and designation of safe routes.

Disposition of surface and aircraft for defense and guard of enemy submarines on vital points of safe routes.

k. It was one of the important lessons experienced frequently in the Japanese Southern Area Invasion that air raids by small forces cost many losses for comparatively small effects. Again it was illustrated that in the engagement northeast off Rabaul in which the Chitose Flying Corps of the 4th Fleet encountered the oncoming enemy task force. The reason why the lst Air Fleet always succeeded in making decisive blows to the enemy with relatively small losses was evidently due to the fact that it used to employ the most powerful force in its attacks. It led me, therefore, to the following conclusion: The disposition of our air force after the Japanese Southern Area Invasion was to be such that fighters and scouting planes were disposed in vital points and land-based bombers were concentrated in one or two points (not less than 50 planes).

5. My opinion about how to force peace upon the Allies at the time of the Japanese Southern Area Invasion being finished. (Translator's Note: He added in his note that he suggested this opinion to both headquarters of the Combined Fleet and the General Staff in Tokyo.)

Our policy should be first to prepare a concrete measure for transporting essential materials gained in the newly occupied area to the homeland, secondly to continue blows actively on vital enemy points.

The fatal blow to the enemy would be, of course, the fall of the British Empire, the weakest point of the Allied Powers. In order to achieve this purpose, there were two measures for us: One was an operation for India and another, an operation for Australia. To launch the former operation, however, there were two conditions. One was that Germany would penetrate Iraq and Iran, thus cutting down oil resources from the British Empire and also threatening India from the rear. Another was that, in order to destroy a powerful enemy encounter, which could be expected, sufficient forces should be employed in this operation.

The Australia operation which aimed to cut the American-Australian lifeline was such a threat to the Allied Powers that they could not but prevent our operation by all means. In this operation also, we should prepare sufficient forces to destroy enemy counterattacks.

Comparing these two operations with each other, the India operation involved such disadvantages as part of our main striking forces being withdrawn from the main theater, the Pacific, which, in other words, would mean our operation would be too widely spread out. The Australia operation, on the contrary, could be regarded as part of our main operation against America and also would have a rich chance of taking hold of American task forces. If those operations had proved successful, they would have done much to contribute to weakening the fighting spirit of the enemy, by continuing accumulation of damages upon him.

At the same time, the submarine operation would be strengthened to sever enemy transportation routes.

6. My opinion which was forwarded to the Commander in Chief of the Combined Fleet when I was informed of the Midway operation:

At that time there were three operation lines which might be taken into consideration. They were: the Midway invasion, one for the Fiji Islands and one for New Caledonia via the Solomons. A Midway invasion would offer us the following advantages, if it were successful: first, that we would always threaten Hawaii, the center of the enemy transportation route, and second, that we would prevent enemy task forces from launching blows against our homeland. Yet it involved no less [sic] disadvantages. Not only would its occupation by Japanese forces mean a spread out of our operation so that its support might involve too many difficulties, but it would necessitate that we maintain a larger number of forces there in order to encounter enemy attacks effectively. Moreover, as enemy preparations for war, especially enemy air forces, increased, Midway Island would be within the reach of enemy land air forces, while, on the contrary, it would not be easy for Japan to maintain a powerful air force there because of a too-long supporting route. Had we only attempted to invade that island and, after a complete destruction of enemy installations thereof, withdrawn from there, apparently it would not have been so difficult for America to restore that island immediately.

The second plan, the operation line for the Fiji Islands, would be the next to the first plan in all respects.

On the other hand, the third plan, the operation line for New Caledonia, would not only involve such advantages as have been mentioned previously, but would have the advantage of being easy to support. In particular, we would gain the utmost advantage of pushing our operation under a powerful air cover operated from a newly constructed airstrip on Guadalcanal Island. I was convinced that the last plan would be the best. (Translator's note: He added that against this opinion the Commander in Chief of the Combined Fleet, Admiral Yamamoto, did not show any sign of adopting it, mentioning that this matter was already a matter of understanding between his staffs and the General Headquarters, so that it was almost impossible now to change it.)

7. My impression concerning the Battle of Midway Island.

a. In past operations, Japan succeeded in launching surprise blows upon the enemy, because Japan only attempted to advance operations, either under the cover of her air forces or after having gotten at least approximate information about the enemy. In the case of Midway Island, however, it was utterly different. We met with fiasco because we did not get any sign of the existence of an American task force near Midway Island. The need of high-speed, long-range reconnaissance planes was badly felt. It was our great regret that we lacked sufficient measures in establishing guard screens by means of submarines both ahead and to the sides of our fleet, as well as the fact that we failed to have some submarines go to Midway Island beforehand to get some information.

b. It seemed that our intention of that operation had been revealed to the enemy. After that battle, I received some information that the American Fleet not only expanded strict air patrol around the island from 21 May, but they concentrated air and surface forces there, in particular disposing carriers in three lines, as well as a considerable number of submarines. Then, it caused us to question whether the secret of that operation had been revealed beforehand, perhaps owing to some mistakes of our communication activities.

c. A rendezvous point of our invasion force was fixed in Saipan, though that place was not adequate from the viewpoint of keeping secrecy. It should have been fixed in Truk by all means, because Truk Island rendered not only such an advantage for us as to disguise our next intention as either for east or south, but gave us the benefit of selecting an advancing route to Midway Island under cover of our air base on Wake Island.

d. The fact that we accompanied slow-speed transport ships apparently made it easy for enemy submarines to track our fleet. In fact, our convoy met enemy submarines twice on their way. Maybe these submarines were those on patrol missions.

e. This operation had such a significant character that a large-scale engagement might be expected between both powerful fleets. From this point of view, our disposition of the fleet was open to the charge of being too widespread. Because Japan intended the Aleutian operation to coincide with the Midway operation, so that it was necessary to share part of our carrier forces with the Aleutian operation [sic]. Even in the Midway operation alone, the covering force for the invasion was too separated from the carrier group force to cooperate with it. In fact, when our carrier group was reported as having received severe damages from enemy carrier-borne craft, the covering force for the invasion (Translator's note: under his command) hurried with increased speed to the engagement area, ordering the convoy to withdraw, but our fleet failed to launch a night action upon the enemy.

8. My impression concerning battles around Guadalcanal Island.

a. The immediate purpose of the present operation had to be stressed in recapturing Guadalcanal Island. In accomplishing this purpose, an operation aiming at the destruction of the enemy fleet had to be given such priority as circumstances permitted. We had to pursue one object. (Translator's note: He expressed this in a Japanese proverb saying that "he who pursued two hares, catches neither.")

Therefore, it was quite necessary that, concentrating the majority of our air and surface forces around the Solomon Islands, we would launch decisive blows upon the enemy with a powerful force and a thorough preparation, thus would continue such attacks as to give the enemy no time to recover. Also at the same time we had to continue night bombardments by cruisers upon that island and to send powerful Army forces there by means of high-speed transport ships or destroyers if necessary. At this critical moment we had to devote all our attention to getting rid of following the policy of doling out our forces as well as of getting into an engagement of exhaustion.

b. An enemy that gave us most pains was a land-air force. Then, its destruction was most urgent, in which a greater role would be played by our land-based air force, too. In order to achieve this aim, therefore, we would launch a decisive blow with sufficient forces, only after having concentrated sufficient forces as well as fuel and ammunition. And, after launching such a blow, we would continue incessant attacks upon the enemy to insure thoroughness.

c. We would endeavor to intercept enemy support and reinforcement to Guadalcanal Island. This would necessitate destruction of enemy bases for patrolling flying boats in that area. Then, first we would scout Espirito Santo, Stewart and San Cristobal to get information about the enemy, and at the same time would utilize these opportunities to attack enemy shipping, concentrating submarines in that theater.

d. We, the Japanese people, have a characteristic of being too simple and also short of tenacity. We could not but recognize these same features exposed in conducting operations, too. For instance, it was rare in our past operations that we continued chasing a defeated enemy completely. Maybe this was because we were often obliged to be in such circumstances that to continue the chase was difficult, owing to a lack of sufficient force, though we should have continued daring chases by all means. We had not a few instances of them, viz. the Battle of Savo Island and the Battle of the Coral Sea. Also we had many instances of them in air engagements. The fact that our naval force carrying out transportation missions to Guadalcanal gave up their missions to return immediately, after meeting enemy interceptions of surface vessels, could not be freed from being considered other instances. In such cases, our forces ought to have removed enemy interceptions with either part or the most part of their covering forces, thus diverting the enemy to them, while, on the other hand, attempting to make landings even with only part of their force.

e. I commanded both the Second and the Third Fleets, maneuvering on the sea off the Solomon Islands in the fall of 1942. However, I got the impression that, in such operations when two different fleets were combined, the commanding officer of the main task force should be assigned to take the responsibility of commanding both fleets. In the operation above mentioned, I endeavored to go along with the intentions of the Commander in Chief of the 3rd Fleet, paying all respect to him, though I might have failed to satisfy him if considered from his point of view.

(Translator's note: He was senior to Vice Admiral Chuichi Nagumo, the Commander in Chief of the 3rd Fleet. The 2nd Fleet, composed chiefly of cruisers and destroyers, was providing the guard for the carrier group, while the 3rd Fleet was the main striking force, composed chiefly of carriers as its nucleus.)

9. My impression concerning the Night Action of 14 November 1942.

a. We misunderstood the enemy because of obscure information in our hands. Owing to information about the enemy which had been received by the evening of 14 December, there were three enemy groups in the area south of Guadalcanal; viz. one consisted of a carrier, 2 battleships, a cruiser and 4 destroyers and last, one of 4 cruisers and 4 destroyers. As to the former two groups, we had had the impression that they used to stay south of that island, particularly at night, to withdraw southward. In the report of that day, they were reported coursing 100 degrees only, and their positions were omitted. As to the last group, it was only reported heading 300 degrees.

Toward eventide of that day, however, another message was received from seaplanes catapulted from our own force. It said that only two cruisers and 8 destroyers were heading at high speed to the island, so that it led us to the conclusion that enemy battleships were withdrawing southward as usual.

I made up my mind, therefore, to strike first the enemy cruisers and destroyers suspected to be in the Guadalcanal Area, and then to launch a bombardment upon air strips, which was the main object of that operation. For this purpose, I had our destroyer group in mass occupied ahead of my main force instead of our screen, in order to get some information about the enemy, before we suddenly collided with them. In case I had only aimed at bombardment, I would have intended to retain a screen of destroyers in order to prevent enemy PT boats from getting in our way.

Anyhow, I expected to meet enemy surface vessels before I would begin a bombardment on the island[;] then, the sudden appearance of enemy battleships in that area was utterly beyond my consideration. Otherwise, I ought to have prepared to launch a systematized night action upon the enemy.

b. So that, when my main force sighted enemy battleships, my destroyer group had already penetrated into the area east of Savo Island, and were coming to fierce grips with enemy cruisers and destroyers. Consequently, in the first stage of that engagement I failed to use our destroyers most effectively to destroy enemy battleships.

c. It goes without saying that I should have launched our oxygen-torpedo attacks against enemy battleships without the enemy's having detected any sign of them, after having certified the formation, the course and the speed of the enemy. But I failed to do so. Because of that, there were some doubts about the existence of enemy battleships in that area, and also we found many difficulties to certify enemy forces in their obscure backgrounds of islands. I ordered searchlights lit in order to illuminate the enemy clearly. Not only did this very action cause us to fail in launching our torpedo attacks without being detected, but to receive enemy bombardment in return.

d. Although we were favored by occupying good positions in launching our torpedoes at about 5,000 meters in the reverse course, I got the impression that our attacks did not prove effective, perhaps because we met the enemy fleet all of a sudden. Above all, it was my great regret that not a few torpedoes fired by our fleet exploded on their unfinished way.

e. The engagement was fought in a narrow area, furthermore, dotted with a lot of dangerous reefs, so that sailing in that area was not an easy task at all. This situation was made worse not only by the fact that visibility was bad owing somewhat to the remains of the smoke screens laid by both fleets as well as to bad weather, but to the fact that our fleet had to maneuver all the time in all directions in view of an accident to a self-tracking instrument. So that our position became very doubtful, and much time was needed to reaffirm it.

f. In order to use effectively such a battleship as the *Hiei* that had high speed but comparatively weak protection would necessitate utilizing its high speed so as to outrange enemy gunfire, thus exhibiting its superior gunfire. Then, when they were employed in such narrow areas as the Guadalcanal slit, we ought to have anticipated such damages as were received in those engagements. In fact, we lost two of these ships in those engagements owing to their weak protection; one being sunk by concentrated gunfire of four battleships whose existence near Guadalcanal was utterly beyond our imagination.

g. The reasons why I gave up the night action unfinished and ordered my command to withdraw northward were as follows:

(1) Our fleet had almost exhausted our torpedoes.

(2) A continuance of that night engagement in the face of still sound enemy battleships as well as land- and carrier-borne air forces, would cause us to subject our fleet to powerful enemy air attacks from early morning of 15 November, consequently would result in sacrificing our important striking force which could hardly be supplemented afterwards.

h. In order to make clear the circumstances of that night engagement, I added the following information concerning damage inflicted upon the enemy, of which I had heard during that engagement:

(1) We observed the first salvo fired by the *Kirishima* destroyed a tower of an enemy battleship and since then that ship was observed to stop firing. Meanwhile, when that ship was illuminated by our searchlights, it was learned that each turret of that ship was turned in different directions, elevating their guns.

(2) The second enemy ship on which our fleet concentrated gunfire and torpedoes was observed submerged to her upper deck. Evidently, the gun-

nery officer of the *Atago,* my flagship, reported to me that she was sinking. Also, the DD *Asagumo* mentioned that she inflicted two torpedoes on that ship at about 2203. Not a few observed at about 2210 that she was sinking, listing to her starboard side.

(3) The *Takao* observed at 2206 two huge columns of flame rising up amidst the first ship.

(4) The DD *Ayanami* reported she sank an enemy cruiser. And another destroyer reported also she sank a cruiser at 2130.

(5) At about 0030, the 4th Sqd. and the 4th Des. Sqd. observed a warship with apparently a battleship tower blown up at the southwest area of Savo Island.

10. My impressions immediately after the withdrawal from Guadalcanal Island. (Translator's note: He added in his note that he proposed this opinion to Admiral Yamamoto.)

We, the Japanese Navy, which had to aim at destroying the majority with the minority, should seek no alternative but to destroy enemy forces successively, always taking such advantages of keeping superiority in a battlefield. For this purpose, there were two matters to be set up at once: one, prompt refitting of airstrips so as to speed up the concentration of our air forces; another, the prompt fortification of our vital islands to enable us to maintain those islands, until our main striking force launched a powerful blow concentrating its forces, either when the enemy came to assault or when we made an operation actively at one theater.

In accomplishing these two matters, we should make it a policy to establish immediately an inner main defense line, then, in accordance with our available capacities, to expand its establishment to outer circles gradually. It would be high time for us to launch "One Decisive Big Battle" against the enemy, in order to change hands in successively losing the balance against us, when the enemy came to assault either Formosa, the Nansei Archipelago or the coast of China. In the face of the bitter experience that our adopted measures always failed to be in advance of the enemy's, and also of the daily increasing difficulties of transportation, we at the first hand strengthen the fortification of the east coast of Japan proper, then, in accordance with available capacities, expand its defense line to the Philippines, the Palau and the Marianas line. Thus, we would aim to get time for preparation, while on the other hand we would endeavor to decrease enemy forces as much as the circumstances permitted.

Index

A

Abe, Genki, 121
Abe, Hiroaki, 293–94
Abe, Nobuyuki, 118, 128, 133
Abukuma (cruiser), 90, 290, 297, 301
Accounting, Bureau of, 47
"A" class competition battle practice, 15–16
Admiralty Islands, 65–66
advanced tactical training, 16–17
Agano (cruiser), 90, 281
Aiko, Fumio, 23
airborne torpedoes, 14, 23
aircraft carriers. *See* carrier divisions
air fleets
  1st, 257, 258, 285–86, 287
  11th, 270, 274, 282, 285
  establishment of, 79–80
  organization of, 83–84
  responsibilities of, 82
air squadrons
  1st, 285, 287
  2nd, 285, 287
  3rd, 284, 285
  4th, 285
  7th, 284
  21st, 285
  22nd, 281–82, 285, 308
  23rd, 285
  26th, 282
Aitoku, Ichiro, 42, 43
Akagi, I.J.M.S (gunboat)
  construction of, 87, 88
  Kiichi Hasegawa as captain, 294–95
  naming of, 300
  specifications, 96
  Tetsutaro Sato as skipper, 10
Akagi-class ships, 95–96
Akazawa, Shijuo, 302
Akebono (destroyer), 276

Akikumo (destroyer), 291, 297, 301
Akiyama, Shinshi
  career of, 9–10
  Kai-Sen Yomu-Hei (Essential Instructions on Naval Battles), 10
Amagi (carrier), 87, 89
Amatsukaze, 274
Anami, General, 52
antisubmarine nets, 238
Aoba (cruiser), 90, 284
Aoki, Shigemasa, 102, 105
Arao, Okikazu, 102–3, 105, 110
Arare (destroyer)
  naming of, 301
  sinking of, 290–91
  Yukei Ogata as skipper, 297
Aratama-maru (supply ship), 235
Ariake (destroyer), 259, 260
Ariizumi, Ryonosuke, 41
Arima, Takayasu, 261
Arimoto, Terumichi, 297
Arisue, Seizo, 102
Arisue, Yadoru, 102, 104, 105, 108–9
Arita, Hachiro, 124, 169
Army
  anti-American attitude, 123, 124–25
  Army-Navy maneuver, 17
  aviation development, 22
  educational policies, 7–8
Army General Staff
  authority of, 26–27
  disarmament agreement negotiations, 28–29
  Operations Section members, 104–5, 106–8
  organization of, 26, 39
  War Direction Section members, 105, 108–9
Army General Staff College, 31
Asagumo (destroyer), 273, 274, 275
Asakaze (destroyer), 278

319